Wins, Losses, and Empty Seats

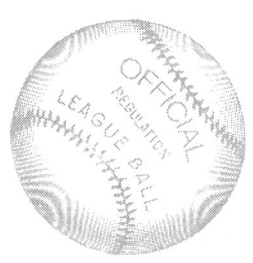

Wins, Losses, and Empty Seats

How Baseball Outlasted the Great Depression

David George Surdam

UNIVERSITY OF NEBRASKA PRESS · LINCOLN AND LONDON

© 2011 by the Board of Regents
of the University of Nebraska
All rights reserved
Manufactured in the
United States of America
∞
Library of Congress
Cataloging-in-Publication
Data

Surdam, David G. (David George)
Wins, losses, and empty seats:
how baseball outlasted the
Great Depression /
David George Surdam.
p. cm.
Includes bibliographical
references and index.
ISBN 978-0-8032-3482-6
(cloth: alk. paper)
ISBN 978-0-8032-7179-1
(paper: alk. paper)
1. Baseball—Economic aspects—
United States. 2. Major League
Baseball (Organization)—Finance.
I. Title.
GV880.S88 2011
796.357'640973—dc22
2011002716

Set in Minion.
Designed by R. W. Boeche.

Contents

List of Tables vi
Acknowledgments ix
Introduction xiii
Prologue: *Clash of Titans*. 1

Part 1: **The Financial Side of the Game** 5

   1. The American Economy and
      the State of Baseball Profits. 7

   2. Why Did Profits Collapse?
      The Revenue Side 27

   3. Why Did Profits Collapse?
      Player Salaries and Other Expenses 59

   4. Farm Systems 95
      Conclusion of Economic Side 109

Part 2: **The Game on the Field** 111

   5. Competitive Balance 113
   6. Player Movement 131

Part 3: **Using League Rules to Aid in the Recovery** 157

   7. Helping the Indigent 159
   8. Manipulating the Schedule
      to Increase Revenue 169

Part 4: Innovations to Boost
Attendance and Profits 195

9. Radio and Baseball. 197

10. Baseball Under the Lights 219

11. Other Innovations 247

12. How Effective Were the Innovations? 279

13. The Inept and the Restless
    Franchise Relocation. 285

    Epilogue: *The End of an Era* 301

    Appendix 1: *Radio and Sunday Ball's
    Effect on Attendance*. 307

    Appendix 2: *Dramatis Personae* 309

    Appendix of Tables. 315

    Notes 353

    Bibliography. 399

    Index 405

Tables

See Appendix of Tables, page 315

1. Economic Indicators, 1929–1943

2. Index Numbers for Various Indicators

3. Major League Attendance, 1925–1941

4. Consolidated Real Net Income
   after Income Taxes, 1929–1941

5. Nominal and Real Net Operating Income

6. Sources of Revenue and Expenses
   across All Major League Baseball Teams

7. Nominal and Real Games at Home Revenue per Attendee

8. Nominal and Real Gross Operating Income
9. Real Games at Home and Games Away Revenue
10. Real Exhibition Games and
    Real Concessions (Net) Revenue
11. Nominal and Real Concessions (Net) Revenue per Attendee
12. Nominal and Real Radio Revenue
13. New York Yankees on the Field
    and on the Ledger, 1926–1941
14. New York Yankees' Revenue Sources, 1926–1939
15. New York Yankees' Total Gate Receipts, 1926–1939
16. New York Yankees' Visiting Share Divided by Attendance
17. Real Team Salaries 1929, 1933, and 1939
18. Nominal and Real Revenue Compared to
    New York Yankees' Player Payrolls, 1926–1939
19. Adjusting the New York Yankees' Payroll, 1930–1934
20. New York Yankees' Core Player Nominal Salaries, 1930–1934
21. Real Gross Operating Expenses and "Other Expenses"
22. Selected "Other Expenses" Incurred
    by the New York Yankees
23. Real Cost of Player Contracts and Farm Losses
24. Measures of Competitive Balance
    in Major League Baseball, 1929–1941
25. Records of Major League Baseball Teams, 1929–1941
26. Records of Major League Baseball
    Teams' Highs and Lows, 1929–1941
27. Population of Cities With and
    Without Major League Baseball
28. Introduction and Movement of Top Players, 1919–1941

29. Main Players of the St. Louis
    Cardinals' Pennant-Winning Teams
30. Estimated Redistribution Due to
    Revenue Sharing in 1929, 1933, and 1939
31. Nominal Games Away Revenue and
    Win-Loss Percentage in the Major Leagues
32. Visiting Teams' and League's Shares, Road Receipts,
    and Revenue Sharing at Yankee Stadium, 1926–1939
33. Average Attendance at American League
    Holiday Doubleheaders, 1946–1953
34. Offensive and Pitching Statistics, 1929–1941
35. Effects of Sunday Ball
    Three Years Before and Three Years After
36. Effects of Radio Broadcasts of Home Games, 1934–1935
37. Effects of Night Baseball
    Three Years Before and Three Years After
38. Per Capita Attendance by City, 1929–1941

Acknowledgments

Claudette Burke, librarian at the National Baseball Hall of Fame and Museum, provided the impetus for this book. She suggested that I examine the New York Yankees' financial records held in the museum's archives. Her suggestion was certainly fruitful.

Professor Louis Cain of Loyola University of Chicago was another source of inspiration, when he suggested a decade ago that I pursue another subject, such as the economics of professional sports, after completing my book on the Union Navy's blockade during the American Civil War. His suggestion, too, was astute.

George Rugg, curator of the Joyce Sports Collection at Notre Dame University, provided me with relevant sports periodicals, such as *Baseball Magazine* and the *Sporting News*, access to the Philadelphia Phillies' financial records, and team scorecards. As with my book on baseball during the postwar era, George's contributions loom large.

Mark Watson and Thomas Stave of the University of Oregon Knight Library provided encouragement and assistance in locating government materials, among other kindnesses.

Professor Erik Craft, of the University of Richmond, assisted me in locating weather data for New York City during the 1930s.

The University of Northern Iowa College of Business Administration provided a teaching reduction for Fall 2008 and funding for research. The college also provided funding for presentations at the Social Science History Association meetings in November 2007 and at Missouri Valley Economic Association meetings in October 2007. Faculty members of the college made useful comments at a Friday workshop. The University of Northern Iowa generously awarded me a Summer 2008 research fellowship.

Farzad Moussavi, Dean of the College of Business Administration, generously matched the University of Northern Iowa Sponsored Program's contribution to the subvention of this book. Department of Economics head Fred Abraham has supported my research throughout the process.

Rob Taylor, sport history editor, gave support and encouragement throughout the review process.

Professor Michael Haupert of the University of Wisconsin at LaCrosse generously shared American League player salary data from his data base, which was carefully and painstakingly gleaned from the National Baseball Hall of Fame and Museum. He also shared Philadelphia Phillies' financial records with me.

Professor Kenneth McCormick of the University of Northern Iowa Economics Department alerted me to a *New York Times* website, which greatly speeded up the process of collecting articles from that source. Professor Kenneth Brown patiently explained the nature of fixed-effect regression estimation.

Professors Louis Cain, John Hoag, Michael Haupert, Stacey Brook, and Rodney Fort and several anonymous referees contributed sagacious comments along the way.

My University of Chicago Department of Economics dissertation committee of Professors Robert W. Fogel (chair), David Galenson, and D. Gale Johnson and Robert D. Clark Honors Thesis committee of Professors Paul Speckman (chair), Richard Koch, and Edward Diller encouraged my interest in sports statistics and sports history.

Notre Dame graduate Sara Szekely helped photocopy articles from the *Sporting News* during one of my visits to South Bend.

My brother, Stanley, instilled a love of sports in me. He taught me to

Acknowledgments

overcome my right-handed proclivity and to bat left-handed. He also urged me to dribble and shoot basketballs with either hand, making me ambidextrous, at least for sporting endeavors.

UNI students Stephanie Easterling, Josh Mahoney, and Adam Koch exemplify the scholar-athlete model for university varsity athletes. Ms. Easterling's enthusiasm for sports research was infectious. Mr. Mahoney was a 2010 recipient of the Walter Byers NCAA scholar-athlete award while majoring in economics. Mr. Koch was a pivotal player in UNI's basketball upset of the University of Kansas in a recent NCAA basketball tournament.

As the project neared completion, I had the pleasure of working with Ann Baker, manager of the editorial, design, and production department at the University of Nebraska Press. Janine Goodwin did an excellent job of editing the manuscript. For the fourth time, Sarah Statz Cords compiled a comprehensive index for one of my books. She has never tired of my Civil War and baseball interests.

Introduction

You own a baseball team during the 1930s. Your customers are facing declining incomes. In addition, the consumer price index is falling. In the words of the old American Express ads, "What will you do?" Before you decide, consider that you also possess both price-setting (monopoly) power for your product and single-employer (monopsony) bargaining power over your primary labor input. How will these powers affect your decisions?

You have these powers because Major League Baseball is a cartel. A cartel is a group of firms that band together to make some decisions jointly for the group's mutual benefit. Members may see greater profits as the cartel tries to establish monopoly prices, although individual firms may find it advantageous to cheat on the cartel agreement. The American League and National League gained an explicit exemption from antitrust laws in a Supreme Court case dating from the struggle with the Federal League in 1914–15. Because the cartel gives you territorial protection against other teams moving into your city, you have price-setting power. You have single-employer power thanks to the reserve clause that binds players to just one team.

Economists and the general public are keenly interested in cartels. Since antiquity, people have suspected conspiracies that injured the public interest by fixing prices and other shenanigans. Since the enactment of the Sherman Antitrust Act (1890) and the Clayton Antitrust

Act (1914), American businesses that wish to indulge in cartel behavior must do so furtively. Because of baseball's antitrust exemption, the owners' actions, while still often cloaked with secrecy, are more open than most. Baseball therefore offers economists greater opportunities to study cartel behavior than do other industries.

The Great Depression created stress for the cartel. Buffeted by declining consumer expenditures and a decline of one-fourth in prices, owners scrambled to keep their teams and leagues afloat. The focus of this book is how a cartel functions under adverse economic conditions.

How did the owners adjust to their fans' dwindling ability or desire to pay for baseball? Did a lifeboat mentality develop, in which the strong teams wanted to toss the weak teams overboard? Did the owners reduce ticket prices? Since the owners had single-buyer power over the players, did they squeeze player salaries? Did the hard times inspire innovation? Potentially helpful technologies such as electric lighting for night baseball and radio broadcasts certainly piqued the owners' interest. Did owners investigate instituting interleague play or divisions and playoffs? These are the issues this book will address.[1]

Not Your Robber Barons' Cartel

Baseball's cartel in the 1930s differed from cartels in other industries because it had the advantages of an explicit antitrust exemption and control over its key input. The joint-production nature of baseball's product also distinguished baseball's cartel from other cartels.

The alternative to a cartel was unappealing to owners of professional sports teams. The early history of professional baseball was dismal. Owners may have boasted of being rugged individualists who personified the virtues of free-market capitalism, but they really meant that free-market capitalism was good for the other guy. A free market in players and games always seemed to result in chaos. As early as 1875, William Hulbert, owner of a Chicago team, decided the sport needed to be rationalized like other industries, in which concentration and limited competition ruled.

Introduction

When individual business owners get together to create a cartel, they confront some basic problems. First, the cartel members have to decide how to divide the potential revenues or profits. Since each owner desires to get the most advantageous agreement possible, a cartel may die stillborn. Second, if the owners succeed in creating an agreement, they must monitor each other's actions to insure compliance. Self-interest does not end with the formation of a collusive agreement. Owners may be willing to break the rules, especially when they are trying to get players. If malfeasance is discovered, the owners also need a mechanism to punish cheaters. Third, if the owners are successful in creating and maintaining a cartel, they can earn handsome profits above the norm, assuming the demand for their product remains healthy. Since handsome profits are not commonplace, other business owners become envious and desire to enter the market. The cartel members must devise ways of deterring upstarts from entering the market. Much of the baseball owners' activity, then, can be seen through the lens of cartel behavior.

Owners had an exceptional element of control over their key input: skilled baseball players. Aside from amateur players who were signing their first professional baseball contracts, there was scant evidence of a free market for players' labor in baseball. The sixteen Major League clubs maintained tight control over the best players via the reserve clause, a system similar to the star system used by motion picture production companies. Once a player signed a contract with a professional team, he was bound to that team or to any subsequent team to which he was traded or sold. The owners conveniently interpreted the reserve clause as being perpetual, even though other observers believed that once a player sat out a season, he became a free agent. Because of the reserve clause, an owner held a superior bargaining position, thereby enabling him (or, occasionally, her) to pay below-market salaries to players.[2]

The owners also controlled players through the adroit manipulation of various agreements with Minor Leagues pertaining to player movement. Teams in higher leagues could draft promising players from teams in lower leagues. Major League team owners eventually started buying Minor League teams to get even more control over promising players. In addition, the Major League owners enforced discipline over players by using blacklists.

Aside from their antitrust exemption and control over its key input, baseball's cartel is somewhat different than, for example, a cartel between auto manufacturers. Economists have noted the unique aspect of professional team sports. The product, a contest, is a result of joint production by two separate clubs. The product literally requires two to tangle. Fans are far more interested in watching a contest between two distinct clubs than they are in watching an intrasquad game. An auto manufacturer may wish the demise of a rival firm, but in professional team sports such desires are sublimated within the need to have rivals, hapless or not, in order to produce games. This joint-production aspect of sports means that owners of stronger teams can be confronted with the necessity of bailing out owners of weaker teams.

Cooperation and competition therefore coexisted in Major League Baseball. Owners clearly understood this dichotomy and sometimes stated it explicitly. In 1901, when the National League owners considered a plan for creating interlocking ownership of teams as a response to the upstart American League, New York Giants owner Andrew Freedman stated, "We are here to-day, with each man trying to clutch his interested partner by the throat and throw him down the baseball abyss as hard and as quick as he can do it. That gets him out of standing in the way of his success with his club and his ambition to win."[3] His rival owner, James Hart of Chicago, put it more bluntly: "We are the only paradoxical business institution in the world. My good is your ill; your good is my ill. We compete for players, we compete for points, we compete for games; it is an antagonistic business from start to finish. If it was not, we would not be in business."[4]

Prior to baseball's antitrust exemption, the two leagues had engaged in cartel-like behavior, including erecting barriers to entry by other teams aspiring to Major League status. New teams or new owners for existing teams could not enter either league without the almost unanimous approval of existing owners. Imagine grocery store chains voting on whether a new grocery store could open in a city. Nor could existing teams move into cities already occupied by other teams, although, as a result of the 1900–1903 struggles between the two leagues, five cities had two or more clubs.

Owners deterred the entry of new teams and leagues not only by voting upon who could join the industry, but by their control of labor. Because of the Major-Minor League agreements, existing Minor League teams had difficulty stockpiling sufficient talent to credibly claim Major League status. The rules insured that any upstart league would have difficulty getting well-known players to join them. Although the Federal League succeeded in enticing several top players into defecting, those players were often aging stars without much to lose. Indeed, the Federal League's leading hitter, Benny Kauff, who believed himself the Ty Cobb of that league, promptly reverted to being an average player when he rejoined the National League.

Owners justified these rules by claiming such strictures promoted competitive balance. Otherwise, they claimed, the wealthy teams would corral all the top talent and make the league a farce. Since some leagues had foundered upon extreme competitive imbalance, there was a veneer of plausibility surrounding their claim. However, fans of the St. Louis Browns and Philadelphia Phillies could be excused for wondering about competitive balance during the 1930s. Many, if not most, economists studying sports are dubious about whether the reserve clause matters much for competitive balance. By the 1950s the American League's chronic competitive imbalance inspired the farcical Broadway musical, *Damn Yankees!*, with a story line implying that the Washington Senators could compete with the New York Yankees only by trafficking with the Devil.

While these cartel actions are malign, there are aspects of the cartel's behavior that contribute to the fans' enjoyment of the game. The cartel standardized the product by creating and enforcing a uniform set of playing rules, although there were some notable omissions (for example, there are no rules requiring identical playing fields, aside from the requirement that there be a diamond of bases). The leagues also set up schedules. Economist Rodney Fort explained the necessity of league scheduling. "If team owners cannot cooperate with each other to set a schedule, then league play, by definition, cannot occur. . . . Thus, leagues need to act in their single-entity capacity [cooperation between team owners that allows competition to occur] to include all teams in the schedule. If only larger teams play each other, smaller-market teams would fail economically."[5] During the 1930s both leagues played balanced schedules in which teams played every rival twenty-two times with equal numbers of home and away games. These measures helped insure that an undisputed champion would be determined, something the fans appreciated.

Despite these potential benefits, the baseball cartel has largely served the interests of the owners. The owners could exploit an element of monopoly power over their consumers via their territorial exclusivity, as well as superior bargaining strength over labor from the reserve clause. By the 1950s, owners learned how to obtain (extort) public money for building new stadiums and how to get favorable tax treatment by claiming depreciation on their players. Other business owners could only envy baseball owners for their advantages. Under normal conditions, how could an owner fail to make profits with these advantages? No wonder baseball owners inspired competition from potential upstart leagues, and no wonder there were usually plenty of people clamoring to become owners.

Because there were uniquely profitable aspects of owning a Major League team that could inspire potential new owners to enter the industry, baseball owners also tried to deter entry by remaining publicly modest. They didn't like to brag about the profitability of owning a ballclub. When it suited their interests, some owners would sing a song of woe, but very few ever boasted of healthy profits. While they sometimes allowed attendance figures to leak out (often when they were battling with a rival league), they usually tried to suppress such information until after World War II. The owners took the stance that their financial records were strictly none of the public's business.

The owners withstood occasional scrutiny of their antitrust exemption, especially as it was applied to player control. A Wisconsin representative, Raymond Cannon, asked the Attorney General to investigate baseball's trust in 1937. "This combination has made it possible for the magnates owning the ball clubs to dictate and impose upon the players such terms as they desire. In order to hoodwink and mislead the baseball public, the baseball magnates each year permit the publication in the press of the salaries of two or three outstanding players on each team, but refuse to let the sporting writers . . . know what salaries they are paying all of the other players." Cannon went on to complain that a well-known owner stated, "it was none of the public's business what salary the players on his club were receiving."[6] The attorney general turned down Cannon's request by repeating Justice Oliver Wendell Holmes's ruling in the Federal League case that baseball clubs were not "engaged in interstate commerce."[7]

Congress would hold almost annual investigations of major league baseball in the 1950s and 1960s, but legislators never touched baseball's antitrust exemption or its right to maintain a reserve clause. In the end, Charlie Finley's failure to pay premiums on Jim "Catfish" Hunter's annuity became the crack in the reserve clause edifice.

How Might Cartel Members React to an Economic Downturn?

Owners of firms in competitive markets who faced a decrease in demand would be forced to accept lower real (inflation-adjusted) prices for their output. As the demand fell for their output, these owners' demand for their labor input would, in turn, also fall, thereby leading to lower wages (in both nominal and real terms).

Because Major League Baseball team owners had territorial protection, which gave them price-setting power, and the reserve clause, which gave them single-employer (monopsony) bargaining power, their ability to earn above-average profits afforded them more discretion than a typical firm in a competitive industry possessed. They could choose whether or not to adjust prices and salaries in the face of declining demand. In a sense, the owners were not as strictly under the iron discipline of the market as owners of firms in more competitive markets. Neoclassical price theory suggests that price-setting owners would set their price in the elastic region of demand, where a price change would lead to a relatively large change in quantity (consumers are sensitive to changes in prices), unless there were significant tie-in sales, such as concessions and parking. Many researchers estimating consumers' responsiveness to changes in prices—the price elasticity of demand—found owners pricing their tickets in the inelastic region of demand, where a price change would lead to a relatively small change in quantity—consumers are not very sensitive to changes in prices—raising questions of whether owners are truly profit maximizers or whether tie-in sales affected pricing decisions.[8]

Owners of professional sports teams rarely portrayed themselves as profit maximizers. Many chose to depict themselves as sportsmen who placed their teams' win-loss record and fans' interests ahead of profits. Thomas Yawkey of the Boston Red Sox absorbed losses for years, pursuing pennants by purchasing top-flight talent. Not all owners could afford to be sportsmen; some, like Connie Mack of the Philadelphia Athletics, had few assets apart from their teams. These owners were under greater pressure to avoid losses, if not to maximize profits. A profit-maximizing owner facing decreased demand for his product might choose to reduce prices and cut salaries, although they would not do so in the same way as would a firm in a competitive industry. Then again, a wealthy owner might not do either and might simply absorb these negative effects upon profits. It does seem unlikely, however, that profit-maximizing owners facing declining demand would allow real ticket prices and salaries to rise.

Introduction xxi

Where'd You Get Those Numbers?

Researchers examining the baseball cartel's behavior have been blessed with some exemplary sources. Although sports teams in all places and at all times attempt to shield their financial records from public view, Congressional hearings held in 1951 forced owners to divulge income and revenue statements for the years between 1920 and 1950, with detailed information on the 1929, 1933, and 1939 seasons, among others.

The New York Yankees will loom large in this book. Not only were they a successful franchise during the Great Depression, but the team donated a large collection of its financial records to the National Baseball Hall of Fame in Cooperstown, New York. This donation was surprising, since a researcher in the late 1940s found such records for sale in a used bookstore.[9] Before he could purchase the records, a Yankees official bought them back and the team refused the researcher's requests to study them. Unfortunately, the financial records at the Hall of Fame do not include profit and loss statements, balance sheets, or other summary documents. Such documents would have required careful analysis, as the accounting rules may have shifted during the subsequent decades. Michael Haupert and Kenneth Winter, two patient researchers with a sound grasp of accounting rules (especially those pertaining to amortization of durable assets), reconstructed profit/loss statements for the years between 1915 and 1937 from the general ledger and cash book information.[10]

The New York City Public Library has a collection of papers left by Jacob Ruppert, owner of the Yankees. These papers include sporadic Yankees board meetings in which Ruppert, his general manager Edward Barrow, and other team officials discussed their decisions. Unfortunately, many of the minutes are not contained in the collection; this reduces its potential to give valuable insights into the officials' rationales for their decisions.

The Joyce Sports Collection at Notre Dame University obtained some of the Philadelphia Phillies' financial records for the seasons between 1935 and 1939. These records allow us to compare a wealthy franchise with an impoverished one. The Phillies' payroll information does not list the salaries of individual players.

Some economists, including Andrew Zimbalist, are skeptical of published team finances.[11] Team owners may feel reticent to show large profits and may report more pessimistic figures in public forums. Since the Yankees officials probably did not anticipate that their records would become public, there is little reason to suspect distortions like those identified by Zimbalist. Because these are the team's actual financial records, there is no reason to suspect that the data are misleading or "cooked." The payments to the league, for instance, coincided with the published attendance figures.

Finally, isolated pieces of financial information circulated in the press from time to time, including franchise purchase prices and player sales prices. Teams printed scorecards that occasionally contained ticket and concession prices throughout the years between 1929 and 1941. The Joyce Sports collection contains a wide array of scorecards from these years. Previous researchers have compiled attendance figures, and, of course, the various baseball encyclopedias have a wealth of the player data and team statistics so beloved by baseball fans.

The National Baseball Hall of Fame has extensive records of individual American League player salaries. Economist Michael Haupert compiled the information, which will be referred to as the Haupert Hall of Fame Salary Database (or Haupert Database).

Enough information exists, therefore, to examine the cartel's behavior during these years. The biggest void is what the owners actually thought about proposed changes.

Past Literature

Charles Alexander's *Breaking the Slump* is a comprehensive description of Major League Baseball during the 1930s; he focused primarily on the game on the field and not on the general ledgers. He made little use of the data presented to the U.S. Congress in 1951. The New York Yankees' financial records may not have been available to him.

Other historians, such as Harold Seymour (*Baseball: The Golden Age*) and David Voigt (*American Baseball*) compiled general histories of the sport, but provided only brief examinations of the financial aspects of the game. Labor historians, such as Robert Burk (*Much More Than a Game*), have woven the events of the 1930s into a tapestry depicting the exploitation of players by owners.

Contemporary sportswriters occasionally wrote articles detailing some financial aspects of professional team sports. These articles often cloaked the information with the phrase, "a representative team," and, of course, the data was sporadic and sparse.

Because owners of professional sports teams generally prevented the public from viewing their financial data, there have been few studies of the business aspects of leagues or of individual teams. Peter Craig, an undergraduate student at Oberlin College, wrote a lengthy bachelor's thesis on the business of baseball in 1950.

Sports economists have rarely examined the events of the 1930s. Fort and Quirk (*Pay Dirt*) studied profitability, franchise values, and competitive balance throughout the twentieth century, but their main focus was not upon the 1930s. Haupert and Winter ("Pay Ball") have reconstructed profit and loss statements from the New York Yankees' financial records. They have also analyzed such questions as the profitability of buying Babe Ruth from the Boston Red Sox and of building Yankee Stadium. Although their reconstructed profit and loss statements extend into the 1930s, they did not emphasize the question of how the team coped with the Great Depression. Members of Congressional investigations probably compiled the most comprehensive report on baseball's finances. This is especially true of especially the committee that met in 1951.[12]

Henry Fetter's *Taking on the Yankees* chronicled the Yankees. He claimed that the team won because of superior management. While the Yankees did well at obtaining players up until the mid-1960s, he did not present evidence that the team was innovative or particularly clever on the business side. He simply assumed that the team's management was superior because the team won the majority of pennants between 1921 and 1964. Daniel Levitt's *Ed Barrow* details that executive's way of obtaining talent, negotiating salaries, and making decisions regarding the team's operations. Levitt believes that because the Yankees reported more profits than any other team in baseball, Barrow and owner Jacob Ruppert made astute choices. He lauds their obsession with winning and Ruppert's willingness to delegate authority to a baseball expert.[13] Hiring Barrow to run the team was an excellent decision. While Levitt examines some of the business side of running the Yankees, he does not ask whether their animosity towards night baseball and radio broadcasts were as wise as their personnel decisions. The duo of Ruppert and Barrow also lagged in implementing other promotions. Although we can never be sure whether they should have implemented these changes sooner, an assessment of their tenure must address these questions. A skeptic might argue that the team's success was due to its formidable drawing power, which enabled its officials to withstand more mistakes than other teams.

Albert Power's *Business of Baseball* is an overview which paints the owners as the villains. His work is badly flawed by shaky economic analysis; for example, he does not use inflation-adjusted player salary figures when discussing the events of the 1930s. He utterly fails to justify his demonization of the owners.

Overview of the Book

I will briefly describe the American economy during the 1930s and its effect on baseball. How did the economic downturn affect attendance and team profits? What did the owners do about player salaries? How did the events of the 1930s affect baseball's competitive balance and the movement of players?

As owners with fewer resources struggled, what did the wealthier owners do to help them during the Great Depression? Did the existing revenue-sharing rules sustain weak teams, or were more drastic measures needed? I will differ from previous writers on the events of the

1930s by discussing a possible remedy which the owners used only in extreme circumstances: manipulating the schedule to increase revenue. During the 1950s owners of teams that were struggling to remain competitive resorted to relocating their teams to more lucrative venues. Did owners in the 1930s consider moving to other cities?

Did owners attempt to innovate in order to attract larger audiences? The new technologies of radio and electric lighting made it possible to reaching new and larger audiences. Baseball rules have rarely remained static; did owners try to revise playing rules to make the games more satisfying for fans? Which owners proved more adventurous? While most of the owners were not revolutionaries or visionaries, nor were they Luddites opposed to any change. The owners' individual and collective responses revamped the game and moved it closer to the version that today's fans know.

Wins, Losses, and Empty Seats

Prologue
Clash of Titans

Two of baseball's most famous teams arrived at Yankee Stadium on September 9, 1928 for a four-game series that began with a doubleheader. The Philadelphia Athletics, managed by Connie Mack, held a one-half game lead over the New York Yankees.

While many writers and fans have since anointed the 1927 New York Yankees as the greatest team ever, the 1928 edition was having trouble defending their title. The team had built a sizeable lead throughout the summer before watching the Athletics roar back. The 1928 team did not enjoy good health, and such standout pitchers as Herb Pennock, Wilcy Moore, and Urban Shocker missed starts throughout the season. In addition, despite the label "greatest team of all time," the Yankees had mediocre players at shortstop, at third base, and behind the plate.

Connie Mack had needed a decade to rebuild his Philadelphia Athletics after he sold most of his star players between 1914 and 1915. Now he had a nucleus of future Hall of Fame players in Mickey Cochrane, Al Simmons, Jimmie Foxx, and Lefty Grove. To provide veteran leadership, Mack signed Ty Cobb, Tris Speaker, and Eddie Collins. By September, however, the Athletics were using the veterans sparingly. Eventually, these seven players and Mack would all be inducted into baseball's Hall of Fame.

The Yankees had manager Miller Huggins, Earle Combs, Waite Hoyt, Herb Pennock, and Tony Lazzeri in addition to Babe Ruth and Lou

Gehrig. The team used Stan Coveleski for a dozen games. Rookie Bill Dickey would eventually make catching a strong point for the Yankees, while young Leo Durocher would become a Hall of Fame manager and baseball character. The two teams had eighteen Hall of Fame personnel between them, including five of the first twelve players selected.

The two clubs had so much talent that a doubleheader played on May 24 featured thirteen future Hall of Fame players in one game, not including those sitting on the bench as substitutes or managers. In the first game of the doubleheader, the Yankees started Combs, Durocher, Ruth, Gehrig, Lazzeri, and Hoyt. The Athletics countered with Cobb, Speaker, Cochrane, Simmons, and Grove. Collins and Foxx played as substitutes. In the second game of the doubleheader, ordinary pitchers took the mound; Simmons, Foxx, and Collins did not play, so the fans only saw eight future honorees.

Over 85,000 fans crammed into Yankee Stadium to watch the September doubleheader. According to the *New York Times*, some 100,000 additional people did not get tickets. The paper reported that the gate receipts amounted to $115,000, which would have been enough to pay the season salaries of Babe Ruth, Waite Hoyt, and another regular player. The team's cash book listed a more modest $75,000, including advance sales.[1] The Yankees swept the doubleheader, 5–0 and 7–3. They won the third game on September 11, before losing the final game of the series. Still, the Athletics left New York trailing by one and a half games. They never caught up. The four games attracted 171,000.[2]

While the Yankees boasted after the doubleheaders, "The same old As; the same old As" (the team had finished second or third for the previous three seasons) and "We broke their hearts today," Babe Ruth would play on only one more pennant winner during his remaining seven seasons as a player.[3] The balance of power was shifting in the American League.

One might argue that the September doubleheader was a high-water mark for the Major League Baseball cartel. In the National League, the St. Louis Cardinals were narrowly defeating the New York Giants and would establish themselves as a dominant National League team for over a decade. The Cardinals, with the disadvantage of sharing a small Major League city, were a "new-model" franchise, using vertical integration by owning or controlling Minor League teams. The 1928 season was one of the rare years in which both leagues had tight pennant races.

Within a few years, Major League Baseball would be confronted with a serious challenge: surviving the Great Depression intact. The severe economic downturn tested the cartel as few previous threats had.

The fortunes of the Athletics and Yankees reflected the economic downturn. The Athletics, who were not well capitalized, struggled after 1931. While the Yankees would endure some losses on the ledger and on the field, they would end the era on the upswing.

1. The Financial Side of the Game

1. The American Economy and the State of Baseball Profits

Major League Baseball was not immune to the effects of economic fluctuations. We can presume that economic activity affected the demand for baseball games, although the relationship was not always obvious. Baseball owners faced a severe economic crisis after the 1929 season. Some contemporary observers felt that the economic downturn and the accompanying unemployment might initially boost baseball attendance, as fans would have more leisure time.[1] An extended economic downturn, however, would more likely erode fans' willingness and ability to attend games, although the immediacy and the magnitude of the response are not well understood.

This chapter provides a description of the national economy and how baseball fared between 1929 and 1941. Although this work places considerable emphasis on profit/loss figures, the reader should recognize that interpreting profit and loss information is problematic at best. Sometimes owners cried "losses" when things weren't so bad. The owners could, of course, camouflage losses through adroit manipulation of accounting rules. I will describe how fluctuations in attendance, revenue, and expenses affected profits and losses in subsequent chapters.

The Economic Downturn

There are different ways of measuring economic activity. Although modern economists prefer to use gross domestic product (all goods and services produced in the United States) rather than the more traditional gross national product (all goods and services produced by Americans, whether here or in other countries), we will use the gross national product (GNP) figures, as they were used more frequently during the era being examined. The gross domestic product and gross national product tend to track closely.

The GNP peaked in 1929 both in nominal and in real (inflation-adjusted) terms (table 1). By 1933 nominal (GNP) was almost halved. However, because the price level fell by roughly 25 percent, the real GNP in 1933 was about 70 percent of the GNP in 1929. GNP rose throughout the remainder of the decade in both nominal and real terms, although there was a downturn in 1937 and 1938. By 1940 real per-capita GNP was above the 1929 level. Thereafter, GNP figures were increasingly distorted by government purchases of military goods and services.[2]

This is the simple story of the U.S. economy. More important for Major League Baseball owners was the extent of the economic downturn in the northeast quadrant of the United States that encompassed the ten cities with Major League Baseball.

There are some crude measures that show how various states and regions, as well as industries, fared. The number of employees on nonagricultural payrolls fell by one-fourth between 1929 and 1932.[3] The number remained stagnant in 1933 before rebounding in 1934. A second drop occurred between 1937 and 1938, after which the number of such employees increased up until the war. The number of employees, of course, is not a perfect measure, since many workers may have had reduced hours or reduced real wages.

Different industries had diverse experiences during the period. Mining, contract construction, manufacturing, and transportation suffered larger-than-average proportional declines in employees. Wholesale and retail employment closely reflected the general decline, but finance, insurance, and real estate and services suffered smaller proportional losses in the number of employees, which was probably good for the baseball owners if their chief clientele was white-collar workers.[4] One industry did well during the era: government. The number of employees in the federal government actually rose between 1930 and 1933, even before Roosevelt assumed the presidency. The employment numbers do not give us definitive clues as to how individual cities fared. A city such as Washington DC might have endured the Depression without too much job loss, given the increase in federal employment.

The U.S. Department of Commerce provides a second clue from its estimates of per-capita income by state beginning with 1929. On average, nominal per-capita income fell by 44 percent between 1929 and 1932. As economists Thomas Garrett and David Wheelock point out, the decrease in nominal per-capita income differed greatly across states.[5] States that began the period with relatively low per-capita incomes generally suffered larger percentage declines than states with high per-capita incomes. During the recovery in the second half of the 1930s, the states with large percentage declines during the early 1930s tended to have larger percentage increases.[6] States dependent upon agriculture and mining often suffered the biggest per-capita income declines. From the perspective of owners of Major League teams, cities in the northeast sector of the country tended to have lower drops in per-capita incomes than cities in the old Northwest, such as Michigan, Illinois, and Ohio, with the exception of Missouri. Of the states with Major League teams, Massachusetts fared relatively well in terms of per-capita income between 1929 and 1932, dropping only 32.3 percent in nominal terms. Michigan's nominal per-capita income fell by half. Michigan's doldrums undoubtedly reflected the auto industry's parlous condition: factory sales of motor vehicles in 1932 were only one-fourth the number sold in 1929.[7] Because these are per-capita incomes by state, the figures are at best crude measures of how the major cities might have fared. A city's experiences might diverge from the statewide estimates. Washington DC was spared the worst of the impact on per-capita income because of the stability of federal jobs. The city's per-capita income fell only 17 percent between 1929 and 1932.

Owners might have been heartened, at least initially, by personal consumption expenditures (PCE). Although these fell in a pattern similar to GNP, the decrease was not as marked. PCE represented 75 percent of GNP in 1929 but the share rose to 83.8 percent in 1932 and remained high in 1933 at 82.4 percent. Thereafter, PCE's share of GNP shrank well into the war, aside from the downturn of 1937 and 1938.[8]

Of course, within PCE, consumers might have maintained their spending on such basics as food, shelter, and clothing while jettisoning trips to ballparks and motion picture theaters. Within personal consumption expenditures, as GNP fell, so did recreational expenditures, but spending on recreation maintained its share of GNP through 1932. Indeed, the proportion rose slightly in 1930 and 1931, giving credence to the idea that unemployed workers did not immediately cut their spending on leisure, and may even have increased it slightly. After 1932, however, recreation's share of GNP fell, reaching a trough in 1935.[9]

Americans did not greatly curb their real spending on motion picture theaters or spectator sports until 1932. Nominal spending on spectator sports and motion pictures displayed slightly different paths. Spending on spectator sports fell slightly in 1930 before falling by 29 percent between 1929 and 1932. The spending began a modest resurgence in 1933 and a more dramatic increase thereafter. By 1934 spending on spectator sports was the same as in 1930. It was 9 percent higher in 1935 than in 1929. Motion pictures initially saw an increase in nominal spending between 1929 and 1930 and held steady in 1931. The industry then experienced a sharp drop that reached bottom in 1933, a year after the lowest point for spectator sports. In 1933 motion picture spending was 28 percent below the 1929 level. While the industry experienced a rebound throughout the rest of the 1930s, nominal spending did not reach 1929 levels until 1940.

Table 2 shows the relative changes for key variables. The table uses 1930 levels as the base levels. In real terms, the situation was bright for both spectator sports and motion pictures. Motion picture theaters experienced a surge of popularity in 1931 compared with 1929, and even spectator sports were off by only 3 percent over the same period.

Spending on spectator sports reached a trough in 1932, but the trough was not as severe as that of real GNP. Real spending on spectator sports rebounded strongly in 1933 and continued to improve throughout the decade. By 1934 real spending on spectator sports exceeded the 1930 level. Motion picture theaters reached a nadir in 1933 before rebounding, albeit more gradually than that of spectator sports. By 1936 and 1937, though, real spending was similar to 1930 and 1931 levels.[10]

How did the economic downturn affect Major League Baseball?[11] As table 3 shows, baseball's attendance slumped from 1930 to 1933. The American League began a rebound in 1934, but the number of fans did not reach 1930 levels until 1937. The National League, with its banner year in 1930, was mired in a slump that persisted longer than did the American League's. In terms of consolidated real net income after income taxes (which we will denote as real profit/loss), the American League collectively lost money in 1931, while the National League's collective losses began in 1932 (table 4). The American League's relative losses surpassed those of the National League by wide margins except in 1934. Both leagues returned to profitability in 1935. The National League's collective profits stayed at less than half of the 1930 level through 1941, while the American League's 1940 profits exceeded the 1930 level. The National League's collective real profits exceeded those of the American League for every season except 1940 and 1941.

According to information presented to Congress, taken from the Department of Commerce's "Survey of Current Business," Major League Baseball's profit performance between 1929 and 1941 compared well with motion pictures and other recreations.[12] The estimated profit margin was based on profit as a percentage of sales, which may not be the best way of measuring profitability since it does not reflect the return on capital. Baseball's profits as a proportion of sales were generally higher than that of other recreations and motion pictures. The industry's decline in 1932 and 1933, though, was deeper than that of motion pictures. By this measure of profit margin, other recreations were unprofitable in every year from 1929 through 1938, with the exception of

1937. Despite baseball's apparently favorable outcome relative to other recreation industries, a key question remains: why did Major League Baseball's profits lag behind the attendance rebound?

False Profits in the Press: True Profits before Congress

Baseball owners reported consolidated net profit and loss after income taxes to Congress beginning only in 1951. The owners reported net income for the years between 1920 and 1950, as well as detailed financial information on revenues and expenses for sporadic years (1929, 1933, and 1939 were the years relevant to this study for which detailed information was available). In addition, the financial records of the New York Yankees and the Philadelphia Phillies allow us to estimate the profitability of these teams. The Yankees' and Phillies' data, found in their cash books and financial ledgers, corresponded closely with the information they supplied to Congress, so there is little reason to think that the owners distorted the records they presented there.[13]

Before these figures became available, observers were largely ignorant of baseball's profitability. The *Sporting News* and the *New York Times* often ran stories on the profitability of individual teams. As in contemporary times, reported profits must be evaluated carefully, and it is worthwhile to compare press reports with information compelled by the Congressional investigation. A reporter wrote in the *Sporting News*:

The broadcasting of how much clubs have lost during the past few years seems to have become general. The bigger the figure, the better it seems to please some to herald the news. And when the figure does not appear big enough, the clubs drag out everything that represents a dollar and chalk it up on the loss side of the ledger, until it would seem that modern business acumen was measured not by the profits that had been made, but by the losses that had been sustained. If this unfavorable publicity served any useful end, it might be justified, but there isn't one single excuse for the practice. It will not bring out more fans to the parks, it will not increase the prestige of the game, nor will it induce players to sign for smaller sal-

aries. . . . *As for the players, all they have to do is to consult the records at the internal revenue offices, which will be open to the public in accordance with a regulation passed by Congress [in 1934], to ascertain what club officials have been receiving in the way of salaries, and then the players will have an argument on their side that all the lamentations at wailing walls will not be able to overcome.*[14]

A letter writer to the *New York Times* succinctly summed up the problem of discussing baseball profits and losses: "Debates about ball club finances are academic as long as the ledgers are not exposed to public view."[15]

One sportswriter characterized the industry as a million-dollar business "fraught with comparatively few possibilities for big profits and many for sizeable deficits. These owners then, must be men of substance who have nerve to take big chances for, in any one year, seldom more than three or four of the 16 clubs in the two leagues make big money or break even." He described one owner's reluctance to sell the club at a big profit (the writer did not explain how a club could be sold for a big profit despite losing money) but concluded, "The game is in his blood; the profits will come later—he hopes."[16]

Sportswriter Dan Daniel got to examine the Yankees' financial books in 1939. He found the team's payroll was in excess of $300,000 for each of the three seasons, 1937, 1938, and 1939, and claimed that Ruppert had paid over $7 million in salaries and $6.5 million to acquire players since he acquired the club.[17] These were fairly close to the actual payrolls shown in the Yankees' financial records, if you include the manager's and the coaches' salaries as part of team payroll.

Whether or not owners attempted to camouflage their profits is an interesting question, but accounting principles may have differed in the past. For instance, the way in which a team expensed player purchases mattered. Before the 1920 season, the New York Yankees paid $100,000 for Babe Ruth (not the $125,000 and $350,000 loan to Harry Frazee reported in most histories) according to the team's cash books.

The accounting rules of the time allowed the club to report the entire $100,000 as an expense for the 1920 season even though Ruth was a "durable" commodity providing a stream of services over a number of years. A business might prefer to expense a player purchase immediately in order to reduce current tax liability.

The Internal Revenue Bureau gave this ruling on the related matter of a player's contract salary in 1936:

The cost of a baseball player contract which, at the time of its acquisition had a period of one year or less to run should be deducted as a business expense in the year in which such cost is paid or accrued, regardless of whether the contract contains a renewal option. The cost of a baseball player contract which at the time of its acquisition has a period of more than one year to run should be amortized over the life of the contract and an annual allowance for such amortization should be deducted each year during which the original contract continues. If an option to renew a baseball player contract is exercised, the arrangement should be treated as a new contract for the period of the renewal.[18]

Owners used the amortization of park improvements as another way to manipulate profit/loss statements. Jacob Ruppert built Yankee Stadium during the early 1920s and made subsequent improvements. The way in which he expensed the construction costs and subsequent depreciation had a large impact on any given year's profit/loss figures. When owners began installing lighting systems, sportswriters acted as though the entire cost of the system could be expensed in the year of construction, even though such systems were durable and would provide light for many years.

Whether an owner paid himself a salary, incurred expenses, or put relatives on the payroll also affected net income. Jacob Ruppert received $1,000 each month for "expenses" during some seasons. Gerald and Mary Nugent also drew salaries as owners of the Philadelphia Phillies.[19]

An example of the difficulty sportswriters had in estimating a club's profitability appeared in the *Sporting News*. The reporter shifted through the balance sheet the Red Sox filed with the state of Massachusetts. He concluded that the way in which the team accounted for depreciation, player contracts, and renovation of Fenway Park made estimating the season's profitability problematic.[20]

Despite these examples, the owners occasionally gave surprisingly accurate, if incomplete, financial information to the press during the Depression. Player salaries reported by the Yankees tended to be quite close to the actual amounts shown in the team's financial books. Ruppert and other owners may have divulged such tidbits to cast a player as being greedy or overpaid, especially when the mass of Americans were struggling to survive. Owners were usually wary about releasing salary information, lest their players cast off their ignorance and acquire a true indication of their value.

An examination of some teams' reported profitability shows the trends during the Depression years. Although owners appeared to downplay gains and exaggerate losses in the press, the trend generally coincided with their reported profits and losses.

Sportswriter F. C. Lane attributed some of baseball's financial woes to overzealous owners. He reported that owners complained of the "wasteful and un-businesslike" behavior of other owners. "Eight clubs have annually indulged in a battle royal for a pennant. Within reasonable limits, that is just what they should do. But limits have long ceased to be reasonable."[21] In a later article, he continued in this vein: "In striving for a pennant, the interests of each individual owner clashes with the interest of the league."[22] Economists identify this problem of owners being too competitive as a variant of the "Prisoners' Dilemma" conundrum: each owner, while pursing his own self-interest, might injure the interests of the group. If each owner expended an additional $100,000 to sign the best players, the overall rankings of the teams might be unaffected, but the owners would be collectively worse off.

The experiences of several teams demonstrate the ebbs and flows of profitability during the 1930s. We will begin with teams in small markets and will then examine teams in large cities.

The St. Louis Cardinals and St. Louis Browns shared the smallest of the five cities with multiple teams. The Browns typically lost money during the 1930s, with their owner, Phil Ball, stating, "The Browns made money for me in 1922, not before, not since. As president I get no salary, and I run the club for the pure fun of it."[23] Ball appears to have exaggerated his losses to the press, as the Browns reported profits to Congress for most of the 1920s.[24] His successor, Donald Barnes, absorbed serious losses during the late 1930s, although he attributed some of the loss incurred in 1937 to investment in a minor league system.[25] The Browns actually lowered their losses in 1933, but the period between 1936 and 1941 was quite costly, with losses exceeding $700,000.

The St. Louis Cardinals, however, usually reported profits from 1926 on. The team paid a reported 10 percent dividend after its first pennant in 1926 and declared a dividend of 20 percent after winning pennants in 1928 and 1931. The dividends would have been even higher if the club had not chosen to reinvest much of its profit into its growing farm system.[26] When the Cardinals won the 1934 pennant, the paid attendance was less than $350,000 for the season, and only a seven-game World Series lifted the club into profitability for the season. Despite the somewhat disappointing profit figure for 1934, owner Sam Breadon, in a rare moment of braggadocio by an owner, claimed, "I have made more money in baseball since 1926 than any man in the business. I say this, proudly, because most of the money I have made has been turned back into the game, into the development of our farming system, toward making the Cardinals a self-sustaining club."[27] The club again paid a dividend, this time of $10.00 per share, after the 1935 season; although it failed to win the pennant, attendance rebounded strongly.[28]

The Cardinals continued to pay dividends of $12.00 per share in 1936 and $8.00 per share in 1937.[29] Their string of dividends ended with the 1938 season, when the team finished sixth and attendance tumbled below 300,000. An observer claimed, "It has been estimated that the average major league club must draw around 400,000 to get over the red line." Even selling a sore-armed Dizzy Dean to the Chicago Cubs for $185,000 failed to move the club into profitability.[30] The team went back to paying dividends after a new crop of young players had developed and Breadon and Rickey had sold or traded several veterans and no longer had to pay their relatively high salaries. Breadon argued that the young players deserved a chance to demonstrate their prowess, while Rickey collected a bonus from the sales of players.[31]

The Cardinals' farm clubs were a mixed blessing. Even though the young Cardinals defeated the Dodgers after a tight pennant race in 1942, Breadon stated that the club would have shown a loss without the World Series receipts. The farm system lost over $100,000. While they won the pennant, attendance was just 550,000: "the club can make a little money with a 500,000 home attendance."[32] The end result was a dividend of just $2.00 per share, the lowest since 1938. The profit picture brightened in 1943, even though the team blew apart the National League pennant race, winning by eighteen games; this development may have squelched attendance late in the season.[33]

The Cincinnati Reds were another team that represented a small city. The team showed dramatic changes in profitability. Larry MacPhail took over as general manager in 1934; his initial efforts did not turn the ink from red to black, as the team lost money in 1934 (part of which was due to $131,500 in player purchases). The team's attendance also faltered in the early part of the 1934 season because the club lost some Sunday home dates after Pittsburgh won the right to stage Sunday games. Powel Crosley Jr. announced in the press that the club earned an indeterminate but modest profit for 1935 ($58,000 according to the information giving to the Congressional hearing), as it reduced running expenses while night baseball and the general excitement surrounding the team boosted attendance. Profits rose from a modest amount in 1935 to over $100,000 in 1936, after which MacPhail left the team. The team's 1939 pennant inspired Crosley to liquidate some outstanding debt, to improve Crosley Field, to buy some players, and to issue a dividend. He said the team made $400,000 in profit ($403,000 according to the information given to the Congressional Hearing).[34]

The Reds discovered that maintaining such profitability was difficult. While the team won the World Series in 1940, profits would be "appreciably less" than in 1939. General manager Warren Giles professed indifference to the diminution in profits: "But who cares for profits? We're champions!" The twin slayers of profits for repeat pennant winners—rising payroll and shrinking attendance—afflicted the Reds. The Reds did climb out of indebtedness and paid a dividend of $12.00 per share based on the $275,000 profit in 1940.[35] The club had difficulty making profits between 1942 and 1945 but declared a token profit of $1.00 per share after the 1942 season. Even during the war, the club spent $87,000 to get new players in 1943, but these efforts could not undo the dwindling crowds or the team's diminishing ability.[36] After the war the Reds would be unable to compete with the Dodgers and Cardinals.

The Washington Senators could be pardoned for wondering whether they picked the worst year to win a pennant. The team's last pennant in 1933 (aside from pennants won after the franchise relocated to Minnesota in 1961) resulted in a tiny loss for owner Clark Griffith. Griffith had earned hundreds of thousands of dollars during the team's successive pennant titles of 1924 and 1925, so the 1933 experience must have been frustrating in the extreme. Naturally he declared no dividend.[37]

The downtrodden teams did not necessarily lose large sums. Although the Boston Braves reported a loss of $150,000 to the press in 1939, the information presented to Congress showed a $41,000 loss. The Braves typically limited their annual losses to less than $50,000 throughout most of the 1930s. Leaving out the 1933 season, the Braves came within $160,000 of breaking even for the thirteen seasons between 1929 and 1941.[38] Even the Phillies broke a six-season streak of losing money by making a profit in 1943, the year their attendance hit an all-time high. The team's largest profit between 1920 and 1949 was in 1932: it was over $100,000. The Phillies issued a small dividend in 1943, preferring to reinvest some of the tiny surplus.[39]

Even under flush economic conditions, owners dreaded the consequences of a pennant rout. The 1929 season featured such routs in both leagues, and the *Sporting News* reported, "With the Athletics and Cubs 'in' weeks before the closing date, there was little enthusiasm shown outside of those two cities. It is an undeniable fact that during the last two weeks of the campaign, some of the clubs did not take in enough money to pay operating expenses." The reporter used the Pittsburgh Pirates to illustrate how the remaining games of the season generated expenses but not matching revenues before concluding, "The club would probably have been in the pocket [black] if the season had ended two weeks earlier than it did." Despite this contention, the Pirates reported an after-tax profit of almost $150,000 for 1929.[40] The season was profitable, but owners might have pondered the lost profits due to the pennant race blowouts.

The Yankees and the Chicago Cubs represented two of the successful teams in large cities. While the *Sporting News* liked to report how much money Jacob Ruppert spent on the Yankees, with one article in 1930 citing a figure of $6 million, the paper did not always match this with revenue. Ruppert did not deny rumors that he had paid at least $2 million to build Yankee Stadium and had spent $1 million to acquire new ballplayers over the previous ten years.[41] He often earned some of the largest profits in baseball.

Ruppert waxed optimistic about baseball's future in early 1937. He attributed the rebounding crowds to "looser money, and more jobs and profits, and . . . to causes inside the game itself. In both leagues we are developing dramatic youngsters." He went on to state his belief that a player such as Bob Feller would someday be worth $100,000 (although he hesitated to label Joe DiMaggio as a $100,000 player). He claimed that the total value of his franchise, including the stadium and the farm clubs, was $8 million. "A two percent return on this would be $160,000. After depreciation, taxes and other deductions which our accountants could tell you about, the Yankees do not make $160,000 a year, net."[42] Since Ruppert was also claiming a healthy appreciation in his franchise's value, one is entitled to wonder how appreciation could be taking place if profits were so low. The Yankees actually earned respectable profits during the late 1930s, so this statement of Ruppert's can be considered dubious.

The Chicago Cubs experienced some of the largest profits and some of the largest losses of the era. The team enjoyed much greater net income between 1929 and 1931 than did the New York Yankees. The Chicago club was just one of two teams to report over $500,000 in real net income after taxes for a season during the period examined, second only to the Detroit Tigers' $634,000 in net income in 1935. Philip Wrigley, who inherited the team after his father William died in 1932, claimed that the team's subsequent losses resulted from declining attendance, "generous" salaries to players, and "tremendous cash expenditures for the purchase of stars." Wrigley believed his club had lost "more money than any major league team in the last three years." He claimed, "I am in the game for the sport of it, whether the club makes money or not, but it is essential that the club break nearly even or show a little profit." The Cubs' reported consolidated profit or loss for 1932 through 1934, presumably the three seasons Wrigley referred to, showed a combined loss of $462,000.[43] The team lost almost $250,000 in 1933, just one season removed from a pennant. It reported a profit for 1935, another pennant-winning season. The profit during the pennant-winning season of 1938 was a mere $39,000.[44] The Cubs spent $185,000 on acquiring Dizzy Dean during the season, getting seven wins (out of eight decisions) from him. They barely won the pennant, so Dean's exemplary win-loss record may have tilted the balance in favor of the Cubs; he may also have drawn large crowds to Wrigley Field. Given the series' brevity, the team may not have made much money from its World Series appearance. The Cubs' pennants of 1932, 1935, and 1938 earned the team a combined net income of less than $300,000; they also had four of the top five biggest net losses in the National League during the period.

The Cubs, like the Boston Red Sox, found that buying star players to remain in pennant contention could be an expensive proposition.

The Red Sox had lost $400,000 in ten seasons with chronically poor teams before Tom Yawkey bought the franchise on February 25, 1933. He reported a loss of over $500,000 in 1933 alone, as he bought star players while refurbishing Fenway Park. The *New York Times* claimed that Yawkey lost $1.6 million between 1934 and 1936, but this is treble the amount shown in the Congressional hearings.[45] The way in which Yawkey chose to amortize the purchase of Fenway Park, his improvements to it, and his purchases of players obviously allowed him a wide latitude in the way he reported his losses. The team reported losses after taxes in excess of $100,000 per season for seven consecutive years and lost $84,000 in 1940 before earning modest profits in 1941 and 1942. Perhaps the military draft had so denuded baseball rosters that there were no stars left for him to buy. The *Sporting News* suggested the club lost $165,000 in 1938, which was nearly the amount reported to Congress, so in this case the reporters got accurate figures.[46]

While the Yankees were consistently profitable, the Detroit Tigers actually earned almost $250,000 more real net income between 1934 and 1940. None of the National League teams' net income for the years between 1929 and 1941 came within $1 million of New York's net income, even though the Yankees reported losses for three seasons. Despite the Yankees' profitability, the National League collectively earned $3 million more in net income than did the American League.

Nine of the franchises reported combined real net incomes in excess of $200,000 each for the period between 1929 and 1941, including six National League teams. Two other American League teams earned more modest profits. Despite these not-so-disastrous outcomes, profitability did not necessarily match the rebound in attendance.

Net Operating Income

Baseball teams divided the revenue and expense information that they presented to Congress in 1951 into operating income and expenses and other expenses, such as the cost of acquiring players and farm-system losses.[47] The net operating income was the difference between the gross operating income (gate revenue from home and away games, exhibition games, radio, net concessions, and other income) and gross operating expenses (player salaries and other unidentified operating expenses). The two Major Leagues had different trends in real net operating income during the 1930s. The National League had higher real net operating incomes or smaller losses than did the American League for each of the three years surveyed.

While both leagues registered declines of over $1.6 million each in collective real net operating income between 1929 and 1933, the National League's rebound was more impressive (table 5). The senior circuit had greater net real operating income in 1939 than in 1929, a claim the American League could not match. The National League's surge occurred in spite of the Chicago Cubs' free fall in net operating income, a reduction of over $675,000. The Cincinnati Reds and Brooklyn Dodgers emerged from the doldrums of the early 1930s with healthy real net operating incomes, surpassing those of the Yankees or Athletics in their heydays.

Thomas Yawkey's infusion of cash, which brought talented players to Boston, may have exceeded a profitable level. The Red Sox suffered during the 1933 season, but Yawkey's money pushed the team to second place in 1938 and 1939. Although attendance increased, the Red Sox still had a negative net operating income in 1939. The Yankees' seventeen-game lead certainly hurt the Sox's late-season attendance, which fell from 640,000 to 573,000 between 1938 and 1939. While the Red Sox would exceed 700,000 in attendance for the next three seasons, the club's inability to turn a positive net operating income did not bode well. Yawkey needed his deep pockets to sustain the team's status as a contender.

While chapters 2, 3, and 4 will look at individual components of teams' revenues and expenses, table 6 provides a glimpse of crucial issues across all Major League Baseball teams. Gate receipts began their slow descent as the major source of revenue, while radio and, later, television began their ascent. Team salaries were not a compelling reason for the owners' inability to regain the peak of 1929 and 1930, nor were the growing farm losses a likely culprit. The rise of other operating expenses, however, will loom large. The Red Sox and Chicago Cubs will also figure prominently in the story.

Franchise Values as an Indicator of Profits

If interpreting the profit figures given to Congress creates ambiguity, another way to think about the health of professional sports teams is to examine franchise values. In theory, franchise values reflect expected future profitability. Expected future profitability is based upon past and current profitability, as well as anticipated changes in tax rules, in market demand tied with changing population, and in technology or rules that create new revenue streams or affect existing revenue streams. If franchises were consistently losing money during the early 1930s, we could assume these losses would be reflected by falling franchise values. When profitability resumed, franchise values might rebound. Ideally, we would like to have yearly values for franchises, but this would require yearly sales. Most sports teams are sold infrequently, so franchise values are established only sporadically and provide only an impressionistic view of the health of the industry.

Quirk and Fort have compiled a list of every franchise sale in Major League Baseball. In some cases, no sales price was reported. In other cases, the quoted sales price was equivalent to a guess. They concluded that franchises were, in hindsight, "relatively overvalued in the 1920s."[48] Those owners who bought franchises during the 1920s could be excused for not foreseeing a decade-long economic slump exacerbated by four years of total war. Conversely, those owners who purchased franchises during the late 1930s and the war might not have anticipated the postwar boom.

While some franchise sales during the period between 1929 and 1941 reflected capital appreciation (at least in nominal terms), the overall impression from Quirk and Fort's list is that of a soft market. The Boston Braves netted a capital loss between 1925 and 1935, but the owners may have broken even in real terms. The team later sold for a real appreciation in 1941. A group headed by Bob Quinn bought the crosstown Red Sox in 1923 for $1.15 million; it is not clear whether Fenway Park was included. They sold the team to Thomas Yawkey in 1933 for $350,000 plus $400,000 for Fenway Park. Although the franchise value clearly fell in nominal terms, Quinn's syndicate may almost have broken even in real terms (assuming they had purchased Fenway Park in 1923). Sidney Weil purchased a majority of Cincinnati Reds stock in 1929 but went broke by 1933. A year later Powel Crosley Jr. bought the team for an unspecified price, so no estimate of the franchise's appreciation or depreciation is possible. The estate of Phil Ball sold the St. Louis Browns to Donald Barnes in 1936. The estate absorbed both nominal and real losses from the transaction. The Philadelphia Phillies depreciated in real value between 1909 and 1943. The Reds, Braves, and Phillies were nearly bankrupt at the time of their sales. The Cleveland Indians also depreciated between 1927 and 1932, although the 50 percent loss in nominal value was cushioned by the falling price level throughout the economy. However, the Detroit Tigers appreciated 4.6 percent per annum in nominal terms between 1920 and 1935 (and more in real terms). Two men purchased a 50 percent share of the team for $500,000 in 1920, and by 1935, 50 percent of the team sold for $1 million. We cannot know whether most of the appreciation occurred during the 1920s. Sam Breadon's inability to sell his St. Louis Cardinals for a reported $1.1 million in 1935 may have been indicative of the soft market for franchises. Given that the Cardinals were a relatively profitable team (albeit in a shared small-city market), his inability to attract buyers was troubling.

Surprisingly, the New York Yankees' franchise value fell between 1922 and 1945, although in real terms the value may have appreciated slightly. Still, given that the franchise was one of the more successful in terms of profits, the meager real appreciation is startling, unless one considers that New York's greater profitability from its quasi-monopoly in New York City had been capitalized in the 1922 price.

After the Yankees' owner, Jacob Ruppert, died in January 1939, the board of directors selected Ed Barrow to become the club's president. Ruppert's attorney estimated that if inheritance taxes were imposed directly on the estate's baseball holdings, the valuation would range between $5 million and $6 million.[49]

The first serious bid to purchase the Yankees was made by a group headed by Postmaster General James Farley. The *Sporting News* reported that the deal had "progressed to proximity of agreement, with the price set at $4,000,000 in cash." Another article in the same issue, though, disputed whether Farley's offer was serious. This writer stated that Ruppert placed a value of $10 million on the Yankees and the farm system. The writer concluded that, "at $4,000,000 the Yankees would be the biggest bargain in the history of the baseball."[50]

In an editorial, the *Sporting News* said baseball officials were stunned by the reported $4 million price tag, since Yankee Stadium alone was valued at $3 million. Ruppert's three heirs, however, faced staggering inheritance taxes of up to 75 percent of the value of the estate. The government allowed heirs up to ten years to pay off the tax but assessed 6 percent interest on the unpaid balance. The total Ruppert estate was estimated to run over $25 million.[51]

Farley and his group had difficulty gathering the capital needed to purchase the club, but as late as January 1941 he expressed hope that he would be able to conclude the deal.[52] Farley failed in his bid to acquire the Yankees. In 1944 a group headed by Larry MacPhail purchased the club for considerably less than $4 million in depreciated wartime dollars.

The sporadic franchise sales support the view that profitability was below normal during the 1930s, as few of the franchises sold appreciated significantly in real terms.

Conclusion

Major League Baseball's experiences during the 1930s mirrored that of the national economy, with slight differences in timing. Owners could congratulate themselves for surviving the decade's upheavals without losing any members, although a number of teams remained in peril on the eve of Pearl Harbor. The industry also appeared to have survived the 1930s in better shape than many of its competitors in the recreation industry.

Owners could ponder why their collective profits did not return to the 1929 and 1930 levels, even though attendance was almost the same in 1940 as in 1930. The next chapter examines the nature of their profit woes in greater details, while subsequent chapters investigate whether increases in player salaries or farm system expenses were the culprits.

2. Why Did Profits Collapse?
The Revenue Side

Why did the owners of baseball teams suffer losses between 1931 and 1935? Was there such a sharp decrease in demand and revenues that owners simply could not adjust their costs quickly enough to maintain or restore profits? Gate revenue was affected by the number of attendees and ticket prices. Was falling attendance the main culprit? A reduction in attendees would tend to reduce revenue, unless it was matched with an increase in ticket prices. Did ticket prices change and exacerbate the declining attendance? A reduction in ticket prices could either reduce or increase revenue, although one must be careful in identifying nominal and real (inflation-adjusted) ticket revenue. What happened to the owners' other revenue sources?

Attendance

Baseball's attendance peaked in 1929–30. The stock market crash and eventual economic downturn did not trigger an immediate diminution in Major League attendance. The *Sporting News* editorialized that baseball was "such a good tonic ... that it can turn the more or less depressed mind to watch its fascinations. If depressing conditions do bring about enthusiasm in baseball, perhaps that is partly the reason why the interest has been so great this year."[1] Such glad tidings proved ephemeral and baseball suffered from falling attendance during the Depression. The fall in attendance reached its nadir between 1932 and 1934.

Owners did not publish accurate or official attendance figures for the first four decades of the twentieth century. By 1943 *The Sporting News* and *New York Times* included attendance in the box scores; however, the attendance figures included people who did not pay full admission. On occasion the periodicals would list both the total attendance and the paid attendance. Throughout the discussion, we will use attendance figures published in Thorn, Palmer, and Gershman (7th edition). Their figures coincide with the gate-sharing rules. These figures reflect paid attendance, the number of seats sold at regular prices. They do not include seats sold at discounted prices, such as those sold on ladies' days, those sold for children's prices, or those given away as free passes. Contemporary sportswriters who wished to determine attendance were forced either to estimate crowd sizes or to rely on owner statements.

When owners were fighting another league, they found it desirable to inflate their attendance figures. After peace was established they might revert to their tales of woe or at least release self-serving figures, although their exaggerations might echo for several seasons. Sportswriter Irving Sanborn claimed that the World Series forced owners to present more accurate figures. "The advent of the World's Series with its hard and fast rules for the distribution of every dollar and fraction thereof, of the receipts among the players and magnates proved a cruel shock to the players and an eye-opener to those who had been swallowing the prevailing press-agent scale of figures of attendance." Sanborn added that after a few World Series the players became suspicious that the owners were shortchanging them based upon the announced attendance at regular season games and World Series crowds. "When word of the players' suspicions reached the national commission, which handled all the coin, that body quickly and wisely removed those suspicions by telling the players to appoint a committee representing both competing teams to come behind the scenes, count all the tickets and the coin, or take any steps they chose to find out if the figures announced through the press were not right. . . . From that time the World's Series has acted as a check on all tendency to overstate the attendance at parks."[2]

Eight years later the problem of unreliable attendance figures still plagued fans. A *Sporting News* editor wrote that some fans were discouraged from attending games because of fears that a game was sold out. The editor took owners to task for consistently exaggerating attendance figures. "It is difficult to understand what purpose is served by this exaggeration of figures, but it is a policy that seems to be general." The editor concluded by noting the owners' failure to "provide enough windows for ticket sellers on those big days."[3] A fan wrote to the *New York Times* advocating publication of official daily and season attendance figures. "I believe these additions would serve two purposes: show what teams draw best and show what type of baseball the fans like best.... They might also serve to arouse some baseball civic pride and create a desire among the fans to have their team outdraw its rivals."[4]

Which teams attracted the largest audiences? Did the New York teams fare best? While the Yankees frequently drew over a million paying customers per season, the club never attained the attendance level it had achieved when it was a tenant of the Polo Grounds. During 1927 two million fans paid to see the team at Yankee Stadium and on the road. That season, however, the Giants had a larger road attendance.[5]

The Yankees were not the attendance champions as the "Roaring Twenties" came to an end. The Chicago Cubs' attendance exceeded 1 million for five consecutive seasons, including a then-record 1.4 million, despite playing in a stadium with less than two-thirds as many seats as Yankee Stadium. Even poor weather during the early part of the 1928 season and the ensuing dropoff from the 1927 attendance could not prevent the club from achieving over a million in paid attendance.[6]

Pennant races affected attendance, of course. At first the novelty of a pennant winner other than the Yankees increased American League crowds in early 1929, but the Athletics' big lead suppressed the crowds as the season waned. The National League, too, had a lopsided race. Some owners attributed the reduction to "a lowering in the quality of playing material," although they recognized that "fans simply refuse to follow, even moderately, clubs that are out of the race, which is a new trend."[7] At least the 1929 World Series proved popular, as both the Cubs and the Athletics turned away thousands of fans.[8]

Major League owners hesitated to attribute the eventual falloff in attendance to the economic conditions. After the National League's crowds shrank by 15 percent between 1930 and 1931, the league's president thought the Cardinals' domination of the race was as great a factor as the gathering Depression.[9] During the first weeks of the 1932 season, owners recognized that attendance was seriously affected, and not just by cold weather. As crowds dwindled and receipts shriveled, National League owners decided to curtail the distribution of free passes to games, limiting the number to five hundred passes per team.[10] A *Sporting News* editorial claimed that the National League style of ball pleased fans: "They like their baseball battles closely fought and they never object to a victory of 4–3. . . . At heart, that is real fan sentiment."[11] The following week the editor observed, "It has been a long time since players, taken generally, have buckled down to earnest effort as they have this year."[12] Despite these factors, National League attendance continued to slump.

As late as June 1932 some baseball officials were still citing factors other than the Depression for the attendance doldrums. "It was the opinion of the owners that 90 percent of the loss [in attendance] was due to bad weather rather than to business depression."[13] At least there was a tight pennant race in the National League at the time of this observation; this may have mitigated the effects of the bad weather.

In the American League, Cleveland fans demonstrated that the game was still immensely popular on occasion. The Indians played their Municipal Stadium debut on July 31, 1932. Newspaper articles cited the attendance as either the largest or the second-largest ever; the September 9, 1928 doubleheader between the Yankees and Athletics was the other contender for the largest crowd. A *Sporting News* editor gushed, "Coming at a time when the croakers would make it appear that baseball had passed its zenith and was on the downgrade, the opening of a stadium capable of seating over 78,000 ought to be sufficient answer to any doubts as to what those in the sport think of its future."[14] Despite this auspicious start, the Indians eventually moved back to their old ballpark, as playing in the spacious stadium was too expensive unless sufficiently large crowds showed up.[15]

The Yankees and Giants continued to attract relatively good crowds on the road. The Giants played to 650,000 paying customers on the road, leading the National League. The American League did not release similar data, but a reporter believed that the Yankees led the league in road attendance.[16]

The *New York Times* observed, "With less in pocket, they [fans] wanted a better article for their money, so to speak. In the major leagues good teams were, almost without exception, well supported. Poor teams were virtually abandoned by their former supporters. This was no time to be wasting money on an inferior product." This rosy prediction for pennant-winning teams would ring false for the 1933 Washington Senators and the 1934 St. Louis Cardinals: they were pennant winners that had abysmal home attendance. The writer also noted that the Minor Leagues were already in financial jeopardy; "But the minor leagues, for various good reasons, were in a bad way financially even before the general depression hit the country. Their sad fate was only hastened by the depression."[17]

Baseball was not alone in facing diminishing crowds. College football suffered from faltering attendance. Colleges reduced ticket prices for the 1932 season, but still experienced a 20 percent drop in attendance. Harvard's director of athletics, William J. Bingham, stated, "The decline in gate receipts for the big games likely will lead to further reduction of prices. It is possible a solution will be found in establishing a wider range of prices for the major contests." The article continued by citing even bigger drops in attendance in the Big Ten. These colleges also dropped their prices, while teams in the Rocky Mountain region banned radio broadcasts as well.[18] The dropoff continued throughout the 1932 season, although a few teams, such as Purdue and Wisconsin, registered increased gate receipts between 1931 and 1932.[19]

Attendance at baseball games sank further in 1933, although some teams attracted larger crowds.[20] During the desperate 1933 season, the *New York Times* reported that owners sometimes threw open their gates, allowing fans in for free or for a nominal amount. Commissioner Landis cited this as evidence that the "American people still love baseball. Many of them now are peering over the fence or through it and they will return as paid customers as soon as they have any money."[21]

The National League's attendance in 1934 was roughly the same as that of the previous year despite a thrilling pennant race between the Cardinals and the Cubs. The American League recovered from its 1933 trough, especially as the Detroit Tigers garnered large crowds while winning the pennant. The data owners presented to Congress in 1951 showed that four American League teams lost money in 1934, and offered a rare case in which a press report on profits was more optimistic than the reality.[22] American League president Will Harridge enthused, "Never before have I seen such enthusiasm and optimism among the baseball magnates. This goes for the minor leaguers [what was left of them] too. At the two baseball meetings this Winter, I noted that all the club owners chose to hold on to their stars rather than to sell them, even though there were several high monetary bids."[23]

The Cardinals won the 1934 pennant but had the smallest crowds for a pennant winner in decades. About a third of a million fans paid to see the team at home, while the road crowds were almost half a million. Fewer than 825,000 people paid to watch what would later be known as one of the most colorful teams ever.[24] While readers pondered the sad fate of the Cardinals, a *Sporting News* editor opined, "the fans want showmanship, aggressiveness, color and a display of a will to win." The description fits the Dizzy Dean and Pepper Martin Cardinals, so the editorial may have missed the mark. The editor also noted that followers of the game want "decent comforts, courteous treatment and such conveniences as loudspeakers and adequate scoreboards." With these factors in place, he concluded, "the front office needn't worry about receipts."[25]

Although contemporary sportswriters thought attendance improved in 1934 (especially in New York) Thorn, Palmer, and Gershman show that the New York clubs had smaller crowds in 1934 than in 1933.[26] The National League showed definite improvement in attendance during 1935. Larry MacPhail's energetic approach to reviving baseball in Cincinnati and Boston Braves owner Judge Fuchs's purchase of Babe Ruth triggered excitement.[27] Cincinnati's encouraging crowds mirrored a general trend in major league baseball: the worst was over by 1935.

The 1936 season brought larger crowds for many teams. The New York Giants had to return money when a doubleheader sold out in September. The World Series between the Giants and the Yankees broke attendance records twice, as 64,842 paid to see Game Four and 66,669 paid to see Game Five at the stadium, surpassing the crowd at a 1926 series game.[28] The St. Louis teams remained stagnant; the Browns were hard pressed to attain an attendance of 100,000 for the season.[29]

Cleveland's attendance hovered around 400,000 between 1933 and 1935 but rebounded over the following three seasons, although not by enough to keep the team playing in Municipal Stadium. Only when the club anticipated a large crowd would it switch to the stadium.[30]

Major League attendance stabilized at around 9 million between 1937 and 1939, with the National League surpassing the American League in 1938 for the first time since 1926–33. The American League might have been hobbled by the Yankees' pennant dominance, as the league's attendance jumped by more than one-fourth when the Tigers ended the New Yorkers' string in 1940.

The *New York Times* heralded the 1938 season as one of the most financially successful. The newspaper attributed the National League's showing to the Cubs' late-season rush to clinch the pennant that buoyed attendance, although in comparison to the team's crowds of 1929 and 1930, the total fell short by 500,000.[31]

Some teams did very well at the gate in 1939. Cincinnati and Brooklyn struggled to reach 1 million in attendance, but fell short in terms of paid attendance. Both teams undoubtedly had over a million attendees if we include those on free passes or discounted tickets. The Dodgers, however, were not as popular on the road, with just 500,000 watching them in other parks.[32]

Attendance rose by almost 10 percent in 1940 and stayed around 9.7 million in 1941 before falling during the first three wartime seasons.[33] The American League had an attendance advantage of 1.04 million over the National League in 1940, the largest gap between the two leagues since Babe Ruth's debut with the Yankees in 1920 boosted American League attendance. Despite a hotly contested pennant race between the Dodgers and Cardinals, the National League's attendance lagged behind that of the American League. The senior circuit's attendance increased by 400,000 in 1941, closing the gap somewhat.

The 1941 National League pennant race triggered a controversy over the two contenders' attendance marks. Cubs fans reportedly rooted against the Cardinals as opposed to the Dodgers, because "St. Louis fans don't deserve a pennant." Apparently Cubs fans thought the St. Louis attendance numbers revealed ennui on the part of Cardinals fans. The reporter pointed out that the Cardinals' attendance of 646,000 was pretty good for a city of 800,000, whereas the Cubs had only 550,000 attendees, despite the fact that Chicago was four times as large as St. Louis. The Cubs, however, were not contenders.[34] The Cardinals' best attendance between 1929 and 1941 was in 1941. The team's three pennant-winning seasons of 1942–44 averaged just over half a million per season, so the team never led the league in attendance. Examination of the per-capita attendance (attendance divided by the metropolitan population) shows that the Cardinals' attendance was more impressive; as owner Sam Breadon boasted, "see for yourself whether they don't make St. Louis the best baseball town in the country."[35]

The first year of the war whittled down the crowds by 8 percent. Even another tense Dodger-Cardinal pennant race failed to sustain the crowds for these clubs, as the two teams attracted 250,000 fewer patrons. The Senators benefited from having more night games.[36]

Baseball's attendance figures roughly corresponded with the economic conditions during the 1930s, although the diminution in crowds lagged behind the progress of the economic slump. The attendance resurgence of the late 1930s should have helped owners regain the profit levels of 1929 and 1930 but profits remained lower than they had been during those halcyon seasons.

Ticket Prices

Attendance figures present an incomplete picture of Major League gate revenue. Not all attendance figures were created equal. Home gate revenue is, after all, a function of attendance and ticket prices. Higher ticket prices could offset a fall in attendance, in which case revenue and profits might not decrease. The deflation of the early 1930s also complicates the task of assessing the trends in revenues. Was falling attendance during the early 1930s exacerbated or cushioned by changes in ticket prices?

Single-game ticket prices generally appeared to have been stable throughout Major League Baseball during the early 1930s. Baseball officials resisted reducing nominal ticket prices. In 1932 both league presidents explained, "during the boom period baseball made no attempt to take advantage of easy money. There can be no logical demand to reduce admission prices at major league ball parks for the simple reason that they have never been increased."[37] The writer quoted National League president John A. Heydler as saying, "Within the last five years, two parks increased the prices of their box seats, but not the regular admission fee, and with the exception of a small additional cost for reserved seats there has been no increase of admission prices in baseball in twenty years." Heydler tied rising costs to the owners' unwillingness to lower ticket prices, pointing out that the stadiums were much better in 1931 than they had been twenty-five years previously and that player salaries and expenses had escalated. He could not see how a fan could accuse owners of gouging when the price of a general admission seat at the Polo Grounds had advanced only from 75¢ to $1.00, a change that had been made years ago.[38] Later, Heydler argued, "When, therefore, it is considered that operating expenses and salaries have increased tremendously in that interval [the previous five years] so that it has come to a point where about half the clubs in our league are finding it almost impossible to meet the enormous overhead, I cannot see how any one can expect them to lower prices."[39] An economist might argue that if customers were sensitive to price changes, lowering prices could have increased revenues. Just as a grocery store might put a gallon of milk on sale (with suitable announcement via advertising) in hopes of attracting much larger crowds and revenues, a baseball owner might have tried a similar tactic with ticket prices.

Owners argued about whether to reduce admission prices. A few owners began to waver after the 1933 season and considered lowering prices on bleacher and pavilion seats, arguing, "from the long point of view, it is better to have those sections filled with customers who can afford to pay the price than it is to have them empty because those who would like to see the games and who would occupy these seats cannot pay what is asked. Then, when better days have arrived, the bleacher customers of today will be the grandstand patrons of tomorrow."[40] The Cleveland Indians, Philadelphia Athletics, and Cincinnati Reds were the only clubs cited by the *New York Times* or *The Sporting* News as having lowered their ticket prices. Prior to the 1933 season the Indians reclassified some grandstand seats as bleachers and reduced the price of box seats by 15¢. The management hinted that it would have preferred to reduce the bleacher and grandstand prices, too, but that they could not without the consent of other American League clubs and "that consent does not appear likely."[41] Connie Mack cut the price of his box seats from $2.20 to $1.65 for 1934 (both prices included the amusement tax). He retained his $1.10 general admission and 55¢ bleacher seat prices.[42] After Larry MacPhail took over Cincinnati Reds, he lowered ticket prices for some games during the season but maintained higher prices for holidays and possibly Sundays. The Reds would continue their policy of charging different prices for weekday and weekend games well into the 1950s.[43]

If teams did not want to tamper with their "list" ticket prices, one may still wonder why more of them didn't offer discounted tickets as a form of modern-day differential pricing. The Boston Braves initiated half-price days for women in addition to their regular ladies' days. As the decade wore on the calls for reduced ticket prices diminished, although a few clubs wanted to allow the right to have discounted days and books of tickets at reduced prices.[44]

Although some people called for baseball owners to lower their ticket prices, the owners fared well in the press. The *Sporting News* editor, for one, lauded the owners for fair dealing with the public in matters of ticket prices. "Baseball stands are vastly different from what they were in the old days, yet the baseball clubs do not begin to ask the patron to pay as much in proportion to their maintenance as the modern theaters demand. The only amusement comparable to baseball is the moving picture show, which is based on cheap distribution and much of it."[45]

The owners could not reduce ticket prices for a significant segment of their patrons: those receiving free passes. In the past owners had cultivated political clout by handing out such passes. During the Depression a *Sporting News* editor suggested that the practice was outdated and that owners should reduce the number of free passes (known in the vernacular as "Annie Oakleys"). The editor expressed little sympathy for a process that had gotten out of control: "It is high time that club owners in both the major and minor leagues took stock of the situation and eliminated the abuse—otherwise, quit complaining about hard times."[46] The National League owners voted to limit the number of passes to 500 per club in 1928, but somehow this did not seem to curb the problem in New York City. A sportswriter estimated that the Giants and Yankees issued more than 170,000 free passes during the 1931 season. The sports editors and writers did not want a total elimination of the free passes, however; they were gratified that "free passes will be limited largely to the metropolitan newspapers which make the big crowds possible."[47]

The federal government added to baseball fans' misery by reinstating a tax on tickets for amusements. The government had levied a 10 percent tax on all tickets costing more than 40¢ beginning during World War I and continuing into 1928. The war tax ended in June 1928, except for admissions costing more than $3.00, such as World Series tickets. The new admission tax took effect June 21, in the middle of baseball season.[48] As with most taxes, sportswriters and fans were confused about who would pay the tax. One reporter said that the reinstated tax differed slightly from the original wartime one in that the government specifically stated that the purchaser of the ticket had to pay the tax (which would be collected by the ball club and remitted to the government), whereas the first tax did not specify who would pay the tax. This handy phrase helped owners avoid charges of "gouging" the fans when they passed on the price of the tax.[49] Economists would argue, however, that the legal incidence of the tax (who has to pay the tax to the government) is not important with regard to the actual burden of the tax (that is, who actually pays the tax in terms of either a higher overall purchase price or of a lower net receipt). Buyers and sellers usually share the burden of the tax. In this case, because the owners did not adjust their ticket prices, fans paid the entire burden of the tax. The owners, however, probably sold fewer tickets than they would have had the tax been shared.[50]

Pity the poor free pass holders, as some of the owners not only charged them the federal tax but also began charging a 25¢ handling fee for the passes, evoking complaints.[51]

The *Sporting News* advised the government to reconsider the admission tax on baseball. "The revenue gained from the levy on the present tax is so immaterial, while the commensurate gains for the enterprises concerned by having it lifted would be so great, that there is little argument in favor of its retention." The editorialist suggested, at the least, the government rescind the tax for tickets priced under $1.00.[52]

Once the federal government successfully reinstated its tax, other governments, city and state, decided to levy their own taxes. While the New York clubs successfully lobbied state legislators against a new state tax on amusements, owners in Ohio and Pennsylvania were not as fortunate. Heydler claimed that one state (probably Ohio, the subject of an earlier editorial in the *Sporting News*) added twenty percent to the cost of a ticket; according to the league president, admissions fell by one-fourth as a result. Since he was referring to the 1934 season, any shortfall in attendance may have been caused in part by other factors.[53]

As though Connie Mack and Gerald Nugent needed more bad news, the Pennsylvania legislators voted to impose state taxes during the 1935 season. The Athletics normally charged $2.00, $1.00, and $50¢ for box, grandstand, and bleacher seats, respectively. The federal tax added ten percent to all seats, while the new Pennsylvania tax added another four percent. The state taxes raised the Pennsylvania clubs' ticket prices slightly above those of their rivals. Even the free pass holders now had to pay 14¢ in taxes. Not only were the ticket prices higher, but the unwieldy tax and admission charges created bottlenecks at the ticket booths because of the change needed for almost every transaction.[54]

The federal tax prompted more discussion about ticket prices. The top Minor Leagues, such as the Pacific Coast League and the American Association, finally decided to reduce the price of bleacher seats to 25¢ for the 1932 season. The *Sporting News* applauded the Minor Leagues' actions and even thought that the Major Leagues might emulate the lower bleacher prices: "something should be done for the bleacher fan. Many persons with the old love for the game haven't the means to go as often as they would like. The bleacher fans, probably, have been the hardest hit by the depression. Wouldn't it be a good idea to let them into the bleachers once a week for a quarter?"[55] Major League owners refused to follow suit. The big league owners claimed that they could not lower their prices in the face of fixed expenses and the federal admission taxes.

Even after the trough of the Depression, fans wrote to the *New York*

Times and complained about high ticket prices. On one occasion an older fan complained about the prices of baseball tickets compared with those of his halcyon youth: "In the old days the grand stand seats at the Polo Grounds cost 75 cents, the right-field admissions were 50 cents and the bleachers in left field sold at 25 cents a seat.... What magic transformed the ball park to make a seat which formerly sold at 25 cents now cost $1.10?"[56] Another fan claimed that the rows of empty seats implied that the $1.10 general admission price was "pretty steep for many to pay" and urged the owners to reduce admissions a little.[57] One fan argued that ticket prices should be reduced "in keeping with the deflationary trend.... A grandstand seat should cost no more than 85 cents, and a bleacher seat, should be obtainable at 40 cents."[58] When Larry MacPhail succeeded in improving Brooklyn's position in the National League and boosted the crowds there, not all Dodgers fans were pleased. One fan wanted more bleacher seats at Ebbets Field, while others criticized the variable pricing practiced by the club. The team reclassified general admission seats as reserved seats for Sunday doubleheaders. John McDonald, the team's assistant to the president, said the policy was established to meet the overwhelming demand for reserved seats. He mentioned that many of the general admission seats that had been reclassified carried the same $1.10 price as general admission seats, although some of the seats now cost $1.65. He concluded by claiming that the average price of grandstand seats at Ebbets Field was 10 to 20 percent lower than the average price at the Polo Grounds or Yankee Stadium.[59]

For some games ticket prices were arguably set too low. Then, as now, some people took the risk that a game would be more popular than anticipated and bought up seats to resell (what people call ticket scalping might better be called ticket arbitraging or speculating; these terms are also free of ethnic prejudice). An editorial in the *Sporting News* characterized the transaction: "First, the buyer, who purchases from willingness to overpay or from compulsion. He is always the primary party. Second, the seller, who disposes of tickets with a desire to squeeze the public, or with the determination to impose an exorbitant and unnecessary super-price on the public and profit by the speculation." The editorial advised clubs to refuse to sell to the speculator, although it did not elaborate how such characters were to be identified, there being no badge of infamy for speculators.[60] Like most observers, the editorial writer misstated the speculator's role. If the owners did not set a market-clearing price, the speculator transferred tickets to people who valued them enough to pay the higher price. The process was fraught with risk, since the speculator might have overestimated the demand for a particular game, have been stuck with redundant tickets, and have absorbed a loss.[61] The presence of large numbers of fans being turned away at some games was proof enough that the owners occasionally set prices below the market-clearing level, which is not to say the owners necessarily acted irrationally. Sometimes they simply underestimated demand; sometimes they knew they could sell out with higher prices but feared antagonizing their fans. Economists Kahneman, Knetsch, and Thaler demonstrated that producers should consider the effects of their ticket prices in the long run, often taking perceived fairness into account.[62]

Certainly owners understood that the increased demand for World Series games justified a much higher set of prices than for regular-season games. The fans apparently acquiesced, even though the change meant many regular-season fans might be priced out of attending while wealthier, less dedicated fans attended the premium contests. In 1932, at the deepest part of the Depression, the Yankees charged $6.60 per box seat for a World Series ticket, three times the normal price. The team set similar proportional increases for reserved and general admission tickets. The bleacher fans caught a break from the club, having to pay only double the regular-season price. Fans could buy tickets for all three potential home games as a set. The club set similar prices for their World Series appearances between 1936 and 1939.[63] Fortunately for the Yankees, their club clinched the pennants early during these seasons and could sell the tickets in a reasonably orderly manner.

When the New York Giants participated in the World Series, the club charged prices similar to those the Yankees charged. Even at $6.60, box seats sold out quickly at the Polo Grounds. A sportswriter claimed that ticket brokers "cornered blocks of seats, as they always do, and they are looking forward to fancy prices and a handsome profit as they dispose of these to those fans who purchase only for individual games. Business organizations here and in other cities are conspicuous in the list of applicants with orders for blocks of tickets."[64] Speculators hovered about Times Square offering World Series reserved tickets at $12.00 per game or a complete strip of tickets to all three potential Polo Grounds games at $25.00. A reporter suggested that the speculators had reached the upper limit of fans' willingness to pay, since "there was no apparent rush for tickets at those prices."[65] The Dodgers later upped the ante by charging a 25¢ handling fee on World Series tickets.[66]

Before the economic depression there was strong evidence that the New York market was willing to demand more tickets at the premium prices than the Yankees had seats for a few games. At a crucial matchup between the Athletics and Yankees in September 1928, thousands of disappointed fans vented their frustrations. "When the supply [of reserved seats] became exhausted the disappointed ones rushed and roared, or rather roared and rushed, in the order named."[67] A month later the St. Louis Cardinals faced excess demand for their available World Series tickets, with the club returning an estimated 75,000 requests for reserved and box seats.[68] The Cardinals and Yankees attracted almost 200,000 paying customers for the four-game series, and their total receipts ran $777,290. Although these figures did not surpass the 1927 World Series, they were still healthy. Even the federal government did well, getting about one-tenth of the receipts via the tax on tickets, which were priced at about $3.00.[69]

Another large excess demand for World Series tickets occurred in 1941, when the Brooklyn Dodgers finally returned to the World Series after twenty-one years. The loyal Dodger fans would easily have overwhelmed the limited seating capacity of Ebbets Field. Larry MacPhail must have been tempted to play the Dodgers' "home" games at either

Yankee Stadium or the Polo Grounds, which had many more seats. He ultimately decided not to ask for the switch, perhaps out of fear of fan reactions but perhaps also because of the difficulty of printing and distributing tickets.[70] His decision may have cost both clubs hundreds of thousands of dollars over a seven-game series. The issue recurred in 1947 and the Dodgers again chose not to switch home fields.

Major League Baseball owners essentially maintained their list ticket prices during the 1930s in the face of a decline in the general price level of roughly 25 percent. This means ticket prices actually rose in terms of purchasing power. The combination of rising real ticket prices in the face of declining consumer incomes seems ridiculous from a sound business standpoint. Were the owners momentarily crazed? I think the answer lies in the owners' belief that fans would vote with their feet. Owners offered three or four classes of seats. They saw their patrons moving to cheaper seats between 1929 and 1933, a change reflected by the lower nominal average home revenue per attendee figures (table 7). In real terms, though, the news wasn't so bad. The inflation-adjusted (real) average home revenue per attendee rose between 1929 and 1933. The shift to the cheaper seats did not fully offset the increase in real ticket prices, so the owners realized higher real home revenues per attendees; this cushioned the drop in attendance. By 1939 the nominal home revenue per attendee had rebounded back to the 1929 level because fans shifted back to the more expensive seats. Owners found that the average real home revenue jumped considerably. Whether this strategy of passively maintaining nominal prices was an astute one is difficult to ascertain. Dropping the nominal (and possibly the real) ticket prices might have lessened the reduction in attendance, but whether such a mitigation would have increased real ticket revenues remains unknown.

Revenue and Ticket Prices

Table 8 shows gross operating income. The nominal figures portray a more dismal situation than the deflation-adjusted figures. Major League

Baseball's real gross operating income jumped sharply between 1929 and 1939. Teams differed in their revenue potential because they derived revenue from a variety of sources. Gate receipts were the main source, of course, but owners also staged exhibition games and sold concessions. As the 1930s ended they also began to get media revenue.

Games at Home and Away Revenue and Exhibition Games Revenue

What happened to collective nominal and real games at home and games away revenue? The revenue information demonstrates the importance of distinguishing between nominal and real (inflation-adjusted) figures (table 9). The American League teams reported just half as much games at home revenue in 1933 as they did in 1929, but in real terms the drop was a more modest one-third. The games at home revenue reflected the gate receipts adjusted for the visitors' share, the league's share, and the federal amusement tax levied for the 1933 and 1939 seasons. The visitors' share amounted to roughly 28¢ and 24¢ per attendee in the American League and National League respectively. The difference in the visitors' share accounts for part of the National League's advantage in average home revenue per attendee shown in table 7. The league's share ranged from 2.5¢ to 5.0¢. Most years the shares were 2.5¢ per attendee in the National League and 3.0¢ per attendee in the American League.

Teams differed in their ability to generate gate revenue. Part of the disparity arose because of varying population bases. The teams in New York and Chicago held an inherent advantage over other teams, although they did not always exploit that advantage.

Ruppert might on occasion get almost $100,000 in gross revenue from a single date at Yankee Stadium. A Memorial Day doubleheader with the Boston Red Sox in 1938 created a gross receipt of almost $92,000. Ruppert had to pay the 10 percent federal tax, visitors' share, and league share, so he netted roughly $57,000.[71] Sportswriter Dan Daniel reviewed this doubleheader two years later. He believed fans assumed

Why Did Profits Collapse? Revenue Side

the Yankees netted $80,000 after taxes and explained why this wasn't so. Daniel also pointed out that Yankee Stadium had 14,000 bleacher seats, each of which gave the club 50¢ in gate revenue; 20¢ per seat went to the visiting team. He cited a figure of 86.4¢ in gate revenue per attendee.[72] The fans spent about $20,000 for concessions, although Daniel did not know how much of this went to the Yankees and how much was kept by the Stevens concessionaire.[73]

Of the other New York clubs, Brooklyn had healthy attendance figures between 1939 and 1941, but the New York Giants' lower figures masked the club's inherent advantage. The Giants' price per seat was probably higher than Brooklyn's, since the Polo Grounds contained a higher proportion of box and reserved seats than Ebbets Field. The Giants also gained more revenue from hosting college and professional football games.[74]

The New York clubs had natural advantages over the Braves and Browns due to their population base. Teams in Boston and St. Louis usually drew far smaller crowds, even on their best days.

Although profits were not as large in 1939 as they had been in 1929, despite similar attendance in the two years, real games at home revenue and real games away revenue were not the culprits. Even in nominal terms, combined home and away revenues were greater in 1939 than in 1929.

Table 10 shows exhibition game revenues. The St. Louis Browns reported receiving no exhibition game revenue, but they may have included such revenue as "other" revenue. As can be expected, the New York Yankees were among the top draws for exhibition games; the Philadelphia Athletics rivaled them in 1929 before becoming an exhibition game irrelevancy. In his prime, Babe Ruth was a big draw for fans in smaller towns. The Yankees recognized this by paying him a bonus based upon exhibition game revenues. Exhibition game revenue accounted for a nickel out of every revenue dollar across the major league teams, although many of the teams probably realized less than a penny or two of each dollar of revenue from this source. At best, many teams may have simply hoped to recoup some transportation, hotel, and meal money during their road trips.

Eat, Eat, Eat at the Ballgame: Concessions Revenue

While concessions represented less than one-tenth of a team's total revenue, they could make the difference between turning a profit and incurring a loss (tables 6 and 10). Net concessions revenue, like other revenue sources, was unevenly distributed. The Philadelphia clubs had poor returns from concessions, while the Yankees reaped the most revenue from this source. National League owners received more concessions revenue than their American League counterparts. The owners watched concessions revenue falter in 1933, although the decrease was relatively mild in real terms. Concessions revenue jumped between 1933 and 1939.

Sportswriter Dan Daniel described how the Chicago Cubs initially rented out its concessions, but when the Wrigleys discovered that the concessionaire made $125,000 a year they changed their minds. Walter O'Malley, later owner of the Brooklyn Dodgers, thought it best to farm out the concessions, since a concessionaire was an expert at the business and the baseball officials were not.[75]

Harry Stevens provided concessions not only at Yankee Stadium but also at the Polo Grounds, Ebbets Field, Fenway Park, and Braves Field. The author has examined team scorecards from 1929 through the 1960s. While the Stevens-produced scorecards were never the worst, they were rarely the best in terms of paper quality or information. The Stevens scorecards rarely, if ever, provided concession and ticket prices for the New York clubs. The advertisements might give the price of Muriel cigars or Schrafft's chocolate bars, but that was all.[76] Stevens discovered that New York City fans favored peanuts, while fans in western cities opted for popcorn. "It cost Mr. Stevens several thousand dollars to learn that while you can lead an Eastern rooter to popcorn, you can't make him eat....Eastern fans eat few sandwiches; they prefer the succulent hot dog. Western fans... go for ham sandwiches in a big way.

They eat hot dogs, too; but not as many as Easterners do."[77] Sundays were not the best days for selling hot dogs, as "your Sunday fan comes from his dinner, or a heavy luncheon and he is not a frankfurter patron until late innings, if then. At night, we sell fewer hot dogs than on week days because most of the customers come from their dinners."[78]

One reporter claimed that fans bought more concessions if the home team won the first game of a doubleheader, an argument that Bill Veeck echoed in the 1950s.[79] As the Depression faded and as night ball spread, owners found growing numbers of fans devouring ever more food. "In Brooklyn, the entire back of the grandstand has been converted into a gigantic eatery. This became essential with the growth of night ball, and the habit of customers dashing direct from their places of employment to the ball park."[80]

If a fan became hungry or thirsty, a dime or two nickels to rub together would provide some satisfaction. Team scorecards provided intermittent information on the prices of hot dogs, soda, and peanuts. Each commodity cost 10¢ at Fenway Park in 1935–36, Shibe Park in 1938, Braves Field in 1941, and Wrigley Field in 1935–40. By 1944, Burk's Franks went for 15¢ at Shibe Park, according to a Phillies scorecard. The Braves also listed beer prices in 1941: 10¢ for draught and 20¢ for a bottle.[81]

Table 11 shows net concessions divided by attendance. This provides a crude estimate of the net amount each attendee spent at the ballpark. There are problems with these figures, of course. First, actual attendance at games included people with discounted tickets and free passes. These people did not count in the official attendance figures. Bill Veeck Jr. once claimed that during his stints as owner of the Cleveland Indians and Chicago White Sox, unofficial attendees totaled more than a million people in a season.[82] These unofficial folks were undoubtedly as thirsty and hungry as regular attendees. A team with a high proportion of unofficial attendees might end up with a high concessions-per-attendee figure. Second, owners had different concessions contracts. A few ran their own concessions, but most hired independent operators, such as the Stevens Brothers, to run the concessions. Because of these issues, the per-attendee concession figures are not necessarily reflective of how much people spent at the various ballparks. The table does not necessarily imply that Philadelphia fans, for instance, were so intent on the game that they eschewed sustenance.

In the American League the Yankees appeared to get more concessions revenues, both in dollars and per attendee, than most of their rivals. The Browns, surprisingly, had the highest per-attendee concessions revenue, whether as a result of a favorable concessions contract or because fans sated their hunger for victories with hot dogs and drinks. The Cardinals and Pirates had hefty per-attendee figures.

Concessions revenues remained a steady source of revenue for baseball owners during the 1930s.

Other Revenue: Radio and Miscellaneous Revenue

Although television and, to a lesser extent, radio revenues comprise an important proportion of modern baseball's revenue, media revenue was just beginning to sprout into a dependable source during the 1930s. Table 12 shows revenue from radio broadcasts. Although some clubs permitted broadcasts of home games, none charged for the rights in 1929. A few teams pocketed small amounts of money by 1933. Most of the owners were wary about radio, as will be discussed in a later chapter. Baseball moguls embraced radio broadcasts only after radio stations began receiving plentiful advertising dollars that they were reluctant to share with team owners. By 1939 the owners received over $850,000 for broadcasting rights. As a percentage of gross operating income, radio revenue quickly achieved parity with net concessions and provided one dollar of revenue out of every fourteen. Significant disparities in radio revenue arose immediately; the Giants earned four times as much as the Reds. The Yankees had a similar advantage over the Senators. Media disparity exacerbated the underlying disparity in potential and actual gate revenue, a trend that endures today.

Teams also had some unspecified revenues, amounting to 6 to 8 percent of total revenues. The Browns' other revenues may have come from exhibition games, as they listed no revenue from this source. Other teams might have gotten revenue from renting out their stadiums to football teams or to Negro League clubs.

The New York Yankees collected hefty fees from hosting other major sporting events. Knute Rockne brought his Notre Dame boys in for a tussle with the Army team in November 1929. The *Sporting News* anticipated a crowd of 90,000 for the game and guessed that the Yankees would collect $100,000, which was, according to the team's cash books, much too optimistic.[83]

Case Study: New York Yankees

Although the New York Yankees may not be representative of all, or even of most, Major League Baseball teams, a case study of their finances is useful. The Yankees' management reported consolidated net income (after taxes) from 1920 until the early 1950s to Congress in 1952 (table 13). They reported annual nominal and real net income figures of over $200,000 between 1920 and 1930, except for 1925. The team reported losses in 1932, 1933, and 1935. Between 1931 and 1935, the team lost about $170,000 in nominal terms. These figures demonstrate trends similar to those prepared by Haupert and Winter (2003), who calculated team profit before taxes.[84]

Even the New York Yankees could not evade the baleful effects of the Great Depression. Table 14 shows total revenue from baseball operations aside from the World Series. Net receipts from home games were the dominant source of revenue, while receipts from away games were the second largest source. Nominal and real total revenue peaked in 1930 before dwindling through 1935. Because of deflation, the diminution was smaller in real terms, and real total revenue for 1929–32 compared favorably with 1921–24 (although the latter period had the advantage of concessions revenues). Still, 1933–35 represented a low point for Ruppert's ownership, whereas overall spending on spectator sports rebounded. The divergence may be explained by the team's performance: they won a pennant in 1932 but failed to do so between 1933 and 1935.

Revenue from spring training and exhibition games fluctuated considerably between 1929 and 1939. As Babe Ruth deteriorated during the Great Depression revenue from these non-counting games dwindled, reaching a low in 1936.

When they were tenants of the Polo Grounds, the Yankees did not report any revenue from sales of concessions. With Ruppert's construction of Yankee Stadium, the team began receiving revenues from such sales. Between 1926 and 1931 revenue from concessions hovered around 9–10 percent of total revenue. Harry Stevens held the contract to run concessions at Yankee Stadium. The concessions revenue per attendee fluctuated throughout the period, generally mimicking the trends in the economy.

The Yankees hesitated to broadcast their games on the radio and were one of the last American League teams to do so. The team eventually broadcast games beginning in the 1939 season and stopped doing so during 1941 and 1943–44.[85] The team got $110,000 in nominal broadcasting revenue in 1939 but failed to get as much in 1940 or in 1942.

We will discuss the player payroll's effects upon net income in chapter 3. For the moment, it is sufficient to note that the team suffered from narrowing differences between revenues and player payrolls.

How did the Yankees' management respond to the dismal revenue and profit figures of the early 1930s? As table 13 shows, attendance at games at Yankee Stadium fell between 1930 and 1935; a decrease in the nominal gate revenue per attendee exacerbated the effects of declining attendance. The average receipts remained close to $1.00 through 1930. As the Great Depression continued, the average receipts fell to a low of $0.88 in 1933 and 1935 before rebounding in 1936 to $0.94 (table 15).

Although nominal ticket prices remained stable (if we ignore the federal tax), the average real home receipts jumped in 1931 and continued to rise through 1933. Real ticket prices rose concurrently with falling incomes. Attendance fell from 1.17 million in 1930 to 730,000 in 1933.

For most of the years examined, the American League did not report attendance either in the daily box scores or on a yearly basis, but

Why Did Profits Collapse? Revenue Side

previous researchers have published yearly attendance figures. The information in the cash books enabled me to reconstruct series-by-series and sometimes game-by-game home and away gate receipts. We can deduce the team's policies regarding ticket prices from the gate receipts. Because of the league-share and revenue-sharing rules, one can calculate the attendance at each home series.

The American League enacted new revenue-sharing rules before the 1927 season. Home teams were required to remit 3¢ per full admission to the league while paying 20¢ per bleacher or general admission ticket and 30¢ per reserved or box seat to the visiting team.[86] Unfortunately, constitutions are difficult to find, and this information came from an amended copy of the December 15, 1926 constitution. The league appeared to levy only 3¢ per full paid admission between 1924 and 1938, with one exception in 1933. In 1933, the league share jumped to 5¢, the level permanently instituted in 1939, which is the amount listed in the amended constitution. I did not find any mention in *The Sporting News* or *The New York Times* of these changes in league funding.

The evidence strongly suggests that the team did not change its prices during the Great Depression. Season ticket prices reported in the team's general ledger remained constant between 1923 and 1944, aside from adjustments for war or amusement taxes. The Yankees certainly tacked the amusement tax onto their season ticket prices in 1933 (they did not retroactively charge the tax on their 1932 season-ticket holders).[87] A box containing eight seats cost $554.40 throughout the period. When the federal government levied the across-the-board 10 percent tax on amusement tickets, the team adjusted the box seat price to $609.84. A single box seat cost $69.30 between 1923 and 1944. Again, when the tax was levied, patrons paid an additional $6.93. A few boxes cost $400.00 but these existed alongside the $554.40 boxes and apparently contained fewer seats.

Evidence on ticket prices implies that bleacher seats cost 50¢, general admission seats cost $1.00, reserved seats cost $1.50, and box seats cost $2.00. The American League Constitution stipulated that a minimum of 50¢ be charged for admission, and Ruppert was quoted in 1933 as charging this amount for his bleacher seats.[88] A Yankees bleacher ticket stub for 1937 showed a price of 55¢, which included the admission tax.[89] Other ticket stubs in the National Baseball Hall of Fame & Museum's collection reveal general admission prices of $1.00 in 1930 and $1.10 (including tax) in 1937. Reserved-seat ticket stubs showed prices of $1.65 in 1936 and 1939. Two ticket stubs from 1929 and 1934 listed on eBay showed prices of $1.50 and $1.65 for a reserved seat; the latter ticket included the federal amusement tax. Another ticket stub shown on eBay from the 1931 season showed a price of $2.00 for a box chair.[90]

Within the Yankees' financial records, the only evidence of ticket prices, aside from the season box seats, was an entry listing refunds in the cash book.[91] A single general admission or unreserved grandstand seat cost $1.10. Reserved seats cost $1.65, while individual box seats were $2.20. No bleacher seats were refunded. These prices reflected the 10 percent admission tax.

The Yankees did not publish ticket prices for individual games or for season tickets in their scorecards. All three New York teams advertised their games in the *New York Times* on days when they played at home. The Giants listed ticket prices for bleachers, general admission, and reserved seats in their advertisements between 1931 and 1934, but the Yankees and Dodgers did not list theirs. A scouring of the *New York Times Index* and the *Sporting News* failed to yield ticket price information.

The New York Giants played in the Polo Grounds, across the Harlem River from Yankee Stadium. The Giants advertised prices of 50¢ for bleacher seats, $1.00 for general admission seats, and $1.50 for reserved seats for the 1931 season and into the 1932 season. When the federal amusement tax resumed on June 21, 1932, the Giants immediately added the 10 percent tax to their ticket prices.[92] The Giants continued to publish ticket prices in their advertisements through the 1934 season, and these prices remained constant.

The Yankees and Giants were not the only clubs to add the 10 percent surcharge onto their ticket prices. National League president John Heydler stated that "clubs in the National League will not assume the burden of paying the extra costs themselves. . . . no club in baseball would be able to undertake the task of relieving the spectator of the obligation to pay the tax"[93] From the fans' perspective, this was equivalent to a 10 percent increase in ticket prices, levied at the depth of the Depression.

The fifty-cent denominations of tickets had an indirect benefit. The ticket sellers would only have to deal with change denominated in quarters or half-dollar pieces. The Yankees purposely supplied their takers with half dollars, both for convenience and to prevent an unscrupulous seller from short changing patrons. "They [the half dollars] are difficult to get, but they are an insurance against loss by the public. A ticket purchaser might not miss a dime or even a quarter, in the hurry of making change, but he would be likely to notice the loss of a half a dollar."[94] The federal admission tax, of course, derailed this simple scheme.

Aside from the tax-induced changes, then, there is little evidence that Ruppert changed nominal ticket prices during the Great Depression.

A more likely explanation for the dwindling nominal average ticket price shown in table 15 was that fans simply moved around Yankee Stadium, switching to the cheaper general admission and bleacher seats and away from the reserved and box seats (and displacing fans who were unwilling or unable to pay even bleacher prices). The gate-sharing rules illuminate this process. Visiting teams received 20¢ per full admission to the bleachers or general admission and 30¢ per full admission to reserved or box seats. In addition, for the relatively few season ticket holders, the team paid the league and visiting shares only if the patron went through the turnstiles.[95] The home team saved the visitor's share from "no-shows." Any discounted ticket price was not assessed the league's or visiting team's shares. These attendees did not count in the attendance figures. For most teams, ladies' day tickets were the main type of discounted tickets, but the Yankees did not begin ladies' day discounts until the 1938 season.[96] The team also did not offer children's prices.

The visiting share divided by attendance ranges from 20¢ to 30¢; therefore the average visiting share immediately reveals the percentage of attendees sitting in reserved or box seats. For instance, suppose there were ten patrons. Six paid for reserved or box seats. The Yankees would have paid $1.80 to the visiting team (six times 30¢) for these six tickets. Four paid for general admission or bleacher seats. The Yankees would have paid 80¢ to the visiting team (four times 20¢) for these four tickets. The Yankees would have paid $2.60 to the visiting team for the ten seats, or an average of 26¢, proving that 60 percent of tickets were sold in the reserved and box seats. An average payment of 28¢ meant 80 percent of the seats sold were reserved and box seats. The percent of bleacher and general admission seats would be the complements, or 40 and 20 percent respectively.

I use only the years 1927–41 (corresponding to the revenue-sharing rules cited in the 1926 constitution) in discussing the share of bleacher and unreserved grandstand (general admission) seats to reserved and box seats. The proportion of cheap seats was well below 30 percent through 1930 (table 15). As the Depression continued the proportion rose above 35 percent in 1932 and peaked at 39.7 percent in 1935. Unfortunately, the data does not allow for finer differentiation within the cheap seats or reserved/box groupings. The Yankees sold 4.1 million seats between 1928 and 1931, of which 3.0 million were box and reserved seats and the rest were general admission and bleacher seats. Between 1932 and 1935 the club sold just 3.2 million seats; although the number of general admission and bleacher seats remained almost constant at 1.2 million, only 2.0 million box and reserved seats were sold. Even within a season, the mix of seats varied considerably, as table 16 reveals. While the sparsely-attended series appeared to attract larger proportions of bleacher fans, statistical analysis shows only a weak relationship between the size of the crowd and the proportion of cheap seats sold.[97]

Since Ruppert doesn't appear to have lowered ticket prices, despite deflation, we can ask, "What evidence did he have regarding ticket prices and demand?" Did he feel that fans were relatively unresponsive to price changes, so any reduction in ticket prices would result in lower revenue?

Because Congress rescinded the war tax midway through the 1928 season and reinstated it as an admission tax during the 1932 season, we can examine the effects upon home receipts. The tax was 10 percent on all seats except for discounted seats, such as ladies' day seats. Therefore, the relative prices (the ratio between prices of bleacher and box seats, for example) of box, reserved, general admission, and bleacher seats remained unchanged. Assuming that customers did not care whether the Yankees or the federal government received either a tax or its equivalent in an increased ticket price, the reinstatement was an across-the-board 10 percent increase in price in 1932. The removal of the tax in 1928 was equivalent to a 9.1 percent decrease in overall price. We can examine how total home receipts that include war taxes were affected by the admission tax.

In 1928 the twenty-eight home playing dates with the tax in force netted an average of $16,300 (including the tax) per date. The remaining thirty playing dates without the tax, including the bulk of the nineteen doubleheaders, averaged $20,900 in gate receipts. Thus the removal of the tax was associated with greater revenues. In 1932 the Yankees had twenty-five home playing dates before the tax resumed. These playing dates averaged $18,000 in receipts. For the forty remaining playing dates, the average receipts were $11,500. In both cases the average receipts for the tax-free dates were higher. Before the team could draw definitive conclusions, however, some thought should be given to the fact that 1928 featured a pennant race that persisted until the final weekend of the season, whereas in 1932 the Yankees had built a large lead by mid-June and coasted to a triumph. The team would have to employ more sophisticated statistical analysis before concluding that lowering prices increased average receipts.[98]

On the basis of this admittedly tenuous analysis, an economist might suggest that the Yankees should have considered lowering ticket prices, but Ruppert apparently chose to operate on another margin: the number of seats within each classification. He eventually chose to encourage bleacher patrons by creating more cheap seats instead of tampering with prices. He did not choose to do so by reclassifying existing seats. There is little evidence that many owners apart from Ruppert or Cleveland's owners reclassified seats during the early years of the 1930s. (Owners did reclassify seats during the 1950s.) Instead, Ruppert revamped the bleachers and grandstands before the 1937 season by replacing the wooden bleachers with concrete ones. Part of the bleacher section was covered, giving the team the "largest 50-cent covered section in the major leagues."[99] Other owners also recognized the popularity of bleacher seats (and their attendant low ticket prices) and chose to create more bleacher seats. The Brooklyn Dodgers decided to add 4,000 more bleacher seats by reclassifying seats for the 1933 season, while the Chicago Cubs added 3,500 bleacher seats for the 1936 season.[100] Given that bleacher seats were inferior goods (in the sense that as a fan's income falls, he buys more of them, or if a fan's income rises, he buys fewer of them), increasing their availability in the face of declining fan income made sense. Ruppert's construction plan, however, developed as fans began to shift back towards more expensive seats during the late 1930s.

The *Sporting News* reprinted an article by sportswriter Joe Williams, who found that the American League sold a higher proportion of bleacher seats than the National League, with the Yankees selling the highest proportion of all: 31 percent in 1932. Williams thought that a key to the Yankees' financial success was the team's willingness to court bleacher patrons, although the *Sporting News* reporter rebutted this example with that of the Cubs, whose bleacher patrons comprised just 7 percent of the total tickets sold.[101] The *Sporting News* nevertheless advocated that owners should try to create more bleachers.

If Ruppert was unwilling to change nominal ticket prices, what else did he do to boost revenues? He was not keen on three of the innovations to boost attendance that some of his fellow owners pursued: ladies' days, night baseball, and radio broadcasts. While women attending ladies' day games did not count in the official attendance, their presence might have triggered increased male patronage or increased female attendance at other games. The Yankees were one of the last teams to have ladies' days, beginning in 1938.[102] The team also resisted playing night games at Yankee Stadium and would not play any until after World War II. Several other teams, though, installed lights and few owners that used night baseball ever reduced the number of such games. Ruppert also delayed broadcasting games on radio.

Aside from building more bleachers, Ruppert proved cautious in implementing steps to boost attendance and receipts at Yankee Stadium. He appeared to be satisfied with fielding a quality product on the field. Given the rebound in the team's fortunes on and off the field during the late 1930s, perhaps he felt justified in his conservatism.

Conclusion

Although real revenues fell along with economic activity throughout Major League Baseball, they rebounded nicely as the 1930s wore on. The attendance decline of the early 1930s was matched by a decrease in the average nominal home revenue per attendee as fans moved to cheaper seats. By holding nominal ticket prices fixed in the face of generally falling prices, however, the owners saw an increase in the average real home revenue per attendee. This increase helped cushion the fall in attendance. By the end of the decade, with a rebound in attendance, real revenues were comparable to, if not greater than, those earned during the peak years of 1929 and 1930. Revenues were not the reason profitability did not return to the 1929–30 levels. Whether owners would have benefited from reducing their ticket prices or from offering more discounts is hard to determine.

3. Why Did Profits Collapse?
Player Salaries and Other Expenses

Owners saw their profits plummet during the early years of the 1930s. It is certain that revenues fell in both nominal and real terms. Profits were sure to fall if owners did not reduce expenses commensurately. How quickly did owners adjust their player salaries and other expenses in response?

Player Salaries

Owners and fans have traditionally blamed player salaries for decreased profits and higher ticket prices. Owners were floundering in red ink by 1933. Did they use their monopsony power to reduce player salaries quickly?

Player salaries were possibly the largest individual expense for owners during the 1930s, but today's owners would envy them. According to information presented to Congress in 1951, player salaries, including managers' and coaches' salaries, comprised roughly a third of the total operating income or gross operating expenses in 1929, 1939, and 1943. The player salaries represented over 44 percent of total operating income and 36 percent of gross operating expenses in 1933, indicating a squeeze on the owners' profit margins. After World War II, these ratios hovered around 20 percent but did not include managers' and coaches' salaries in most cases.[1] As a comparison, modern owners provided a blue ribbon committee with payroll and revenue data for the 1995–99 seasons. This reliable information, which is rarely provided, showed that player salaries usually averaged more than 50 percent of revenues.[2] For the owners, the years centered on 1933 proved to be the worst in terms of payroll-to-revenue ratios. No wonder owners sought to reduce payrolls between 1931 and 1935.

Until the mid-1970s major and minor league baseball players labored until the reserve clause, which essentially bound them to one team unless an owner chose to allow a change. In his pathbreaking paper, Simon Rottenberg noted that under baseball's reserve clause, owners possessed single-buyer (monopsony) power in setting player salaries, which "can have the effect of depressing salaries."[3] Because of the players' weak bargaining position, there is a strong presumption that players were not paid commensurate with the additional revenue (in economic terms, the marginal revenue product) that they generated for a team.

Salaries of baseball players are usually a matter of conjecture although, given the relatively small salaries of the era, the estimates were usually within a few thousand dollars of reality. Reporters' estimates of Yankees player salaries were remarkably accurate, but their estimates of other teams' player salaries were less accurate. The Haupert Hall of Fame Player Salary Database has American League player salaries which can be compared with newspaper reports. Sports economists would greatly appreciate having voluminous salary data, so they could decide whether owners paid players based on their productivity or whether the players were exploited and, if they were exploited, how severe that exploitation was.

Were the Players Overpaid?

Although owners were keen to cut salaries during the early 1930s, they had always seemed interested in reducing payrolls. The reserve clause gave the owners the upper hand during salary negotiations. Researchers Robert Burk and John Helyar have contributed just two of the more recent accounts of the unhappy history of labor and management relations in baseball. The Congressional committee of 1951 also compiled a litany of player and management strife.[4] Most observers argued that the reserve clause was necessary to promote honesty and competitive balance, but the chronic disparity between the Yankees and Browns undercuts the latter argument. One owner, Philip Wrigley of the Chicago Cubs, admitted that he admired a player who held out, since holdouts were confident of their abilities and wanted to be paid commensurately.[5] A *Sporting News* editorial claimed that the average player benefited more from the reserve rule than did a star player, "who hardly needs protection, even if his club does, that the rule is favored and looked upon as a sort of a benevolent protection."[6]

Despite the strong presumption held by economists that players were underpaid, sportswriters, possibly due to subconscious envy, appeared to believe that the players were overpaid. An editorial pointed out that "an advance is paid to the athlete of this type for a succeeding year and instead of playing better, he cannot play as well, and often plays abominably bad. Yet, we cannot recall that such a player ever volunteered to have his salary reduced to the sum of the preceding year." In another editorial the writer claimed, "If players were paid exactly on the value of their performances, we feel quite sure that more of them would receive less than they do."[7] The players made much more than the average manufacturing worker of the era; according to information presented to Congress in 1951, the players' average annual earnings were between five and six times those of workers in the "all industries" category.[8] It is also true that few people, sportswriters included, would have paid money to watch even the best worker on an assembly line. Top baseball players attracted large crowds of paying customers. Occasionally the *Sporting News* editorial page reflected this aspect, as when it analyzed whether Jim Bottomley was worth a reported $150,000. The editor tried to figure out just how much more in gate receipts per game an acquiring club would need in order to break even with its purchase.[9]

The editorialists for the *Sporting News* generally assumed a patronizing attitude towards the players, as evidenced by a discussion regarding baseball players and automobiles. While the editorial writer did not favor prohibiting players from driving cars, even in spite of the "menace to thousands of dollars' worth of personal earning ability," he suggested the players be "perfectly satisfied to run his machine with the same careful adjustment as he tries to run bases."[10] While it is understandable why owners were concerned about their players' off-the-field activities, players chafed under restrictions. Baseball owners, of course, were not the only employers to probe into their workers' private affairs. Automobile manufacturer Henry Ford had long sought to keep his workers thrifty and sober, even to the extent of employing spies.

Owners tried to discourage players from earning extra income from barnstorming during the winter. They worried, of course, that players might be injured while playing against amateurs, but they also worried that the players might become less reliant upon their regular salaries. Commissioner Landis suspended Babe Ruth and Bob Meusel when they barnstormed following the 1921 World Series.

The players did not respond by forming a union. In an editorial, the *Sporting News* cited the difficulty of setting a wage scale to cover the disparate abilities and popularity of different players; more importantly, "It is the lack of public sympathy, however, that probably would represent the greatest obstacle to the formation of a players' union."[11] Players were decades away from having their consciousnesses raised by astute labor experts such as Marvin Miller. The *Sporting News* editorial page pontificated against a proposed player organization to protect their rights: "Keep out of it. Every time that such a plan has been attempted it has resulted in utter failure. There is not a player today in the major leagues who is receiving an inadequate salary."[12]

The players also lacked a pension, and there was no Social Security program for much of the era. When someone suggested creating a pension plan for the players, the *Sporting News* editorialist sniffed in 1937, "Ball players come within the provision of the Social Security Act, just as do workers in other lines of endeavor. There appears to be no particular reason for special consideration to major league performers."[13]

Why Did Profits Collapse? Player Salaries

Larry MacPhail convinced his fellow owners of the wisdom of creating a pension plan for the players a decade later. The players would discover, however, that the pension could be used to keep them in line and to prevent new leagues from entering the market.[14]

The Economic Downturn and the Path of Salaries

Even before the stock market crash in October 1929, the *Sporting News* reported that players were getting nervous because they suspected owners would devise some way to lower their salaries. Players worried that owners would claim publicly that the pay cuts were necessary because of rising operating costs and losses.[15]

The economic downturn created a difficult situation for owners and players alike. Because of the decline in the general price level, even maintaining a player's nominal salary was the equivalent of giving him a pay raise. When the demand for baseball declined, the demand for baseball players should have decreased as well, implying lower real wages. Cutting the nominal salaries by amounts commensurate with the declining price level was troublesome enough; actually reducing the real salary proved even more contentious. Few observers explicitly mentioned the price deflation. Instead, they assumed that a reduction in nominal salary was a wage cut in reality. Even researchers working after the fact made this assumption. Reporter F. C. Lane recognized the effect of deflation. He also believed that the salaries of 1929 were the result of the postwar inflation "which stalked nationwide in the boom days of '28 and '29." He admitted that writers who had received cuts in pay or who faced layoffs "will waste little sympathy on a ballplayer whose twenty thousand dollar salary has been sliced in half."[16]

Inflation or not, player payrolls at the height of baseball's prosperity seem minuscule to today's readers. Philadelphia's Connie Mack reportedly paid about $125,000 for the nine key players on his 1929 club, with pitcher Lefty Grove receiving the highest salary at $20,000. Grove apparently did not receive $20,000 until the 1931 season; he received $12,000 in both 1929 and 1930 according to the Haupert Player Salary

Database.[17] As this core of players continued to win American League pennants, Mack undoubtedly saw his payroll increase, although not by as much as modern fans might surmise. Al Simmons, one of the better negotiators among the players, went from $25,000 per season to signing a three-year contract for $100,000, starting in 1931. This was only a one-third increase in his salary despite stellar production.[18]

By early 1931 the *Sporting News* editorialists were claiming that even had the players "been scaled down 25 percent for the season of 1931 [and they had not been scaled down 25 percent], they would not have been treated more harshly than men have been treated in other employments."[19] The editor admitted in another issue that a player would resent a decrease in his salary "because he looks upon it as the first tendency toward the period in his career when he is on the decline."[20] The editor still could not resist a swipe at some of the players, especially a star on a poor team who "is invariably too high in the appraisement of his own services. It is a case of looking into the mirror and saying, 'how handsome I am and how ugly are the others.'"[21] In another slap at the players, a *New York Times* editor said, "When so many people are economically adrift in a yawl, they behold yachtsmen becalmed without feeling too deeply distressed."[22]

Part of this reduction in payroll came from layoffs. Some observers suggested shrinking the twenty-five player roster as early as 1929.[23] Major League owners voted to cut player rosters from twenty-five to twenty-three from May or June to the end of August for the 1932 season. Many of the owners wanted to cut their rosters from the existing level of twenty-five players, but each team hesitated to do so out of fear of operating at a competitive disadvantage. Each owner was reluctant to be the first to cut his roster.[24] By making a roster limit mandatory for all clubs, team owners solved the coordination problem of who would be the first to cut his roster size. While some owners disliked the roster limitation, the *Sporting News* editorialists thought the idea a useful way to cut redundant players without a loss of quality. One editorial noted that "none of the players cut loose to get within the limit was claimed by any other club, which would indicate that the surplus was not considered good enough to make the grade in the big league." The writer suggested that the extraneous players "decrease individual responsibility and sometimes intensity of individual loyalty."[25] Of course, the players cut were often the least valuable ones, so the savings in salaries was not proportionate to the 8 percent reduction in the number of players. Players earning the twenty-fourth and twenty-fifth highest salaries on the Yankees usually earned less than $4,000 each per season. The owners also saved by having two fewer mouths to support with meal money, to transport, and to house on the road. A month later the editorial writer urged the owners to cut their rosters to twenty players, although he admitted that managers would resist further cuts due to their quest for reserve pitchers.[26]

When economic conditions improved, the owners voted to restore the twenty-five-man roster for the 1939 season. Owners had failed to approve a similar measure at the 1937 meetings. During World War II, with the constant shuffling of players and reduced talent level, some baseball officials wanted the player limit expanded to twenty-eight or thirty.[27]

While the major league owners succeeded in reducing their rosters by two players at the December 1931 meetings, they failed to enact a salary limit either for individual players or for a team's total payroll. They passed a resolution urging a reduction in general operating expenses. Reporters cited teams such as the Senators as having especially inflated payrolls relative to results.[28] Owners also considered a proposal to set a maximum salary. The Yankees apparently did not support the proposal, as Ruppert argued that "each club owner was privileged to pay what he pleased."[29]

As another example of the coordination problem, an individual owner might have hesitated in being the first to reduce not only nominal but real salaries across the board, lest he create dissension among his players. The Yankees decided to cut Babe Ruth's salary after the 1932 season. Ruth was finishing a one-year, $75,000 contract. The Yankees offered him a one-year salary of $50,000 (the two parties settled for $52,000). C. C. Spink, editor of *The Sporting News*, suggested, "Ruth is the bellwether of the salary rolls; if he takes a cut, other players must do likewise, proportionately; if he doesn't, others cannot see why they should be asked to accept a reduction."[30]

The Path of Team Payrolls

How well did the roster cuts and individual owner efforts to reduce payrolls work? Owners provided team salary information (combined salaries of players, coaches, and managers) for selected seasons to Congress in 1951. Table 17 shows that owners did not collectively reduce real team salaries between 1929 and 1933. Half the American League teams and five of the National League teams had higher real team salaries in 1933 than in 1929. The Cleveland Indians, for instance, made a point of mailing contracts with pay cuts before the 1933 season, but the team was unable to curb its real salaries.[31] Burk shows that nominal average salaries fell through 1935 before rising, but he did not convert these into real salaries.[32] Since the Consumer Price Index rose slightly between 1933 and 1935, his figures imply that real average pay fell between 1933 and 1935.

Real team salaries increased between 1933 and 1939. Between 1929 and 1939, salaries rose by 26 percent in the American League and 13 percent in the National League. The American League teams increased their total real team salaries by $475,000 during this period, while National League teams increased their collective real salaries by $245,000. The American League's increase in payrolls exceeded the drop in total after-tax profit, making payrolls a convenient scapegoat for the owners' diminished profitability. The National League's increase was less than half the decrease in average profits between 1929–30 and 1939–40, so these owners needed other explanations. Because real operating income for both leagues increased by greater amounts than the real payrolls, it is specious to make increased payrolls the culprit. The increasing payrolls of the late 1930s may have reflected owners' ability to spend more on real salaries in the face of rejuvenated demand and increased revenues. The proportional increases in real payrolls lagged behind the proportional increases in gross operating income between 1933 and 1939.

While team salaries varied, the relative disparity was much smaller than it was in 1995–99. In the latter period the New York Yankees' payrolls were often more than five times the team salaries of small-market clubs. In some cases the Yankees might have a team payroll nine times greater than that of the team with the smallest payroll.[33] For the 1929, 1933, and 1939 seasons, no major league team had a payroll more than two and a half times that of any other team.

The *New York Times* reported baseball officials' claims that clubs would cut their combined payrolls by $1 million for 1932, or roughly $60,000 per team. Clark Griffith thought the "slash will be general among the more highly paid men." Some clubs had the misfortune of having few high-salaried men to slash. After the 1932 season, a *Sporting News* editor guessed that aside from some significant pay cuts for individuals, there would not be any wholesale reduction in salaries.[34] Not all of the owners cut their stars' salaries. Paul Gregory reported that Pittsburgh maintained the nominal salaries of its top three stars—Pie Traynor and the Waner brothers—between 1931 and 1934.[35] Two months later a reporter painted a more dismal picture for players, suggesting that "retrenchments for 1933 will far exceed those of 1932 and that stars and average players alike will feel the paring knife of the club owners."[36]

Some owners again tried to legislate a mandatory 25 percent reduction in salaries, but they were opposed by others who felt a mogul's right to set salaries was sacrosanct. Clark Griffith tried to save money by making Joe Cronin a player-manager, combining two salaries into one. Other owners shortened spring training and sent fewer players there.[37]

Clubs also sought ways to save money on other player costs, such as meal money and hotel charges. Sportswriter William Brandt described the new economy. Teams used to give players $4.00 per diem, but were now requiring players to meet the headwaiter and sign the checks. In this way owners only paid for what the players actually consumed; players could no longer pocket the difference between the per diem and the actual cost of the meals. Other owners lodged their players in hotels where the meals were included in the price of the room.[38]

Owners cast about for other ways to save money on non-playing personnel. The American League decided not to "kill the umpire" but to cut the umpire, reducing the number of umpires from eleven to ten. Other owners began cutting the number of coaches, and the *Sporting News* approved of such measures, noting that in previous times players had acted as third base coaches. The editorial writer called coaches "expensive appendages, who apparently toil not, neither do they spin, and if economy must come, it seems that the club owners might well begin there."[39] The Cleveland Indians' owners even tried to reduce their general manager's salary from $30,000 to $12,500. The general manager, Billy Evans, balked but settled for $12,500 plus $5,000 if the team made a profit of $100,000 in 1934.[40]

Baseball commissioner Kenesaw Mountain Landis took a hefty pay cut: his salary dropped from $65,000 to $40,000 between 1931 and 1933. He volunteered to cut $15,000 off his salary for 1932 and accepted an additional $10,000 cut for 1933. A sportswriter for the *Sporting News* and an editorial in the periodical both pointed out that Landis' pay cut was necessary to induce Babe Ruth and other players to take a large cut, since "[Ruth] shouldn't accept a reduction if the commissioner didn't." National League president John Heydler also took a voluntary pay cut.[41]

The *Sporting News* ran article after article covering individual teams' efforts to cut their payroll during the early months of 1933. The Cardinals hoped to cut their payroll by 25 percent. The Indians gave only two or three raises and planned to reduce all the other players' salaries. The *Sporting News* editor claimed that "the slashing wasn't generally so heavy as predicted." Whatever cuts occurred were not enough; some teams, such as the Cincinnati Reds, started releasing players and trainers during the season, while the *Sporting News* encouraged more salary limitations.[42]

After the season, American League president William Harridge proclaimed that owners would have to further reduce salaries, if only to stay "out of the red" in 1934. Sportswriter F. C. Lane seconded Harridge's proclamation by saying, "[The owners'] only error is that they did not begin sooner and cut more drastically."[43] Because the Phillies and Pirates won the right to play home games on Sunday for 1934, the Brooklyn Dodgers lost several Sunday home games and faced bleak prospects. The club definitely planned to reduce salaries in 1934. Even winning a pennant did not insulate players from pay cuts, as the Washington Senators discovered to their chagrin. A reporter claimed that because the 1933 World Series ended so quickly (five games instead of seven), Griffith missed out on tens of thousands of dollars that could have been used to grant pay raises while remaining profitable.[44]

As the teams headed into spring training for the 1934 season, observers believed that at least half the major league teams planned further reductions in their players' salaries. The observers estimated that payrolls had been reduced by one-fourth in the past two seasons.[45] A reporter claimed that Lefty Grove was the highest-paid pitcher at $18,000, but the Haupert Player Salary Data Base indicates Grove earned $20,000 for the 1932 season.[46] In this case the reporter was below the true figure.

The 1934 season may have been the ebb of nominal payroll levels. There was some optimistic news regarding salaries in 1935. The *Sporting News* reported that the Cleveland Indians planned to increase their payroll by $30,000. The club unexpectedly finished third by winning ten more games and turned a profit, even though attendance was nearly the same in 1934 as it had been in 1933. The following season the *Sporting News* editorialized that salaries had touched bottom and were ready to rebound. "It is understood that the Chicago Cubs and Cincinnati Reds are passing out general salary boosts this spring, and it is announced that there will be no slashing by the New York Giants."[47] The *New York Times* suggested that the Red Sox had the largest payroll of 1935 at $300,000; in comparison, the Yankees and Athletics had payrolls of $400,000 each in 1931. The New York Yankees' financial records suggest a player payroll of well below $300,000 in 1931, but the newspaper account may have included the manager's and the coaches' salaries, which could have totaled an additional $60,000 or more. The newspaper account also did not adjust for the fact that price levels were lower in 1936 than in 1931.[48]

A *New York Times* article touched on a subject that would persist until the 1950s: Tom Yawkey's generosity towards his players. Year after year sportswriters would refer to the Red Sox players as working in a country-club atmosphere. The *Sporting News* referred to them as "millionaires" as early as 1937. Perhaps Yawkey paid his stars more than other owners would have, but his reported player payroll in 1939 was far smaller than those reported by New York, Detroit, and Cleveland in the American League.[49]

As the Depression lifted, articles reported resurgent payrolls. Heading into the 1937 season thirty-six players had salaries of $15,000 or more, with two-thirds of them playing in the American League. Eleven managers were the highest-paid person on their teams. Dan Daniel wrote that the Yankees' 1937 payroll would be around $300,000, and he thought it might exceed the Cubs' payrolls of the late 1920s. Yankees players weren't alone in getting higher salaries than in previous years, as Daniel had estimated the combined Dodger, Giant, and Yankee payrolls would exceed $700,000.[50]

Progress towards higher salaries was not uniform. The Chicago Cubs, formerly a high-paying team, decided to hold the line on salaries for 1939, even though the players had won the 1938 pennant. Billy Herman was identified as a likely candidate for a pay cut.[51]

As the Yankees made a mockery of American League pennant races, even Ed Barrow decided to grant more pay raises. He had earned a reputation for hard-headed negotiation, "Barrow is a hard-boiled citizen who has been jousting with ball players for nigh on to 50 years. ... He remains in the cold offices in New York, his outlook tinged by the snows in Bryant Park." With Jacob Ruppert dying, sportswriters predicted that Barrow would ease up during negotiations; "[he] is going to see that the boys get all the traffic will bear and cut down the squabbling, as he does not want Colonel Ruppert bothered by player affairs."[52] The Yankees' cash books show that their player payroll rose from $283,000 in 1938 to $303,000 in 1939.

St. Louis Cardinals players anticipated pay raises for 1940. The players expected that the advent of night ball in the city would boost attendance. Sam Breadon stated that the 1939 payroll amounted to "close to $200,000." He recalled that the 1931 club had the highest payroll at $290,000. Not all of the players enjoyed repeated raises; the salary of slugger Johnny Mize had taken a roller-coaster ride during the late 1930s.[53]

The Cincinnati Reds' management rewarded its players for winning the 1939 pennant by giving out almost $50,000 in raises. "We'll have a payroll as high as any team in 1940, even though our club represents the smallest city in the major leagues. Another season like that of 1939 and we'll encounter no financial difficulties. But a bad year could put the Reds plenty in the red." Club official Warren Giles also pointed out that the Reds did not have the revenue cushion that the New York teams did. Those teams earned revenue from renting their stadiums for football and boxing. They also earned more money from radio broadcasts than did the Reds.[54]

Even Connie Mack gave out pay raises for the 1940 season, although his best player, slugger Bob Johnson, would only earn $15,000 for 1940. Haupert's data indicates that Johnson's contract also included a bonus clause promising payment of $1,500, if he refrained from "intoxicating liquor during the season."[55] Johnson, a greatly underrated player, had driven in 90 or more runs in every one of his eight seasons. For the previous six seasons, he had driven in more than 100 runs in each for an offense that frequently ranked seventh or eighth in the league in runs scored.

The St. Louis Browns continued their penurious ways. "The Browns came in for some embarrassment late last week when it became known at the capital in Jefferson City, Mo., that three members of the club had applied for state unemployment relief. The players were revealed as Berardino, Glenn, and Cole. . . . The relief fund pays $15 per week for 12 weeks during the period of unemployment."[56]

World War II disrupted players' lives and generally halted player salary increases. The government enlisted many of baseball's best players. The remaining players found themselves being encouraged to give up part of their salaries to buy defense bonds. Baseball owners wondered whether the government's freeze on salaries would apply to their employees. The owners might have been attracted to a salary freeze that would completely deprive players of bargaining strength, but the Director of Economic Stability ruled that baseball could continue to operate as before.[57]

That's No Way to Treat a Star: Individual Cases

Star players fought hard to get pay raises that would lift them far above the salaries of mere mortal players. The sporting pages reveled in salary negotiations. The spirited holdout of a star such as Babe Ruth or Dizzy Dean fueled interest in baseball during the winter months. Some players proved adept negotiators, while others were more passive or acquiescent. All the players, of course, operated under a disadvantage when bargaining. In the words of a 1950s baseball executive, A. C. Allyn Jr., owner of the Chicago White Sox, "The players, it is true, either have to sign a contract with us or not at all, but they do have *the privilege of not at all*, [italics mine] and we are not permitted to cut their salaries more than a nominal amount at any time."[58]

While Lou Gehrig is revered for his courage, he was not an aggressive negotiator. He signed for $25,000 after his breakout 1927 season. Before the 1927 season, he had signed for $8,000. The *New York Times* pointed out that perhaps only four other players had ever made $25,000 in a season—Ruth, Rogers Hornsby, Ty Cobb, and Tris Speaker. After this one-time jump in his salary, Gehrig advanced very slowly toward the $30,000 level, despite being a consistently productive hitter; however, his salary rose in purchasing power throughout the early 1930s. According to the player contract books in the Yankees financial records,

Gehrig signed for $25,000 per year for each season between 1928 and 1932. Gehrig attempted to hold out for $30,000 for the 1931 season but reportedly signed a one-year contract for $25,000.[59] In his biography on Gehrig, author Jonathan Eig suggests that the first baseman was a passive negotiator, whose wife, Eleanor, helped him to demand and to get pay raises in later years.[60] Upon returning from an overseas trip before the 1935 season, Gehrig declared he was holding out for more, perhaps for as much as $35,000. The team had cut his salary to $23,000 for 1933 and 1934. Eventually the team raised it to $31,000 for 1935 and 1936.[61] Eig depicts Ruppert as being condescending. "Gehrig, it is a pleasure to do this. You are one of the few players who always does his work without a murmur. Since you have been with this club you never have given us a moment of worry. We always know where you are and what you will do. You run out every play, hustle every minute and always are on the job." Ruppert then mentioned to one writer, "That Gehrig is getting to be a real man." Eig believes that the underlying context was a comparison of Gehrig's behavior to that of Babe Ruth.[62]

By 1937, Gehrig was the highest-paid player in baseball, according to the *New York Times*. His salary peaked at $39,000 in 1938, at which point he had one of his worst years.[63] During the 1939 spring training season, Gehrig was visibly deteriorating. As the *Sporting News* put it, "The big worry of the camp. . . . Legs seem to bother him. He looks harassed [sic]."[64] Baseball fans know the sad denouement: amyotrophic lateral sclerosis (ALS, which has been known ever since as Lou Gehrig's Disease). The club paid him $35,000 for 1939, even though he retired in May.

In contrast to Gehrig, Joe DiMaggio was keenly aware of his value. He was willing to demand large pay raises and to hold out for more if necessary. According to the Yankees' player contract books, Joe earned a hefty rookie salary of $8,500 in 1936. The team paid him $15,000 in 1937. After proving that his solid rookie season was no fluke by having an even stronger sophomore season, Joe held out. Some sportswriters claimed that he was holding out for $40,000, an unprecedented amount of money for someone with just two years in the Major Leagues, no matter how wondrous those years were. The Yankees initially offered $22,000. During the holdout Ruppert resurrected one of his old ideas and proposed paying players on a twelve-month basis instead of just during the six-month season. Earlier he thought the proposal would give owners even more control of the players and stop them from earning money barnstorming.[65] Now he wanted the proposal because "There is no effective way to prevent a player from dodging training or from holding out through the whole training season, and that is not fair to the club and the other players, and in the final analysis, to the dodger himself. Paying the player monthly for 12 months, would make him pay for remaining out of camp."[66] To put pressure on DiMaggio to sign, the club and reporters began talking up Myril Hoag as a replacement, along with the continuing development of Tommy Henrich. The negotiations became acrimonious, and the team succeeded in persuading the public that the young player was greedy.[67] The team and DiMaggio agreed to a salary of $25,000, but the club docked him for the time he spent holding out. While he did not have as great a season as he had in 1937, he still drove in 140 runs and made a mockery of the necessity of spring training.[68] He received continued pay raises thereafter. By the time he left for military service, he was making $43,750.

National League stars also struggled to get bigger pay raises. Before the 1928 season, the league's best hitter, Rogers Hornsby, signed a three-year deal for a reported $121,800, the third-largest package of the time after Babe Ruth's five- and three-year contracts. Hornsby received $40,000 a year in salary from the Boston Braves. The team also paid him $600 per season to be the team captain.[69] The Braves only paid Hornsby for one season before trading the cantankerous star to the Chicago Cubs, his fourth club in four years.

New York Giants first baseman Bill Terry struggled to raise his pay after hitting .401 with power. His initial request was for $30,000 a year for three years but he later reduced this to a one-year, $25,000 contract. Club owner Charles Stoneham responded with a top offer of $22,500.[70]

After he slumped from .401 to .349, the Giants wanted to cut Terry's salary by $9,000, which was roughly 40 percent. The Giants eventually settled with Terry by making him a player-manager. Terry made a reported $30,000 for the 1933 season, and, after winning the 1933 National League pennant, received a raise to $40,000.[71] Terry ended up on the other side of negotiations when he became general manager of the Giants. Even when the team had a disappointing season in 1935, he announced that no player would get a pay cut and a few deserving ones would receive increases.[72]

Dazzy Vance became baseball's highest-paid pitcher when the Brooklyn Dodgers signed him for $20,000 in March 1928. The *New York Times* thought that only Herb Pennock of the Yankees received more money for pitching. The newspaper quoted $22,000, but the Yankees' financial records show him making just $17,100 in 1928 and $19,250 in 1929, although he also received bonus payments of $1,000 per year. A year later, Vance negotiated a $5,000 raise for the 1929 season. Vance's $20,000-plus salaries proved ephemeral. A few years later, Vance would fight to keep from accepting a 40 percent cut in his reported 1931 salary of $22,500. Apparently he ended up signing a contract for only $15,000. The following year, Dodger management wanted to cut him to $10,000 for the 1933 season.[73]

Other pitchers, such as the Yankees' Lefty Gomez, struggled to reach $20,000. After winning the pitchers' Triple Crown (wins, strikeouts, and ERA) in 1934, Gomez wanted $20,000, but sportswriter Dan Daniel claimed that no Yankee hurler had ever made more than $17,000 (this is refuted by figures in the team's cash books and player contract books). Apparently the Yankees acceded to his request for an $8,000 raise. The *New York Times* disclosed that a Treasury report listing Americans with high incomes in 1935 showed Gomez making $20,000 and New York Giants ace Carl Hubbell earning $17,500.[74] The Yankees' records confirm that Gomez earned $20,000 for 1935 and 1936. The team cut his salary to $13,500 for 1937, after he had a mediocre season in 1936.

He bounced back to earn $20,000 for two more seasons before taking a permanent cut in salary.

Of all the stars, though, no one's salary loomed larger than Babe Ruth's. Ruth had signed a three-year contract for $70,000 per season for 1927–29. When the contract ended after the 1929 season, he hinted that he wanted $85,000 for one year or $75,000 a year for two years. He later changed his demand to $85,000 a year for three years. The Yankees countered with a two-year contract at $80,000 per season or $85,000 for 1930 alone.[75] The paper pointed out that President Hoover made just $75,000 and Commissioner Landis $65,000. The episode gave rise to the legend that when Ruth was told he was demanding more money than the President of the United States earned, he replied that he should get the sum because "I had a better year."[76]

Sportswriter Joe Vila reported that the Yankees had paid Ruth $530,000 over the years and that Ruppert had not made much money off of the Yankees; "since that time [opening of Yankee Stadium] the overhead has eaten up the profits. Whether that assertion is true or not, the impression has been created that Ruth has been amply repaid for his efforts with the bat, and that in offering him a new contract for $75,000, Ruppert is extremely generous." Researchers Haupert and Winter would controvert Vila's assertion, as they calculated that the Yankees made a handsome return off of their investment in Ruth.[77] The Yankees acquired former home run leader Ken Williams on waivers, a move some believed was a negotiating ploy to force the Babe's hand. Ruth eventually settled for the two-year, $80,000 per year contract. Given the federal income tax laws of the time, he would have paid over $10,000 a year in such taxes, a low tax rate that might make modern-day players envious.[78]

Ruth and the Yankees sparred over his salary again after the 1931 season. Although he would be thirty-seven years old at the beginning of the 1932 season, he had shown no signs of slipping, with 46 home runs and a .373 batting average. Despite these stellar numbers, Ruppert wanted to reduce his salary because, "Baseball—no, not even the

Why Did Profits Collapse? Player Salaries

Yankee management—cannot afford to pay such a salary. We realize the Babe is a big asset, but he isn't the big drawing power of the Yankee baseball club by a good, long ways." He claimed, "Never again will any player get that much money [$80,000] for a year's play."[79] Some observers thought the Yankees offered Ruth a one-year contract of $50,000 to $60,000.[80] Ruth himself claimed that the Yankees offered $50,000 on a one-year contract, a cut of one-third. He stated he was willing to absorb a reduction of 10 or 15 percent but felt that the one-third cut was not fair. Sportswriter Joe Vila sided with Ruppert, citing the Yankees' overhead. Ruth eventually settled for $75,000 for the 1932 season.[81] Vila wrote that Ruppert was justifiably wary of offering a two-year contract, "feeling that such a move would be a trifle risky in view of the advancing years of the homerun king," so Ruth signed his first one-year contract with the team.[82]

Ruth had his last great season in 1932. This time Ruppert was serious about trimming the Babe's salary to $50,000. Ruth resisted by stating that he would not play for only $50,000.[83] A *Sporting News* editorial suggested that the public was shifting their sympathy from Ruth to Ruppert in the negotiations,

the ground being taken that all owners of ball clubs were more or less hard taskmasters who measured their awards too niggardly for the value they received. This is not true, but public opinion is fascinated into molding itself in favor of the employee as against the employer, especially where there is popular idol in the foreground of the picture.... For the first time there has been a slight undercurrent of opinion in favor of the owner. Even the ball players in a mild way are inclined to believe that Ruth was the exorbitant party.... These players had believed that a high salary for Ruth meant high salaries for them.[84]

Ruth's holdout probably damaged both the club and himself, as attendance at the spring training games dwindled without him in the lineup. Eventually he settled for $52,000.[85] The *Sporting News* editorialist suggested that Ruth's previous $80,000 salary was a high-water mark that would never be attained again. "The Babe came into prominence at a period that was made for him.... But the times are changing and Ruth's drawing power and his ability on the diamond are waning."[86]

With Ruth slipping in 1933, the Yankees were determined to further reduce his salary. Ruth signed a one-year contract for $35,000 in January 1934, thereby avoiding protracted negotiations. Despite his salary reduction, he reportedly remained the game's highest-paid player.[87] The San Francisco Seals minor league club offered to pay Ruth's salary if he would play for them in the Pacific Coast League: "We make our offer in good faith, based on the esteem we hold for Babe Ruth and taking into consideration what baseball the world over owes to him."[88] Naturally nothing came of their offer. After another mediocre season (by his standards), Ruth was looking for a managerial position. The Chicago White Sox and Boston Braves were interested in signing him, but not necessarily as a manager. The Braves' owner, Judge Fuchs, hoped the slugger would prove boffo at the box office and sustain the Judge's precarious finances. Fuchs assured current manager William McKechnie that he would remain in the position.[89] Rumors abounded that the White Sox wanted Ruth as a manager and were willing to pay up to $100,000 for his services.[90] The Braves eventually landed Ruth, relieving the Yankees of a potential headache, since Ruth wanted manager Joe McCarthy's job. Initially Ruth attracted large crowds to National League parks, but he was clearly finished. Like a dying sun, he had one last brilliant flash; he hit three home runs in one game on May 25, 1935. He retired shortly after that game. The Judge was left with his financial woes.

Babe Ruth was not alone in having his salary slashed. His slugging counterpart in the National League, Hack Wilson, experienced an even more rapid salary decrease. Wilson played for the Chicago Cubs and had set a major league record for runs batted in during 1930, as well as the National League home run mark. The Cubs, who reported greater profits between 1928 and 1931 than did the Yankees, raised Wilson's salary to $33,000 for 1931.

Unfortunately for Wilson, between the new, deader baseball used after the 1930 season and his personal problems, his performance plunged. Rather than pay anything near his $33,000 salary for 1932, the Cubs traded him to the St. Louis Cardinals. The Cardinals offered him $7,500, plus a verbal agreement to add more if he had a good year. Wilson naturally balked at the huge cut, so he was promptly traded to Brooklyn. Eventually he settled for $16,500.[91]

Wilson's chief National League slugging competitor was Chuck Klein. The Philadelphia Phillies traded him to the Chicago Cubs after the 1933 season. Phillies owner Gerald Nugent bleated, "we were forced to make the trade through continued and heavy loss of money, not only last season but the season before as well."[92] The article did not disclose Klein's salary demands.

Ruth's closest imitator, Jimmie Foxx, must have wondered what it took to get a pay raise from Athletics owner Connie Mack. After hitting 106 home runs, driving in over 330 runs, and hitting .360 during 1932–33, Foxx was disgruntled with Mack's offer of $15,000 for 1934 and a bonus based on attendance. Mack eventually signed him for $17,500 and no bonus in 1934, according to the Haupert Player Salary Database. Observers estimated that he had achieved his prodigious slugging for 1931–33 under a three-year contract paying $50,000 (which tallied with the Haupert data). Foxx wanted $25,000. He understood that the Athletics could not pay as well as other clubs, but as Mack apparently lowered his offer to $11,000 the slugger balked. Eventually he signed a one-year contract for 1935 at $18,000.[93] According to sportswriter James Isaminger, Mack went so far as to insert a bonus clause based on attendance in Foxx's contract, in lieu of a higher salary; Foxx's contract on record at the Hall of Fame does not show this bonus clause. Foxx was reportedly displeased, especially since the clause required an attendance mark of 900,000, a figure the club had never attained. Isaminger believed this was the first time the owner had ever inserted an attendance clause into a contract and thought it reflected the team's desperate financial condition.[94] Mack later admitted that he could no longer pay high enough salaries to his stars, so he traded or sold them to wealthier teams.

Owners sometimes paid extra for players with "color." Lou Gehrig was a marvelous hitter, but he was bland. Babe Ruth exuded charisma. Pitcher Dizzy Dean had marquee value in addition to his pitching prowess. From the start, Dean had a high estimate of his value to the St. Louis Cardinals, and he staged chronic holdouts in an effort to get more pay. Dean's negotiating antics made Babe Ruth's efforts at bargaining appear positively dignified. Authors Robert Gregory and John Heidenry chronicle Dean's antics.[95]

After his 30-7 record in 1934, Dean naturally expected some payback from the Cardinals, say $25,000. He often used his younger brother, Paul, as a pawn in his negotiating tactics, and demanded $15,000 for him. Paul had won nineteen games that season, fulfilling the preseason boast that the brothers would win forty-five games between them. Dean had already staged a strike of sorts during the 1934 season, and Cardinals management, experts in the art of paying minimal salaries to or trading their veterans, anticipated his antics. Dean threatened to leave baseball and go to Hollywood to make a movie in December. Whether or not this silly threat had an effect, the club eventually more than doubled his 1934 salary of $8,500 but stopped well short of his requested $25,000. Breadon and Rickey, who already had reputations for tight salary negotiations, had an excuse to limit salary increases. Colorful as the Gashouse Gang may have been, the team hadn't drawn well in 1934. Players on other teams reputedly referred to the Cardinals as "coolie help," reflecting the team's reputation for paying relatively low salaries.[96]

After following his 30-win season with 28 wins in 1935, Dean demanded $40,000. At one point he suggested he might go into the furniture business instead of accept the same $18,500 salary he received in 1935. "While I'd be making my money [selling furniture] Mr. Rickey would be losing close to $250,000 because the Dean boys weren't out there winning his fifty games for him."[97] The following month the *Sport-*

ing News reported that Dean had signed for $23,000 and his brother for $10,000.[98] Dean won 24 games in 1936 and asked for $50,000 for 1937. This time he remarked that Branch Rickey was reputed to have placed a value of $400,000 on the pitcher for purposes of trade or sale: "Since he's got that kind of tag on me, I ought to be worth $50,000 to him next year and that's what I'm asking from now on."[99] The *Sporting News* reported that Dean settled for $22,500 for 1936, although he could have made more if the team's attendance had topped 500,000. The article mentioned that only Lou Gehrig received more for the 1936 season and that Dean's salary was the second highest ever for a pitcher, exceeded only by Dazzy Vance during the 1920s.[100] Dean may have employed bombast, but the previous quote reveals a keen sense of his value. Even after his career-altering injury in the 1937 All-Star Game—he was struck on the toe by a line drive—the Chicago Cubs paid $185,000 and three players for him. Dean went 16-8 for the Cubs over four seasons.[101]

Although reported Yankees players' salaries tallied closely with the team's financial records, reporters and fans rarely knew exactly what salaries players received. One of the few glimpses fans got of actual salaries occurred during the late 1930s. Congress passed a Revenue Act in 1935. Part of the act required disclosure of salaries of $15,000 or more paid annually by corporations. The House Ways and Means Committee released this information for the years 1934–37. It is a pity that the threshold wasn't $5,000, because researchers would have salary information on most of the regulars in the major leagues if it had been. Branch Rickey was the highest-salaried person in baseball during 1934, earning $35,000 in salary and $14,470 in bonus pay. Babe Ruth was the highest-paid player. Lou Gehrig was the highest-paid player in 1935 and 1936. The Tigers had three players making in excess of $15,000 in 1937: Hank Greenberg, Charlie Gehringer, and Tommy Bridges. The number of players making over $15,000 was lower in 1937 than in the previous years. Publication of the top players' salaries may have helped star players in their negotiations, since secrecy surrounding salaries tended to redound to the owners' advantage. Congress eventually voted to stop publication of the salaries.[102]

Bonus Payments

Owners facing deflation might have rewarded good performances with bonuses rather than salary increases. A bonus had the virtue of being perceived as temporary, so the owner would not create ill-will by not paying a bonus in a subsequent season if the player's performance fell or remained constant. Economist Michael Haupert suggests that bonuses were more prevalent throughout major league baseball in 1934 than in 1924.[103]

Clark Griffith preceded most of his fellow owners in trying to reduce salaries after the 1929 season. He implemented a system in which base salaries would be lower, but players could augment their pay by meeting performance bonuses. Charles Comiskey of the White Sox had used bonus payments a decade earlier. Pitcher Ed Cicotte was allegedly promised a bonus for winning 30 games in 1919. Cicotte won 29 and was aggrieved when the manager didn't start him late in the season, thus denying him a chance to win the bonus payment. Some historians think this perceived malfeasance on Comiskey's part motivated the pitcher to conspire to throw the 1919 World Series. Eliot Asinof's *Eight Men Out*, later made into a motion picture, made this claim, but Haupert reports that the information on the pitcher's contracts at the Hall of Fame did not show any such bonus clause. Bonus payments thus had a mixed history. The *Sporting News* editorial page was dubious about Griffith's plan: "it is doubtful if the bonus contract gives mutual satisfaction more often than once in 25 instances. A bonus contract implies distrust, although the pretext often is put forward for it that it incites zeal and ambition . . . the bonus contract will appear to [the player] as an indirect expression of lack of good faith."[104] In Griffith's case, his star slugger Goose Goslin disliked the plan. The slugger won the American League batting title in 1928 with a .379 mark but slumped to .288 the next season. He continued to play poorly in 1930, so the owner banished him to baseball's Siberia, the St. Louis Browns.[105]

Griffith might well have been pleased with his plan, because the Senators rebounded from their lackluster 71-81 mark in 1929 to 94-60 in 1930, starting a run of four straight seasons of 90 or more wins. The *Sporting News* reported that some pitchers were the chief beneficiaries of the bonus payments in 1930. Griffith decided to continue the bonus plan for the 1931 season.[106]

Phil Ball, owner of the Browns, tried a bonus system in 1931 by offering rewards for exceptional feats. After the team recorded essentially the same win-loss mark in 1931 as in 1930, he decided that offering monetary carrots was ineffective. An anonymous sportswriter in the *Sporting News* claimed, "In the tight places something crawled up into the necks of the boys and they became nervous and worried when they realized that cash money hung in the balance." The reporter claimed that both Ball and his players agreed it was best to suspend the bonus payments and just rely upon negotiated salaries, and he mentioned, "[The players] also have agreed they would work just as hard without the bonus arrangement."[107]

Thomas Yawkey of the Red Sox began offering bonus payments in 1934. His players would earn bonuses if the team finished first, second, or third in the standings. Apparently Yawkey's fellow owners were displeased by this style of bonus, but the players reportedly liked the plan. The team improved its record by 13 wins in 1934 but failed to collect the bonus, finishing fourth. Commissioner Landis required Yawkey to revise the plan by eliminating the bonus for winning the pennant. The commissioner said it was permissible to offer a bonus for finishing second, third, or fourth, but not first.[108]

For the 1934 season Larry MacPhail offered a "profit-sharing" plan based on attendance to his players on the Cincinnati Reds. If home attendance exceeded 275,000, each player would get a 5–15 percent boost to his base salary. Unfortunately for the players, the Reds' attendance was only 206,000, so none of them received a bonus. MacPhail's biographer, Don Warfield, could not ascertain whether the general manager offered a similar bonus plan for 1935.[109] The *Sporting News* editors thought poorly of MacPhail's plan, with the usual argument that bonuses were demeaning to players and created dissention among the ranks. Even if the bonus inspired a shirking player to play harder, the editorial admonished him that he "should have enough pride in his work and enough intelligence to know that only his own performances will keep him from fading out."[110] The Reds' bonus plan backfired in 1936 when Babe Herman temporarily quit the team after manager Charley Dressen claimed the player did not hustle sufficiently to earn his $500 per month bonus. MacPhail tried a less lavish bonus scheme during the 1936 season. Players earned $2.00 for driving in a run in a relatively close game, while they paid $2.00 for failing to do so.[111]

The Chicago Cubs explicitly disdained a bonus system of payment. "Many clubs offer players, particularly pitchers, bonuses for games won over a minimum number, or for home runs beyond a predetermined limit. But the Cubs' management feels that it works to the disadvantage of pitchers, particularly. If an opposing pitcher is particularly good, the bonus pitcher may develop sore arms in order to avoid pitching against him. So the Cubs players are paid what the management thinks they are worth, without any strings attached."[112] After Philip Wrigley took over for his father, William Wrigley, who died early in 1932, he began offering spontaneous bonus payments. Manager Charlie Grimm would determine who deserved such bonuses for "meritorious performances." Sportswriter Irving Vaughan was dubious of the venture and editorialized, "a lot of the boys will think they deserve extra compensation when the club thinks otherwise, and this difference of opinion naturally will stir up discontent."[113]

After winning pennants in 1934 and 1935, the Detroit Tigers offered a bonus to their players based on winning a third consecutive pennant. This time the league president quashed the plan, saying it would be detrimental to baseball. Senators owner Clark Griffith backed Harridge's move: "The plan would put clubs of lesser financial resources as those backed by wealthy owners to a great disadvantage."[114] The *Sporting News* editorial writer also applauded Harridge's move, claiming, like Griffith, that only wealthy teams could afford to offer such bonuses and this would trigger envy and even more inequality.[115]

As the Depression waned, baseball owners continued to use bonuses. The St. Louis Browns and Brooklyn Dodgers paid bonuses. The Dodgers gave out bonuses to ten players, a coach, and manager Leo Durocher after the team won fifteen more games in 1939 than in 1938.[116] In July Donald Barnes offered his floundering Browns a bonus if the team finished fourth, fifth, or sixth. The plan called for players to either divide $10,000, $15,000, or $20,000. Sportswriter Dick Farrington sneered at the bonus: "What was their answer to this act of generosity? They stuck loyally to form, that's what they did, and their answer to Barnes was eight straight defeats, seven after his generous offer." Farrington admitted that the players had to contest the Yankees during the losing streak and suggested Barnes might have waited until an easier foe appeared before making his offer. An editorial in the same issue of the *Sporting News* remarked that no other owner had ever offered a bonus for finishing sixth.[117] The carrot proved ineffective, as the Browns won just 43 while losing 111. They were 13 games behind the seventh-place Athletics and 23 behind the sixth-place Senators.

Although these examples show that bonuses were fairly common, the owners eventually decided to outlaw them. Both leagues approved a rule stating, "No contract shall be approved by the President of the League that shall provide for the giving of a bonus for playing, pitching or batting skill; or which provides for the payments of a bonus contingent on the standing of the club at the end of the championship season." The only bonuses permitted were the attendance clause and the retention by the club clause. As Herbert Simons pointed out, even the attendance clause created disagreement, as the club's official attendance often deviated from the figures shown in newspapers. The latter figures included the "pass gate" where favored people got in for free. The owners naturally interpreted any attendance clause in terms of official attendance.[118]

A Case Study: The New York Yankees

How did the New York Yankees adjust team payroll during the 1930s? Because researchers have access to the team's financial records, its actions during the 1930s allow a good case study, although the Yankees may not be representative of all teams. The financial records also allow us to address how a team owner with single-buyer power over his players determined salaries.

In the face of falling revenues, did the Yankees exercise their monopsony power and cut salaries?

As table 18 shows, the Yankees' player payroll increased dramatically between 1926 and 1929. The payroll remained high in 1930. Between 1930 and 1933, however, consumer prices dropped almost 25 percent.

Table 18 also shows the difference between total revenue and player payrolls. As a percentage of total revenue, payrolls burgeoned during the early years of the Great Depression and fell thereafter. The difference between total revenue and player payroll appeared to mirror trends in the consolidated net income after taxes reported to Congress; the two variables, when stated in real values, had a correlation coefficient of 0.79, implying a high correlation. Because the revenues fell more rapidly than did the payrolls, the smallest differences between the two variables occurred in 1933 and 1935. These two seasons were the years of the largest losses reported by the team during the Great Depression.[119]

The period between 1929 and 1935 was one of the most disappointing of Ruppert's ownership, with just one pennant. The Yankees reduced their payroll by almost $69,000, or almost 25 percent, between 1930 and 1934 (table 19). Most of the reduction took place between 1932 and 1933. These cuts were not enough to reduce real salaries between 1930 and 1933; indeed, the 1932 real payroll was the highest to date of Ruppert's ownership. The Yankees' pennant in 1932 did not deter management from cutting both nominal and real payroll in

1933. Management finally succeeded in reducing real salaries below the 1930 level by 1934.

Did the team rely upon an across-the-board cut in salaries? The nominal salaries of twelve players who comprised the core of the Yankees between 1930 and 1933 peaked in 1931 at $207,000 (table 20). In 1932 their nominal salaries approximated the amount paid in 1930. Ruth absorbed the bulk of the reduction in combined nominal salaries. The Yankees largely maintained the nominal salaries of their regulars aside from Ruth between 1930 and 1934 by cutting his salary. Given the deflation, the core group aside from Ruth experienced an increase in real pay. Although the deflation cushioned Ruth's pay cut, his real pay fell from $80,000 in 1930 to less than $45,000 in 1934. His salary's free fall mirrored his declining prowess as a home run hitter: from 49 in 1930 to 22 in 1934.

The Yankees did not try to reduce salaries by unloading many expensive, aging stars as Philadelphia Athletics owner Connie Mack eventually did. However, Ruppert indicated there was a limit to his willingness to absorb losses by stating candidly, "Should it ever become necessary to sell some of the Yankees because of diminished patronage here I would follow Mack's example."[120] The Yankees traded two regulars in 1930: Waite Hoyt and Mark Koenig. The two earned a combined $25,000. They were replaced by Lyn Lary and rookie Lefty Gomez, who made less than half the amount earned by Hoyt and Koenig. This move may have been motivated more by a desire to improve the team's performance than to save money.

Owners could also adjust salaries of employees who were not players. The Yankees incurred salaries for a manager and his coaches, and these salaries were reported in the team's financial records. Longtime manager Miller Huggins died near the end of the 1929 season. He earned over $39,000 during that season. His temporary replacement, Robert Shawkey, only received $15,000 for the 1930 season. The Yankees then hired Joe McCarthy away from the Chicago Cubs for the 1931 season. McCarthy had won the 1929 National League pennant for the Cubs.

According to the Yankees' financial records, he earned $35,000 per season between 1931 and 1935, but an article in the *Sporting News* claimed he had signed a three-year contract at $50,000 per year in the wake of the team's 1932 World Series triumph. After several seasons without a pennant, his salary fell to $27,500 per year. The team's resurgence boosted his salary back to $35,000 in 1938. As a comparison, the Brooklyn Dodgers paid their manager, Casey Stengel, roughly $10,000 to $12,000 during the mid-1930s. Stengel's record, of course, was not as illustrious as McCarthy's.[121]

The team usually had three coaches, although there were only two shown in 1930 and 1931. Art Fletcher was the best-paid coach and received $7,500 in 1928 and 1929 but $10,000 between 1930 and 1932. His salary fell back to $8,000 in 1933, even though the team won a pennant in 1932. Fletcher's cut in pay was not unique among his fellow coaches, as the other two received similar reductions.

If the Yankees' management had wanted to reward exceptional performance but had not wanted to "lock in" higher salaries in the face of deflation, they could have opted for more bonuses. The Yankees' player contract books show that the team offered fewer potential and actual bonuses during the 1930s. The team had reduced the prevalence of bonus payments during the 1920s; in the years before 1927, only two or three players per season usually had bonus clauses. The team increased its use of bonus clauses in 1929, with fourteen players having such clauses. Three players received signing bonuses, including two players who did not play for the team in 1929. Seven players received bonuses only if they remained with the club all season. Three players had incentive clauses. Benny Bengough was offered a bonus for catching seventy-five games, while pitchers Waite Hoyt and Herb Pennock had bonuses incumbent upon winning twenty or twenty-five games. Even before the stock market crash and economic downturn, therefore, the team had increased its use of bonuses. Sixteen players had bonus clauses in 1930, although the largest bonuses were signing bonuses. The number of bonuses declined to ten and eight in 1933 and

1934 respectively. The potential bonuses in 1930 totaled over $20,000, but bonuses were less than $10,000 in 1934 (excluding Babe Ruth). Ruth had a bonus based on exhibition game receipts: he got 25 percent. By 1934 six of the eight bonuses required that the player remain on the roster all season. There were no concrete performance clauses between 1932 and 1934.

One can construct earnings profiles for Yankees players. Given a team's ability to control salaries, how did teams determine what to pay players? Productivity? Seniority? An owner's whims? Brown, Gabriel, and Surdam performed statistical analysis of New York Yankees player salaries between 1919 and 1942. The New York Yankees apparently based current payroll on the previous season's total revenue and on previous win-loss record.[122] In agreement with economist Gerald Scully's 1974 work, Brown, Gabriel, and Surdam found that age and experience were important determinants of player salaries.[123]

It appears that the Yankees paid their hitters partly based on offensive productivity (home runs) and also on labor market experience, as measured by age and previous at bats. Yankee pitchers were also paid on the basis of productivity (wins, win-loss percentage, and innings pitched) and age.

Were the players paid their marginal revenue product? Statistical analysis suggests that star players earned less than their marginal revenue product.[124] These estimates imply that the marginal revenue from an additional win, an improvement in win-loss record of .006, was roughly $15,900 split between the two seasons. Thus a player with a marginal productivity of two additional wins would have a marginal revenue product of over $30,000. Aside from Ruth, Gehrig, and DiMaggio, few players on the Yankees ever attained such salaries. Gehrig often earned less than $25,000 per season. As it is likely that his marginal product was more than two games per season, these results suggest that he, along with most star players other than Babe Ruth, was not fully capturing his marginal revenue product.

Conclusion of Player Salaries

As late as 1933, baseball owners had not slashed real player salaries below pre-Depression levels, even though demand for baseball fell. Their reluctance to do so is a mystery, given their strong bargaining position. Owners may have faced a coordination problem similar to that of cutting the roster limit. Being the first team to cut real payrolls might have lowered player morale. The Yankees' highly-publicized salary battles with Babe Ruth may have served to help other owners cut their slumping stars' salaries, but cutting the rank-and-file players' real salaries proved more difficult.

Baseball owners were not unique in having difficulty cutting real salaries. Economist Christopher Hanes found that employers facing the economic downturn tended to "hold nominal wages rigid if they were in industries characterized by relatively high earnings per employee, capital intensity, and product-market concentration."[125] Major League Baseball reflected some of these conditions, although the owners eventually succeeded in cutting nominal salaries. Several of the owners owned stadiums that represented hundreds of thousands of dollars of capital. The owners' barrier to the entry of new teams also implied an artificially concentrated market. Even with their limited bargaining power, Major League Baseball players received higher salaries than the average worker. Truman Bewley reviewed many theories explaining wage rigidity during recessions, including relative wage comparisons where workers are loath to have their wages cut relative to other workers in the industry, creating a coordination problem for firms in cutting wages. He also found that morale effects acted as a brake on wage cuts.[126]

While the top stars chafed under their inability to get higher salaries, there appeared to be no sentiment for unionization. The 1930s were marked by labor strife in many industries, but baseball players did not organize. A New York representative, Vito Marcantonio, attempted to agitate for a union of ball players, but his efforts were futile. An unctuous *Sporting News* editor said his attempt "exposes his ignorance, not only of present conditions but of baseball history. Furthermore, Marcantonio isn't likely to gain much support from what he is pleased to call his constituency, for the ordinary man isn't likely to lose any sleep over whether the major league player gets $40,000, or even $7,500, the average salary, if either figure is far from said ordinary man's own earnings."[127] Marcantonio's efforts occurred just as nominal salaries began to rebound after 1935.

Although owners possessed bargaining strength due to the reserve clause, they did not cut salaries sufficiently to stave off revenue losses between 1931 and 1935. The decrease in real revenues was not met by any widespread decrease in real salaries until possibly 1934. Real payrolls rose between 1933 and 1939 but the increase in real payrolls did not exceed the increase in real revenues. The owners' inability to return to the profit levels of 1929–30 was not entirely the result of higher real salaries.

Other Expenses

Salaries comprised a minority of total expenses. What happened to other expenses?

Owners claimed other expenses rose during the Depression and throughout the 1930s. National League president John Heydler claimed that owners faced higher expenses, including travel, hotel, taxes, park upkeep, and executive salaries. He did not explain why such a variety of expenses would increase when the nation was experiencing a major deflation.[128]

The owners' remarks about rising other expenses appear to be accurate. Table 21 shows that real gross operating expenses increased by one-third in both leagues between 1929 and 1939 (in the American League the comparisons are based on the teams aside from the Chicago White Sox, who did not provide information on real gross operating expenses for 1929 and 1933). We have seen that real payrolls increased by 26 percent and 13 percent in the American League and National League respectively during the ten years. Since real payroll increases were smaller than the overall changes in real gross operating expenses, the real other expenses accelerated faster than salaries. These expenses increased by 38 percent and 45 percent in the American and National Leagues respectively. In dollar amounts, the seven American League teams had $909,000 more in real operating expenses between 1933 and 1939, while the National League had $1,258,000 more in such expenses. The increases in other expenses certainly consumed a large proportion of the increase in real operating income, and, as table 6 suggests, became relatively more important (rising from 46.4 percent to 53.7 percent of real gross operating income). Since team salaries comprised a slightly smaller proportion of real gross operating income in 1939 than in 1929, other operating expenses are the key suspect in the Major Leagues' failure to return to the profitability levels of 1929–30.

Since real other expenses are net of team payrolls and include transportation, baseball equipment, hotels, office expenses, office salaries, and ballpark expenses, one might think such expenses might be roughly similar across teams. Owners did not provide as detailed financial records for the Depression seasons as they would for 1952–56; aside from the records of the Yankees and the Phillies, we have no breakdown of other expenses. Table 22 shows some selected expenses for the Yankees. Other teams would have similar expenses, but, of course, the amounts would vary. The reality was that other expenses were as widely divergent as were revenues. The Yankees actually spent more dollars on some items in 1933 than they did in 1929, so the owners' complaints about rising expenses were not fictitious. Ruppert took out $12,000 in salary or expenses during 1933 but took nothing in 1929. The Yankees also incurred an additional officer's salary in 1939: George Weiss, farm director.

The New York clubs generally had much higher other expenses than teams in St. Louis or Philadelphia. The Phillies reported only $67,000 of other expenses in 1929. The Yankees spent $42,500 on hotels and transportation and $14,000 on baseball uniforms, balls, and bats, and one shudders to think what sort of hotels the Phillies lodged in on the road.[129] Did Phillies ushers wrestle fans to retrieve each and every ball hit into the stands? The Phillies' cash book showed that the team actually stayed at hotels similar to those patronized by their National League rivals and the New York Yankees in 1939. The club incurred less hotel expense than did the Yankees ($7,500 versus roughly $17,000). The Yankees, of course, did not have to pay for hotels in New York City, although the hotel charges in that city may not have differed from other cities as much as they do today. One might have expected that the Phillies, having to remain in New York City to play two rivals, would have had higher hotel expenses. The team's principal owners, Gerald and Mary Nugent, paid themselves salaries but on a sporadic basis. Mary, the team's vice-president and treasurer, received thirteen payments of $416.66, but she sometimes went months without receiving a check. She allegedly said, "Gerald does all of the talking for this family." Gerald paid himself almost $16,000 in salaries during 1939. According to the *Baseball Blue Book* for 1939 the Phillies had a secretary, Robert Irwin, and a traveling secretary, James Hagan. The team also hired Johnny Ogden to run the farm system and employed J. J. "Patsy" O'Rourke as its scout (the Yankees had several scouts on their payroll). Hagan received twice-monthly checks for $148.50 and O'Rourke received $164.99. There were some other personnel listed, presumably office staff. The team paid almost $5,000 for railroad fares, far less than the Yankees' transportation bill. The Phillies also spent much less on bats and balls in 1939 than did the Yankees.[130] By 1939 both the absolute and proportional differences in other expenses between the Yankees and Giants versus the Browns and Phillies increased.

Conclusion

While owners struggled to reduce real team salaries between 1929 and 1933, they allowed such expenses to rise during the remainder of the decade. According to regression equations based on the 1929, 1933, and 1939 seasons, teams had different real gross operating expenses for three reasons. Winning teams incurred higher expenses, partly because of payrolls. Teams in New York City and the Chicago Cubs incurred more operating expenses. The Yankees, Giants, Cubs, and Dodgers incurred greater operating expenses for the same win-loss record. For the first three teams the increased amount was $288,000 or more. These clubs' advantages in revenue were apparently offset by the higher cost of doing business in their cities. Teams spent an average of $175,000 more on operating expenses in 1939 than in the other two years, a reflection of the stronger economic climate.[131] Detroit, Brooklyn, Cincinnati, and the Boston Red Sox stand out as teams outside of the Yankees and Giants that experienced big jumps in real other expenses. These teams had vigorous new ownership or management who refurbished the teams' stadiums and made other improvements. Brooklyn and Cincinnati installed lights that might have increased electrical expenses and incurred amortized construction costs. These owners' willingness to incur even larger absolute and proportional increases in other operating expenses sometimes boded ill for their profits.

So far we have examined the operating side of team revenues and expenses. Teams incurred significant costs in acquiring players. During the 1930s, teams developed farm systems. Did this development hike expenses and erode profits? The next chapter answers these questions.

4. Farm Systems

One development during the 1930s may have raised Major League expenses: the burgeoning farm system. Major League owners began buying or subsidizing Minor League teams in the 1920s. The owners had previously purchased players from Minor League teams, sometimes in open bidding and sometimes through fixed prices via a draft of Minor League talent.

Owners could negotiate a working agreement with a Minor League team whereby a Major League team would get first dibs on promising Minor League players on that particular Minor League team. The Minor League team might get a subsidy or other support in return. Some Major League owners disliked the potential of a Minor League team owner reneging on an agreement and sending a talented youngster to another team. These owners might choose to purchase a Minor League team and the accompanying players. The Major League owner would then have greater control over the players but would also be liable for the expenses of the Minor League team. In either case, both Major League and Minor League team owners were subject to the Major-Minor agreement pertaining to players. The key question was whether the expense of sustaining Minor League teams was less than that of having to engage in open bidding for new talent. Even if the expense was greater, the Major League owners might still consider the endeavor worthwhile if it meant greater security over the flow of talent from the Minor to the Major Leagues.

If all the Major League teams had invested in farm systems, however, they might have found themselves collectively worse off. The Yankees were likely to triumph with or without farm teams. The Major League pecking order might have been unaltered if all teams had invested. The owners would simply have incurred greater expense in order to maintain the same competitive balance.

The Free Market for Minor League Players and Branch Rickey's Innovation

Major League team owners were keenly aware of how expensive it could be to purchase talented Minor League players could be. The Yankees, for instance, purchased Lyn Lary and Jimmy Reese for $125,000.[1] Daniel Levitt documented some of the more expensive signings during the 1920s, before the Major Leagues gained leverage over Minor League owners in terms of drafting minor league players. Leavitt believes that the American League owners' more aggressive bidding for promising Minor League players helped that league's top teams become paramount in World Series play.[2] The St. Louis Cardinals demonstrated a different approach. The club's executive, Branch Rickey, recalled that whenever he evinced an interest in a young player, other owners would swoop in and offer the Minor League owner more money for the player. "When the Cardinals were fighting for their life in the National League, I found that we were at a disadvantage in obtaining players of merit from the minors. Other clubs could outbid us; they had money; they had superior scouting machinery; in short, we had to take what was left or not at all. The New York Giants, a wealthy club, became the worst thorn in the side of our open negotiations for players."[3] He decided the team should control a large number of players, so they would not be continually outbid. In a sense, his vision of a farm system was a classic example of what economists call "vertical integration," whereby a firm acquires a company producing a key input for its product. Rickey garnered a personal advantage from the farm system, as he got a percentage of the sales price on the surplus players he sold to other clubs.

At first the other owners scoffed at the Cardinals' willingness to invest significant capital into a set of Minor League teams, especially given the precarious nature of such teams. They predicted financial disaster for owner Sam Breadon, but an editor for the *Sporting News* noted the Cardinals' success, claiming that rival owners bemoaned the team's cornering of the talent market: "What can we do to strengthen? Every time we see a ball player to help us, he is owned or controlled by the [Cardinals]."[4]

After the team won additional pennants in 1928 and 1930–31, other owners began to see the wisdom of controlling players and directing their training. A sportswriter wrote:

there is being wrought a change in Minor League conditions, a change that should bring many benefits to all concerned, and yet an element of danger, in that this change . . . may permit greater freedom for the practice of abuses. The big leagues are beginning to take the financial burden of minor league baseball off the home-town fellows' back. It is from no philanthropic motive they are doing this, but because in this age of great demand and short supply of able ball players, they have come to see the advisability of controlling their own base of supplies. So big league club owners are buying up minor league clubs to use as farms for the schooling of their undeveloped playing talent, and from which to draw their replacements when needed.[5]

An extra benefit of running a farm system was that a player could be "indoctrinated thoroughly all his baseball life in the particular style of play and winning psychology of the parent organization."[6]

The Cardinals also pioneered the player tryout system, as Rickey recalled:

It was then I hit upon the idea of tryout camps, inviting all the boys in a locality to turn out for a week's workout under the eyes of experienced observers. . . . *Mass production has given us 50 per cent of the men we have signed in the last few years, and well over half of that 50 per cent were pitchers. That is why the Cardinal organization today is so strong in reserve pitching.* . . . *More patience and care are required in making the right selection among pitchers than in choosing players at any other position. They'll fool you more often than any other type of player. When making our camp eliminations, there is no dismissal of any pitcher as long as even one of half a dozen men in charge questions the wisdom of letting him go.*[7]

The Cardinals' farm system enabled Branch Rickey to unload veteran stars before their deterioration lessened their value. He cut salary costs by replacing higher-salaried players with youngsters. By 1939 he could boast that every player on the current roster was either a Cardinal farmhand or had been acquired for one.[8] Rickey and the Cardinals maintained a strong farm system up through World War II. The team would attain its peak success by winning four pennants in five years between 1942 and 1946. By then, however, Rickey was with the Dodgers, and the Cardinals went into eclipse. The Dodgers' farm system and Rickey's integration of baseball catapulted the Dodgers to the top of the National League.

As late as the 1950s, some baseball observers still felt that it was cheaper for Major League owners to purchase talented Minor League players than to operate a farm system, but Leslie O'Connor, former assistant to Commissioner Landis and later White Sox official, stated, "It [just purchasing players] would leave too much to chance, and good businessmen like Walter O'Malley of the Dodgers, Lou Perini of the Braves, and Del Webb of the Yankees are not going to buy very much of that."[9]

Imitation Is the Sincerest (and Sometimes Most Profitable) Form of Flattery

The Cardinals' success inspired the Yankees to imitate the farm system. As early as 1928 the *Sporting News* reported (perhaps prematurely) that the Yankees and Browns had successfully developed farm clubs, with Cleveland poised to join them. Daniel Levitt documents that Ruppert bought the Chambersburg, Pennsylvania Minor League team in late 1928.[10] The *New York Times* and the *Sporting News* gave conflicting accounts of the Yankees' initial foray into Minor League ownership. The newspaper reported that Ruppert was considering buying the Jersey City Minor League team, while several months later, the sports periodical reported that Ruppert and Barrow were going to develop players via farm clubs. Sportswriter Frank Graham claims that Ruppert bought Newark in November 1931 after a persuasive sales pitch by the Minor League team's owner, an account seconded by Ed Barrow in his memoirs.[11]

The brouhaha over the Yankees' purchase of outfielder Myril Hoag from the Sacramento Pacific Coast League club may have confirmed the wisdom of Ruppert's decision to own farm teams. The Sacramento club reneged on the Hoag deal when they returned pitcher Fay Thomas to the Yankees, possibly in the hope of sending Hoag to the New York Giants. The controversy highlighted the advantage of owning versus maintaining a working agreement: owning gave tighter control over Minor League players.

As late as 1932, a *Sporting News* editor stated that the Yankees were about to enter a system of Minor League ownership. This was odd, since the publication had reported the club's purchase of the Newark Minor League team for roughly $500,000 back in the previous November. In any event, the Yankees were quick to acquire the Springfield, Massachusetts team, which they bought in 1932.[12] George Weiss, who would soon become the Yankees' director of farm clubs, stated, "The figures show that it cost the Yankees no more to operate and assist five clubs last season, try out 190 ball players, come into contact with hundreds of other prospects and give good minor league baseball to five cities, than it would to purchase outright one outstanding minor league player."[13] He persuaded Ruppert and Barrow that they needed a farm system and not just a couple of farm teams. Throughout the 1930s, the Yankees continued to expand their farm through purchase or affiliation.[14] Ruppert stated, "Chain baseball is really a salvation to the game, as it makes it possible for a small town to have a team which it ordinarily, would not have, because of the cost." He asserted, for instance, that he lost $17,000 on the Wheeling team, but that he gained some players that would repay his investment. Ed Barrow remained ambivalent about the farm system, writing in his memoirs, "I have never been very strong for the farm system, but since I was in it I did not want to overlook any opportunities of getting young players."[15]

If imitation was the sincerest form of flattery, the Yankees' fecund farm system was a fitting tribute to Rickey's vision. Although the Yankees had difficulty developing durable pitchers aside from Lefty Gomez and Whitey Ford, the team's success at developing position players enabled it to obtain sufficient pitching from other teams.[16]

Other teams began farming. The Cleveland Indians purchased the Toledo Mudhens. After his initial buying spree of established players, Red Sox owner Thomas Yawkey decided to invest in a Minor League system and acquired the Reading team. He preferred to buy teams rather than maintaining working agreements. Some Major League teams were reluctant to buy farm teams. The New York Giants hesitated to buy any Minor League teams, preferring to maintain "working agreements" with a few teams.[17] By late 1936, Horace Stoneham, son of Charles Stoneham, had decided to start purchasing clubs. "We are convinced that our old system of relying on deals and purchasing players has outlived its usefulness. As things stand now, we cannot compete with clubs controlling large farm systems. The case of the Indians with Bob Feller is just another instance of what a club operating minor leagues can do. We have no chance of obtaining any such players in the open market. So, as we will have to do it sooner or later, we're going to start [a farm system]."[18] The Brooklyn Dodgers quickly followed suit; their actions included the purchase of the Montreal Minor League club, at which Jackie Robinson would make his organized baseball debut some years later.[19]

By 1935, the *New York Times* could state that every Major League club was associated with one or more Minor League organizations which acted as a proving ground for the development of young players.[20]

Backlash against Farm Systems

Some observers believed the farm system would redound to the advantage of the wealthy clubs; this was amusing when we consider that the pioneering team was one of the ne'er-do-well clubs. The *Sporting News* editor reminded readers that the Cards were hardly well-heeled in the 1920s.[21] Once again, we see the argument: "Four or five rich clubs would buy up and control all of the most valuable sources of recruiting ball teams, and lop-sided races, loss of interest, and financial depression would result." Senators owner Clark Griffith, mindful that his club was ill-equipped to compete in buying Minor League teams, was opposed to the system. Another American League owner suggested that he purchased a Minor League team in "self defense," in order to be able to "switch players with a reasonable degree of intelligence and surety."[22] The Yankees' opponents kept trying to figure out ways to curb that team's dominance. Griffith suggested limiting the number of Minor League teams any big league club could own in the higher classifications, as well as a ban on pennant winners' player trades. The owners did not enact the farm limit but did pass the trade ban. Ed Barrow remarked that the ban, while discriminatory, was probably temporary and was a sop to Griffith: "the other magnates wanted to compliment [him] on his seventieth birthday."[23] Some owners suggested limiting each Major League team to ownership of two Minor League clubs, but the editor of the *Sporting News* was dubious, citing the owners' willingness to circumvent any limitation enacted. Even Griffith began farming; he bought his first Minor League team in 1929.[24]

In the 1950s the Chicago White Sox demonstrated that a team did not have to maintain a strong farm system in order to remain competitive. "If the [small number of future Major Leaguers signed by the White Sox] is an indictment of [them] as farmers, though, at the same time it is proof positive of their genius as traders."[25]

The concern over competitive balance was not the only issue created by the existence of farm systems. Landis clashed with Rickey and other owners over the farm system. At the end of the 1928 season, he investigated the new phenomenon by canvassing all of the Major League owners to discover how many teams they controlled or owned.[26] Major League teams developed agreements with Minor League teams, which were normally denoted as "working agreements;" clandestine agreements devised to cover up the existence of prize talent also became common. All this, in the words of a *Sporting News* editor, brought "contempt for the rules and evasions which sooner or later [are] to bring down the law."[27] Many critics worried that wealthy clubs such as the Yankees would stockpile players and keep some of their surplus talent from advancing to the big leagues. During the 1950s congressional investigators wanted to know how many players each team controlled. They feared that a talented Minor League catcher in the Yankees' system, for instance, might stagnate for years behind current star catcher Yogi Berra. The team did develop catchers Elston Howard, Sherm Lollar, and Gus Triandos during the postwar era. Rickey of the Cardinals fought allegations that the chain store system prevented players from advancing as rapidly as they should. He pointed out in 1934 that there were forty-three players from the Cardinals or their chain system performing on other teams throughout the Major Leagues and that Minor League players advanced to higher classifications either by promotion or via the draft.[28]

Economists might be skeptical about the rumors of talented players languishing in the Minor Leagues. Simon Rottenberg and Ronald Coase, working independently, have each developed the concept that talent would be distributed similarly under either the reserve clause or free agency. Their insights apply to farm systems and to independent Minor League teams. For example, if Lollar had been a Major League talent, the Yankees might have foregone additional revenue (perhaps from selling him) by keeping him in the Minor Leagues beyond a reasonable time for seasoning. In fact, however, the Yankees sent Lollar and Triandos to other big league teams and temporarily converted Howard to the outfield while bringing him to the Majors. Certainly such stars as Robert "Lefty" Grove might have felt exploited by their independently owned Minor League teams. The Baltimore Orioles hung on to him until a Major League team finally met Jack Dunn's demands. Dunn insisted on maintaining a major-league caliber roster for his International League team: "I'll give Baltimore a Major League team, even though it still operates in the International League. Nobody is drafting my players, and I'm not selling. We'll keep our good players right here in Baltimore."[29] He was an anomaly among Minor League owners.

The player draft was designed to help good players advance, as Major League teams or teams in higher Minor Leagues could pick players from lower classifications.[30] The draft was also designed to help Major League owners get top Minor League talent at fixed prices that were lower than those on the open market. "To pay $100,000 for a Minor League player is wretched business, nor is it much better to experiment with a Major League player to that extent."[31] Minor League owners, facing a draft, were compelled to sell their top players. Owners sometimes used the draft for nefarious purposes. Sometimes they drafted players from their own farms, which Commissioner Landis found reprehensible. "Selection of a player from a club's own farm is wholly inconsistent with the draft."[32]

Major League owners used ownership of farm teams and "working agreements" to manipulate the rules so that they could cover up players in order to prolong their control over them and for other purposes. Owners shuttled players between their teams. Cleveland broke the rules by signing Robert Feller before he had graduated from high school. To camouflage their violation, the team arranged for some phony transactions via their Minor League teams. Lee Keyser, owner of the Des Moines Minor League club, protested and claimed he wanted to sign Feller. Eventually Commissioner Landis acceded to Feller's preference, allowing him to remain with the Indians. The team also arranged for

Tom Henrich to be sold by New Orleans to Milwaukee, thereby keeping him from advancing until the Indians so desired.[33] In this case the club lost a fine player when Landis declared him a free agent.

Farm systems helped keep Minor League teams from achieving major league status despite their wish to do so. Some Minor Leagues made futile attempts to resist the draft.[34] The Pacific Coast League recognized this and wanted an exemption from the baseball draft after World War II in order to accumulate sufficient talent to become a third Major League. The Majors would also use their control of players to stymie the nascent Continental League in the late 1950s.

By the early 1930s the farm system was entrenched. At the 1932 meetings the owners adopted legislation approving the so-called chain-store system. Their action was a direct affront to Landis.[35]

Landis continued to fight the farm system. He believed that abuses had become so rampant that he played a baseball version of Moses, proclaiming "Let my [young] players go!" by freeing ninety-one Cardinal farmhands in 1938 and a similar number of Tiger farmhands in early 1940. (One wonders how Charlton "Moses" Heston would have played the commissioner, given the actor's penchant for playing strong-willed characters such as Andrew Jackson and Charles "Chinese" Gordon). The Cardinals lost Harold "Pete" Reiser, while the Tigers lost Benny McCoy and Roy Cullenbine. After fining the owners of the Cardinals' minor league affiliates, Landis freed most of the Cedar Rapids roster. A total of twenty-five Minor League teams were involved. While Rickey undoubtedly fumed, his fellow owners hoped he would remain silent and avoid a potentially embarrassing feud. "Some of the other owners doubtless were hoping Landis would content himself with one spring sensation and go on about his golf."[36] The Cards retrenched in the aftermath with actions that included releasing manager Frankie Frisch, whose salary was reported to have been $18,000. Breadon remarked, "We cannot operate as we once did, and this makes it necessary for us to cut down somewhat."[37]

Reports began surfacing as early as May 1939 that Landis was investigating the Tigers' farm system. At the end of November he fined the Tigers and the Dodgers for concealing player contracts from his office. He freed five Tigers and eighty-seven Minor League farmhands, although he later rescinded Paul "Dizzy" Trout's freedom. He awarded restitution to some former Minor League players. He also fined the Cubs and the Browns for "meddling" with the Tigers' player property rights when these clubs heard that McCoy and Cullenbine were involved. Some Major League sources estimated the Tigers' loss at half a million dollars.[38]

Landis established a schedule of fines and other punishments for future misdeeds, including placing guilty officials on the ineligible list. The Yankees, among other teams, hastened to return working agreements within their farm system, pending clarification of his ruling. Other teams reacted, too. The Indians had to sell their Owensboro, Kentucky team, because Landis decreed that no Major League team could own or control more than one team in any Minor League.[39]

Landis's decisions and the chicanery surrounding player movement affected the Minor Leagues. The Minor Leagues disagreed with the commissioner's proposals to stop abuses of the Major/Minor agreement with regard to player contracts and movement. The International League regarded the commissioner "with fullest appreciation ... [but] they feel the remedy can be worked out in the present successful structure of baseball."[40] The commissioner and the Minor Leagues finally agreed on a new rule, stipulating a three-year limit on a club's right to option a player to clubs of lower classification, applicable to the entire chain system. "Thus it no longer will be possible to prolong a player's stay in the Minors merely by selling his contract from one club to another in the same chain."[41] The reader is entitled to imagine how clever owners circumvented the newest set of regulations when it suited them.

Was Farming a Cheaper System?

Some observers continued to maintain that owning a farm system was an expensive way to obtain stars. One reporter recalled how Detroit signed Ty Cobb for $700 and the Cardinals signed Rogers Hornsby for $500. "Valuable players could be practically picked up in yesteryear and scouting was an adventure, like prospecting for gold."[42] The reporter conveniently forgot the contrary instances of big-league clubs overpaying for Minor League talent.

As a proportion of expenses, Minor League subsidization remained stable in 1929 and 1933.[43] Minor League subsidization consisted of purchases of contracts and farms' operating losses, although some of the purchases were of Major League players and had nothing to do with Minor League subsidization. In 1929 very few teams had farm operating losses, but by 1939 several teams reported some losses. Some owners sold enough player contracts to report a gain, and a few had positive balances from their farm operations. Table 23 shows the cost of player contracts and farm losses. Because the White Sox did not report either category for 1929 and 1933, the American League comparisons will pertain to the other seven teams in that league.[44]

The farm systems' reputation for being a drain probably originated from the results during the trough of the Depression, as nine teams reported losses. The Athletics, Cubs, and Senators had fairly significant losses, while most of the remaining losses were relatively small. The combined cost of player contracts and farm losses exceeded the amounts of 1929, even though both leagues reported smaller real player contract costs in 1933. The Major League owners' exposure to potential farm losses were undoubtedly tempered by the relatively small number of farm teams owned or subsidized in 1933. The number of Minor Leagues and teams reached its nadir in 1932–33.

The National League featured a tight pennant race in 1938, with four clubs finishing within six games of the top. All four teams aspired to capture the pennant in 1939 and each spent over $125,000 in acquiring players. The seventh-place Dodgers outspent all of them. The end result was that the National League's real cost of player contracts rose by $500,000 between 1933 and 1939. American League teams had higher real costs of player contracts in 1939 than in 1929, but the rise was relatively modest.

As teams developed their Minor League systems, some Major League owners found them to be profitable. The Yankees, Giants, Red Sox, and Cardinals reported negative real farm losses for 1939, which means they made a profit on their farms. The Yankees, under George Weiss, had taken Rickey's idea and turned it into a profit center. The Yankees' real after-tax profit for 1939 was $460,000, so their $274,000 farm profit was a large proportion of the team's overall gain. The Yankees paid their farm director Weiss under the category of officers' salaries in their general ledger. His salary could reasonably be deducted from the farm profit as an expense of maintaining the system. The team also began spending more on scouts and their associated expenses, some of which was incurred scouting youngsters for their Minor League system (see table 22). While the Yankees would not always have a positive return from their farm system, they did well in 1946. By 1950, most teams lost money on their farm systems, with some clubs losing almost $500,000 in a season; those dollars were, of course, depreciated by the wartime and postwar inflation.[45]

American League teams trimmed their real Minor League subsidization in 1939 compared with 1933, mostly because of the Yankees' farm system success.

Conclusion

The Major League owners' farm systems did not appear to be a major expense during 1939. The overall cost of player contracts and farm system losses did not increase in the American League between 1929 and 1939. The National League experience was different, but the added expenses of 1939 were the result of a doubling of spending on player contracts. Farm losses were negligible in 1939. Because such information was only provided for 1929, 1933, and 1939, we cannot state whether 1939 was representative of the late 1930s. At the least, the evidence does not indict the farm systems as large expenses.

Conclusion of Economic Side

Increases in real other expenses appear to have been a major cause of the Major League owners' inability to regain the profit levels of 1929–30 by 1939–40, despite increases in real operating revenue. Real payrolls increased, but lagged behind real other expenses. In the National League, an arms race between five clubs spurred spending on acquiring players that reduced profits. The burgeoning farm systems were not a big expense for most teams.

Two teams created the bulk of the collective drop in profits between 1929–30 and 1939–40: the Boston Red Sox and the Chicago Cubs. While Connie Mack, Clark Griffith, and Donald Barnes might grouse about their declining fortunes, the Cubs went from being the most profitable team in baseball to becoming one of the biggest financial losers. Under Yawkey, the Red Sox, which had formerly lost money in dribs and drabs, spent most of the mid-1930s losing hundreds of thousands of dollars. At least he stanched the losses in 1939–40, limiting them to a mere $228,000 for two seasons. The other fourteen teams in the major leagues earned almost the same amount of profit for 1939–40 as they had a decade before.

2. The Game on the Field

5. Competitive Balance

Competitive balance may well be the most contentious issue in professional baseball. The current era features wealthy teams, such as the New York Yankees, which seem able to alleviate all their weaknesses by buying the appropriate free agents. Fans have long bemoaned free agency as a vehicle that helps the rich. Middle-aged fans of today, though, can remember baseball's so-called "Golden Era" of the immediate postwar period (1946–64). Mickey Mantle, Willie Mays, and the Duke (Snider) were great centerfielders for some of the most storied franchises in the games. All, of course, were New York players. Many, if not most, of the authors who rhapsodize about this golden era grew up in New York City. Looking back at that era, we can see it glittered its brightest for fans in the Big Apple. In the American League, Cleveland and Chicago fans occasionally got to see a World Series, while the National League was somewhat more balanced. Few teams in professional sports have paralleled the Yankees' domination of the American League. Between 1947 and 1964 the Yankees failed to win the pennant only three times, losing twice to Cleveland and once to Chicago. The Yankees won in the absence of free agency. This was no halcyon period for competitive balance.

Did the 1930s feature better competitive balance than the postwar era? How did competitive imbalance during the 1930s affect attendance and profits?

How to Measure Competitive Balance

How do economists measure competitive balance? Fans and sportswriters can easily look at the standings and get a rough idea of competitive balance. How many games the pennant-winning team is ahead of the second-place team gives a crude measure of how tight the pennant race is. To encompass the entire league one might examine how far back the last-place team is. One could also use win-loss percentages. While answering only 70 percent of test questions may result in a barely passing grade, in baseball such a record would stamp a team as truly great. Winning fewer than 30 percent of your games would be a mark of infamy.

Is optimal competitive balance in the eye of the beholder, as beauty is said to be? Or is there a more mathematical representation? A more sophisticated yet readily understandable measure of competitive balance is the standard deviation of the win-loss percentages. Consider flipping a fair coin. As you know, there is a 50 percent probability of the coin will land showing heads and a 50 percent probability it will land tails. In a coin-flipping league, the average win-loss percentage would, of course, be .500 (note that the so-called "win-loss percentage" is a misnomer, as it is not stated as a percentage). If we made 154 tosses to mirror the 154-game schedule played during the 1930s, the standard deviation would give you a range around the mean of 77 wins. Through sheer luck you might get, for example, 85 wins out of 154 tosses. A few more than two-thirds of the teams would be within one standard deviation in either direction of 77 wins. About 95 percent of the teams would be within two standard deviations of the mean. The standard deviation of a 154-game coin-flipping season is 6.2 games. In roughly two-thirds of the seasons you would fall between 70.8 and 83.2 heads. You would have between 64.6 and 89.4 heads about 95 percent of the time. The standard deviation is .0403. If baseball teams were evenly matched, 95 percent of the teams would be between .419 and .581. You will note that this spread of two standard deviations is not too different than the spread between teams in a typical baseball season. Baseball teams are not equal, of course, so the standings are not equivalent to random coin tosses, though they are not as far from random as fans and pundits might think. Economists use the actual standard deviation as one measure of balance.

While season-by-season standard deviations and the other measures are useful for ascertaining the balance or imbalance within a season, these measures don't reveal an equally important facet. Is there churning in the standings across seasons, or do the same teams consistently win or lose? Fans might tolerate runaway pennant races if their team has a reasonable chance of contending in some or most seasons. Conversely, even if the within-season standard deviation was small, fans might lose interest if their team lost consistently.

Competitive Balance between 1929 and 1941

Sports economist Rodney Fort presents data that suggests that Major League Baseball was more unbalanced during the 1930s than it was in subsequent decades, including 2000–2003.[1] Unfortunately, his data did not extend to earlier decades. In another work, Fort teamed with James Quirk to examine competitive balance from 1901 through 1990 using different measures. The period between 1930 and 1939 was the least balanced of any decade in the American League, while the National League was more in line with other decades.[2]

Table 24 shows various measures of competitive balance on a season-by-season basis rather than working on the basis of decades, as Quirk and Fort have done. The reader can quickly see that baseball was not akin to a coin-flipping league. The standard deviations were consistently much higher than .0403, sometimes three times as high. The American League had standard deviations which were consistently higher than those of the National League during the period under study.

The American League's standard deviation in 1932 exceeded even that of the 1954 season, when the Cleveland Indians set an American League record for win-loss percentage (.721). The Yankees and Chicago White Sox also won over 60 percent of their games during that season. The remaining five teams all fell forty games or more behind the Indians. The standard deviation that season was .147, almost the same as the 1932 season.

Other measures of balance confirm the standard deviation measures and suggest that the American League not only had greater standard deviations but more runaway pennant races. The American League pennant winner finished an average of more than twice as many games ahead of the second-place team as did their National League counterpart. The American League pennant winner typically had a higher win-loss percentage as well. Four of the top seven win-loss records in American League history for 154-game seasons occurred during the Depression era. On the other hand, in the sixty-odd seasons with 154-game schedules, American League teams had three of the seven worst records ever between 1929 and 1941, while the 1935 Boston Braves (then temporarily known as the Bees, but referred to here as the Braves for clarity) had the worst National League record ever. The 1941 Phillies had the fourth worst win-loss record in National League history.

What about churning? During the postwar era, the American League had tighter standard deviations than during the 1930s, but since the Yankees won fourteen of sixteen pennants between 1949 and 1964, fans of other teams might not have found much comfort in the lower standard deviation. Table 25 shows the cumulative win-loss records of the sixteen teams between 1929 and 1941. Both leagues had similar standard deviations (.068 and .069). The National League had three teams with similar records at the top: Chicago, St. Louis, and New York. This era might strike modern-day fans as bizarre, as the Chicago Cubs had the best record in the National League and even appeared in four World Series. Of course, this was prior to the Billy Goat curse.[3] The National League also had the team with the worst win-loss percentage, the Philadelphia Phillies. While the St. Louis Browns were perennial losers in the American League, the Phillies, due to a late-era rush, lost more games.

More than half of the sixteen teams appeared in the World Series between 1929 and 1941 (table 26). In the American League, four teams won pennants. This compares favorably with the immediate postwar era, in which four teams won pennants in the nineteen seasons between 1946 and 1964. Most of the teams experienced significant fluctuations in their win-loss records. Table 26 also shows that every team had at least one winning record during the thirteen seasons surveyed, although some of them barely qualified. Every team except the Yankees had at least one losing season. Most teams went up and down. The Philadelphia Athletics and Washington Senators began the era with excellent teams and ended as the dregs of their league. Indeed, the 1929–31 Athletics were one of only two teams to post three consecutive seasons with more than 100 wins per season. The Cleveland Indians and Pittsburgh Pirates were typically solid teams with winning records, although neither franchise won a pennant. The Boston Red Sox, Detroit Tigers, Cincinnati Reds, Brooklyn Dodgers, and Chicago White Sox improved during the second half of the era.

The Philadelphia Phillies and St. Louis Browns merit special consideration. These franchises set records for ineptitude. The Browns finished a record 64.5 games behind the Yankees in 1939 and went 18-59 at home.[4] The Phillies set National League records for most consecutive seasons with more than 100 losses and for last-place finishes (five seasons between 1938 and 1942), although they fell short of the 1915–21 Athletics' feat of finishing last seven straight times. Philadelphia fans watched their two teams finish last forty times between 1901 and 1961.

Sports economists might nod politely at these facts. They would be more interested in the reasons teams experienced fluctuating performances. Because of their larger fan bases, teams such as the New York Yankees, New York Giants, and Chicago Cubs had an inherent advantage over teams in smaller cities or teams sharing markets in Boston and St. Louis. Over time, as injuries and surprise performances evened out, the Yankees, Giants, and Cubs would field better win-loss records on average than the Browns, Braves, Red Sox, and Reds. Teams do experience fluctuations in their fortunes. If a city's population increases or decreases relative to that of its rivals, its baseball team may benefit or suffer at the gate and on the field. Occasionally, a new stadium or some innovation may spark sufficiently increased demand for a team to rise in the standings because of its increased revenues. The ebb and flow of an owner's finances may affect his or her team's ability to field a winner. On rare occasions, a team with a new owner, flush with cash, may transcend its usual position in the standings. Some owners, such as former ballplayers Connie Mack and Clark Griffith, may have possessed an extraordinary ability to identify and to sign top talent. Otherwise, aside from variances due to surprising performances and injuries, the relative status of most teams would attain an equilibrium over time.

We can rule out two explanations for fluctuating team performances during the 1930s: changing populations and the building of new stadiums.

Table 27 shows the population of cities with Major League Baseball teams. There was surprisingly little change in the population of these cities between 1930 and 1940, aside from Detroit, Washington DC, and New York. The other cities were within a percentage point or so of their 1930 population. Even with three teams, New York City was much larger than Cincinnati or Pittsburgh. The two-team cities of Boston and St. Louis lagged noticeably behind New York City, Chicago, and Detroit. Given Washington DC's relative increase in size, one might have expected an improvement in the team's record across the 1930s, but the opposite occurred. Based on city populations, the New York City teams appear to have maintained, if not increased, their edge.

Cleveland had the only new stadium but didn't play there often. Detroit increased its stadium size in 1936 in response to the large crowds attendant upon its pennants of 1934 and 1935. These two teams remained contenders during the mid- and late 1930s. Other teams, such as the Red Sox, made minor changes to their stadiums.

Did Competitive Imbalance Matter?

As the Yankees and Athletics battled down the stretch of the 1929 pennant race, they attracted large crowds. As sportswriter F. C. Lane wrote,

"The baseball public is interested in a contest between two well matched opponents."⁵ The Yankees' deteriorating pitching continued through 1929, with the staff's earned run average increasing by almost one full run between 1927 and 1929. When the Athletics crushed the Yankees three games in a row in early September, essentially ending the race, interest and attendance dwindled and New York sportswriters speculated on how the Yankees would reload. The club had brought up catcher Bill Dickey during the season, though some observers thought the team needed at least a new backup receiver in addition to the overhaul of the pitching staff.⁶ The Yankees would eventually improve their pitching staff but the improvement was not evident during 1930, when their ERA soared towards the 5.00 mark. Although the team scored 1,062 runs, it gave up almost 900. This ratio insured a winning record but put the team sixteen games behind the Athletics (and eight games behind the surging Washington Senators).

The Yankees turned the tables on the Athletics in 1932, as the teams' pitching staffs went in opposite directions. The Athletics gave up almost a run more per nine innings than it had in 1931, while the Yankees reduced theirs to below four per nine innings, a fall of not quite one run per game from the ill-fated 1930 staff. This time the Yankees won by thirteen games instead of losing by thirteen and a half games. These pennant-race blowouts did not help American League owners. For the four seasons between 1929 and 1932, the National League owners boasted collective profits of almost $2 million more than the American League. With the exception of 1931, the National League had tighter pennant races and lower standard deviations than did the American League.

The four consecutive pennant-race blowouts worried American League owners. The National League featured tighter races and while not all the teams in the league made money in 1931 and 1932, "the others were not in dire distress."⁷ A *Sporting News* editorial could suggest "some scheme . . . should be evolved that would give the weak clubs a chance to strengthen themselves." The writer made it clear that he was not advocating "syndicate baseball," in which an owner might have interests in multiple teams, "but equitable ways and means can be devised for aiding chronic tail-enders.... There can be no question that such action would be to the profit of every club in the leagues."[8] A fan in New York wrote to the *New York Times* advocating letting "Boston have some of the real stars coming up from the minors," since "the treatment of Boston is a disgrace."[9] From time to time, sportswriters suggested that teams had voluntarily helped weaker clubs with an occasional favorable player transaction, such as the Yankees sending third baseman Joe Dugan to the Boston Braves or the White Sox and Tigers giving the downtrodden Red Sox veterans Smead Jolley and Dale Alexander, but such moves were mere sops.[10] While teams sharing St. Louis or Boston and teams in smaller cities, such as Cincinnati, were at a chronic disadvantage because of their limited drawing power, energetic ownership that was willing to invest large sums of money could change a franchise's fortunes quickly. Population size was not necessarily destiny; as an editorial in the *Sporting News* maintained, "it has been proved, time and again, that money is not the sole consideration in putting together a pennant-winning team."[11]

Some Major League owners, such as Jacob Ruppert, excoriated critics who suggested transferring some players from wealthy to impoverished teams. "I found out a long time ago, that there is no charity in baseball, and that every club owner must make his own fight for existence.... I want to win the pennant every year, if that is possible."[12] The prior owners of the Yankees had accepted charity in the form of some players from other owners, as the nascent American League recognized the importance of a strong team in New York City. Ed Barrow recalled how American League president Ban Johnson forced Detroit to trade starting shortstop Kid Elberfield to the New York Highlanders (Yankees) for two washed-up players, Ernie Courtney and Herman Long. Johnson wanted to ensure that the New York club would be strong enough to compete with John McGraw's National League New York Giants.[13]

While the American League did little to redress the competitive imbalance, some owners took the initiative. The 1933 season was the dividing line in fortune for many of the teams. The Washington Senators won the pennant by only seven games, a tight margin by American League standards. Despite the relative closeness of its pennant race, the American League remained far less profitable in 1933. The National League's combined loss was $614,000 less than the junior circuit's losses. The Athletics already showed signs of deteriorating, finishing about twenty games behind. The fortunes of the Athletics and the Senators were about to ebb permanently. While the Tigers and Red Sox did not show improvement in 1933, both clubs were about to ascend rapidly. The Red Sox benefited from a change in ownership. Tom Yawkey proved an aggressive owner willing to spend to acquire topnotch talent, while the Detroit Tigers benefited from astute signings of Minor League talent, including Hank Greenberg and Schoolboy Rowe. The 1934 and 1935 races were relatively close, which helped American League attendance rebound after the 1933 low. The White Sox's acquisition of three of the Philadelphia Athletics' regulars boosted attendance at Comiskey Park in 1933. The Red Sox's attendance more than doubled between 1933 and 1934, reflecting both the general rebound in attendance throughout the league and the fact that the club won thirteen more games in the latter season.[14] In terms of competitive balance, the St. Louis Browns remained weak even though they had a 31 percent increase in attendance.

While some clubs rebounded from prolonged mediocrity, other clubs, such as the Phillies and Browns, appeared hopelessly mired. The *Sporting News* editorial page suggested palliatives for the competitive imbalance. One writer bemoaned the tendency of bottom-dwelling clubs to sell star players in order to stay afloat. Aside from the St. Louis Cardinals, who perfected the art of selling players and remaining competitive, most clubs found such short-term remedies a vicious circle: "the loss of the star or stars not only usually results in sinking the club deeper in the mire, but also in weakening the morale of the team and lessening fan interest." The writer suggested using broadcasting money from the World Series and All-Star games as a revolving fund that could be loaned to teams with temporary financial problems.[15] The leagues occasionally lent money to such franchises as the Braves, Phillies, and Browns. The loans kept these franchises afloat, though they rarely affected the owners' ability or willingness to improve their clubs. The Browns did buy a few players from other clubs in 1939 and 1940, but they financed these purchases with influxes of capital from their board of directors.

Another possible way to help the weak teams while hindering the strong teams was to restrict the latter teams from acquiring players through midseason trades. The *Sporting News* editorial page advocated such trade restrictions in 1935. Players and fans also made suggestions for increasing competitive balance. Burleigh Grimes, longtime pitcher, proposed that second-division clubs be allowed to carry twenty-five players after June 15 for the remainder of the season, while the first-division teams continued with the usual twenty-three.[16]

A fan wrote to the *New York Times* and urged New Yorkers and fans elsewhere to boycott the Yankees and force Ruppert to break up the team.[17] The following week, another fan echoed the lament, implying that the Yankees made their "team so superior to all others that the element of competition is all but eliminated, then baseball suffers."[18] A third fan facetiously suggested, "As a matter of good sportsmanship and also for the purpose of encouraging other teams to remain in the baseball business, the Yankees could well afford to give their opponents four outs and a base on balls in each inning."[19] The most revolutionary proposal came from a fan suggesting that Major League Baseball teams completely divest themselves of Minor League farm systems and operate the "entire minor league structure as a hatchery for major league stars . . . [with] free competition and open bidding for minor league players not eligible for the draft."[20]

Nothing came of these suggestions. The Yankees, with their new rookie Joe DiMaggio, charged back to win the 1936 pennant. The club won the 1937 pennant and the 1938 pennant . . . and the 1939 pennant. The club won the last pennant even though its consistent slugger, Lou Gehrig, bowed out early in the season before his thirty-sixth birthday. His absence hardly created a ripple in the team's record, as the club scored one more run in 1939 than in 1938 and won more games. "Lose a Hall-of-Fame player? Who cares?" they might have said. The Yankees won the 1939 pennant by a mere seventeen games, with the Browns finishing 64.5 games behind them (they were eliminated after their 110th game on August 22). While attendance in the American League did not sink to 1933 levels, it fell 10 percent from the 1937 peak. A reporter in the *Sporting News* attributed the Yankees' attendance decline from 998,000 to 860,000 to a variety of factors, including the 1939 World Fair and radio, before asking, "Is New York tired of a winner? Would New York turn out to see a Yankee team which would be threatened with a drop into second or third place?"[21]

Although American League profits exceeded those of the National League for the 1934 and 1935 seasons combined, the Yankees' runaways in 1936–39 ushered in another period of lower profitability for the other teams in the league relative to their National League peers. The National League's collective profits were $2.15 million, doubling the American League's $1.08 million. None of the National League's pennant races were won by more than 5 games, while the Yankees' smallest margin was 9.5 games.

Naturally American League owners wrung their hands over this discrepancy. Even before the 1938 season, Ruppert decried proposals to break up the Yankees: "If we ever get to that [breaking up the Yankees], we can lock our ball parks. Baseball . . . is a sporting proposition. If we have to make races synthetically, we will have to drop the game. We will have forfeited the support of the public. . . . The Yankees intend to keep developing, to keep winning pennants, by as big a margin as they can be won, without regard for the effect it may have on other clubs. Now that sounds very selfish, doesn't it? But I know that the destinies of the game lie in building up, not breaking down." He concluded by advising other clubs to imitate the Yankees' system.[22] After the 1938 season Ruppert again reiterated, "We're going to win pennants just as long as we can. What do they want me to do, deliberately weaken my ball club? Wouldn't that be dishonest?" He also dredged up some history, citing the original calls to break up the Yankees (and Giants) after the 1923 World Series, the club's third consecutive appearance. The Yankees failed to win the pennant in 1924 and plummeted to seventh place by 1925. "Our attendance dropped nearly in half. It was then Barrow, Huggins and I decided we always must have suitable replacements on hand even for our strongest clubs. You never know when even the best club will crack up." Again he urged his rivals to strengthen themselves: "That would raise the caliber of American League baseball, not lower it."[23]

While the Yankees were obvious threats, American League owners recognized the future dangers posed by that franchise's Newark Bears, a minor league club that won pennants easily in 1937 and 1938 and also won the first Minor League World Series in 1937. A few observers thought the Bears could give the St. Louis Browns stiff competition. The New York club had a surfeit of talent and was rumored to be considering selling some of its Minor League talent, although it promoted Charlie Keller to the big leagues.[24]

Acrimony flared in the American League councils in 1939. The Yankees were cruising while their rivals were fuming. Clark Griffith suggested in late July that the pennant-winning team (which he assumed, correctly, would be the Yankees) be barred from trading with another league rival until the club was dethroned, saying, "As things stand now, a team can stay on top for several years." He denied that his proposal was aimed solely at the Yankees: "Connie Mack's great team won three years in a row. My Senators won twice in succession in 1924 and 1925." He also wanted to limit farm systems, which had been a bête noire of his for years; a cynic might argue that he knew he could never compete in building such a system with clubs in bigger cities. Out of consideration for Ruppert's illness (which would lead to his death in January 1939), Griffith agreed to postpone a vote on the matter. There was a large loophole in his proposal: the pennant-winning club could obtain players from their farm systems, off the waiver list, and from trades with teams in the other leagues.[25] In the postwar decades, the Yankees often obtained veteran help, such as Johnny Mize, Enos Slaughter, and Jim Konstanty, from National League teams.

Despite the postponement of the intraleague trading ban, Ed Barrow was perturbed by Griffith's proposal. He turned down offers to sell some of his talented Minor Leaguers, including Phil Rizzuto, Walt Judnich, and Gerald Priddy, by saying he was not selling to anybody. Sportswriter Dan Daniel reported, "Up to this time, Ed had adopted a policy of appeasement. He had tried to placate the have-nots. But now our local Chamberlain has laid aside his umbrella and his diplomacy, and he is ready to fight."[26]

While the National League leapfrogged the junior circuit in terms of attendance for the 1938 and 1939 seasons, teams in that league also worried about the Yankees' superiority. The Yankees won sixteen of nineteen World Series games between 1936 and 1939, matching the American League record of 1927–30. The Yankees won all eight games in 1938 and 1939. Some observers attributed the National League's woes in the series to tight pennant races that sapped the energy of the eventual champion. After the Yankees shut out the Reds in the 1939 World Series, both teams lamented the loss of $300,000 in ticket receipts for hypothetical Games Five, Six, and Seven.[27]

In the aftermath of the series, the Yankees continued to seek players to improve their club. First baseman Babe Dahlgren was hardly an adequate replacement for Lou Gehrig, and shortstop Frankie Crosetti was aging. As one fan wrote to the *New York Times*, "Now Ed Barrow is reported to be demanding George McQuinn, .320-hitting first-sacker of the Browns, in exchange for a generous amount of cash."[28] The Yankees failed to get McQuinn at this point; they would later obtain him for the 1947 season. Just before the December meetings, Barrow decided to "make a concession to the rest of the American League clubs and stand pat."[29]

Barrow's concession did not dissuade Griffith from proposing his pennant-winner trading ban, which passed. He did withdraw his proposed restriction on the number of farm clubs a Major League could own to one in each Minor League classification, a limitation which most clubs would accept voluntarily by the 1960s. The American League accepted the trading ban unanimously. By that point, Barrow may have decided to maintain goodwill and go along; as Dan Daniel wrote, "[Barrow] regards [the ban] with tolerance and a laugh." While Joe McCarthy remained irritated by the discriminatory policy, Barrow was bemused by the sudden outpouring of fan support for the Yankees. "Now the fans feel we do merit moral support." He suggested that a "gentleman's agreement" would have been a better approach.[30] He continued to appear placid about the ban: "This ball club has not made an emergency trade since it got Ruether and Severeid back in the Huggins regime, so why get excited?"[31] He neglected to mention the important midseason acquisition of Red Ruffing in 1930.[32]

Branch Rickey decried the American League's trading ban. "Sure, the National League wants to beat the Yankees in World's Series competition.... But that type of legislation is not on the square. It destroys initiative and puts a penalty on enterprise.... They've gone communistic in that league. Socialistic, I should say—trying to curtail enterprise ... and it's a bad thing for the game."[33] Rickey's National League colleague, Larry MacPhail, chimed in, "It has made the American League a laughing stock in baseball. It is an effort to drag the entire league down to the level of the cellar club, and it is to the credit of the National that it refused to go along on that legislation."[34] Some American League owners had second thoughts about the ban, and within a month, Detroit officials pushed to rescind the ban in the near future. The Tigers' move showed itself to be ironic in retrospect, as they would win the 1940 pennant after a tight three-team race.[35]

Because of the loophole in the ban, Barrow could afford to be magnanimous. The Yankees swapped pitcher Joe Beggs for veteran Lee Grissom of Cincinnati in January.³⁶ Grissom hurled four scoreless innings for the Yankees before they sent him across town to the Dodgers. Perhaps because of the trading ban, or perhaps because of a temporary stumble, the Yankees slumped to just 86 wins and finished third, two games behind Detroit and a game behind Cleveland. The following season, Detroit faced the trading ban and an unsympathetic draft board that transformed the slugging Hank Greenberg into a GI. The Tigers collapsed, and the Yankees began yet another run of pennants, winning by seventeen games. One sportswriter predicted that the Tigers would struggle in 1941, since the pennant-winning club depended heavily upon veterans and Commissioner Landis had stripped the club of ninety-one players, most from the Minor Leagues.³⁷ The Tigers appeared to be unlucky. While the 1936 Yankees can be thought of as being among the greatest teams ever, the defending champion Tigers were hobbled by player-manager Mickey Cochrane's nervous breakdown and Greenberg's injury. Had these two stars remained healthy, the 1936 race might have turned out very differently. With the loss of so many Minor League players, including eventual big-league players Roy Cullenbine and Benny McCoy, the Tigers lacked replacements for Greenberg and declining pitchers Bobo Newsome and Schoolboy Rowe in 1941.

In July 1941, American League owners barely approved ending the trading ban as of season's end, too late for the Tigers. News accounts suggested that at least three owners voted to retain the ban. In the end, the Yankees clinched the pennant sooner than they ever had, after the 137th game of the season."³⁸

The Tigers' surprise championship after a close race in 1940 boosted American League profits to the highest level of the years between 1929 and 1941. The Cincinnati Reds blew away their National League peers, and that league's profits dwindled. The American League had almost three times as much profit as did the senior circuit in 1940. Despite a Yankee pennant runaway in 1941, the junior circuit still earned more profits than did the National League. The spirited pennant race between the Dodgers and the Cardinals lifted profits by less than $50,000.

During the 1950s, observers attributed some of the Yankees' superiority to morale factors—to an esprit de corps, if you will. As early as 1942, sportswriter Dan Daniel began to identify this alleged element by using the example of Buddy Hassett, who had played for Brooklyn and the Boston Braves before finishing his career playing for the Yankees in 1942. After claiming that Hassett was amazed at how much better he threw the ball and pulled the ball, Daniel concluded, "In short, the Yankee uniform did something to Buddy. It not only reclaimed him, it not only turned him away from the detour that led back to the Minors, but it made a real Yankee out of him. Ask Buddy what that NY on your blouse does for a player and he never will stop."[39] One wonders what telephone booth Buddy used to change into his uniform with the NY on the blouse. Buddy's record with the Yankees included a lower batting average, higher slugging average, and same fielding average he had with the Braves. This is not meant to disparage the idea that being a Yankee bred confidence. Certainly David Halberstam's anecdote about veterans pulling Yogi Berra aside early in his career and chastising him for not taking things seriously enough suggests a professionalism greater than that of other teams.[40] Red Ruffing was only the first of several Major League pitchers who experienced the rejuvenating effects of hurling for the Yankees, thanks to the team's generally superior defense and strong hitting.

Over in the National League, the Philadelphia Phillies continued to suffer from a lack of capital. The league is said to have loaned the team some funds, and some of the owners suggested selling players to the Phillies at $5,000 each. Branch Rickey, now with the Dodgers, ridiculed the idea and echoed Jacob Ruppert, saying that there was no room in baseball for charity. One can only imagine Tom Hanks (in much makeup and a body suit) imitating Rickey and yelling, "There's no charity in baseball!" Pious though he was, Rickey was a competitor on the level of Ty Cobb and no fan of turning the other cheek or helping the meek and the poor; he simply employed more genteel weapons, remarking "In the 100 years of baseball there never has been any other practice than to boot the other fellow when he is down."[41] A few officials disagreed. Cincinnati general manager Warren Giles suggested that the waiver rules be altered to allow the Phillies to claim more players from that source.[42]

Conclusion

Competitive balance had an effect on the profits of individual teams and of the leagues as a whole. During the Depression years, the American League had two of the most dominant aggregations in baseball history: the 1929–31 Athletics and the 1936–39 Yankees. The 1932 and 1941 Yankees also cruised to easy pennants. These runaways may have accounted for the league's poorer profit record for most of the period. The relationship between competitive balance and collective profits was not perfect. The National League's tight race of 1934 did not spur profitability, perhaps because the small-market Cardinals were one of the contenders and, of course, because of the dismal economic conditions. The Cardinals also contended in 1941, which was another of the National League's disappointing seasons in terms of profits.

In terms of the other aspect of competitive balance, churning, many teams kept their usual place in the standings: Yankees, Giants, Cubs, Browns, Phillies, and Braves. Other clubs, such as the Red Sox and the Tigers, benefited from increased owner willingness to spend cash in order to get talented players. The one city with a significant increase in relative population, the Washington Senators, did not improve. The era was unkind to the wily former players turned owners, whose ability or willingness to maintain strong teams appeared to have eroded as the decade wound down. The Reds and Dodgers benefited by astute management that increased crowds and afforded the clubs sufficient capital to obtain star players, as will be shown in the next chapter.

6. Player Movement

How did the New York Yankees, New York Giants, and Chicago Cubs achieve winning records year after year? Why did other teams, such as the St. Louis Browns, Philadelphia Phillies, and Boston Braves, seem to flounder forever? Did winning teams succeed because they had some prescient ability to sign the best rookie players, or did they buy and trade for stars from downtrodden clubs? What was the pattern of player movement in an era without formal free agency and without a draft of amateur players?

Baseball players toiled under the reserve clause during the Great Depression. Once a player signed a professional contract the team could sell, trade, or terminate him almost at will. While owners may have desired a completely controlled labor market, amateur players still faced a relatively free market for their services. Highly desired youngsters sometimes received modest bonuses or higher monthly pay in the Minor Leagues. In Donald Honig's *Baseball When the Grass Was Real*, players described how they were signed by teams. Baseball commissioner Judge Kenesaw Mountain Landis occasionally released Minor League players from their contracts upon finding that a Major League team had broken a rule, sometimes by signing players before they turned eighteen years old. In these cases we can see free agency roughly similar to the modern version, albeit with untried players. The National Football League introduced the reverse-order player draft during the 1930s; baseball lagged by three decades in implementing such a draft.

Trades and sales of established big-league players and acquisitions of talented Minor League players by purchase or draft were the main ways of transferring players between teams during the Depression. With the advent of free agency during the 1970s, many pundits and fans, as well as owners, bleated that "rich teams will buy pennants." Usually the charge was that the Yankees were the team buying the pennants (fans seemed less concerned about the Mets or the Dodgers buying pennants). The Yankees had obviously done well for much of the reserve clause era, although they had floundered between 1965 and 1974.

Although some teams consistently finished with poor records, upward mobility was a reasonable possibility. Between 1929 and 1941 almost half of the teams in Major League Baseball experienced a 30-win improvement in their records over a two- or three-year period. To put this in perspective, such an improvement would be the equivalent of going from 66-88 to 96-58 in a couple of seasons.

Player transactions could change a team's prowess. They also had tax implications. Owners fought off the Internal Revenue Department's attempt to alter the law on expensing player purchases. Owners had written off the entire purchase price of a player in the year the expense was incurred, even though the players frequently served beyond that year. The IRS recognized this and wanted to force the owners to spread the expense over an arbitrary three-year period. The courts did not uphold the revenue department's interpretation, and owners were free to expense the purchase price as they had before.[1] A decade later owners won a favorable interpretation on the depreciation of player contracts they acquired when they purchased a franchise.

General Pattern of Player Movement

What was the general pattern of player movement during the 1930s? Did the pattern differ from modern ones? Modern fans may recall how the Florida Marlins rid themselves of star players after the team's first

World Series title. Middle-aged fans will remember Charlie Finley, who disposed of most of the stars from his Athletics through trading them, selling them, or losing them to free agency. Older fans will recall Connie Mack's actions. Mack, the owner of the Philadelphia Athletics, anticipated Finley's antics on two separate occasions. He broke up successful teams after 1914 and 1932. The latter situation was perhaps baseball's biggest dispersal of stars. These were owners of teams without strong drawing power. When we see teams in smaller cities or sharing medium-sized cities losing top talent to teams in larger cities, we are not witnessing a new phenomenon.

Table 28 shows several crucial points. In 1919–41, the New York Yankees introduced the largest number of what we shall denote as productive players (as identified by the Total Baseball Rating listed in the *Total Baseball* encyclopedia) of any team in the Major Leagues between 1919 and 1941.[2] The team's nineteen productive players had a combined Total Baseball Rating appreciably higher than that of the St. Louis Cardinals. While the table is not a measure of a farm system's productivity, as most teams had no farm clubs during much of this period, it is an indication of how perceptive scouts were in identifying, and the owners were in signing, top talent. Some teams were inept due largely to their inability to sign top young talent. The Braves, Browns, Phillies, Reds, and Senators combined produced only about 10 percent of the total ratings and won a total of five pennants between 1919 and 1941. Most of the teams playing in smaller cities or sharing a medium-sized city fared poorly in signing top talent, although there were exceptions in both directions. The Dodgers and White Sox introduced relatively few top players, while the Cardinals were adept at introducing good young players.

The table reveals another key point. There was never a time when stars stayed put. During this time period, without free agency, less than a quarter of the players played their entire careers with the same team. Players moved frequently. The teams playing in small cities or sharing medium-sized cities rarely kept their star players. The Braves, Reds,

Phillies, Browns, and Senators kept just two of their twenty debutantes. The Philadelphia Athletics kept only Eddie Rommel of the star players Connie Mack signed (most of whom he acquired in the 1920s), a trend that he had started even before the 1920s. Even the big-city Dodgers and Cubs rarely kept their star players. The St. Louis Cardinals almost never kept any of their stars. The two players that remained with the Cardinals for their entire careers, Stan Musial and Whitey Kurowski, debuted in 1941. The Boston Red Sox began keeping their stars once Thomas Yawkey bought the club, while the Chicago White Sox kept two of their three stars. Of the teams introducing a large number of productive players, the New York Giants and New York Yankees retained the largest proportion but still kept less than half of them throughout their careers. The general rule, then, was this: A talented player beginning with a team in a small city or sharing a medium-sized city was less likely to stay with his original team than one who made his debut with the Yankees or Giants.

Individual Teams' Experiences

By examining the experiences of several teams, we can see how the Yankees remained paramount for extended periods and how other teams improved or floundered continually. We have seen in previous chapters that some teams had inherent advantages which allowed them to maintain strong teams and some had disadvantages which kept them weak, a few clubs demonstrated more volatility because of wealthy new owners or newly impoverished owners. Other clubs might hope to transcend their inherent population base and put a better product on the field because the owner or his general manager was especially good at identifying talent.

How to Remain Competitive: The Yankees' Experience

After buying most of the top players from the Boston Red Sox between 1919 and 1923, the New York Yankees began focusing on purchasing top Minor League talent. The team eventually began buying farm teams and making arrangements with some Minor League teams in order to develop young players. When the need arose, the Yankees were also willing to buy Major League players. The 1928 team epitomized the process. While the 1927 version cruised to the pennant, the following season was quite different. The team's pitching staff, beset by injuries and ineffectiveness, needed reinforcements. They bought Tom Zachary from the Washington Senators for $8,000, and bought ex–New York Giant pitcher Rosey Ryan from the Toledo Minor League team the next day. A few days later, they acquired Ed Wells from Detroit for $15,000. On September 8, they bought Fay Thomas from Oklahoma City for $12,500.[3] In addition to bolstering their pitching staff, the club obtained a backup catcher, Arndt Jorgens, from Oklahoma City.[4] These acquisitions did not appreciably help the Yankees, and the club won the pennant by a scant 2.5 games.

The Yankees' deteriorating pitching staff forced the team to search for new hurlers, and the team turned again to their frequent trading partners: the Boston Red Sox. The Red Sox initially resisted the Yankees' overtures for Charles "Red" Ruffing. Bob Quinn refused to sell Ruffing, "saying that if money can not get the Yankees and other clubs what they want, then it's playing strength, and not money, that the Red Sox want for any athletes they may let go." Eventually the Yankees persuaded Boston to relinquish the pitcher in return for second-line outfielder Cedric Durst and $10,000.[5] Ruffing found pitching for the Yankees to his liking. Given the team's usual solid defense and, of course, its renowned slugging, he found it much easier to win than he did with Boston (he was 39–96 with Boston). He won 231 games for the Yankees while losing just 124 games with them.

The Yankees often paid as much for Minor League talent as they did for Major League players. Tony Lazzeri cost $50,000 and five Minor League players; Earle Combs also cost $50,000 (but no players). The Yankees paid $125,000 for Minor League players Lyn Lary and Jimmy Reese in 1928. The price paid for these two mediocre players seems excessive compared with the $100,000 that the team paid for Babe Ruth, especially when adjusted for the higher price level of 1920.[6] Years later Ed Barrow called the deal the "biggest flop" the team had made. He admitted in his memoirs, "In fact, I've got to be ashamed of it."[7] Bill Dickey and Joe DiMaggio proved real bargains, as the Yankees paid a combined $37,500 and three players for the two future Hall of Fame players. By 1932, when the Yankees finally overtook the Athletics, most of the Yankees' on-the-field players had been acquired as Minor League talent. The talent signings culminated with DiMaggio in 1934. The club also picked up George Selkirk.[8] Still, buying Minor League talent was an uncertain process. In addition to the dubious purchase of Lary and Reese, the team paid $25,000 for Tom Padden.

The Philadelphia Athletics crushed the defending champion Yankees during the 1929 season. Connie Mack built his team by purchasing top Minor League talent such as Lefty Grove and George Earnshaw. Mack paid $50,000 and gave up two pitchers for Earnshaw.[9] The Yankees responded by starting rookie Bill Dickey at catcher. The next season the Athletics continued to dominate the Yankees, but the latter team added two new pitchers in Vernon "Lefty" Gomez and Ruffing. Dickey, Gomez, and Ruffing became Hall of Famers. Between 1930 and 1934 the core players remained essentially the same. The team won the pennant in 1932 but faltered the next three seasons.

After 1932 the Yankees didn't have to fear the Athletics anymore, as Connie Mack began selling his star players. We will examine his diaspora of players shortly. Why didn't the Yankees acquire any Athletics players? After all, buying a star player from the Athletics had a double benefit: it strengthened the Yankees while weakening their strongest rival. Certainly having Lou Gehrig and Bill Dickey made acquiring Foxx and Cochrane redundant, but it is hard to imagine today's Yankee management passing on Lefty Grove, quite possibly the dominant pitcher of his generation. Ruppert claimed that he would have been willing to pay $150,000 for Grove if he had been allowed to bid. "Lefty Grove would have meant at least two pennants for the Yankees." He also evinced an interest in Foxx as "He [Foxx] would be sort of a new Ruth for the Yankees."[10] Although Mack stated that he would not sell any of his stars to front-running teams, it is difficult to imagine him turning down good Yankees dollars, especially since the Red Sox gave just $125,000 for not only Grove but pitcher Rube Walberg and infielder Max Bishop.[11]

During Mack's dismantling of the Athletics, Ruppert admitted that if demand for Yankees games fell sufficiently, he would emulate Mack and sell star players. He added that the fans still demanded a winner in New York, and he intended to satisfy them.[12]

The 1936 Yankees continued the trend towards building upon judicious purchases of and trades for Minor League players who became Major League regulars. Of the starting lineup, only Jake Powell did not debut with the Yankees. The pitching staff was comprised of a greater proportion of acquired Major League veterans: Ruffing, Monte Pearson, Bump Hadley, and Pat Malone. The team did not have a formal farm system during much of the 1930s and relied instead upon year-by-year agreements to make loans or give money up front to Minor League teams in return for priority in acquiring promising players at set prices.

Barrow's choice of players reveals an interesting pattern. The Yankees led the league in walks twelve times, on-base percentage nine times, and slugging average ten times during the fourteen seasons between 1926 and 1939.[13] While fans might say, "How hard can it be for the team to lead the league in walks with Babe Ruth and Lou Gehrig?" it is important to note that the remaining players on the team sometimes drew more walks than a majority of American League teams. Whether or not Barrow looked consciously for patience at the plate, he found it.[14]

The Yankees rarely sold players. It is ironic that Ruppert's first outright sale of players was to the Boston Red Sox. Thomas Yawkey was in a hurry to transform the Bosox from the dregs to the cream of the American League. Most fans recall his purchases of stars Lefty Grove, Jimmie Foxx, and Joe Cronin. He paid good money for fading or second-line Yankee players, including Billy Werber, George Pipgras, and Lyn Lary.[15]

In general, Barrow used Ruppert's money wisely in building and maintaining the Yankees.

The Former Contenders: Athletics and Senators

Within a span of little more than two years, the American League's balance of power was permanently changed by trades. The powerful Philadelphia Athletics and Washington Senators traded themselves into perpetual mediocrity, while the Boston Red Sox and Detroit Tigers rejuvenated themselves. Both the Athletics and Senators were owned by former ballplayers turned owners. Connie Mack and Clark Griffith had sparse assets outside of baseball. While their baseball acumen might have enabled them to overachieve on occasion, their relative lack of capital became a greater detriment as the decade ended.

Mack had built three championship aggregations: 1905, 1910–14, and 1929–31. He had a keen eye for talent but was bedeviled by slender capital reserves. He had acquired some money in the stock market by the mid-1920s and decided to complete his rebuilding by acquiring such veteran talent as Ty Cobb and Eddie Collins. Griffith had earlier refused to meet an aging Tris Speaker's salary demands for a reported figure of $40,000 to $60,000. He released Speaker, one of the earliest inductees to the Baseball Hall of Fame. Mack signed Speaker for the 1928 season. According to Haupert's information, Speaker earned $30,000 in 1926 and 1927 before ending his career with $15,000 in 1928. Speaker joined Cobb and Collins on Mack's sentimental journey of aging stars.[16]

The economic downturn and the dominance of Mack's 1929–31 clubs hurt attendance at Shibe Park; it fell from 839,000 to 627,000. He was also hurt by the fact that his club could not play home games on Sundays. Because the club was successful and had several stars in their primes—Lefty Grove, Mickey Cochrane, Al Simmons, Jimmie Foxx—the payroll rose, too.

After a disappointing 1932 season, in which the team finished second and attendance fell by over 200,000, Mack's financial woes mounted. He sold Simmons, Mule Haas, and Jimmy Dykes to the Chicago White Sox for a reported $150,000.[17] In a poignant announcement, he stated, "We went into the red heavily. ... We had one of the highest salaried clubs in the league, including even the Yankees, with Babe Ruth's $75,000, and our attendance figures were far below those of last year. I feel also that I've been a failure, not in playing results, but financially. And that failure forced me to sell those players. Any man who can't make both ends meet must be a failure. And I didn't make ends meet for the A's." Mack's deals differed from those of Charles Finley, owner of the team during the 1960s and 1970s, who attempted to sell or trade his stars to front-running Boston and New York. Mack, conscious of the effects of his transactions upon competitive balance in the American League, stated that he hoped not to sell any more players, but if he had to do so, "it will be to an American League club in the sixth, seventh or eighth position in the standings. None of the five ranking clubs in the league will ever be able to buy or trade with me for a player as long as I'm a manager ... [the leading clubs] are always well supplied with players ... that's as strong as I'd want to see them."[18] An editorial in the *Sporting News* commented that the Simmons deal was not a "setup," with its suspicions of syndicate baseball—both clubs got what they needed.[19]

A year later, with no relief in sight and a disappointing delay in the approval of Sunday ball, Mack sold several more players in 1933, including Grove and Cochrane, for hundreds of thousands of dollars. Mack indicated at first that the bankers were pressuring him but later claimed that it was that he did not want to pay his players the money they demanded. Trying to put things in the best possible light, he said, "But now we have the funds with which to rebuild. In fact, we already have spent a considerable portion for new players."[20]

The Athletics' entire starting lineup and the top three starting pitchers were sold or traded by the end of the 1935 season. Mack also traded some of the developing stars he initially used to replace his 1929–32 players: Doc Cramer, Pinky Higgins, Johnny Marcum, Eric McNair, and Sugar Cain. He retained only one of the new stars that he developed during the 1930s, Bob Johnson, whom he kept until 1943. Mack claimed that he intended to rebuild the team quickly, but he failed. The Athletics would field losing teams from 1934 to 1946 before a brief flirtation with winning in the late 1940s. His dispersal of stars affected the competitive balance in the American League. Strangely, he did not send any of his stars to National League teams.

Who obtained the players sold by the Athletics? Boston took Grove and Foxx, arguably the brightest of Mack's stars. The Red Sox later acquired Cramer, Marcum, Higgins, and some other Athletics starters in the mid-1930s. Red Sox fans who bemoan the Yankees' acquisition of all their stars in the 1920s might take solace in that reversal of fortunes. Detroit got Mickey Cochrane, who promptly led them to two pennants before a terrible injury ended his playing career. The White Sox picked up Al Simmons, the other Hall of Fame player from the Athletics, as well as some other starters. White Sox owner Charles Comiskey believed that the acquisition helped boost attendance, which rose 160,000 between 1932 and 1933.[21] Even the St. Louis Browns scavenged the carcass of the Athletics, carrying away lesser players such as pitcher Roy Mahaffey and Cain. Cleveland and Washington also acquired players from Mack in time.

While Mack intentionally dismantled his club, the Washington Senators could be pardoned for wondering what happened. Despite the clever line, "Washington: first in war, first in peace, and last in the American League," the Senators had been a solid franchise during the 1920s, with two pennants in 1924 and 1925. Senators owner Clark Griffith ran the franchise during its most successful period. He did this despite having little capital apart from the team. Although the club reported profits for every season between 1920 and 1928, it lost almost $100,000 between 1929 and 1932 despite three winning seasons. Griffith had been willing to spend large sums of money to obtain players, including a reported $154,750 during 1929 alone. The Senators won the 1933 pennant easily, but he reported a loss of $500.[22] The team's pennant in 1933 was the culmination of eight winning seasons in the previous ten years. Compared with Griffith's 1925 pennant winner, the 1933 champions attracted almost 400,000 fewer attendees, which suppressed revenues. The club's attendance was the lowest for an American League pennant winner since World War I, so Griffith had the misfortune of winning what would be his last pennant in one of the worst financial seasons in the game's history.

Without many roster changes, the club plunged from a 99-53 record to a 66-86 mark between 1933 and 1934. The major player transaction was trading Goose Goslin for John Stone. These two players had similar batting records in 1933 and 1934, although Stone undoubtedly received less pay than Goslin. The real reason for the club's collapse was pitching. The top three starting pitchers went 71-34 in 1933 and 36-47 in 1934. The team quickly traded most of the pitching staff by the end of the 1935 season.

A year later, Thomas Yawkey of the Red Sox approached Griffith with an offer to buy star shortstop and manager Joe Cronin. Yawkey offered $250,000; in terms of purchasing power, this was close to three times the amount the Bosox received for Babe Ruth. The Senators' slump in 1934 and the attendant drop of 100,000 in attendance made Yawkey's offer tempting. Griffith claimed he owed banks $125,000. He initially resisted selling Cronin, who had married his adopted niece. Griffith hardly ever sold his star players, but Yawkey was persistent and pointed out that he could pay the player-manager more money.[23] Eventually Boston obtained Cronin for $225,000 and Lyn Lary on October 26, 1934, although newspaper accounts at the time estimated a sale price of between $150,000 and $200,000. Griffith claimed the sale price was twice as much as any one had ever paid for one player, but some sportswriters, such as Richard Vidmer, viewed the claim as exaggerated.[24] Washington fans might have been placated by the fact that "'Griffith would never have parted with Joe if he was not convinced it was for the best interests of his new kin-in-law,' [Red Sox General Manager Eddie] Collins said. 'In fact it appeared that Griff was more concerned about Joe's welfare than he was about that of his ball club. He dreaded telling his Washington public of the deal.'"[25]

The Athletics and Senators exemplified downward mobility. Mack's rebuilding process floundered despite his discovery of longtime big league players such as Bob Johnson, Doc Cramer, and Eric McNair. His efforts were frustrated by his inability to find good pitchers. By 1939 he was rebuilding again and was willing to transfer all of his players except for the aforementioned Johnson and his catcher.[26]

The seventh-place Senators never regained their baseball respectability. Aside from a couple of seasons during World War II, they had few winning seasons between 1935 and 1960. Red Sox fans liked to bemoan the "Curse of the Bambino," a silly fantasy concocted by bored sportswriters, but Senators fans might wonder about the "Curse of the Cronin," which is at least alliterative.

The Carrions (aka the Nouveau Riche): Tigers and Red Sox

The Detroit Tigers were the first team to reap the benefits of buying a former Philadelphia Athletics star. Although the team brought up Hank Greenberg and pitchers Schoolboy Rowe and Eldon Auker in 1933, they still fell short of a pennant, although their performance was clearly superior to the 61-93 record they posted in 1931. The Tigers obtained Cochrane after the 1933 season and, two days, later, traded for future Hall of Fame outfielder Goslin from Washington. The Tigers won 101 games in 1934, completing a 40-game improvement. Five of the starting players and four of the five pitchers with the most innings pitched in 1934 started their careers with the Tigers. The team won another pennant in 1935 before getting run over by the Yankees in 1936.

Since the Red Sox had traded most of its team to the Yankees during the 1920s, they languished at the bottom of the American League. When Yawkey purchased the team in 1933, he infused money into the franchise. The Red Sox rebounded from their 43-111 record in 1932 to 76-76 in 1934. In an amusing twist, the Red Sox bought or traded for several New York Yankees players, including Lyn Lary, Billy Werber, George Pipgras, Dusty Cooke, Gordon Rhodes, Hank Johnson, and

Ivy Andrews. Unfortunately for the Red Sox, these were largely second-line players.

While Griffith pocketed the money from selling Joe Cronin, Yawkey continued his free-spending ways. After improving Fenway Park and buying Athletics stars Lefty Grove, Rube Walberg, and Max Bishop in late 1933 and Cronin in 1934, the enthusiastic owner added Athletics slugger Jimmie Foxx after the 1935 season, adding three future Hall of Fame players to his team while each was still in his prime. Breathless reporters calculated the millions he spent in trying to win a pennant. American League fans would chafe at the Yankees/Athletics set of deals in the late 1950s, but Roger Maris, Clete Boyer, and Ralph Terry were at best pale imitations of Grove, Cronin, and Foxx.

Yawkey was coy about purchasing Foxx, claiming that after the disappointing 1935 season that he was through spending "big money" for "big names." Manager Cronin stated that the team preferred to spend the reputed $200,000 asking price for Foxx on young players instead.[27] The rumors did not disappear, and this time Mack publicly denied any potential sale to Boston: "I have denied it so often that I will neither confirm or deny it now. Everybody is taking a hand at selling my players. It's a great game and I have stopped being amused at it."[28]

The problem was that Foxx, a slugger whose stature was only slightly lower than that of Ruth, wanted more money. He stated that if another team acquired him, they had to pay him more, "[That] contract with Philadelphia was based on Shibe Park receipts and I knew that the Athletics could not pay any more. Now, if some American League club owner puts up a fortune for me in release money, he will have to give me a contract for more than I ever received before, even though my contract has two more years to run."[29] Mack could stop denying rumors after December 10, when he sold the slugger to Boston for a reported $150,000–$200,000. He also completed a second transaction with the Red Sox, sending budding stars Eric McNair and Doc Cramer there for Carl Reynolds, a player to be named later, and another large sum of money.[30]

By now sportswriters were claiming Yawkey had poured $3.5 million into the team since 1932, including the $1 million purchase price and $1.5 million Fenway renovation project.[31] Despite all his expenditures, Yawkey only succeeded in making the Red Sox almost perennial runners-up during the late 1930s and early 1940s.[32]

The Woebegone: Phillies and Braves

National League teams also experienced significant fluctuations in their records, although few endured gyrations comparable to those experienced by the Philadelphia Phillies. The Phillies vacillated between terrible and barely respectable between 1928 and 1934, with records of 43-109 in 1928, 71-82 in 1929, 52-102 in 1930, 78-76 in 1932, and 56-93 in 1934. The team would achieve a dubious consistency thereafter, losing more than one hundred games in five of the six seasons during the late 1930s.

Pity the poor Philadelphia fans. They not only watched Mack dismantle his great Athletics team, but saw the cross-town Phillies become the era's equivalent of the post–World War II St. Louis Browns and Kansas City Athletics, teams that consistently traded or sold their best players to the wealthier Boston Red Sox and New York Yankees.

The Phillies set National League records for futility during the late 1930s; however, the team's talent scouts were reasonably productive. The team introduced Hall of Fame hitter Chuck Klein during the late 1920s. Although his hitting numbers were inflated by the Baker Bowl's tiny dimensions, Klein was a genuine slugger whose effectiveness ended all too quickly. His first six seasons with the team resulted in four home run titles and a batting title. Despite the fact that he was the reigning batting champion, the Phillies sold him to the Chicago Cubs for three players and $65,000 or more. Klein had been one of the players freed from the St. Louis Cardinals' farm system during the 1920s, and a sportswriter mentioned how the Cardinals must have been gnashing their teeth at the reported sum paid by the Cubs for him in 1933.[33] Phillies fans might have been distraught at losing their star player, but

Klein struggled to hit .300 with the Cubs, who sent him back to Philadelphia in 1936. Perhaps it was clever of the Phillies to trade him before the decline became too apparent.

The Phillies had been trading stars for years. They had already traded Lefty O'Doul, who was Klein's sidekick for two years, to the Brooklyn Dodgers for some players and cash. In a weird parallel to Babe Ruth's career, the Yankees debuted Lefty as a pitcher. He didn't fare well and was traded to the Boston Red Sox. After disappearing from the majors, he resurfaced as an outfielder. In a short but memorable career Lefty compiled a .349 batting average. While his numbers were somewhat inflated by the Baker Bowl, he did win a batting title with Brooklyn. Throughout the 1930s the Phillies usually sold whatever promising players they acquired. During the late 1930s the team traded or sold four pitchers who would quickly become 20-game winners for their new teams: Curt Davis, Bucky Walters, Claude Passeau, and Kirby Higbe. The first three were on the staff in 1936. One can imagine Phillies fans crumpling their scorecards in anguish after watching the rapid improvement in these hurlers' performances for other teams. Another standout was shortstop Rowdy Richard Bartell. Pittsburgh traded Rowdy Richard to Philadelphia, where he compiled some good batting statistics for a shortstop. The New York Giants had bought shortstop Dave Bancroft from the Phillies in 1920. When the Giants needed another shortstop during the 1930s, they returned to the Phillies and obtained Bartell for $75,000 and four players.[34] His slick fielding and good hitting helped them win pennants in 1936 and 1937.

Brooklyn scavenged the Phillies by buying slugger Dolph Camilli, while even the nouveau riche Reds swooped down and acquired top pitcher Walters for two players and cash.[35] As a fan complained in a letter to the *New York Times*, "such deals do not appear fair to either the Philadelphia fans or the club itself." The fan urged owner Gerald Nugent to obtain "other men who might possibly inject new blood and strength into his dead team."[36] A sportswriter reviewed Nugent's player sales and estimated the owner had received $0.5 million dollars over the past ten years.[37]

The Phillies were able to find good players, but they were hard-pressed to keep them. The Boston Braves rarely signed good Minor League players. While the Reds and Dodgers transformed their teams from mediocrity into champions, the Boston Braves could only aspire to mediocrity. The club finished with a humiliating 38-115 record in 1935 but improved quickly to 71-83 in 1936 and 79-73 in 1937 before sinking back into ineptitude. The Braves' continued improvement in 1937 rested upon two rookie pitchers, who each won twenty games: Lou Fette and Jim Turner. Boston also relied on trades and waiver purchases to field a respectable club for 1937. Just two of the starting lineup and two of the reserves debuted with the Braves. The club introduced a DiMaggio in 1937, but it was Vince, not Joe.

The Big Spenders: Larry MacPhail's Reds and Dodgers

Larry MacPhail reversed the fortunes of two moribund franchises: the Cincinnati Reds and the Brooklyn Dodgers. His Reds and Dodgers actively pursued the star players given up by the Phillies, Cardinals and Braves. Because night baseball proved lucrative for the two franchises, MacPhail and his successor in Cincinnati, Warren Giles, could rapidly improve their clubs by buying players. The aforementioned Walters and Camilli deals, as well as a deal for Joe Medwick, reflected the financial health of the two teams. While not all of the players the clubs obtained proved useful, the teams' fans were excited by the management's efforts to improve performance.[38]

MacPhail and Giles used money which was generated in part by electric lighting to transform the Cincinnati Reds from the cellar dwellers of the National League (56-98 in 1937) to pennant winners in 1939 (97-57). Many Reds players were introduced by the team, but the two best pitchers were acquired from National League rivals Philadelphia and St. Louis. Catcher Ernie Lombardi had been obtained in 1932 from Brooklyn before attaining stardom. The team also got established big league players Wally Berger, Lon Frey, and Bill Werber (the latter two for cash) during the 1938 season and before the 1939 season.

If any team could be accused of buying a pennant (aside from the Boston Red Sox, who merely attempted to buy a pennant), that team would be the Brooklyn Dodgers. Larry MacPhail quickly transformed the Dodgers into a strong club. The team had a 62-91 record in 1937 but won its first pennant since 1920 in 1941 with a 100-54 mark. Although they introduced Pee Wee Reese and Pete Reiser in 1940, most of their best players—Dolph Camilli, Billy Herman, Joe Medwick, Mickey Owen, Kirby Higbe, and Curt Davis—were all paid for in players and cash. The club also acquired Dixie Walker for the waiver price and got two pitchers, Whit Wyatt and Hugh Casey, for practically nothing. The team was a collection of clever signings and purchases. By 1947, when the club won its next pennant, Branch Rickey's farm system had begun to produce a plethora of big league players. Only two of the regulars and the best relief pitcher on the 1947 team came from other teams.

The Dodgers bought Medwick, Owen, and Davis from their chief rivals, the St. Louis Cardinals. The Cardinals were in the midst of transforming their team and were happy to unload veteran stars who were demanding pay raises. The two clubs would fight for pennants for the rest of the decade. The Dodgers acquired some of their other players from the Chicago Cubs, Pittsburgh Pirates, Washington Senators, and Philadelphia Phillies.

A Tale of Two Teams (in the Same City): Cardinals and Browns

The St. Louis Browns usually did not have money to buy fancy stars in their prime, as even the Braves did on occasion (Rogers Hornsby). When Hornsby ended up with the Browns as a fading player turned manager, he blasted the "selfish" rich clubs and insisted that the club would no longer just sell players. "I don't think I change this [selfish] attitude, but they'll have to do something to help the Browns while they are helping themselves."[39] After Browns hitter George McQuinn had two solid seasons, rumors circulated that the Yankees would acquire him. A sportswriter described the Browns' dilemma: "their only hope is to keep on trying to build with youngsters. McQuinn will be 30 years old. . . . He isn't a kid anymore, as ball players go." The Browns kept him through World War II before trading him to the Yankees.[40] When Donald Barnes acquired control of the team, he bought players whenever he had some spare cash (usually obtained from an infusion of capital from the board of directors). His purchases included Eldon Auker and Walt Judnich. He wasn't able to acquire enough quality players until the war stripped the top teams of most of their talent, thus leveling the field for the Browns.[41]

The Browns achieved a dramatic turnaround near the end of the era; they improved from 43-111 in 1939 to 82-69 by 1942. Theirs was a special case. With the Browns playing poorly and drawing terribly, fellow American League owners responded as though to the imaginary plaint, "Isn't anybody going to help that [poor] team?" American League president William Harridge requested that the wealthier teams help the Browns by selling top Minor League or young Major League players to the Browns for modest prices. The Browns picked up Chet Laabs and Myril Hoag from frontrunners Detroit and New York.

The St. Louis Cardinals, with their growing system of Minor League farm teams, were the very model of a modern franchise in 1920s terms. The team rose from genteel mediocrity to claim its first twentieth-century title in 1926. Five of the eighteen players listed as regular performers in the *Macmillan Baseball Encyclopedia* started their careers on teams other than St. Louis, but the leading hitters and pitchers all made their debuts with the Cardinals. Two pitchers, Jesse Haines and Grover Alexander, were acquired relatively cheaply; Alexander was obtained for the waiver price.

The team's next pennant winner, the 1928 edition, featured more acquired starters from other teams than did the 1926 club. The Cardinals changed personnel fairly quickly (table 29). The 1930 team differed greatly from the 1928 team. Between the 1930 and 1934 pennant winners, the only major holdovers were player-manager Frank Frisch and veteran pitcher Bill Hallahan. The team's top four pitchers in 1934 were all Cardinal farm products. The club continued to churn players throughout the 1930s.

The St. Louis Cardinals sold many players, but its practices differed from those of the Browns, Phillies, Athletics, and Braves. The Cardinals sold stars before their value declined too greatly and used the money to replenish the farm system. The club sold Dizzy Dean to the Chicago Cubs after his injury. The Cubs paid well over $150,000 for Dean. The Giants and Dodgers bought sluggers Johnny Mize and Joe Medwick. At first Cardinals owner Breadon was reluctant to part with them, but he eventually capitulated, saying, "Sure, we took money in those deals. We had to have money. You can't run a big organization like ours on a home gate of 332,000 admissions." The owner claimed (accurately, as it turned out) that the farm system had plenty of replacement players. The cash deals helped the club declare a dividend for 1940.[42] Despite having sold the three future Hall of Fame players for a combined $360,000, the team rebounded to win three consecutive pennants from 1942 to 1944. The Cardinals were an anomaly; they shared a small city and they drew fewer than 500,000 fans per season, yet they consistently fielded winning teams.

The Vagabond: The Travels of Rogers Hornsby

If you were a team owner seeking a talented hitter, you had a reasonable chance of picking up one of the all-time great ones during the late 1920s and early 1930s. While the wondrous Babe Ruth was traded or released twice during his career, his National League counterpart, Rogers Hornsby, far exceeded him in wandering around the Major Leagues. After a decade with the Cardinals, Hornsby became a traveling man. Most associates of the outspoken Hornsby might have used a variety of "A words" to describe him: abrasive, acidic, arrogant. He began his peregrinations after the Cardinals' 1926 World Series win. He went first to the New York Giants, after demanding $50,000 for his services as player-manager of the Cardinals. Rickey and Breadon opted not to accede to Hornsby's demand and traded him for Frankie Frisch and Jimmy Ring. At least the Cardinals got a star player in return.

After Hornsby's first year with the Giants, John McGraw traded him (despite his .361 batting average) to the Boston Braves for two nonentities, Shanty Hogan and Jimmy Welch. No cash was involved. Apparently the slugger incurred owner Charles Stoneham's ire by hinting that he was to be the future manager of the club, a story hotly denied by the owner: "I wish to say that the deal was made in order to avoid any future conflict in the management of this club." As an aside, the New York Giants had been accused of buying pennants during the club's consecutive titles of 1921–24. The *New York Times* story on the Hornsby trade resurrected suspicions about the relationship between the Braves and the Giants that recalled syndicalism, a situation in which owners had interests in multiple clubs. The Giants had obtained pitchers Art Nehf and Hugh McQuillan from the Braves several years earlier, and those two hurlers were crucial in the team's pennant runs.[43] Hornsby lasted a season in Boston, hitting .387, before being traded to the Chicago Cubs for five players and $200,000. He had just one more productive season left; he helped the Cubs win the National League pennant in 1929. Thereafter, injuries limited his playing time. He bounced from the Cubs to the Cardinals and finally landed with the St. Louis Browns as a player-manager.

Owners, even penurious ones such as Boston's Fuchs, could aspire to acquire a top star on occasion, as Hornsby's itinerary demonstrated.

Good, Old-Fashioned Free Agents

Modern free agency began in the 1970s with Jim "Catfish" Hunter, Dave McNally, and Andy Messersmith. Before these players pioneered free agency as we know it, other players had been free agents. These players were occasionally Major Leaguers released by their teams or, more likely, Minor League players set free by Commissioner Landis when he discovered that Major League teams had violated the rules governing the control of players.

In 1927 two of the game's greatest players became free agents: Ty Cobb and Tris Speaker. Cobb, of course, remains famous in baseball. Pete Rose's quest to best his record for number of base hits and the appearance of a Cobb character in several baseball movies in the 1980s and 1990s ensured that Ty remained in the public's consciousness. Speaker was almost as good a player as Cobb. The Red Sox had sold him to Cleveland after winning the pennant in 1915. His price was worth more in purchasing power than the amount they received from selling Babe Ruth. Fortunately for the owner, Joe Lannin, his club won pennants again in 1916 and 1918; had they not done so, sportswriters might have coined the term, "Curse of the Speaker."

When Swede Risberg broke the ugly scandal in which Detroit Tigers players received payment from the White Sox for beating the Boston Red Sox in 1919, Cobb's and Speaker's names came up. Both were cleared by the evidence, or, at least, by the lack of any incriminating evidence. Commissioner Landis pressured Detroit and Cleveland to grant the two stars their releases, and they became free agents. Historian Charles Alexander discusses Mack's pursuit of Cobb. Mack hoped that Cobb would provide a necessary boost to his young ball club as it pursued of the New York Yankees. According to the Haupert Player Salary Database, he signed Cobb for $50,000 to play during 1927.[44] The Senators signed Speaker. Both players hit well over .300. The following year Mack signed Speaker, too.

Most free agents were Minor League players whose owners had broken some rule. As early as 1929, Landis made nine Major and Minor League baseball players free agents because of their employers' violations.[45] Major League Baseball barely avoided a revolutionary situation when he decided that the Cleveland Indians' signing of Bob Feller violated the Major-Minor sandlot agreement on signing amateur players. Owners simultaneously worried and hoped that Landis would declare the youngster a free agent: they worried because the bidding might have triggered a "spending orgy, which might have run as high as $100,000" and they hoped to be the lucky owner who might nab the obviously talented pitcher. Although Feller was content to remain with the Indians, he and his father recognized his value and vowed to get a $20,000 salary for the 1937 season.[46] Feller got $14,000 for 1937. He did not get his $20,000 salary until 1939, according to Haupert's data. After World War II talented amateurs would command signing bonuses in excess of $100,000 (in depreciated postwar dollars).

Cleveland had to pay the Des Moines Minor League club $7,500 for its chicanery in the Feller case. The club was hit even harder a few months later. Landis declared Tom Henrich a free agent, claiming that Cleveland and the Milwaukee Minor League club conspired to cover up the player. New York Giants manager Bill Terry claimed that his club had offered $20,000 for Henrich. Henrich had been suspicious of Cleveland's and Milwaukee's actions.[47] He signed with the New York Yankees and became a consistent power hitter for the Yankees, earning the nickname "Old Reliable."

Landis freed seventy-three players from the St. Louis Cardinals farm system in March 1938, including Harold "Pete" Reiser, later star of the Brooklyn Dodgers.[48] Landis also investigated the Detroit Tigers' relationship with Minor League teams, and later released ninety-two players in 1940. Infielder Benny McCoy and outfielder Roy Cullenbine were the top Major Leaguers now declared free agents. Connie Mack signed McCoy to a two-year contract at $10,000 per year with a signing bonus reported to be as high as $45,000; he also met the player's stipulation that he would be played regularly at second base.[49] The St. Louis Browns and Brooklyn Dodgers pursued Cullenbine. The latter team eventually signed him for a $25,000 bonus and a $7,500 salary. Larry MacPhail indicated that there was a bandwagon effect involved, as "[the Browns' Fred] Haney said he'd go higher if his club would let him. That's important because Haney's a smart baseball man and he had Cullenbine a couple of years at Toledo."[50] Other free agents at that time included Rick Ferrell and Hank Borowy.[51]

Not every potential free agent situation ended to the player's satisfaction. Yankee infielder Joe Dugan was hoping to become a free agent; the club tried to get him waived out of the league in order to give him an unconditional release and grant his wish. The team eventually traded him to the Boston Braves for the waiver price, an action that angered Dugan.[52] A sportswriter explained, "the feeling persists that there is a bit of gentlemen's agreement to give the Braves a lift wherever possible"[53] (especially since the team was going to get Sunday home games in 1929). Sportswriter Ira Irving bemoaned the situation in which such wealthy teams as the Giants and the Yankees received help during the pennant races of the early 1920s: "the other owners were desperately trying to solve the problem of how to prevent [the New York clubs] from obtaining material from their friends, the Boston clubs. They had secured all the stars on these clubs by the winter of 1923, and the pennant races threatened to become boresome if some remedy was not forthcoming."[54] The Braves might have been better off if they had obtained a scout or two from the Yankees; a few years later, another reporter stated the club had spent $600,000 since 1929 for ballplayers "without getting much in the way of result." The reporter thoughtfully included a list of the disappointing purchases.[55]

While Landis's actions against the Cardinals and Tigers may have affected both franchises' long-term ability to compete, free agency did not directly affect many pennant races.

Integration

Owners of downtrodden teams might have considered another pool of talent: players laboring in the Negro Leagues. Cuban players had performed in Major League Baseball for several years. No one asked whether any of them might be of African descent. New York Giants manager John McGraw wanted to hire an African American infielder, Charley Grant, and pass him off as a Cherokee, but was not able to pull it off.[56] While there were no written strictures against black players, Commissioner Landis was a staunch foe of the idea, and it is likely that many owners, if not players and fans, also opposed mixing races on the ball field.

By the 1930s, however, Major League owners had greater difficulty in pleading ignorance of the talent pool that sometimes graced their own parks (some owners rented their stadiums to Negro League teams). Walter Johnson recognized the talents of Josh Gibson, the legendary slugging catcher. Dizzy Dean extolled pitcher Satchel Paige's ability: "He could pitch anywhere and I'll put him right behind me 'n Carl Hubbell."[57]

While Adolf Hitler and Nazi Germany's racist polices gave impetus to postwar America's examination of its racial legacy, activists before the war began calling for an end of discrimination against Negroes (to use the contemporary term). The American Youth Congress passed a statement to this effect in January 1938.[58] Yankee player Jake Powell's outrageous remarks about beating up black people while serving as an off-season police officer also infuriated many people. A fan, responding to the Powell incident, wrote to the *New York Times* urging a major league "all-colored club."[59] New York state senator Charles D. Perry introduced a resolution disapproving discrimination against "colored players." Collegiate press representatives also worked to organize opposition to Major League Baseball's exclusion of black players.[60] A fan, perhaps overly optimistically, wrote to the *New York Times* that, "If [the owners] could be shown that business would improve with Negroes in uniform, they would fall over one another to break the ban. Actually, the ban is an insult of the purest sort to sports fans."[61] An occasional fan opposed integration, with one writing the *Sporting News*, "It is not difficult to imagine what would happen if a player on a mixed team, performing before a crowd of the opposite color, should throw a bean ball, strike out with the bases full or spike a rival." The writer went on to suggest that taking the top black players from the Negro Leagues would jeopardize the viability of those leagues and thereby cut off the flow of talent, a circuitous argument at best.[62]

As America fought racist regimes in Germany and Japan, Major League Baseball began to show signs of recognizing African American players. Jesse Owens's performance at the Berlin Olympics in 1936 and the collegiate talent on display at UCLA and other schools reinforced recognition of the abilities of top African American players. The Pittsburgh Pirates and Cleveland Indians announced that they would hold tryouts of black players, but nothing came of these announcements. Labor unions also advocated an end of the discrimination.[63] Not until 1947 would Jackie Robinson break baseball's color line and play in the Major Leagues, and the reader is encouraged to consult Jules Tygiel's book for an excellent account.[64]

Conclusion

Player movements during the 1930s demonstrated that teams with sufficient funds and a good eye for talent could transform themselves and increase their win-loss records by 30 or more wins within two or three seasons. While some teams retained their superiority by signing top rookie talent, other teams with ample bankrolls could stay on top by buying or trading for stars from teams with less prosperous owners. Wealthy owners could also afford more mistakes than their less well-to-do peers. The reverse was true, too. Such former contenders as the Athletics and Senators ended the era in a baseball version of Palookaville; unlike Terry Malloy, they were at least able to claim that "we used to be contenders."

Modern-style free agency would be hard pressed to duplicate Tom Yawkey's purchases of Grove, Cronin, and Foxx in three consecutive years, although the Seattle Mariners' loss of Ken Griffey Jr., Alex Rodriguez, and Randy Johnson rivaled Connie Mack's loss of his stars. The analogy ends there, however, as the Mariners would set a record for wins before sinking back into mediocrity, while Mack's Athletics sank into chronic decrepitude.

Teams with deeper pockets could easily prosper under either the reserve clause or under free agency. Such teams could easily prosper by buying established stars or a large number of promising Minor League players. Teams without sufficient funding received scant benefit from the reserve clause in terms of competitive balance. Depression-era owners without much cash could only content themselves with saving some money on salaries by using the superior bargaining position given them by the reserve clause.

3. Using League Rules to Aid in the Recovery

7. Helping the Indigent

Some owners were trying desperately to keep their clubs out of bankruptcy during the 1930s. One method of helping teams in small cities survive was through cross-subsidization, which was typically achieved through revenue sharing. Both leagues had gate-sharing rules. Did such rules provide much succor for struggling teams?

Many people believe gate sharing exists to redress inequalities in revenue and to promote competitive balance. Gate-sharing rules reflect the tension within a professional sports league. Owners are self-interested, but they also have to consider the effects of their actions upon rival owners. While most industries winnow out the weak, modern sports leagues often prefer to maintain weak clubs. However, some owners, especially of successful teams, appear to downplay or disagree with the "helping the weak" argument. If you owned the New York Yankees, your attitude might be, "I should get a large piece of the pie when I visit Kansas City, since I'm bringing in a strong (well-paid), attractive club. When the Royals start bringing in a strong, well-drawing club to Yankee Stadium, I'll be willing to share more revenue."

The prevailing belief is still that revenue sharing exists to transfer money from wealthy teams (primarily in the biggest cities) to poorer teams (primarily in the smaller cities). Certainly the Great Depression era looms as an era in which revenue sharing would have been of utmost importance.

Brief History of Revenue Sharing

Revenue sharing was present at the birth of professional baseball, as the competing clubs had to divide the gate. Baseball historian Harold Seymour and witnesses at the 1951 Congressional hearings claimed that gate-sharing rules redressed revenue differences between teams that drew well and those that did not, but the owners often sang a different tune. Seymour wrote, "Appreciating the results of inequality of markets, the owners tried to compensate by sharing gate receipts."[1] He also described the underlying animosity between owners of large-city teams and their peers. The National League had difficulties with its New York and Philadelphia clubs during its inaugural season of 1876. The large-city owners refused to travel west to play some teams; they offered to pay the western clubs handsomely to come east instead. The National League eventually (but only temporarily) settled on a fixed guarantee of $125 instead of a percentage split in 1886. Owners of teams in smaller cities favored the percentage split, with the Detroit manager complaining, "We should be nice suckers ... to go to Boston or to Washington and put big money in their treasuries for $125." Chicago owner Albert Spalding retorted that wealthier clubs were "tired of carrying along a club like Detroit."[2] An editorial in the *Sporting News* claimed that the National League's equal split of the basic 50¢ admission was a key to its longevity, as the teams in the smaller towns could now survive and compete with teams in the larger cities.[3] The editorial writer, like so many other observers, did not ask whether teams should remain in smaller towns or whether they should relocate (or even fold).

Effects of Gate Sharing

Some sports historians believe gate-sharing rules can promote competitive balance. Leifer makes explicit his belief of the link between the National Football League's generous gate-sharing rule and its competitive balance: "The main reason why the National Football League did not experience high performance inequality, and early baseball leagues did, was the liberal revenue-sharing policies adopted by the National Football League."[4]

While sports economists debate whether gate-sharing rules have much effect on competitive balance, most agree that such rules may ensure the survival of teams in smaller cities. When leagues faced a crisis, they sometimes adjusted the revenue-sharing rules to benefit struggling teams. In the Pacific Coast League, one of the top Minor Leagues, the club directors voted to allow Sacramento an additional 5 percent.[5] Major League owners tended to make loans to teams in financial straits. In addition, most economists assume that gate sharing transfers money from wealthier teams, typically those in larger cities, to poorer teams, typically those in smaller cities, creating a Robin Hood effect. Scully and Quirk and Fort also share a belief that the "more equal the gate-sharing plan among the teams, the more equal the revenues."[6] Underlying their argument is the implicit assumption in their models that the stronger the team is the more it draws at home but the worse it draws on the road (because the rival team is, all things equal, weaker): "Intuitively, gate sharing lowers the value of an additional win-percent to a team because the team only captures a fraction of any increased revenue at home games. On the road, the team generally loses revenue because, on average, the win-percent of its opponent has fallen."[7]

There may be other motives underlying gate sharing. Rottenberg and Quirk and Fort argued that increased revenue sharing should have little effect on competitive balance but may serve to suppress player salaries by reducing the revenue gain from winning additional games.[8] Canes argued that revenue sharing and other league rules may help owners, because "their absence may encourage team owners to produce higher team quality than is socially efficient." He described the externality problem (in which a third party is affected by other parties' transactions): "Since the owner's profits are not affected by decreased demand for games in which his team does not play, he will not take such effects into account; that is, they will be external to the owner's cost and revenue calculations." While owners could compensate each other for the revenue losses caused by fielding too strong a team, "this would require difficult decisions about which teams should be compensated and to what extent. Moreover, if not all team owners were party to the agreement, some could increase the quality of their teams and so displace the others, or could threaten to increase quality in order to be compensated not to do so."[9] Therefore, a properly designed revenue-sharing plan could reduce the incentive (in terms of additional revenue from improving a team) to overinvest in team quality and could also help owners sidestep the potentially disputatious process of determining the compensation described above.

Gate Sharing's Effects between 1929 and 1941

How did gate sharing work during the Great Depression? According to the 1933 and 1936 versions of the National League constitutions, home teams had to pay 25¢ of each full admission (50¢ or more) to the visiting team.[10] Sportswriter John Drebinger claimed National League teams had to pay 26¢ to the visiting team. During the immediate postwar period, the National League required the home team to pay 22.5¢ per admission to the visiting team. The league's revenue-sharing rules thus appear to have changed over time.[11]

From the information provided by owners to Congress in 1951, it appears that National League teams collectively paid between 23.6¢ and 24¢ per home admission to the visiting teams during the 1930s. It is not known whether all teams paid the same flat rate per admission, but it is reasonable to assume that all teams paid close to the average. The American League revenue-sharing plan required the home team to pay 20¢ per bleacher or general admission seat and 30¢ per reserved or box seat.[12] Table 30 shows the estimated redistribution. The amounts are estimates because teams did not report how much they paid to visiting teams but did report how much they received as the visiting team. Given the rigid sharing rules in the National League (roughly 24¢ per home attendee) and the rough average of 27¢ to 28¢ per home attendee in the American League, one can derive estimates of the actual distribution. The New York Yankees' financial records also offer a reasonably complete record of their revenue-sharing experiences.

Because ticket prices were lower between 1929 and 1941 than they were in the postwar period (during which the rules were still similar), the proportion of total gate revenue that was redistributed was greater in the earlier period. Although the Chicago White Sox (1929 and 1933) and Pittsburgh Pirates (1933) did not contribute games away revenue figures, with which will be used to examine the effects of revenue sharing, their shares can still be estimated. American League teams shared almost 29 percent of total gate revenue. National League teams shared 25.8 percent in 1933 and 22.7 percent in 1939. Between 1946 and 1964, the proportion shared among major league teams was between one-seventh and one-sixth.

Whatever the minor ambiguities in the actual plans, the amounts transferred to the Philadelphia Phillies, Cincinnati Reds, Pittsburgh Pirates, and St. Louis Cardinals in 1933 represented proportionally larger shares of those teams' overall gate revenue than the transfers of the 1950s. Philadelphia, a dismal team, probably earned roughly $130,000 in gross home revenue during 1933. Thanks to a net transfer of almost $50,000, the Phillies had $179,000 in actual gate revenue. In 1939 the Boston Braves received a net transfer of $61,000 from revenue sharing. Without revenue sharing, the Braves' gate revenue would have been below $260,000. The revenue-sharing plan dropped the standard deviation of shares of league revenue in 1933 and 1939 (from 0.059 to 0.045 in 1933 and 0.068 to 0.058 in 1939). In cases of extreme distress, such as the Great Depression, the National League's plan succeeded in transferring relatively large amounts of revenue from healthier to weaker clubs. Even with the revenue-sharing plan, the Phillies relied on player sales to remain profitable.

The table shows that revenue sharing corresponded to the fans' and pundits' ideal in the National League. On net Brooklyn, Chicago, and New York paid money to the teams in smaller cities. St. Louis and Philadelphia received net benefits from gate-sharing in each of the three seasons surveyed. Although Pittsburgh did not report games away revenue, a residual method of estimating their net share yields results that imply the club lost $63,000 in 1929. Note that St. Louis and Pittsburgh generally fielded winning teams during this period. There were some aberrations; the 1933 Boston Braves were so lousy a draw on the road that the club paid more than it received despite mediocre home attendance.

The American League's revenue-sharing plan did help the moribund St. Louis Browns and Washington Senators, but the New York Yankees did not lose much from revenue sharing and gained in two of the three seasons shown. The Detroit Tigers were the biggest contributors to revenue sharing.

The revenue-sharing rules' efficacy in transferring revenue from rich to poor teams was reduced for two reasons. First, teams did not contribute the same proportion of their home gate revenue to visiting teams. Table 7 shows that home revenue per attendee differed between American League teams. The Red Sox had the lowest home revenue per attendee, while the Tigers and Indians took turns having the highest. The Red Sox may have sold a smaller proportion of reserved and box seats, causing their average gate-share amount per seat to have been smaller. Without the actual amounts paid to the visiting team, we cannot decide this issue definitively. In the National League, with its flat gate-sharing amount per attendee, the Chicago Cubs paid a smaller proportion of their gate revenue to visiting teams than did the Boston Braves or Philadelphia Phillies.

A second and more important reason the revenue-sharing plan did not redistribute larger sums was the relationship between a team's record and its ability to draw on the road. As table 31 shows, winning teams tended to draw better on the road in general. The New York Yankees' ability to draw well on the road tempered the team's losses from revenue sharing. In contrast, the Brooklyn Dodgers drew reasonably well at home but weren't a particularly strong draw on the road; this contributed to the team's relatively large negative return from the plan.[13]

Because of the relationship between win-loss record and ability to draw on the road, which is shown in table 31, the usual solution of increasing the revenue share would not necessarily have redressed the "perverse" outcomes. Doubling the per-admission revenue share in the American League, for instance, would have doubled the Yankees' positive payoffs in 1929 and 1939 and doubled their loss in 1933. A better way to redistribute revenue would be to put the visitors' share into a common pot and then split the proceeds evenly among the teams. Such a plan would have severed the link between a team's win-loss record and its ability to draw on the road. The last column of table 30 shows the estimated transfers for 1939 from such a pooling plan. The American League already had a prototype of such a plan. In addition to paying money to the visiting team, the home club paid 5¢ per admission to the league to defray the organization's expenses, although in most seasons the assessment was just 3¢.[14] If any money was left over at the end of the season, the league disbursed the sum equally among the teams. Since the American League seems to have temporarily increased the per-attendee rate to 5¢ in 1933, presumably to defray a deficit in operating expenses, there was probably not much to disburse in most years.

The suggestion of a pooling technique for the visitors' shares might have encountered resistance. The Yankees might have argued that the purpose of revenue sharing was to reward clubs that brought in attractive teams. The Yankees typically drew the largest crowds in St. Louis, while the Browns often killed the gate at Yankee Stadium. Middle-class teams such as Cleveland and Detroit might have recognized the potential for smaller net losses from such a plan and might have supported it.

By comparing the visiting share paid to opposing clubs and the road revenue earned by the Yankees, we can get a more detailed idea of how the team fared under the rules (table 32). Revenue sharing did not greatly affect the Yankees' revenues. The Yankees of 1926–28, including the 1927 team often touted as the "greatest of all time," lost just $109,000 to revenue sharing over those three years. In 1936–39, when the team won four consecutive pennants, the Yankees lost less than $15,000 combined from revenue sharing. Between 1937 and 1944, the club gained $84,000 in nominal terms from revenue sharing. The plan was not particularly effective in redistributing money from the powerful Yankees to their rivals. The amounts transferred through the existing revenue-sharing plan were tiny relative to the Yankees' gross home gate receipts.

The author has examined the revenue sharing between the Yankees and the woebegone St. Louis Browns, the perennial "sick man" of the American League, during the 1930s. Although the Yankees were suffering from the economic downturn, they were never in danger of bankruptcy, unlike some of their American League brethren. Since a sports team needs rivals with whom to stage contests, the Yankees and wealthier American League teams needed to sustain their rivals in smaller cities. The Browns were by far the worst franchise in the American League in the 1930s; they had a losing record for every season between 1930 and 1943. The team never had even 200,000 in season attendance during the decade and drew fewer than 100,000 in attendance three times. The Yankees and Browns represented the extremes in the league.

Revenue sharing worked in the case of New York and St. Louis. Although Yankee road receipts from games played in St. Louis are incomplete for 1932 (only eight of the eleven games were reported in the cash book), it appears that the Browns received a net gain of at least $11,000 each season from their contests during the 1930s. In some years the Yankees paid the Browns $25,000 more than they received for traveling to St. Louis. The amount transferred was reduced, however, because of the Yankees' ability to draw on the road. During the decade the Browns rarely accounted for 10 percent of New York's total gate receipts, while the Yankees were quite likely the biggest attraction at the Browns' home park. By dividing Yankee road receipts from games at St. Louis by 28¢ (close to the average paid per attendee to visiting teams), we can get a rough estimate of the attendance. In every season except 1935, attendance at games in St. Louis against the Yankees attracted more than one-seventh of the Browns' season attendance (the average share in an eight-team league). In 1934 the Browns had over 25 percent of their total home attendance from games with the Yankees (evidence that Browns fans preferred the absolute quality of their rivals to relative quality). The fact that the Yankees were the best draw in St. Louis diluted the effectiveness of the revenue sharing, especially coupled with the Browns' inability to draw well in New York or elsewhere.

Gate sharing and other subsidies presented potential problems. An ineptly designed plan might entice some owners to save expenses by fielding lousy teams. American League baseball owners were familiar with franchises that held "fire sales" of players with the ostensible purpose of remaining solvent. After World War II, the St. Louis Browns sold most of their best players. The owners, the DeWitt brothers, pleaded poverty but some rival owners grumbled about the brothers being "parasites, who feed on the drawing power of the better teams while on the road and keep themselves weak and without support at home."[15] A local sportswriter observed, "The [DeWitt brothers'] theory is that a major league franchise has a certain minimum value that can't be reduced even if no players of established major league caliber go with it . . . [they] recognize they can't draw much more poorly with no big leaguers in their lineup than they have drawn with a few, and that they may as well take advantage of their rivals' prosperity and cash in while the cash is good."[16] National Football League owners limited their vaunted generosity and guarded against the potential temptation to field terrible teams and save some money by maintaining a minimum guaranteed payout that operated against the Chicago Cardinals and Green Bay Packers during the 1950s.[17]

Conclusion

Owners of poorer teams probably saw revenue-sharing rules as a mechanism to offset the differences in revenue potential between teams in large cities and those in small cities. Owners of the Yankees, Giants, and Cubs may have viewed revenue sharing as a way to compensate them for bringing strong, well-paid clubs into smaller cities. Baseball owners were not unique in struggling with the underlying tension between teams with varying levels of gate appeal.

A plan that transferred more revenue from the Yankees and Giants to the Browns and Phillies could have easily been implemented. Simply changing the rule from sharing the per-attendee amounts with the visiting team to putting the same amounts into a common fund to be evenly divided among all of the teams would have increased the amount of revenue transferred to the struggling teams. As the Yankees, especially, drew well on the road, such a plan would have injured them more than it would most other teams. It is unlikely that the owners of teams in smaller cities had the political clout to enact such changes.

The effects of the gate-sharing plans during the 1930s corresponded more to the general view of such plans than they would during the 1950s, when the Yankees and Dodgers might well have benefited from even a 100 percent gate-sharing plan, given their popularity on the road. As long as baseball fans preferred to see stronger visiting teams than weaker ones, the effects of revenue sharing would be muted unless the money was put into a common pool. As it was, the gate-sharing plans may have provided sufficient succor to keep the Browns and Phillies going during the Great Depression but did little to promote competitive balance.

8. Manipulating the Schedule to Increase Revenue

Fans often take scheduling for granted. At the beginning of the season, they may glance at a schedule to see when the most desirable opponents will come to town. College football and basketball fans pay attention to strength-of-schedule rankings, since not all team schedules are created equal.

Economists have applied the Coase Theorem to the movement and distribution of playing talent in professional team sports. The theorem states that resources will be efficiently deployed as long as property rights are well defined and there are low transaction costs. Transaction costs are the costs of finding someone to deal with, the cost of negotiation, and the cost of monitoring and enforcing an agreement. Economists have not applied the theorem to other aspects of team sports. For instance, how does the theorem apply to allocating another valuable property right: holiday home dates in major league baseball?

For much of major league baseball's history, holiday doubleheaders have been among the best-drawing playing dates. During the 1930s and the period immediately following World War II, the Major Leagues usually allocated the three holidays—Memorial Day, Fourth of July, and Labor Day—on an equal basis. Teams would alternate having home games on Memorial Day and Labor Day one year and then the Fourth of July the next. Due to the differences in on-the-field abilities of the teams, as well as the large disparities in stadium capacities and population bases, the teams had significant differences in drawing power. Rearranging holiday home dates toward the New York Yankees, Detroit Tigers, and Cleveland Indians and away from the St. Louis Browns and Washington Senators held potential to increase the league's total revenue and profits.

In this chapter we will compare the American League's experiences before World War II and for a brief period after the war. If ever a professional team sports league needed revenue-enhancing innovations, the American League needed them during the Great Depression. After the war, while several American League teams had unprecedented attendance, three American League teams struggled to remain profitable.

Leagues and Schedules

Many economists have noted the hybrid nature of professional team sports leagues. The leagues acted as cartels in protecting territorial rights, setting minimum ticket prices, and creating a standardized product. Within the league, however, teams competed for playing talent and other property rights. As James Hart of the National League Chicago team stated in 1901, "We compete for players, we compete for points, we compete for games."[1] This chapter focuses on his statement, "we compete for games." A league could let teams arrange games among themselves, with only a few stipulations, such as equal numbers of road and home contests with each opponent. The National Association of Base Ball Players (1871–75) followed this procedure, but the league faced a problem. Owners of teams in large cities desired to play other large-city teams on the best dates.

George Halas, owner of the Chicago Bears in the National Football League, testified before Congress: "Naturally each team wanted to play a team which would draw the most fans. . . . It reached the point where the Giants, Green Bay, and the Bears became the most sought after teams to play. . . . We had to have official scheduling. . . . By making the season more interesting to the fans, this action benefited each member club and helped to stabilize each club."[2] Second, acceptable scheduling appeals to fans, who desire a clear-cut league champion. While these may be laudable goals, another key question arises: Do leagues use scheduling to increase and maximize collective revenues and profits?

Initially professional sports leagues evolved from individual clubs that paid top players. These teams did not play within a league framework and were essentially free agents.

Certainly the primitive, laissez-faire approach to professional sports, as exemplified by the Cincinnati Red Stockings of 1869–70 and subsequent barnstorming clubs in professional team sports, had drawbacks. Harry Wright, the organizer and business manager of the Red Stockings, must have spent much of his time as a modern-day athletic director does: sending and receiving telegrams as he scheduled games, negotiating apportionment of the gate, and arranging for travel and accommodations. Since the Red Stockings took on a wide variety of baseball clubs, one could argue that the team's famous lengthy winning streak was somewhat dubious. Some New York or Philadelphia clubs, playing only stronger, eastern teams, might have argued that they were superior teams even though they might have lost an occasional game (at least until they met the Red Stockings).

The National Association of Base Ball Players was an early attempt to operate under a loose league framework. The association failed to create disciplined scheduling, allowing teams to arrange matches. Since many teams folded early in the season, any hope of maintaining a balanced schedule was stillborn. Since the Boston club thoroughly dominated the league, there was at least little controversy as to the identity of the champion.

The 1920 season of the American Professional Football Association, the immediate predecessor of the National Football League, was fraught with the same haphazard scheduling we have seen in baseball's National Association. The league champion was decided by a vote of the member teams, which implies that win-loss records were not sufficiently uniform to be the sole basis of determining the champion.[3] Indeed, several teams had similar records, but their records were compiled under very different conditions. Some teams played almost all their games at home, while other teams played a majority of their games on the road.

Major League Baseball settled on a 154-game schedule for almost sixty years, except in time of war. In both leagues, each team had seventy-seven games at home and seventy-seven games on the road, playing every other rival twenty-two times during the season. In addition the American League was split into four eastern teams (New York Yankees, Boston Red Sox, Philadelphia Athletics, and Washington Senators) and four western teams (Cleveland Indians, Detroit Tigers, Chicago White Sox, and St. Louis Browns). The National League had a similar geographic split. Teams generally made three road trips west or east. The symmetry certainly was easy for fans to understand and contributed to the idea that the schedule was fair in the sense that no team gained an obvious advantage from it, either competitively or at the gate. Teams played intraregionally on holidays.

The Schedule during the Depression

By the 1930s Major League Baseball's schedule was set in the two leagues' respective constitutions, if not in stone. Scheduling was deceptively simple.

Pity the poor schedule maker. Scheduling was a headache for Major League Baseball. The schedule maker had to apportion Sunday, Saturday, and holiday home dates on an equal basis for all teams. While Sundays were the best-drawing days of the week, not all teams could play home dates on Sunday, creating additional complications. Teams made three cross-sectional road trips per season during the late 1920s and early 1930s. In addition to these strictures, there was another rule which was almost a taboo. In cities with two teams, both clubs were never to have home games on the same day. In New York City, which had three clubs, the Giants and Yankees did not share home playing dates, nor did the Giants and Dodgers (the Yankees and Dodgers, therefore, shared many playing dates). In general the schedule makers complied with this edict, and only on rare occasions did teams in the same city have conflicting dates.[4]

Both leagues decided to have four intersectional road trips instead of the usual three for the 1936 season. With better economic conditions, owners decided that a more varied and interesting schedule would offset the increased traveling. The leagues would revert to three road trips during wartime.[5]

Sometimes individual teams made special requests of the schedule maker. The woebegone Red Sox hoped to minimize their early exposure to the Yankees, Athletics, and Senators in order not to be blown out of the race early in 1933. Remember, these were the Yankees of Ruth and Gehrig, the Athletics of Foxx and Grove, and the soon-to-be pennant-winning Senators, a stellar set of rivals (as the heretofore woebegone Tampa Bay Devil Rays competed with the Yankees and Red Sox). The Bosox were not the only team worried about the 1933 schedule, and the league adjusted it to hasten intersectional contests (east versus west) in an attempt to try and prevent a pennant-race blowout. The National League had to agree to the plan in order to avoid intracity conflicting dates.[6] The owners continued to move up the intersectional contests for the 1935 and 1936 season. The *Sporting News* favored the new schedules, as the schedules supposedly spread the risk of bad weather—a team on the move was unlikely to find rain in every city—and to promote fan interest even in a tail-ender by "at least presenting new faces for the customers." The 1936 schedule did increase the travel mileage, but this was offset by a new railroad fare schedule that featured lower rates.[7]

With the advent of night games, a new complication arose. Owners instituted a rule that the day following a night game would be an open date, but this policy created congestion within the schedule and led to more doubleheaders, often on Sunday.[8] The situation inspired Cardinals owner Sam Breadon to advocate his plan of six-day-a-week baseball, in which Sundays would be doubleheaders and teams would officially take Mondays off. Owners might well have filled open Mondays with exhibition games, leaving scant rest for weary players. The Pacific Coast League had used a six-day week partly out of necessity because travel times were long in the league and partly because it was profitable. National League president Ford Frick favored the idea: "I'd rather have the twin bills placed in the regular schedule than let the teams call off a game at the last minute to make a synthetic doubleheader."[9] Although Breadon's plan was not adopted, the leagues allowed owners to place Sunday doubleheaders in the official schedules. Breadon's Cardinals and the St. Louis Browns scheduled the most Sunday doubleheaders.[10]

During this era concerns about sharing playing dates with professional football in the fall were not as pronounced as they would be during the postwar period, although owners worried about conflicting dates with college football. Clark Griffith was concerned about the Washington Redskins football team when that team relocated to the city in 1937. The two clubs were headed in opposite directions; the Senators were moving toward perpetual mediocrity and the Redskins toward frequent division titles. The Redskins opened their home season on September 15 in 1940, well before the end of the baseball season.[11]

Although teams occasionally played just one game with an opponent, the norm was a three- or four-game set, a practice instituted partially to conserve travel expenses. Teams playing in cities that prohibited Sunday games might take a one-day trip to another town to squeeze in a game on Sunday: for example, Philadelphia teams might schedule a Sunday game in New York. Since the railroads often charged by the mile, unlike today's airlines with their Byzantine fare calculations, owners were acutely aware of mileage costs. In the National League the western teams compiled more mileage (up to four thousand miles more in the case of the Pittsburgh Pirates) than did the eastern clubs during 1931. The Dodgers and Giants, of course, had the smallest mileage.[12]

Even after schedules were completed, owners sometimes tampered with them to schedule special events such as heavyweight boxing matches at Yankee Stadium or to create synthetic doubleheaders. Phil Wrigley of the Cubs excoriated the synthetic doubleheaders, arguing that the "fans had a right to expect a [scheduled] contest would be staged, if weather conditions were at all favorable."[13]

Because there were no domed stadiums, all teams faced the possibility that games would be postponed due to rain or snow, especially early in the season. Open dates could have been used to make up these postponed games, but baseball owners sought to wring as much revenue from their teams as possible by scheduling exhibition games on off days.[14] Some owners made up the rained-out games by setting up doubleheaders. The official schedules usually listed three doubleheaders per team, all on the major holidays. The league constitutions generally prohibited doubleheaders before Memorial Day, although occasional exceptions were made for teams that were struggling or that lacked Sunday ball.[15] Teams often played as many as a dozen or more doubleheaders during the latter half of the season, creating havoc within pitching rotations and fatiguing players.

Attempts to avoid inclement weather by starting the season later were often foiled by the natural variation in April showers. Sometimes the season went too long in the sense that there were too many open dates, or that the World Series started too late in October. Judge Fuchs of the Boston Braves wanted a 168-game schedule that would fill all of the open dates.[16] Even the 154-game schedule, a tradition for almost sixty seasons, was not sacrosanct; the owners reduced the 1919 season voluntarily, only to discover that they had underestimated the game's resurgent popularity.[17]

While doubleheaders attracted more gate receipts for the Yankees and Phillies (and probably for all teams) than did single games, it is not clear that they were profitable, and a better comparison might have been between a doubleheader and two single games, netting out the cost per game of ushers and park employees. Some owners believed doubleheaders were beneficial and became notorious for setting up synthetic doubleheaders. Charles H. Ebbets, owner of the Brooklyn Dodgers, was quick to cancel a game. "If it rained in Canarsie, which lies by the sea adjacent to the habitat of the soft clam, and which is but a short distance from Ebbets Field, Mr. Ebbets would abandon his game for the afternoon and play two the next day, or when the opposing team next came to town. It seemed to matter little to Mr. Ebbets what the condition of the National League race might be."[18]

The *Sporting News* inveighed against synthetic doubleheaders, arguing that they created chaos and ill will; it called them "Doubleheaders created in major league baseball to upset the dignity of the schedules and the leagues, to play for the immediate gate receipts at possible injustice to six other clubs, to make paramount the issue of commercialism." Fans were upset by questionable postponements of games. "Such an experience . . . is doubly disappointing to out-of-town fans, many of whom travel considerable distances to attend games. The tendency . . . is to turn from baseball and seek entertainment elsewhere."[19] Regular customers, too, were disgruntled. "Unexpected and unnecessary postponements cause week-day customers to return disgustedly to their homes, swearing, 'Never again.'"[20] The editor disputed whether a doubleheader drew more fans than two single games but warned that making the fans used to a two-for-one offering would induce them to avoid single games: "whether approximately the same number of fans wouldn't be attracted by single games on Sunday as by doubleheaders, except, possibly in cities where the fans have been educated to expect the twin bills."[21]

The owners struggled in deciding how to handle the problem. At the December 1931 meetings the owners voted to ban synthetic doubleheaders unless they were approved by the league presidents.[22] The league presidents did not enjoy exercising such authority. "Naturally, no league head desires to take that responsibility upon his shoulders, so the prevailing sentiment of the club owners will be probed to decide what policy shall be followed."[23] The owners quickly rescinded the ban, causing the *Sporting News* to worry that baseball "is going to become a week-end sport, instead of a daily affair."[24]

After the 1933 season the owners voted to ban all Sunday doubleheaders until after June 15, which was a compromise as some owners favored a ban extending to July 4 while others wanted individual discretion. The issue wouldn't die. Some proponents, such as Breadon of the Cardinals, advocated for a six-day-a-week schedule, but the owners voted to maintain a rule similar to the one they had approved in December 1933.[25] Breadon and his supporters continued to agitate for regularly scheduled Sunday doubleheaders as a way to boost the gate, especially early in the season. The *Sporting News*, echoing a previous editorial, warned that "It is probably true that a number of Sunday twin bills prior to June 15 would bring out the fans in greater throngs on those occasions but if the practice is once started, it must be continued without interruption throughout the remainder of the season—else the fans, accustomed to bargain matinees, will shun single games."[26] As late as 1942 Connie Mack urged regular Sunday doubleheaders.[27]

Using the Schedule to Generate Additional Revenue

Table 33 and Surdam (2009) show that Sundays and holidays were big draws. Having a Sunday or holiday home date was a valuable property right. Was the even division of holiday and Sunday home dates optimal in terms of generating collective revenue for the owners? Would a reapportionment have been mutually beneficial?

If the Coase Theorem is to apply, property rights to desirable home dates need to be well defined. By the twentieth century the National and American Leagues created the schedules and clearly defined which team had property rights to home dates. The American League Constitution read, "The championship games for any season shall be arranged in a written schedule prepared by the President and presented to the League at its spring schedule meeting for that season. The schedule shall provide for an equal number of return dates of each series of games."[28]

The National League Constitution was similar, except that it explicitly stated, "The President of this League in conjunction with the President of the American League shall jointly prepare or cause to be prepared a schedule of games, avoiding as far as possible conflicts in championship [regular season] games in cities in which rival clubs are located."[29] According to the American League Constitution, teams had some discretion in altering the schedule:

No date in said schedule shall subsequently be changed except, (1) by written consent of the two members of the League whose clubs are to play the game in question, from a date fixed by the schedule for a game between such clubs to another day either prior to the first or subsequent to the last date of the same series between such clubs; or (2) as provided in Section 5 of this Article [pertaining to making up rainouts]; or (3) by the written consent of three-fourths of all the members of the League. Any violation of this provision shall subject the offending members of the League to a fine of $200.00 each for each offense.[30]

The constitution was ambiguous about exchanging home dates, although the third clause suggests that the Tigers and Browns, for example, could petition to switch a holiday doubleheader scheduled for St. Louis to Detroit. In the National League Constitution, switching home sites for games that needed to be made up late in the season was permissible.[31]

The Good Dates: Why Can't Every Day Be Like the Fourth of July?

What dates were the most desirable? Large crowds attended most holiday doubleheaders. Attendance at such doubleheaders exceeded the average attendance for two games during the 1930s. Fans got to see two games for the price of one rather than paying separate admissions for two games. One team in particular received large windfalls from hosting holiday doubleheaders. The Yankees reaped large revenues on Sundays, but holiday doubleheaders did best of all.

Equations for 1929, 1933, 1939, and 1943 also showed that holiday games boosted the home receipts by tens of thousands of dollars.[32] Unfortunately, game-by-game revenue figures for other teams are not available, so we will rely upon attendance figures in the subsequent discussions.

As shown in table 33, teams such as the Browns did not receive nearly as large a boost as did the Yankees, but American League teams still averaged almost 17,000 more fans at a holiday doubleheader than they did for two average single games, including Sunday games. This understates the situation, as many of the single games would have been weekday games that typically drew poorly.[33]

League gate-sharing rules also reflected the desirability of holiday games. The National Association stipulated in 1871 that visiting teams receive one-third of the total gate receipts, but holiday gate receipts were to be split 50-50. The American Association of the 1880s stipulated that the home team guarantee $65 to visiting teams, except on holidays. For games played on holidays, the teams split the gate evenly. The American and National Leagues made no special provisions for splitting holiday gate revenue, probably because they assigned the holidays evenly between the teams in the seasons after 1933, at which point all teams had Sunday ball.[34]

The Major Leagues had another model for assigning holiday playing dates. The Southern Association Minor League assigned holiday games to teams with stronger drawing power. The weaker teams in that league acquiesced to such a plan because revenues from the holiday games were shared evenly among all the teams.[35]

Other top-drawing days, such as Sundays, were also apportioned evenly among teams when possible. Giving the St. Louis Browns the same number of Sunday home games as, for example, the Detroit Tigers or New York Yankees created mutually advantageous opportunities for these teams. The Browns and Tigers might have been better off shifting a Sunday home game from St. Louis to Detroit.

How Assigning Holiday Doubleheaders Might Affect Revenues

Suppose a sports league wants to maximize collective profits. The question of who has the property rights for holiday doubleheaders is not important in determining where the games will be staged, but it is important in establishing the distribution of the gains. To maximize collective profits, the league might create a schedule where all holiday games are played in large cities with spacious stadiums. Suppose we consider the Detroit Tigers and St. Louis Browns of the American League. Detroit drew much larger crowds than did the Browns during the era under consideration. If Detroit received the rights to all three holiday playing dates, the team would keep all of the home receipts, net of the amounts mandated by the gate-sharing rules. If home receipts are positively related to the home team's record, such a situation would increase Detroit's gate receipts or, in economics parlance, its marginal revenue product. Because Detroit could field a stronger team, it would benefit more from this situation than it would from the division of holidays or from a situation in which St. Louis received the rights to all holiday playing dates.

If St. Louis received the rights to holiday home dates, it could then sell those rights to Detroit. While St. Louis would not get all the gains from having the rights to the holidays, it would gain more than it would under the equal allocation of holidays and more than it would if Detroit had the initial rights. The advantage Detroit would gain from fielding a stronger team would presumably be less if the Browns had the rights than it would be if Detroit possessed the initial rights to holiday home dates. If the Browns had owned rights to holiday home games, they might have seen a boost in their revenues, depending on Detroit's ability to draw on the road. We note in passing that empirical evidence suggests that attendance at games was usually positively related to the visiting team's record during the 1930s and 1950s.[36] In other words, the system of trading or selling property rights to holiday playing dates might affect competitive balance. If Detroit had a strong team, it would draw a large crowd in St. Louis. If the St. Louis Browns had a stronger team than usual, they might have attracted more fans to games in Detroit. If the Browns had still found it advantageous to give up a holiday home game to Detroit, their gate revenues would have been boosted by the swap. If a team's ability to draw on the road had been inversely related to its record, swapping holiday home games would have had perverse effects upon revenues.[37] The league's allocation of holiday home dates therefore does not only affect the distribution of the rents from holiday games; it is also likely to change the competitive balance.

Given the observation that Detroit usually draws better, all the holiday games should have been played in the Tigers' ballpark without regard to the initial ownership of the holiday home dates unless the St. Louis team was so strong on the field that it could override Detroit's population advantage.[38]

The Potential Gains from Swapping Holiday Playing Dates

Were there potential gains from trading rights to holiday home doubleheaders, and, if so, how large were the gains?

The Tigers and Browns exemplified the potential gains from swapping holiday home dates. The Browns were the American League's weakest franchise. During the 1930s the team struggled to attract even 100,000 fans a season, while the Tigers occasionally drew in excess of 1 million. St. Louis played five holiday doubleheaders in Detroit during the 1936–40 seasons. These doubleheaders had an average of 33,700 in attendance; that average was lowered when only 12,000 attended a 1939 doubleheader. The two teams played two holiday doubleheaders in St. Louis with a total of 16,400 fans attending. For simplicity's sake, let us suppose the averages were 10,000 in St. Louis and 30,000 in Detroit.

In 1939 Detroit averaged $1.07 per attendee, while St. Louis averaged $0.97.[39] We will assume gate-sharing revenue of $0.28 per customer, which was close to the average paid by American League teams. We can create the following scenario for a home-and-home holiday schedule:

Doubleheader at Detroit:
Gate receipts	$32,100
Paid to St. Louis	$ 8,400
Net to Detroit	$23,700

Doubleheader at St. Louis:

Gate receipts	$ 9,700
Paid to Detroit	$ 2,800
Net to St. Louis	$ 6,900

Two holiday doubleheaders total:

Detroit	$26,500
St. Louis	$15,300

If, instead, the two teams played both doubleheaders in Detroit, they would split $64,200:

Detroit	$47,400
St. Louis	$16,800

Even without negotiation, playing both games in Detroit appears to improve both teams' revenues. If the teams split the proceeds of the transferred doubleheader evenly, the split would have been:

Detroit	$39,750
St. Louis	$24,450

Suppose the teams had in fact split the proceeds of the transferred doubleheader. St. Louis would have had an additional $9,150 more than it would have had if one doubleheader had been played in each town. There would also have been increased concessions revenue to share.[40] A similar story unfolds if we examined Cleveland and St. Louis. Given that the Browns had less than $184,000 in home and road receipts for the 1939 season, the swap of just one holiday doubleheader could have increased its gate receipts by 5 percent.

The Browns were not the only team that stood to gain from trading holiday home dates. The New York Yankees were potentially the biggest beneficiaries of holiday home date swaps. The three other eastern clubs played in ballparks seating less than 35,000, while Yankee Stadium seated twice as many by the late 1930s. While teams occasionally crammed in more fans than the listed capacity (40,100 at Fenway

Park in Boston for a 1937 Memorial Day doubleheader with the Yankees and 83,533 at Yankee Stadium for the following Memorial Day), the Yankees and their rivals stood to gain up to 25,000 additional fans from each swap of holiday home dates.[41]

The largest Washington crowd was 38,000 for a 1936 Fourth of July doubleheader. On Memorial Day the two teams drew almost 72,000 for the doubleheader in Yankee Stadium. Both games were nearly sellouts, but the differing stadium capacities created the disparity. The potential gains from swapping were larger than for the Detroit/St. Louis doubleheaders. However, given that Washington was able to fill its stadium, team owner Clark Griffith might have hesitated to switch a holiday doubleheader from Washington to New York.

During the 1933–40 seasons New York played twelve holiday doubleheaders at Yankee Stadium. These doubleheaders averaged almost 55,000 fans, while the ten holiday doubleheaders the Yankees played on the road (two other doubleheaders were rained out) averaged just 29,500. For the 1939 season the Yankees' three eastern rivals had less net home receipts than Detroit, Cleveland, or Chicago. In fact, Detroit had more net home receipts than Boston and Philadelphia combined. The gains from swapping holiday home dates should have been tempting. From Washington's point of view, the potential gains from playing a holiday doubleheader in New York and getting half the gate receipts promised to rival the amounts they received from New York as their visitor's share for an entire eleven-game slate at Yankee Stadium without a holiday doubleheader.[42]

Clearly, then, there was potential for teams to increase revenue and to improve competitiveness by swapping rights to holiday home games.

Why Didn't They Trade Holiday Home Games?

If there were potential gains to trading holiday home games, why didn't the owners create a system of tradable rights? Under the Coase Theorem, the presence of significant transaction costs could derail the efficient allocation of a scarce asset. The cost of negotiation should not have been too onerous, especially since the league had clearly established the initial property rights to holiday home games.

Owners might have worried about the inherent uncertainty of their teams' performance on the field. If the Browns were unexpectedly strong and the Tigers were unexpectedly weak, transferring a holiday doubleheader from St. Louis to Detroit could backfire.

Transportation costs might have increased if the two teams had to take a detour from their usual travel pattern in the eight-team American League. Since holiday doubleheaders took place between intraregional teams, we can assume that clubs would not have been traveling inordinate distances. Someone usually had to travel to a game in any event. Even if we assume both teams had to make a special trip from, for example, Washington and Boston to New York, the increased transportation and lodging costs in the late 1930s probably amounted to $2,500 or less. For example, the Yankees paid the NY & NH Railroad $489.45, presumably for the round-trip fare for the team to play at Fenway Park in Boston. The Yankees played three games at Fenway over three days and apparently incurred a hotel expense of $427.00 at the Copley Plaza.[43] For a three-day road trip, therefore, the team paid less than $1,000 in travel and lodging. Presumably there would be per diem expenses for the team. Teams in western cities might have incurred moderately higher costs.

A potentially larger cost was fan antipathy to the idea of missing their chance to see the hometown team on holidays. We must recall that even the Senators and Red Sox sometimes sold out their small stadiums on holidays, while the Browns might not have had many fans to antagonize.

Fan antipathy might have also arisen from another source. Fans and participants might have worried about "unfair" competition arising from a situation in which the Yankees got more home games than the Senators. If we take two seasons at random, we find that the home team won 55 percent of the games in the American League during 1933 and 1938. If this had been a concern, the league could have created tradable home dates with the stipulation that each trade required an equal number of home games to be swapped. For example, New York could approach Washington in hopes of getting a Fourth of July doubleheader between the two teams switched from Griffith Stadium to Yankee Stadium. In return, the Senators would pick up two games which had originally been scheduled for Yankee Stadium. The Yankees would agree to pay the Senators for the switch. The league could also stipulate that gate-sharing rules would remain in place.[44]

A restriction requiring that home dates be swapped could have reduced the potential gains from trading holiday playing dates. If the Senators always drew as many fans to Yankee Stadium as they did on holiday dates, there would be no purpose in making such a swap. Since most teams drew badly on Mondays and Tuesdays, these would be the likely dates swapped for a holiday doubleheader. Before the Fourth of July in 1938 the Yankees and Senators played two games at Yankee Stadium on the first and second of July. These games generated $15,500 in gate receipts. A 1939 Fourth of July doubleheader at Yankee Stadium between the two teams brought in $64,400. Forcing teams to swap home dates for other home dates might have caused only a moderate reduction in the gains from the swap. We have not considered the hypothetical home receipts at Washington for the transferred July 1 and 2 games.

Another barrier to swapping holiday home dates goes back to the National League Constitution. The clause, "avoiding as far as possible conflicts in championship [regular season] games in cities in which rival clubs are located," comes into play here. While the clause presumably referred to the New York Giants and Brooklyn Dodgers, in practice it held for the Giants and Yankees. Yankee Stadium was located across the Harlem River from the New York Giants' Polo Grounds stadium. Typically, when the Yankees played at home, the Giants were on the road and vice versa. The Giants would certainly resist having the Yankees obtain a holiday doubleheader when the Giants already had a scheduled doubleheader at the Polo Grounds. Were the two teams close substitutes for each other? Would the specter of congestion and delay caused by throngs of fans deter some people from attending either game? Apparently the owners believed so. The Detroit Tigers and Cleveland Indians, though, faced no intracity competition. This third barrier might have required finesse to resolve.

While baseball owners may have been wary of creating unbalanced schedules, whether in terms of home and away games or of playing rivals, professional football has made a selling point of its skewed schedules. To promote parity, the National Football League overtly gives weaker teams a softer schedule for the next season. Even before such shenanigans, the NFL had an unbalanced schedule during the postwar era. Teams played home-and-home series with rivals in their conference and the remaining two games with teams outside their conference. The interconference games were not randomly selected. The Chicago Cardinals and Chicago Bears played interconference games almost every season. Since the Cardinals were perennial losers, the Bears gained from having them as annual fodder. One could plausibly argue that the NFL's form of imbalance was more unfair than relinquishing a pair of holiday home games in Major League Baseball. Whatever antipathy football fans may have held for the unbalanced schedule, it didn't prevent the league from enjoying growing popularity.

Major League Baseball now features unbalanced interdivision and interleague schedules. Even in the American League, teams sometimes played unbalanced schedules during the periods surveyed, often because of weather-related postponements such as rainouts. In 1925 the Yankees and Tigers played 13 games at Yankee Stadium and only 10 games in Detroit. One of the games at the Stadium was a tie game, but the other extra home game was the result of an earlier rainout in Detroit that couldn't be made up there. In 1926 the Yankees played 75 games at home and 79 games on the road. The team played 10 home games and 12 road games each with Chicago, St. Louis, and Cleveland, while playing 12 home games with Boston and 10 games in Boston.

Near the end of the 1939 season, the Boston Red Sox and New York Yankees were scheduled to play several games. The teams were to play single games in Boston on September 26 and 27, but rain washed out both games. The teams were scheduled to end the season with single games on September 30 and October 1. Although both teams had an off day before September 30, they agreed to make up the two lost games as two doubleheaders in New York. Boston agreed to exchange two home games. The teams completed a doubleheader on September 30. Rain washed out the second doubleheader on October 1. The fans probably didn't worry too much about competitive fairness even though the Red Sox were in second place, as they were 17 games behind New York.

Teams did move playing dates. On at least one occasion the Yankees paid to have a home date moved in order to reserve the Stadium for a more lucrative boxing match. On September 24, 1935, Joe Louis fought Max Baer at Yankee Stadium. The Yankees played the Senators in Washington on the 24th, as scheduled. The two teams were to resume their competition at Yankee Stadium on September 25 and 26, but the Yankees had paid the Senators to switch the September 25 game to an earlier date. The teams played a doubleheader on July 28 instead of the single game that had already been scheduled. The Yankees paid the Senators an additional $1,000 after the September 26 game as a bonus for agreeing to the transfer.[45] Although few leagues have brazenly scheduled unequal home and road games for teams, these examples are at least intermediate steps towards the concept of trading holiday home dates.

In the National League there was at least one example in which teams switched a game to get increased revenue. The Brooklyn Dodgers hoped to exceed 1 million in attendance for the 1939 season. The Dodgers' Larry MacPhail sought to insure this feat by transferring a September 25 game at Philadelphia to create a September 30 doubleheader in Brooklyn. A single game in Brooklyn was already scheduled for the 30th. The league agreed to the swap, but sources do not reveal whether the Dodgers paid the Phillies for the switch. Given Philadelphia's low attendance, the team may have agreed to the swap simply for the visitor's share from a much larger crowd.

Whatever scruples the American League may have held regarding competitive fairness, the league did in fact switch holiday doubleheaders under dire circumstances. Detroit and Cleveland seem to have obtained some of St. Louis's holiday playing dates, as the Browns had just 3 holiday doubleheaders instead of the customary 6 between 1937 and 1940. No wonder! The two teams ventured into St. Louis for 4 holiday games during the 1936–39 seasons. The 4 doubleheaders drew fewer than 30,000 in total attendance, which was less than either of the St. Louis/Detroit holiday doubleheaders played at Tiger Stadium in 1936 or 1937. The 1938 Memorial Day doubleheader between the two clubs had 49,500 in the Detroit stands.

The 1940 schedule showed the Browns playing on the road for all three holidays. *The Sporting News* commented snidely, "The Browns do not get a single holiday booking at home this year, possibly because it was figured that, from an attendance standpoint it might be to the advantage of the club to play away from home on such occasions."[46] Unfortunately, contemporary sources such as *The New York Times*, *The Sporting News*, and *The Detroit News* did not reveal whether there was a trade between the Browns and their western rivals. We have noted that the standard visitor's share from playing in Detroit and Cleveland might have been sufficient inducement for the Browns to forego holiday home games. The league did allow the Browns to schedule a home doubleheader before Memorial Day, which was normally forbidden.

St. Louis did not have any home holiday dates through the 1942 season, although they got their 77 home games each season. The St. Louis owners may well have decided to risk antagonizing their fans, since the team never drew even 150,000 fans in any season between 1932 and 1939. Ironically, without any holiday doubleheaders, the Browns' attendance doubled in 1940, perhaps because of a better record and more night games.

The Struggle to Make Money Playing Ball on the Lord's Day

Professional and college football fans have made a fetish out of examining schedules, primarily in terms of strength-of-schedule rankings.

Baseball fans have been less curious about how scheduling affects attendance and competitive balance. Owners coveted Sunday ball. They recognized that many workers could not attend weekday afternoon games. The big Sunday crowds enabled some owners to field stronger teams. Teams without Sunday ball could be at a disadvantage.

Professional baseball on Sundays dated from the 1870s and originated primarily in the western cities with their relatively large proportions of German immigrants. Harry Wright, English-born pioneer of professional baseball, eschewed Sunday ball: "the money from Sunday games didn't justify the moral struggle . . . and in the long run failed to raise annual figures enough to warrant engaging in legal and moral controversies." Wright believed that big Sunday crowds simply siphoned off attendance on other days, an argument that future owners would use in different contexts.[47]

Old-line Protestant churches opposed professional sports and theater, as well as many other activities, on Sundays. Members of some churches were scandalized by the attitudes and actions of more recent immigrants, although some ministers countenanced amateur contests, even when a hat was passed to pay for the game. At times the ministers acquired some unlikely and unseemly allies: saloonkeepers. Both groups felt that Sunday ball cut into their "business," with the latter claiming that ball games diverted thirsty patrons from saloons. Cleveland was a hot spot for the Sunday ball controversy in 1897, with a spokesman for saloonkeepers saying, "Men and boys, instead of LINGERING IN BARROOMS [caps in the original], visiting, playing cards or shaking for drinks will go to the games and spend the 75 cents or a dollar each, they would otherwise leave with us."[48] The Lord's Day Alliance of the United States, fearing a loss of influence in the contemporary culture war, struggled to keep Sunday a day of worship free of commercial amusements. What the alliance loathed were actors and ballplayers performing for filthy lucre on the Lord's Day. The unease was so great that the Protestant ministers sometimes made common cause with Catholic priests in trying to maintain Sunday as a holy day.[49]

Status of Sunday Ball in 1929

Eleven of the sixteen Major League teams played home games on Sunday by 1919. The Pennsylvania and Boston teams could not play home games on Sunday during the 1920s. The five teams without Sunday ball often made special trips to play a single Sunday game in New York City, Detroit, or Cleveland. Such trips created hardship for the players. "Last season the Athletics played 22 Sunday games abroad. They were idle only on two Sundays during the race. This worked a hardship on the Athletics who had to leave Shibe Park in the midst of a series to rush to Detroit or Cleveland on four occasions for Sunday games and then immediately return to Philadelphia." Because the trip was so taxing, Connie Mack sometimes left hurlers Lefty Grove and George Earnshaw in Philadelphia. The Braves often played single Sunday games in Brooklyn, giving that club extra Sunday home games.[50]

Since Sunday was the best-drawing day of the week, the five clubs' inability to stage Sunday home games put them at a financial disadvantage and may have affected their ability to be competitive as well. By 1929 the Boston clubs hoped to get Sunday ball. The *Sporting News* suggested that although most clubs drew quite well on Sunday, "[the] advent of Sunday ball [in Boston] would be of financial assistance to the Braves and to the Red Sox, but, at the same time anybody who knows his Boston can testify to the fact that a first division team for the Tribe would be as big a money maker as a first division Red Sox outfit, and that such a team would go over big whether there was Sunday ball or not."[51]

Another reporter was not so optimistic: "Sunday baseball will draw well in Boston for a while anyway. Neither the Braves nor yet the Red Sox are what could be called a box office attraction. The more they play the greater grows their supporters' distaste. But until the novelty of some place to go Sunday afternoons wears off Boston will be a good money town."[52]

Judge Fuchs, owner of the Boston Braves, energetically sought permission to stage Sunday home games. Author Charlie Bevis recounts Fuchs's efforts to get Sunday ball. Bevis believes that the Judge spent nearly $250,000 to sway Boston voters.[53] Although the Red Sox stood to gain, too, that club's officials chose to watch Fuchs instead of actively petitioning. The Boston city council, aware that growing numbers of Bostonians engaged in playing amateur sports or attending the theater or movie houses on Sundays, began to accept the idea of playing professional baseball on the Lord's Day. Fuchs or his minions allegedly used financial persuasion in getting the council to approve the license. The council approved a motion to allow the Sunday Professional Sports law to apply to Boston by a shutout vote, 23–0.[54] Fuchs filed an application for a permit to play Sunday ball, paying $2,500. The council assessed the Red Sox only $1,000, ostensibly because Braves Field had almost twice as many seats as Fenway Park but also to punish Fuchs for his overzealous pursuit of Sunday ball.[55] The council tabled the Braves' application for a week in "one of the stormiest executive sessions the Council has ever witnessed," but approved it a week later.[56] The Boston municipal court later fined the Braves $1,000 for violating the corrupt practices act.[57]

The council voiced some concern that the Boston clubs would charge premium prices for Sunday games, but as the *Sporting News* pointed out, no team had ever engaged in such a prototypical version of today's variable pricing. During the 1950s the Brooklyn Dodgers would reclassify seats from general admission to reserved for weekend games (possibly as a convenience for their fans), while the Cincinnati Reds would begin charging higher prices for Sunday games.[58]

Another stipulation facing Boston owners was that the licensee had to "furnish free drinking water on the premises as approved by the health commissioner."[59] The edict may well have provided a prime bribery opportunity for some lucky health commission inspector.

The Red Sox had to play their Sunday home games at Braves Field, paying a rental fee, because Fenway Park was located within a thousand feet of a church. Braves Field had a larger capacity than Fenway Park. Presumably either the church relocated or the thousand-foot rule changed, as the Red Sox eventually played Sunday games at Fenway.[60] We'll see what Fuchs got in terms of an attendance boost from his $2,500 license and $1,000 fine in a later chapter.

Pennsylvania Opts for Sunday Ball

Sunday baseball may well have affected competitive balance in the American League. Philadelphia Athletics owner Connie Mack desperately wanted Sunday ball. Mack, a taciturn gentleman who rarely swore or drank, practiced civil disobedience in 1925 by staging a Sunday game between the Athletics and the White Sox within the city limits. The game attracted a large crowd despite poor weather, and Connie was arrested on a technicality but presumably did not serve jail time.[61] Former Athletics owner John Shibe testified that the team "lost at least $20,000 a game by not being able to play on the Lord's Day." A police inspector testified at the same hearing that although the crowd cheered loudly there was no disturbance or disorder.[62] Mack testified in 1933 that his club was going to have a "desperate struggle for existence.... We cannot meet our payrolls playing only on seventy-seven weekdays at home. Last year we ended the season with a big deficit, although finishing in second place, and that's why I had to sell Al Simmons, Jimmy Dykes, and George Haas to get the money to make up for our losses."[63]

Shibe had even tried an end run through southern New Jersey, threatening to stage games there on Sundays. Hopes were high for Sunday ball in Pennsylvania as the 1933 season neared; unfortunately for Connie, the opponents succeeded in delaying the change until 1934. Pennsylvania voters approved Sunday ball in that year, just as they had approved the repeal of Prohibition earlier. The clergy suffered major defeats on both issues.[64] Some of the clergy eventually admitted that Sunday sports, in the words of sportswriter Dan Daniel, "tend to make the people see the brighter side of life, and live a brighter life, and a cleaner one."[65]

Mack hoped the approval of Sunday ball would allow him to retain the remainder of his stars, so he would not have to peddle them to nouveau riche teams such as the Boston Red Sox and Detroit Tigers.[66] His hopes were dashed as the continued economic downturn and a declining ball club limited attendance. He ended up selling his remaining stars.

Pittsburgh owner Barney Dreyfuss was lukewarm about Sunday ball. As sportswriter Irving Sanborn wrote, "Barney is sitting pretty geographically. Because his team can play no Sunday games at home it is scheduled to play in Chicago or Cincinnati whenever possible on Sundays. And in return for not being able to get the big Sunday receipts at home, the Pittsburgh club is favored with all the holiday dates and as many Saturdays as possible."[67] His successor, William Benswanger, wanted Sunday ball and petitioned for it alongside Mack.

The Phillies did not get much of a boost from Sunday ball, although such games may have cushioned the team's free fall from the mediocre to the pathetic. Pittsburgh appeared to be the only Pennsylvania team that saw attendance increase in the wake of Sunday ball.

When the Pirates and the Phillies got Sunday ball, the Dodgers ended up being a big loser, as instead of getting "23 or 24 Sabbath engagements . . . at home, the Brooklyn club from now on must be content with anywhere from 11 to 13 and thus join the common people of the Major Leagues."[68] The Dodgers saw attendance fall by 90,000 between 1933 and 1934.

Sunday Ball Too Late to Help Connie Mack

One is tempted to say that Connie Mack, a devout man, was the biggest victim of the lack of Sunday ball. It is still uncertain whether he would have been able to retain his stars even if Pennsylvania had permitted Sunday ball in 1929 or 1930. Mack's slender financial resources may have made it inevitable that he would be overwhelmed by Yankee (and later Red Sox and Tiger) dollars. While he was an astute judge of talent, the wealthier owners could compensate by buying players in bulk and relying upon Branch Rickey's dictum, "Out of quantity comes quality." Like his fellow player turned owner, Clark Griffith,

Mack may have been more a victim of deep pockets than he was of old-fashioned beliefs.

Conclusion

During the Depression and the immediate postwar period, other potential gains might have been realized by trading weekend series. Sundays and (to a lesser degree) Saturdays were often better-drawing days than weekdays, although owners often bolstered the advantages by scheduling doubleheaders on weekends. A league might also have opened up trading of home dates during the last days of a pennant race in September. Teams in contention, which could have been defined as being within ten games of first place after Labor Day, could have been given the right to negotiate with teams out of contention to swap home games. While no league has ever pursued such a radical plan, one could imagine owners being tempted if the potential revenues involved were large enough. Disentangling the short-term gains from potential long-run adverse effects on fans' behavior would be difficult, however.

Despite potential box office gains from swapping holiday home dates, American League teams appeared hesitant to do so during the period under study. Such a reaction is difficult to explain under the Coase Theorem. The leagues had performed a valuable service by clearly defining property rights to holiday home dates, so the owners were either willing to forego profits or perceived significant transaction costs of swapping holiday home dates. Transportation costs do not appear to have been a crucial factor. The New York Yankees were probably stymied by the agreement with the National League that the New York Giants and Yankees would never share a holiday. The more likely candidates were concerns about fan reaction and perceived fairness. In extreme cases, such American League teams as St. Louis, Detroit, and Cleveland resorted to rearranging holiday home dates.

4. Innovations to Boost Attendance and Profits

9. Radio and Baseball

Cheap newspapers had been the new mass medium of the nineteenth century. Baseball owners gradually reached a mutually beneficial accommodation with the medium. During the 1920s a new mass medium arose: radio. By the end of the Depression era another mass medium, television, threatened to supplant radio.

Baseball owners were not sure how to deal with radio broadcasts of games. Some owners believed that radio broadcasts would strengthen their drawing power, as broadcasts would serve as a form of advertising and would whet the fans' appetite for tickets. Other owners feared that radio broadcasts would be too good a substitute for actual attendance at a game and would decrease the gate. Some observers disagreed with the idea that a broadcast could substitute for attending in person. Sportswriter Harry Hartman claimed that, "A sport fan will not be content with a broadcast if he is able to attend . . . [but if for any reason a fan is not able to attend a sporting event, he tunes in and remains sport conscious."[1] Another observer wrote, "Their show [baseball games] is a spectacle. It isn't something to be heard, but to be seen. Only the ear properly attuned can hear at a baseball game and become rhapsodized."[2]

Entrepreneurs had already broadcast games using telegraphs and large billboards. These endeavors often attracted large crowds on city streets. There was, of course, a delay between the action and the reporting. In many cases, radio broadcasts suffered from similar delays.

Two decades later baseball owners would struggle with television. In retrospect, television was a much better substitute for live attendance, as it engaged both eyes and ears; however, owners jumped in wholeheartedly when it came to telecasting home games. By the mid-1950s, some of the owners restricted telecasts of their home games.

Coping with the New Medium on the Block

Owners discussed radio broadcasts at most of their annual meetings between 1928 and 1934. The owners of the western teams in the National League embraced radio as early as 1928; the owners of the eastern teams did not. The Chicago Cubs and Chicago White Sox began broadcasting their home games in 1925.[3] Despite some initial misgivings, Chicago Cubs owner William Wrigley allowed five radio stations to broadcast games. He later reported that he did not believe that the attendance at games suffered; in fact, he believed it increased because radio created new fans. In later years Wrigley almost singlehandedly kept the other owners from banning radio broadcasts.[4]

Initially radio stations did not pay the team owners for the broadcasts, and stations frequently engaged in a free-for-all. As team owners began granting exclusive broadcasting rights to stations, rival stations that had been shut out were sometimes accused of trying to "bring the club into disfavor with the fans."[5] Before that, however, many radio station owners appeared to believe they had a right to broadcast baseball games, and these station owners were aggrieved when the baseball owners began charging for broadcasting rights.[6]

The reader might think that an owner's willingness to broadcast games from his stadium was his business and not that of his fellow owners. While one owner might benefit from broadcasting his home games, the other owner would be hurt due to the gate-sharing rules if the broadcasts cut attendance at his ballpark. Suppose the Cubs' broadcasts of games reduced attendance by 80,000 during the season. This would represent roughly $80,000 in gate revenue, of which about a quarter would be shared with the visiting teams, leaving the Cubs' owner with $60,000. If he got $70,000 for broadcasting rights, which he did not have to share, he would gain from broadcasting. If all the owners pursued similar policies, however, all would be worse off. The owners thus had reason to consider acting collectively.

At baseball's meetings in December 1929, American League President E. S. Barnard suggested that the owners could ban radio broadcasts entirely, stipulate a mandatory $50,000 fee for each station, or leave broadcasting to each owner's discretion. Barnard stated that he was "inclined to favor charging $50,000 for each broadcast, with the club to receive $25,000 and the league $25,000 from each station. The broadcasting of baseball is purely a commercial proposition. The broadcast stations are in it for the money.... There is no reason why baseball should not share in the profits of a venture that it makes possible."[7]

Although the Major League owners were primarily concerned about the effects of radio broadcasts of their games upon home attendance, the Minor League owners, too, were concerned. These owners blamed broadcasts of Major League games on small-town radios for the diminution of Minor League attendance. As one observer noted, Minor League teams in the South experienced "a very perceptible decrease in attendance in midseason, because the fans would prefer to sit on the veranda and drink cool drinks rather than go to the ball game." This observer, like others, thought Major League teams should charge the radio stations for the broadcasts and then disburse the revenue to the Minor Leagues.[8] The Minor Leagues' struggles against broadcasts of big league games would persist for two more decades. By 1934 the Minor League owners were calling for an investigation to discover whether the broadcasting of Major League games hindered Minor League attendance.[9] It was difficult to ascertain whether radio broadcasts of Major League games in particular hurt attendance at Minor League games or whether the drop in attendance was due to the fact that general radio programming was taking attention away from baseball. In the 1930s Minor League owners were also affected by decreased consumer purchasing power, which was not true of the 1940s and 1950s.

Some observers were skeptical about the Minor League owners' complaints. In the Pacific Coast League owners attempted to ban broadcasts of Major League baseball games in Los Angeles, but a *Sporting News* editor wondered, "how the broadcasting of games that begin four hours earlier . . . is going to affect Coast attendance, unless it is accepted that the broadcasting of any games is a detriment to baseball."[10] Eventually the radio broadcasts stopped. Some Minor Leagues took strong measures. The Texas League owners decided to ban radio broadcasts at their meeting in early 1930.[11] Minor League owners sometimes protested radio broadcasts of certain games. "The minor league clubs playing night games have not objected, as they figure the broadcasts [of Major League games] stimulate interest. Those playing afternoon ball, however, very strenuously object."[12] Commissioner Landis was concerned enough to announce, "before next year we must do something to protect the minors. Otherwise they will be ruined. . . . It is amazing how many small radio stations in minor league territory have started to broadcast major league games by telegraphic descriptions."[13] He advised that no more arrangements to broadcast Major League baseball games be made, pending further discussion.[14]

Even broadcasts of Minor League games might hurt attendance in the Minor Leagues. In the Southern (Minor) League, owners claimed that radio broadcasts of their games cut into the attendance figures, as "It breeds an indolence which keeps fans away from the parks at the slightest provocation."[15]

The radio broadcasters replied that radio would publicize baseball as newspapers always had, giving the sport what amounted to free advertising. Radio advocates argued that the medium made fans out of women and out of people living far away from any cities with big league baseball. "Letters coming in to the broadcasting stations prove without a doubt that a large part of the baseball audience lives miles beyond the pulling range of any ball park. But when they do come to the city there are two things they always want to see above all else: the studios of their favorite radio station and a ball game. . . . Why, if the clubs had to pay for the time on the air at the regular station rates, their bill would be something like $1,500,000 annually."[16]

Club owners who embraced radio did, in fact, credit the medium with making fans out of women. "No one can deny the fact that radio ... is responsible for the wholesale attendance of women at the games." Not only did women attend games in greater numbers, but some observers thought the presence of women exerted a positive effect upon the crowd: "[it] has tended to make men more careful of their speech. Consequently you have a more orderly crowd."[17]

In addition to the owners' suspicions that radio broadcasts hurt the gate, owners groused about negative portrayals of actions on the diamond. Interestingly, National League owners objected to "alleged editorial comments by the broadcasters on umpires' decisions, which tended to incite the public mind against the arbiters."[18] Other critics of radio announcers, such as newspaper sportswriters, claimed that the broadcasters distorted the game by making it more exciting than it was and by providing so-called expert opinion. Newspaper sportswriters had an inherent antagonism toward their radio brethren, and would later develop the same antipathy toward television announcers. To use an anachronistic analogy, the critics wanted a Joe Friday "just the facts, ma'am" approach to announcing the games.[19]

Broadcasting suggested that baseball radio announcers develop an attitude of independence similar to that of newsmen. "The broadcasters are too willing to 'sell out' to sports promoters, who feel they are in a position of command. If radio is to achieve a definite and wholesome result in the field of baseball and other sports, it will have to stand on its own feet as newsmen had had to do to gain their position. Radio will have to fight for its right of freedom of speech."[20]

Critics of radio broadcasts accused baseball owners of enforcing a strict code of censorship and biased reporting. An editorial alleged that contracts with the owners "prohibited mention of rain or cold weather, errors and poor decisions, and warned that baseball broadcasts set a dangerous precedent for 'twisting other news.'" Sponsors and owners, of course, denied that censorship occurred. Decades later, the New York Yankees fired their television announcer, Red Barber, because he had his camera operator pan Yankee Stadium to show a crowd of roughly 400 late in the 1966 season. The Yankees denied that Barber's firing was related to his actions.[21]

College football also struggled to reconcile radio broadcasts with healthy gate receipts. When attendance fell in the early 1930s some football administrators blamed radio broadcasts, although they sometimes acknowledged the economic downturn as a contributing factor. The Eastern Intercollegiate Association banned radio broadcasts for the 1932 season. West Point administrator Major P. D. Fleming claimed, "It has been definitely established that radio cuts into attendance." He admitted that the association cut the broadcasts reluctantly but felt the need to protect football gate receipts, which funded all athletic programs (some things haven't changed for decades), outweighed the public ill-will. Radio officials predicted that "the public demand and a diminished interest in collegiate football will force the institutions to request radio coverage."[22] *Broadcasting* made the possibly hypocritical claim that college football officials were mainly interested in gate receipts and not in the amateur spirit. The periodical also denied that broadcasts hurt gate receipts, without providing data. Instead, the writer argued that the broadcasts maintained interest in and loyalty to the sport in tough economic times when many fans could not afford to attend games in person. He concluded, "We predict a further falling off in attendance this autumn that will immediately be traceable to the loss of radio publicity."[23]

Collegiate alumni complained about the ban on broadcasting and the Eastern Intercollegiate Association voted to rescind its ban just before the season started. The other college football leagues had not imitated the Eastern and had never enacted a ban.[24]

College football officials continued to blame radio broadcasts for attendance problems at college stadiums around the country as late as 1936, but at least the collegiate game attracted sponsors such as oil companies. The public universities found themselves in a difficult situation, as banning radio broadcasts upset taxpayers who "feel they support these schools and have a right to hear the reports of the games." Broadcasting officials, of course, again disputed the allegations regarding ill effects on attendance.[25]

The *Sporting News* polled fans on the topic of whether radio hurt attendance at Major League baseball games. The poll results suggested that radio created interest in baseball among women, retained interest among children, and provided useful publicity. The vast majority of fans responded by saying radio did not hurt attendance. The poll was inherently flawed, of course, as the respondents had an incentive to deny any adverse effects from radio broadcasts; doing so might induce owners to pull the plug.[26] The pollsters also erred in not asking whether general programming on the radio provided a strong substitute for baseball. The 1930s were, after all, the heyday of such stars as Jack Benny, Edgar Bergen, and many others. In another survey, a magazine asked, "Do you prefer radio accounts to attending the games in person?" and "Do you believe broadcasts tend to lessen attendance at games?" *Broadcasting* was skeptical of the result: "Every person answering knew well when he wrote his 'No' that it would be silly to write anything else. Had the answers been overwhelmingly 'Yes,' the demise of baseball broadcasts would have been hastened. There was only one answer possible, assuming of course, that thousands of sports fans do enjoy these broadcasts." *Broadcasting* suggested that radio stations pay for the right to broadcast games: "The broadcaster should be willing to pay a fair sum for the privilege of making the broadcast. After all, these broadcasts are almost invariably sponsored by an advertiser. The club owner is entitled to a fair sum in return for supplying any advertiser with a high class show."[27]

Who were these advertisers? Beer and baseball. Economists use the term "complements" for commodities that are consumed together. Beer and baseball are a great example of complements. Beer companies are some of the most loyal sponsors of baseball. When Prohibition came to an end in 1933, however, some baseball observers feared the resurgence of beer drinking combined with the new phenomenon of broadcasting games on the radio. "Why, they'll [baseball fans] sit in the cafes sipping lager and listening to the games. They won't think of coming out to the park."[28] Early in 1933 Congress allowed beer companies to advertise. Prima Beer decided to sponsor baseball games. "Baseball broadcasting had been decided upon for the obvious reason that sports fans generally are beer drinkers."[29]

Beer wasn't the only vice sponsoring baseball. The Yankee Network (a New England radio network broadcasting Red Sox and Braves games) lined up Penn Tobacco Company and Kentucky Club pipe tobacco to sponsor games.[30] Other industries sponsored baseball games as well. The Philadelphia clubs sold broadcasting rights to Atlantic Refining. General Mills was a prominent sponsor.[31]

While sponsors were in plentiful supply, baseball owners' enthusiasm toward radio broadcasts was not as plentiful. Major League owners' interest in radio broadcasts of their games tended to split along geographical and league lines. The western teams tended to be more favorably disposed toward the new medium. National League teams were more supportive of broadcasts in general. The Chicago Cubs were the foremost proponents of radio broadcasts, having broadcast their home games since the mid-1920s. The Cubs were arguably the most successful team in baseball as the 1920s closed. The team set attendance records, created by periodic pennants and adroit promotions. The club allowed WGN, WBBM, and WMAQ to broadcast games. Owner William Wrigley was confident that radio broadcasts boosted his gate; given that the team frequently led the National League in attendance, it is possible that his crowds would have been even larger had the club banned radio broadcasts.[32]

Owners who were agnostic about radio in the late 1920s became warier as their attendance slid in 1932–34. Although the economic downturn was an obvious culprit, some of the owners didn't need much persuasion to indict radio broadcasts of games. The owners did not, however, accuse non-baseball programming of being a detriment. By the 1932 meetings American League owners, especially Jacob Ruppert, Connie Mack, and Clark Griffith, were set to impose a ban on broadcasting games. These clubs went so far as to ban telegraphic reports that were filed out of the park for broadcasting elsewhere.[33] One of the American League teams that favored radio broadcasts, the Cleveland Indians, made radio stations pay for the broadcasting privileges (although they did not do so in 1933, according to material presented to the U.S. Congress in 1951), and the *Sporting News* suggested this would be the ultimate solution of the problem.

Yankees owner Jacob Ruppert frequently blasted radio broadcasts. "The idea of spending money to provide a healthful form of outdoor recreation and then let everybody in free, of course, is ridiculous. Radio broadcasting comes under that head. Giving out details of games over the air to thousands of fans who otherwise would pay admission to the Stadium is a menace to the National Game." In a later interview, he stated, "The broadcasting company does not pay a proportionate share of the expense of maintaining any sport. Its financial outgo is ridiculously absurd as compared to the cost of the sport, yet in many cases the broadcasts are commercialized."[34]

The *Sporting News* took a middle position with regard to radio. The editor astutely recognized the difficulty of disentangling radio's effects from the economic downturn, "the extraordinary economic conditions that have thrown all measuring rods out of kilter." The editor suggested that baseball limit broadcasts to a few games per week or "put it on a strictly commercial basis." In any event, the editor believed that completely eliminating radio broadcasts would be harmful.[35] A year later the editor took a more nuanced view:

[B]roadcasting helps those clubs that are winning, or have personalities who can be exploited, but that it 'murders' losing clubs. However, none of the baseball officials can deny the fact that as ballyhoo and advertisement of the game, the radio has no equal. Even the daily newspapers have

not given more time and space to the game . . . it is free advertising that would cost the clubs a pretty penny if they had to pay for it at standard rates. Anything done in the matter of restricting broadcasts must be accomplished in such a way as not to alienate such a publicity medium.[36]

The Major League owners' winter meeting of December 1931 may have been the climax of the radio controversy. American League owners wanted to ban broadcasts during the 1932 season or at least levy heavy charges for the broadcasting privileges, but one owner had already signed a contract to broadcast games, causing a delay in the policy. Ruppert and Cleveland owner Alva Bradley opposed broadcasts, even though the latter's team charged for broadcasting rights. The Boston teams and the Chicago Cubs were the strongest proponents of radio. Eventually the owners decided to leave radio broadcasting decisions to the discretion of each team owner.[37] Although the controversy continued for some time, the owners came closest to eradicating broadcasts at these meetings.

The four Chicago and Boston teams definitely planned to broadcast home games during 1933. The Philadelphia teams and New York Yankees planned not to broadcast. The Tigers, Browns, Reds, Cardinals, and Giants decided to broadcast during the 1933 season, although the Giants only broadcast their games to other cities.[38]

Although the Yankees remained vehemently opposed to radio broadcasts, the 1933 meetings were not as contentious on the subject. The owners decided to continue to allow local discretion. The biggest news was the decision by the owners of the St. Louis teams to stop radio broadcasts of their games for the 1934 season despite the fact that the Browns had received payment for broadcasting rights in 1933.[39] These owners issued a statement:

There, no doubt, was a time when the microphones did us some good. That was in the high times. But now we are at a point where we are willing to experiment a season without the 'mikes.' Mind you, I do not say that the radio has not been a boon to the game during certain years. It has had a great advertising value from time to time in the way of propagation and development.... While the broadcasting of games in St. Louis has not been entirely without profit to the ball clubs from a point of actual pay—a certain station having paid as much as $10,000 for the privilege in 1931—it is known that this inducement has decreased with the falling times during the last two or three years.[40]

The *Sporting News* thought that the St. Louis teams' defection from radio might lead to a renewed showdown on radio at the 1934 meetings. The Cardinals, despite having won a pennant in 1934, experienced even more erosion in their attendance. The Browns had somewhat greater attendance, so no firm conclusions could be drawn. The teams reinstated radio broadcasts for 1935. The *Sporting News* suggested that the teams incurred much ill will from their decision to cancel broadcasts. "It is significant that the parking spaces near Sportsman's Park did not contain as many out-of-town license plates as in previous years."[41]

Radio broadcasts rebounded. By the 1936 season eleven clubs broadcast their home games. The Pittsburgh Pirates and Washington Senators broadcast their road games. The Philadelphia teams broadcast all their home games except Sunday games. General Mills and Socony Vacuum Oil were the most important sponsors. The *Sporting News* attributed the new enthusiasm over radio to "the increasing tendency of clubs to grant radio privileges in return for fixed sums of revenue."[42]

The controversy over the effects of radio broadcasts on attendance was not quelled. The Cincinnati Reds' attendance faltered during the 1936 season; some observers attributed the team's doldrums to radio. MacPhail cited a different and rather bizarre reason for the downturn: "at least part of the cause is that the club has been away for almost two weeks and that it takes games at home to build up the interest in the big days."[43] In Detroit, sports editor H. G. Salsinger claimed that the Tigers used to draw 1 million customers a year at Navin Field "before anyone heard of radio." Since the Tigers' official attendance exceeded 1 million in a season only in 1924 and 1935, Salsinger was either exaggerating or including people who did not pay a full admission. The Tigers' gate fell below 500,000 for both 1932 and 1933, which Salsinger considered prima facie evidence of radio's deleterious effect. A local manager of Detroit radio station WJBK retorted, "There is much ground for the contention that radio furnished priceless publicity and saved the baseball industry from a much worse licking than it actually took during the depression days."[44] Despite the arguments regarding radio's effects on attendance at Tigers games, the team continued to broadcast games in 1937 with station WWJ celebrating its thirteenth year of broadcasting baseball games.[45]

Researcher Lowell D. Smith concluded, "The money wielded by advertisers, or sponsors, solved the disputes over broadcast rights and revenue loss for club owners. . . . Unintentionally, advertising minimized the conflict between radio and professional baseball interests."[46] Although a few teams had already charged radio stations for the right to broadcast games, more teams began pursuing remuneration. The Chicago teams planned to begin charging for radio broadcast for the upcoming 1937 season. To help teams in the process, the American League created a standard contract for teams to use in signing radio stations. Observers believed that the National League would quickly follow the junior circuit's example. The Cubs and White Sox signed WGN and WBBM, as well as WCFL and WIND (yes, there was a radio station with those call letters, presumably in Indiana). Each station paid $15,000 or less for the rights.[47] The *Sporting News* reported that "the Bees and the Red Sox derive quite a decent revenue from the radio people."[48] As they headed into the 1937 season, all the Major League teams except the New York clubs were broadcasting games (Pittsburgh and Washington again chose only to broadcast their road games). General Mills and its Wheaties product, as well as Socony-Vacuum Oil Company and Atlantic Refining Company, remained key sponsors. The Kellogg Company also sponsored games. Teams used reconstructed play-by-play from wire reports instead of live reporting in some cases.[49]

The same set of teams would broadcast their games in 1938. The

Senators finally acquiesced and began broadcasting home games in the 1938 season, while the Pirates began allowing broadcasts of home games during the middle of that season.[50]

Broadcasting reported that General Mills was planning to spend $1 million on sponsorship of baseball games during 1937. The company promoted Wheaties and insisted upon a strict decorum in the announcing of games: "under your broadcasting agreements you have simply and solely the right to give a play-by-play account of the game. That is the only right conferred. If this thought is kept in mind during your baseball broadcasts, if you are fully alive to the full extent of the privileges conferred under your broadcasting contracts, conduct your broadcasts in a manner consistent with the privilege, I am persuaded deeply that unhappy situations will be avoided." Included in the edict was no criticism of "umpires, players, managers, or anyone else, or to visit the dugouts or mingle with players on the field."[51]

General Mills was aggressive in its pursuit of players for testimonials regarding the desirability of consuming Wheaties. "No player was signed who was not actually a Wheaties' [sic] eater. . . . If a player becomes an ex-Wheaties eater . . . notices will be sent to the announcers not to use his name in testimonials since General Mills insists that testimonials be authentic."[52]

The Kellogg Company sponsored the Boston, Chicago, and St. Louis teams, as well as the Athletics and Tigers. The cereal manufacturer also sponsored the games of twenty-five Minor League teams. The company ran afoul of the Cubs, however, when it tried to sign an exclusive contract with the White Sox for a reported $75,000. P. K. Wrigley of the Cubs objected to this tactic and threatened to broadcast the Cubs' road games into Chicago; those broadcasts would have conflicted with White Sox home games. The White Sox backed down and allowed multiple stations to carry their games; both clubs got double the revenue from WGN and WBBM as they had for 1937.[53]

Fans in New York City remained the only ones not receiving broadcasts of home games. One fan wrote to the *New York Times* suggesting that the clubs could broadcast home games without fear of losing attendance at the park, since "a broadcast still is a poor substitute for a first-hand view of the game, which is what a real fan always wants, but unfortunately cannot always get."[54] A mere fan's desire for radio was not enough. What was needed to prompt the Giants and Yankees to broadcast home games was a visionary.

After installing lights in Ebbets Field, Larry MacPhail proceeded to outrage his staid neighbors by signing contracts with radio stations for broadcasts of the Dodgers' home and away games. His action irritated Ed Barrow, who insisted that the three New York clubs had a gentlemen's agreement not to broadcast games (or to light up their stadiums). "The agreement among the three clubs still has two years to run, but since MacPhail has seen fit to violate it, the other two clubs are no longer bound by it and can move as they see fit."[55] MacPhail later denied that he was privy to any such agreement. The Giants quickly announced that they would allow broadcasts of home games for 1939.

The *New York Times* reported that fabulous sums were being offered for broadcast rights of New York baseball. A writer claimed Brooklyn would receive $77,000, while the Giants were offered $250,000. The Yankees were reportedly offered $200,000. The reporter thought that Brooklyn night games might not be suitable for radio broadcasts, given the crowded airways. Horace Stoneham figured that his club could expect $150,000 or more for the broadcasting rights.[56] The reality for the Giants and Yankees was less lucrative than Stoneham's hopes. According to figures presented to Congress in 1951, the Giants got $110,000 for broadcasting rights in 1939. With the Giants and Dodgers signed for radio, the Yankees finally succumbed and received the same $110,000 as the Giants. MacPhail got just $87,500 for Dodger rights.[57] Minutes from the team's board meetings show that the Yankees' management hoped to get enough revenue from the radio broadcasts to offset what they thought the team lost at the gate. In some years, the club did not get any satisfactory offers for broadcasting rights, so the Yankees did not broadcast home games consistently until after the war years.[58]

Ruppert capitulated to the demand for radio broadcasting with little grace, grumbling that he was doing it for "the benefit of the other shut-ins."[59] Once again, General Mills, Socony Vacuum, and Procter & Gamble were prominent sponsors.[60]

The agreement between the three clubs is easy to understand. The National League schedule maker made sure that the Dodgers and Giants never played in New York on the same day (unless there was a Dodgers-Giants game). The Giants and Yankees never played at home on the same day either, so the Dodgers and Yankees shared many playing dates. The owners of the three clubs certainly feared that they were substitutes for each other, and such fears naturally led to concerns that radio broadcasts of each other's games would erode the gate of another club. In game theory terms, the radio broadcasting situation presented a potential "Prisoners' Dilemma" situation, in which each team could hurt the collective earnings of all teams by seeking its own best interest. The New York clubs and the other teams in multi-team cities did get the uniform contract to include a clause barring broadcasts of road games in such cities. The Giants and Yankees, who were still suspicious of radio broadcasts, agreed not to broadcast Sunday games and hoped that the Dodgers would follow suit.[61] The Dodgers apparently chose to broadcast Sunday games; as the *Sporting News* reported, they found some evidence that radio cut into the gate when only 14,000 paying guests came to watch the Dodgers host the Giants. "At all the beaches portable radios poured the story of New York's victory over the Dodgers. Had that game not been broadcast, the park would have been packed. The evidence lies before the club owners, incontrovertible." The previous games had drawn well, however, and to cite one game as proof of radio's deleterious effects seems specious.[62]

With the three New York teams in radio's embrace, baseball finally came to terms with the medium. Certainly radio stations' payment of fees for broadcasting rights helped change baseball owners' attitudes, as even owners "who still consider the air reports as harmful figure that they can make up the difference through receipts from the radio and in the good will engendered."⁶³ The *Sporting News* cited a survey by the National Association (of baseball teams) that showed that "59 per cent of the baseball clubs (major and minors) were airing their home games . . . and 68 per cent allowed road games to be broadcast. These percentages are expected to be considerably increased the coming year. . . . Seventy per cent [of the club owners] considered [radio broadcasts] beneficial, 13 per cent held them harmful and 17 per cent still were uncertain. Of these, the higher classification clubs were much more favorable than the smaller minors."⁶⁴

When the three New York clubs began broadcasting games, such advertisers as Atlantic Refining and General Mills increased their baseball budgets, the latter company now spending $1.5 million on baseball. A later article in the *Sporting News* scaled back General Mills' reported expenditures to around $1 million. The Kellogg Company pulled out of baseball. In a development that proved wise in retrospect, General Mills purchased exclusive broadcasting rights for National Football League games.⁶⁵

Although the Chicago and Philadelphia teams received increasing revenues from radio, the Giants and the Yankees found radio broadcasting somewhat vexing.⁶⁶ The two clubs met with the Dodgers' officials to discuss radio. While the *Sporting News* thought the Giants and Yankees each got $125,000 for broadcasting rights and the Dodgers only $65,000, the periodical reported that any such figures were likely to be whittled down for 1940. New York radio stations complained that their baseball broadcasts got low ratings in comparison with those in other cities (35 percent in Chicago; 12 percent in New York). Although New York City's much larger population meant the audience was similar in size to Chicago's despite the lower percentage of listeners, the radio stations offered less for the rights. The Giants and Yankees owners retorted that "by permitting their games to be broadcast they cut the intake at the gate. They are not so sure that even at the 1939 rates, this loss is compensated for by the fees from the sponsors." Barrow claimed to have conclusive evidence that radio hurt the Yankees' gate (the team's attendance fell between 1937 and 1939 but this could have reflected the ennui experienced even by Yankee fans in the wake of a fourth consecutive runaway pennant winner or the economic downturn of 1937–38). The teams lined up a similar set of sponsors with the exception of Socony-Vacuum, which was replaced by Camels cigarettes.[67] The two clubs broadcast games during 1940 but discontinued broadcasts in 1941 when they could not get their desired fees from the radio stations.[68]

Owners also worried that their embrace of radio alienated their original suitor—the newspaper industry. The *Sporting News* reported that afternoon newspapers had changed their deadlines, thereby keeping the box scores off page one. The papers also devoted less space to baseball. Barrow, while admitting that one season was not enough for a judgment, took a shot at the publicity value of radio broadcasts, claiming that newspapers "beat the air all hollow."[69]

Radio Raises a Vexing Question

Despite the growing trend toward broadcasting games, some clubs, such as the Giants, continued to fight a rear-guard action.

In addition to the Giants' refusal to broadcast home games until 1939, the team, like others, was addressing a simple question: who owns a baseball game? The answer seems obvious, but a legal battle proved otherwise. The Giants tried to prevent the Teleflash Company from broadcasting play-by-play reports of ball games at the Polo Grounds. "Teleflash had obtained the information from outside the ball park by locating a man and apparatus on adjoining property overlooking the fence surrounding the park."[70] The New York Supreme Court ruled that "there is no legal barrier to the broadcasting of games from points outside of the park. . . . The ruling that clubs must make their games more exclusive in order to establish their news value and to prevent indiscriminate broadcasts of the contests, is a particularly interesting point."[71]

The question of whether enterprising radio stations were pirating Major League baseball games came before the Federal Communications Commission. The baseball owners wanted the FCC to revoke station WMCA's license. The owners wanted the station to stop "pirating, appropriating, using or disseminating... all or any part of the baseball games conducted by the complainants." The station responded that it informed listeners that they are broadcasting "their 'versions' of the games and do not state that the broadcasts are direct from the parks."[72] Perhaps Ronald Reagan was pirating games when he recreated baseball games early in his media career. The FCC finally ruled that stations rebroadcasting play-by-play descriptions of games "without the consent and authority of either the league or the originating stations" could lose their licenses.[73] This may have been the genesis of the statement that sports fans have heard for several decades: "Any rebroadcast, reproduction, or other use of the pictures and accounts of this game without the express written consent of Major League Baseball is strictly prohibited."

Baseball owners continued to pursue radio stations that they felt were infringing on their property rights. In a 1938 case, the Pittsburgh Pirates and its radio sponsors, including General Mills and Socony Vacuum Oil, and NBC sued Pittsburgh radio station KQV for pirating the Pirates' home games. The judge ruled in favor of the team and its sponsors, arguing that the sponsors had "co-sponsorship of exclusive play-by-play broadcasts, they have a property right with which KQV is interfering, despite the station's contention it is within its rights in broadcasting descriptions secured by its own observers stationed at vantage points outside Forbes Field."[74]

With their property rights clearly defined and defended in the courts, team owners and radio stations found it easier to enter into mutually beneficial exclusive contracts.

Radio and the World Series

Radio stations had broadcast the World Series since the mid-1920s. By the 1930s radio networks covered the games. The National Broadcasting Company (NBC) and the Columbia Broadcasting System (CBS) broadcast the 1933 series. The Ford Motor Company bought broadcasting rights for the 1934 World Series by paying $100,000. NBC and CBS would again broadcast the games. Commissioner Landis stated that the competing players would get $42,000, which would be divided evenly between the players, and the owners of the competing teams would receive the balance. The company sponsored the 1936 series, too.[75] Henry Ford changed his mind thereafter and declined to sponsor the 1937 series. John Royal, vice president of NBC speculated that "It may be that he felt there was not sufficient national interest with two New York teams in the series to warrant him spending another $300,000 for the radio facilities and time on the air."[76] Although most modern observers figure that television wants at least one New York team in every major sporting championship, apparently two teams were too much of a good thing. Commissioner Landis and baseball again found no sponsors willing to pay the $100,000 fee for broadcasting rights in 1938, so he granted free rights for any stations that were interested.[77]

Baseball finally found a new sponsor for the 1939 World Series between the Cincinnati Reds and New York Yankees when the Gillette Safety Razor Company agreed to pay the $100,000 fee. The games would be broadcast exclusively by the Mutual Broadcasting System. The Mutual Broadcasting System's exclusive rights to broadcast the games came under FCC scrutiny as a possible monopoly.[78]

The Gillette Safety Razor Company again agreed to sponsor the 1940 World Series, with an option for the 1941 series. The company again paid $100,000 for the rights. Observers thought the money well spent even with the expense of broadcasting the game, as an estimated 30 million people listened to the 1940 games, a number exceeded only by presidential addresses. The large audience was especially impressive since most of the higher-rated radio shows aired around the dinner hour instead of during the afternoon, when World Series games were played.[79]

Coming Soon, the Future Medium

Visionaries began to consider television and sports. In an early article on the topic in the *New York Times*, an observer thought that "present television pick-up equipment is sufficiently responsive to light to be generally successful for baseball, which is played in the brightest months of the year and usually in fair weather." The observer thought that football would be less satisfactory, given the fading autumn light.[80] On August 26, 1939 the Reds played the Dodgers at Ebbets Field. Although the Reds were on their way to winning the pennant, the game was most notable for being the first televised to the handful of television owners throughout New York City. The telecast was "improved 100 per cent since the Princeton-Columbia game was viewed on the air through a single camera in May of this year. Now the ball can be seen; the players are no longer white dots on the screen." The reporter concluded, "the baseball enthusiast sitting in a comfortable chair at home gets a more intimate glimpse of the players than do the majority in the grandstands. Baseball by television is no long-range view from the bleachers. It's a clear close-up, with face-to-face views."[81] The reporter addressed the question of who would pay for telecasts. The FCC banned advertising on television channels in 1939 but the reporter thought that clever baseball owners could sell billboards on the fences, which the cameras could not avoid showing. The FCC, of course, eventually allowed advertising on television. The *Sporting News* warned that television "is likely to raise a more serious problem [than radio], but baseball can cross that bridge when it is reached."[82]

World War II delayed the dissemination of television, but baseball owners were willing to jump in wholeheartedly when the opportunity arose.[83]

A weekly sports program was another augury of the future. Modern-day sports fans who have been weaned on 24/7 sports coverage thanks to ESPN and other networks would be amused to learn that a fledgling weekly sports program met skepticism. "Immediately skeptics arose to point out that a 15-minute weekly program on Saturday night would not survive and that its success to that point had only been due to the intense interest in football."[84]

Conclusion

Disentangling baseball's attendance woes in the early 1930s remains a difficult task. Radio broadcasts of home games certainly made a convenient scapegoat, but the attendance rebound of the late 1930s, concurrent with widespread broadcasts of Major League Baseball games, undercut the argument that such broadcasts were the chief culprit. Baseball owners' attitudes toward radio became friendlier when the radio stations opened their wallets and began paying for broadcasting rights. Baseball owners apparently regretted their hesitance to embrace radio broadcasts and the accompanying revenue. When television became commercially viable in the late 1940s, owners rushed to televise their home games. Several of them would later retreat from this policy and begin to concentrate on telecasts of games on the road.[85]

10. Baseball Under the Lights

Baseball's other technological challenge dealt with electric lights. While poets and the occasional baseball commissioner rhapsodized about baseball under the sun, daytime was not always a convenient time for fans. Encroaching darkness also wreaked havoc upon lengthy games, creating conduct unbecoming to the game as players employed delaying or hurry-up tactics depending upon whether they were winning or losing.

In retrospect, most baseball historians seemed to view lights as inevitable and owner resistance to them as baseball's version of Luddite behavior. The reality for an owner was much more difficult. Electric lights represented a major investment of scarce capital, and Major League owners had plausible reasons for thinking that what worked in Minor League towns might not work in big league cities. (In some ways theater owners faced a similar dilemma with the advent of talking pictures: whether to invest in the sound system or to see whether talkies were a passing fad.) An economist might recognize elements of a positive externality. The fact that an owner was unable to capture all the gains from increased attendance under the lights because of the revenue-sharing rules was an additional deterrent to assuming the financial risk of putting in lights. The installation of lights might have been beneficial to baseball as a whole, but an individual owner might have found it to be against his self-interest.

This chapter describes the introduction of night baseball and addresses some questions. Why did some owners resist installing lights? Was their hesitance primarily a concern about costs? Did night ball raise both attendance and profits? The questions of how night ball affected attendance and profits are examined in chapter 12.

For a more complete history of night baseball, the reader is encouraged to read David Pietrusza's entertaining (but, sadly, deficiently documented) book, *Lights On!*

Coming to a Small Town Near You

Minor League team owner Lee Keyser noticed that night football brought in much larger crowds than daytime football. He thought, "Why not night baseball? It will draw and offset the use of the auto and give the working man a chance to attend."[1] In addition, night baseball would not have to face the chilly night weather that accompanied night football.[2]

Keyser's proposal met resistance. The *Sporting News* suggested some rather bizarre arguments against night ball: "The night air is not like the day air; the man who goes to baseball after he has eaten a hearty meal is apt to have indigestion if he is nervous and excited; the disturbed and misanthropic fan will not sleep well after a night game."[3] Opponents of night baseball raised health issues. Would inadequate lighting injure batters' vision or cause more frequent accidents on the field? Players had mixed feelings about night ball. They understood the value of the larger crowds, such as those attracted to night games (especially when combined with ladies' day promotions), but they "complain[ed] it upsets their routine, eating and sleeping hours are juggled and it is difficult, at times, to see the ball."[4]

The *New York Times* reported a more optimistic opinion regarding Keyser's staging Minor League baseball under electric lighting, including "an increase in attendance as the result of night schedules was forecast by veteran baseball men who believe the innovation will be practical."[5] A reporter believed that night baseball had only one advantage, aside from broadening the fan base; a night game allowed fans to avoid being "roasted alive on a hot day."[6]

Keyser's experiment was an immediate success, drawing over 10,000 fans, and even interesting fans in New York City: "The first broadcast of a night baseball game in history [that] went on the air last night and New York fans received a detailed account of the Des Moines-Wichita contest at Des Moines, Iowa, over the NBC's stations WJZ and WEAF." The fans in attendance claimed the "contest was viewed as clearly as a game played under daylight conditions."[7]

The *Sporting News* called the game a success, but cautioned against passing judgment as the second night game had greatly diminished attendance: 1,200 fans. Poor weather may have kept the crowd small at that game. Over a number of games, the average attendance was 2,300.[8]

Despite the drop-off in attendance in Des Moines, other Minor League teams quickly installed lights, including Springfield and Quincy, Illinois. Indianapolis claimed to have tripled the average attendance at its night games, which was pretty good for a cellar-dwelling club.[9] The Cincinnati Reds were interested enough in night baseball that the team paid to install lights in its Peoria, Illinois ballpark, perhaps echoing the old Groucho Marx quip, "Will it play in Peoria?"[10]

Even New York City residents could sample night ball by traveling to Jersey City. Yankees owner Jacob Ruppert joined the 10,000 fans who endured rainy weather at the inaugural Jersey City night game. Ruppert thought "night baseball was still a trifle too early in its development to pass judgment upon it or determine how far it will go in supplanting baseball under sunlight. 'From what I heard and what I see here,' said the Colonel, 'I imagine night baseball will prove a great benefit to the minor leagues, and if it becomes definitely popular in the minors I don't see why some day it should not become part of major league baseball.'"[11]

New York City got a taste of night ball, albeit night football, in 1930. Manhattan College and Oglethorp University planned a night football game at the Polo Grounds for October 1930. The denizens of the Polo Grounds, the New York Giants, consented to play the Cincinnati Reds in a night exhibition game in Bridgeport, Connecticut in August 1930.

The game may not have taken place, as a March 1931 article in the *New York Times* claimed that the Giants and the Chicago White Sox played the first night game in the Major Leagues, albeit an exhibition game.[12]

Sam Breadon, owner of the St. Louis Cardinals, favored night ball for Minor League teams but not Major League teams. "There are not enough of the leisure class in the small towns to keep the golf courses and automobiles busy and still make baseball a playing proposition. But night baseball will make it possible for the working people to attend a game.... It is a question, however, whether it ever will be advisable to have night baseball in the big leagues." Breadon did cite another advantage of night ball: "There would be no variation of visibility, such as is encountered on cloudy afternoons ... it never would be necessary to stop a game because of darkness."[13] He revised his opinion the following month after his Houston Minor League team did well with lights. "When we opened under lights at Houston we played to 15,000 fans, and it might surprise you to know that in every Texas League city where lights have been installed the attendance is up 100 to 200 per cent. Vote that down if you will." He was confident that National League owners would eventually install lights.[14]

After the 1930 season, Minor League teams with night ball reported large proportional increases in attendance for their games, with many claiming a doubling or tripling of attendance. The manufacturer of Giant Floodlight Projectors boasted that the Springfield, Illinois team had tripled its attendance with the arc lights. The company advertised its product aggressively in the *Sporting News* before the 1931 season: "YOUR club, too, will make bigger profits than ever before with GIANT floodlights." The company cited the Wheeling, West Virginia team's experience with night ball. Average attendance rose from 200 to 1,140, almost a 600 percent increase [sic].[15]

In the Minor Leagues, a few teams reverted to day ball. Jersey City chose not to continue night baseball for the 1931 season. Oklahoma City's owner decided to reduce the number of night games, since he feared it "retard[ed] the development of young players."[16] Other owners worried about whether night ball distorted players' statistics and requested that "records be separated into night records and day records."[17] In the Texas League, batters struck out more and had lower batting averages at night during the first seven years of night ball.[18] The desire for more refined records presaged the rise of SABR metrics decades later.

Women and night baseball mixed well. An observer wrote, "An interesting phase of night baseball has been the interest of women. At some games the attendance has been 50 per cent feminine."[19]

Many more teams decided to install lights. Sixteen Minor Leagues had teams playing night ball in 1931. The Major League owners, while hesitating to launch night ball, removed an administrative hurdle against it by revising its code. "The old rule that required every championship game to be started at least two hours before sunset has been omitted entirely."[20]

A manufacturer of lighting equipment claimed, "We anticipate that 80 per cent of all Minor Leagues and semipro ball clubs will have their parks illuminated for night play in 1931."[21]

Creating night baseball meant significant capital investment for both Minor and Major League teams. The San Francisco Seals built a new stadium for the 1931 season and reported that the lighting system cost $75,000. The Seals' stadium was the first stadium to be built after night ball started, and the team installed more lamps than had been used in any park before. Unfortunately for the Seals, the capital investment coincided with declining attendance (attributed partly to competition from dog racing) during the 1932 season, so the team announced it would stop playing night games in late May.[22]

San Francisco's experience was not unique. After the 1931 season, some observers felt night ball had proven to be a novelty; of course, disentangling the cause of the smaller crowds in 1931 was not an easy task. One observer, Walter Holke, asked, "If such an attendance was made possible during these dull times by the lights, what would be the possibilities in prosperous times, when everybody has money to spend?"[23]

Night baseball had not proved a passing fad; Minor League teams, despite a few disgruntled owners, generally remained supportive of night baseball. George Trautman, president of the American Association, stated that, "Night baseball has proved financially profitable with all our clubs." The Negro Leagues, too, were using lights well before most Major League owners.[24]

Lights, Action, Play Ball! Night Ball in the Majors

Despite Minor League successes with night baseball, Major League owners remained skeptical. *Baseball Magazine* interviewed a number of the owners. Bob Quinn of the Boston Red Sox cited the large population of night workers as well as the businessmen and tourists in the Major League cities that guaranteed reasonable-sized crowds for afternoon games. Given the earnestness which Boston and Pennsylvania owners fought for Sunday ball, one would have thought the logical connection between attracting working people on Sundays and at night obvious. A reporter wrote, "The great majority of... baseball fans... work during the day. Generally they are able to attend only the Saturday, Sunday and holiday contests... these days have always been baseball's lush money days. In the theatre, indeed, this has always been a recognized fact, utilized by shrewd showmen who count on their evening shows for their big receipts, and make price concessions in many cases for their afternoon shows."[25] Barney Dreyfuss of the Pittsburgh Pirates admitted that night baseball would attract new patrons who were unable to attend during the afternoon, but he felt that while football was a good candidate for night games, the smaller ball used in baseball would create difficulties. In a typically unsubstantiated statement, Clark Griffith of the Washington Senators claimed, "People there [bigger cities] are educated to see the best there is and will stand for only the best. High-class baseball cannot be played at night under artificial light." (A few years later, people might have wondered whether the Senators played high-class baseball.) William Veeck Sr., president of the Chicago Cubs, uttered one of the few positive remarks: "Night baseball in cities where afternoons are warm, should be much more popular than afternoon baseball." Bob Shawkey, manager of the New York Yankees, was positive about night ball: "In some ways, night baseball is a *positive* peril. . . . At night [inside pitches] would be far more hazardous." Others, including John McGraw, disputed whether the ball was difficult to see under the lights.[26] Five years later, Connie Mack, venerable owner-manager of the Philadelphia Athletics, and Joe McCarthy, manager of the New York Yankees, still thought night games were a passing fad and believed that baseball was a daylight pastime.[27]

While Minor League attendance might have been bolstered by night ball, big-league owners remained wary. "The cost of installing and maintaining the equipment has placed many clubs so far in the red that profitable operation would require more paid admissions than the clubs could hope to add through nocturnal games. The expense of merely turning on the lights varies from $17 to $100 a night."[28] The *Sporting News* and other observers may have neglected to amortize the cost of installing lights across several seasons. Regardless of how the editors thought owners might amortize the cost of installing a lighting system, a *Sporting News* editorial concluded, "if [the past few years' experiences] have taught anything, they have demonstrated that baseball is essentially and fundamentally a day-time game."[29] The editorial page displayed inconsistency towards night ball; by August 1934 it suggested, "Light systems cost money, but if adequate, they are worth the price." The writer thought night games would be better draws than afternoon games on "blue Mondays." He also suggested that playing night ball instead of day ball in Washington DC, St. Louis, and Cincinnati would receive favor from the players and fans. The key reason for his optimism regarding night ball was the changing work week: "the financial and attendance argument is irrefutable. The growing trend toward an intensive work-week with more leisure at the weekend . . . makes the weekday attendance a problem deserving serious consideration."[30] Another writer in the *Sporting News* suggested that Major League Baseball was a better candidate for night ball than the Minor Leagues, since the big-league clubs could afford to put in better lighting systems.[31]

Leland "Larry" Stanford MacPhail used night ball at Columbus, Ohio when he ran the club. When he assumed control of the Cincinnati Reds, he decided night ball was necessary to revive the franchise.[32] Powel Crosley Jr., owner of the Reds, showed that 70 percent of the team's gross home attendance for the year occurred on only fifteen playing dates: opening day, holidays, and Sundays. The *Sporting News* suggested that while night ball might boost the Reds' gate, a better method would be to put a better team on the field: "the lighting system they intend to install at a cost of at least $40,000 will illuminate the field so thoroughly as to wipe out all criticism of night ball by the players and fans ... but a more certain way for Crosley and MacPhail to raise their week-day attendance is to get a winning team." The reporter continued by stating that the Reds drew about 675,000 paid admissions at home in 1926, with an average of nearly 6,000 a day for weekdays without any night ball or artificial doubleheaders and also without a championship club. He concluded, "Last season's home attendance did not reach 300,000. But the Reds of 1935 do not figure to be in the running for the flag, so perhaps night ball will be a boon to the club's treasury."[33] The comparison was flawed, of course, because of the differing economic conditions.

The *Sporting News* reported that the Reds' officials estimated that seven night games would increase the season attendance by over 100,000 fans, giving them "enough additional funds to make them equal competitors with their rivals for available baseball talent." MacPhail claimed the seven night games would give them "seven additional Sunday crowds."[34]

The National League owners probably were not swayed by the vacillating opinions of the *Sporting News* editors. They gave permission for night ball for the 1935 season. Charles Stoneham remained a foe of night ball but abstained from voting. The *Sporting News* reported that New York, Brooklyn, and Pittsburgh (then a relatively successful club) opposed night ball but reserved the right to adopt it if proved successful. The agreement stipulated a maximum of seven night games per season. In addition, the agreement prohibited night games on Saturdays, Sundays, and holidays, nor could an owner have a night doubleheader or an exhibition game. To enforce these prohibitions, the league could fine an offending club up to $15,000.[35] While New York Giants manager Bill Terry thought the club would agree to play a night game in Cincinnati, owner Charles Stoneham vehemently denied this, citing both his fears of increased injuries and wasted expense, as well as his personal preference: "Nothing doing . . . baseball is strictly a daytime sport, and I will not be a party to any scheme that tries to make it anything else."[36] In the other league Jacob Ruppert professed to keep an open mind regarding the subject: "If the National League test proves that night baseball is popular, and is needed, I will build an electric plant at the Stadium, and urge the experiment on the American League."[37] The *Sporting News* editorial page suggested that, based on the Minor Leagues' experiences, MacPhail's "Cincinnati plan would not fail. Night ball, in every instance, has demonstrated its ability to attract interest and support."[38]

Although baseball was beginning to emerge from the trough of the Depression, one can understand the owners' reluctance to invest tens of thousands of dollars in an endeavor fraught with perceived risks. Letting Crosley and MacPhail bell the cat probably seemed astute to the other owners.

MacPhail claimed it cost $150,000 to install lights at Crosley Field. An article in the *Sporting News* suggested a somewhat lower figure; "The contract for installing the greatest lighting plant ever devised for a sports enterprise was awarded by the Cincinnati club last week to General Electric Co. on its bid of $45,600 which does not include the cost of the 632 1500-watt mazda lamps which will be used to light the field nor many other items in connection with the plant. All told, the cost of the lights will exceed $50,000."[39]

The Reds were not the only Major League team considering night ball. Phil Ball of the St. Louis Browns investigated installing lights at Sportsman's Park, but found that the park's limited space required towers or standards to be placed on the playing field or in the stands.

The latter approach would have required going through the roofs and would have added to the initial $50,000 estimate. Ball declined to put in lights.[40]

The Reds, long moribund, seemed to be inspired by the prospect of night ball. MacPhail had already kindled interest in the Reds. He made several player transactions that created optimism among Cincinnati residents, although they did not greatly improve the team's performance. "They are presenting a flashy, scrappy, heads-up enthusiastic brand of ball that has the fans sitting on the edges of their seats and whooping it for [manager Charlie] Dressen's men."[41] The editor noted that the Reds already had 6,000 reservations for the inaugural night game a month before the game was to be played.

MacPhail's efforts had already boosted attendance, as over 75,000 people had already attended the team's first seven home games. His efforts revised the old saying, "'Cincinnati is the town where the season opens and closes on the same [day].' This is in reference to the fact that the biggest crowds here in late years have been those at the openers."[42]

The initial night game played on May 24, 1935 was successful. MacPhail, a master promoter, arranged for President Franklin Roosevelt to turn the lights on. As the *Sporting News* reporter wrote, "It always has been good journalistic practice to put the score first in the account of any game, but the result of the contest was only of minor importance in this event." What was more important was the attendance of over 20,000.[43] The magazine's editorial page described the game: "the arrangements left nothing to be desired. The lights adequately covered the field, there were no blind spots, the ball was as easy to follow at bat and in the field, both for players and spectators, as in the daytime, and there was no glare," before concluding, "The management at Cincinnati deserves all the rewards that may accrue from their pioneering venture in the light movement. They had the courage of their convictions, fought for the adoption of their ideas, and ... put on a show, the like of which never has been seen in the game."[44] Despite this laudatory editorial, the *Sporting News* took a cautious approach before advocating night ball in general: "the skeptics have shifted to new objections. They contend that the adoption of the night game, even to a limited extent, by the majors means the disintegration of baseball, the changing of the game from a competitive contest into a circus-like exhibition and the ruining of the physical well-being of the participants." The editor believed night ball should be limited to once a week at most, to attract fans who could not attend weekday games.[45]

Three games into the experiment, the Reds' night game attendance remained stable at around 20,000. The *Sporting News* admitted that, "In the light of three crowds of 20,000 each that attended the games played at Crosley Field—one of them coming after a 13,000 attendance the previous day, when it was Sunday and Dizzy Dean, the most publicized player of today, was the attraction, it must be apparent that the majority of fans—at least in Cincinnati—will support night ball as strongly as the daylight brand."[46] The Reds' seven night games attracted 130,000 patrons out of 448,247 for the season.

In addition to the increased gate receipts, the Reds did handsomely with concessions. For a night game on a Monday night (traditionally a slow day in baseball), the Reds drew 33,468 fans and turned away 2,500 additional people. "Admissions totaled about $45,000. Some 7,000 persons came from adjoining or distant towns by train for estimated fare of $15,000. The big crowd spent approximately $3,800 for drinks, $800 for ice cream and $500 for sandwiches. 6,000 autos were parked outside the grounds. 'Counting all these things it is fair to say that directly and indirectly this one baseball game put $100,000 into circulation.'"[47]

The *Sporting News* suggested that the increased attendance was sufficient to pay off the installation costs, so that "next season, with the installation cost wiped out, there will be a juicy profit from the mazda contests."[48] The *Sporting News* concluded, "Opponents of the night game cannot laugh off those figures [130,000-plus attendance for seven night games], amassed by a second-division club."[49]

Although owners did not state it openly, there was a possibility that night games simply concentrated attendance upon a few games without a net increase for the season. To counter this argument, MacPhail revealed figures showing that the night games did not siphon attendance from Sunday or weekday games: "both our Sunday and weekday attendance is materially larger than a year ago. Instead of hurting our attendance at day games, we are of the opinion that the six night games has [sic] helped our attendance at day games, because night baseball has been responsible for creating new fans, especially among the women and the young generation."[50]

The Reds had continued success during the second year of night ball, attracting a combined 275,000 spectators to the fourteen night games of 1935 and 1936. They surveyed their fans and found that men preferred day ball by 52 percent to 48 percent, but 86 percent of the women preferred night ball—apparently "I don't know" and "I'm indifferent" were not survey choices.[51]

Night ball at Cincinnati was an enduring attraction and provided funds to improve the team, including the purchase of ace pitcher Bucky Walters. The team took the initiative and improved the ticket-selling process, so that fans could get tickets easily.[52]

Larry MacPhail, taking a stance he would maintain for the rest of his life, opposed any increase in the seven-game allotment per season. He made a comparison with Sunday doubleheaders: "if the number of doubleheaders that are played is not limited and kept within bounds serious injury results. There might be a tendency due to the increased gate to overdo night baseball."[53]

Oops, I Did It Again: MacPhail's Second Night Ball Triumph

After Cincinnati's success with night ball, did the other owners contact electrical suppliers for equipment? Ford Frick declared that night baseball would become more general in the following season.[54] Frick was prematurely optimistic. Larry would have to demonstrate night ball's potential a second time before other owners would invest.

MacPhail's success did not impress many of the owners. Most still considered night ball bush-league stuff and felt it was not necessary for the big leagues. The Red Sox and Giants owners disdained night ball. William McKechnie of the Braves was in favor of installing lights in Boston, but the club lacked funds to build a system. Brooklyn Dodgers president Stephen McKeever stated, "It would be impossible to say whether or not night baseball would increase the patronage in Brooklyn. Night baseball has never been played in the larger cities.... There is not doubt that it has increased the patronage in some of the smaller cities, but in the larger cities there is a serious doubt whether or not it would increase the attendance after the novelty had worn off; unless, you had a top-notch ball team and if you had a top-notch ball team in Brooklyn, you would not need night baseball to increase your attendance."[55]

Former skeptic Clark Griffith began to consider night ball, perhaps out of desperation. Since Griffith's main, if not his only, asset was his ball club, he had reason to be cautious. He is said to have seen the light when a charity donkey ball game attracted 10,000 under the lights. Griffith would eventually become one of the strongest proponents of night ball. (In the 1940s and 1950s Griffith would criticize Branch Rickey for integrating baseball, but once the experiment succeeded, the Senators' owner searched for capable African American players.) Even Connie Mack began to think about installing lights, as had Phil Ball of the Browns. The American League thus had three owners who were at least interested in letting someone try night ball, though they might not try it themselves. Griffith remained wishy-washy about installing lights, "yet he is in favor of night ball, and lastly, he generally does not approve of it anywhere. With Griff, baseball under lights merely is the lesser of two evils and the other—synthetic doubleheaders—still is his pet peeve."[56]

Over in the National League, other struggling teams were not as disdainful of night ball. "The Brooklyn club is eager to go in for nocturnal ball, but lacks the $70,000 essential for payment of the lighting contractors."[57] Some owners decided that the improving national economy and attendant rebound in demand for baseball would make night games moot. The lukewarm support for night ball evaporated in the American League as the owners voted for "an unalterable ban" on night ball. "Why? The answer is obvious. The majors believe that they can continue the game as a daytime sport and that economic conditions, not only in the national pastime ... do not make it necessary to adopt a measure they regard as a drastic departure."[58]

American League owners gradually and grudgingly began to reconsider their unalterable ban on night ball. When Donald Barnes acquired the struggling St. Louis Browns, one of his requests was for night ball, as the Cardinals' owner, Sam Breadon, wanted the Browns' park, which the two teams shared, to have lights. The two teams had difficulty in arranging for lights and faced repeated delays. Barnes was undecided about the desirability of night baseball. Since St. Louis, unlike Cincinnati, had two teams, he wanted just four night games for each team. Breadon wanted more than four. The two team owners finally agreed to install lights. Because of their protracted negotiations they could not install them in time for the 1937 season, and they did not want to install them during the season. Part of the delay arose when Breadon and Barnes could not decide which team would host the premiere of night ball in St. Louis. Delay followed delay, and the estimated cost of the system rose to $150,000, a cost that troubled Barnes.[59]

Barnes did not buy the Browns with a large surplus of capital. In hindsight, night ball seems an obvious choice for increasing attendance, but Ford Frick thought the owners exhibited a justifiable caution, stating that "Baseball owners, as a class, are conservative and rightly so. Any man who invests a fortune in a Major League franchise is entitled to be conservative."[60] For Barnes, the choice was quite stark, as a *Sporting News* reporter quipped: "To do or not to do, that is the question. Whether it is more glorious to put in floodlights at Sportsman's Park or spend some $50,000, which he and the 900 stockholders have in the treasury, for minor league players is the burning question with Barnes." Although Cincinnati had drawn well at night games with a mediocre team, MacPhail had previously created excitement about the team with a series of player transactions. Barnes could not both infuse talent and install lights, so he worried about the baseball version of the "chicken and the egg" question: which came first, a winning team or large crowds? Barnes wasn't sure putting a mediocre team under the lights would work in St. Louis. "The Browns aren't drawing, which is nothing new, and Don seems to be of the opinion that a few night games here wouldn't help much, unless he had the team to bring out the fans. He leans more to the idea of spending his little nest egg for players than for light towers and bulbs. Yet, when one considers the kind of money men like Wrigley and Yawkey have spent for players, how far would $25,000 or even $50,000 go in building up the Browns to the contender class?"[61]

The Yankees and Giants remained adamant foes of night baseball, not only continuing to refuse to install lights but also claiming they would refuse to play night games on the road. In the American League, any existing willingness to countenance night ball disappeared when the league voted to ban night ball for the 1938 season, even though Cleveland wanted to install lights. The Browns' and Cardinals' inability to install lights squelched support for Cleveland's bid.[62] Clark Griffith, ever mercurial on the subject of lights, now opposed night games. The league refused night games, except as "an emergency measure for a club in financial straits."[63]

Larry MacPhail had to demonstrate night ball's potential yet again. The struggling Brooklyn owners selected MacPhail to run the team. At first he claimed that Brooklyn didn't need night ball, just a winning club. "I would say that night baseball isn't important in Brooklyn—not as important as other things. The situation in Cincinnati was different. Out there . . . night baseball was a life-saver. We averaged 22,000 attendance in the seven games the first year and did as well the second year. But I'd say that Brooklyn doesn't need night baseball, considering the potential patronage there. All it needs is a winning club."[64] Within a few months MacPhail changed his mind and announced that the club would install lights, estimating that the General Electric Company could do so for roughly $110,000.[65]

"He [MacPhail] contacted the General Electric Company again and soon had committed to the expenditure of $72,000 for new lighting equipment. The Giants and Yankees were unhappy about it, complaining that New York City was not Cincinnati and that the sophisticated residents of a city the size of New York would never go for baseball at night."[66]

Could MacPhail succeed with night ball a second time? The *Sporting News*, rarely consistent in its estimation of the innovation, took an optimistic view: "If MacPhail had a team to go along with the idea, he would be compelled to build additions to the park for the night games, but even with the Dodgers in the second division, Larry might pay off the cost of the lights, which are to be the most expensive ever installed, in the first year of their operation."[67] Such optimism was not misplaced, as Brooklyn fans filled Ebbets Field to capacity for the June 15, 1938 game between the Reds and the Dodgers. "The game was a sellout, with fans arriving long before dark. It was preceded by typical MacPhail fanfare—a huge fireworks display, brass bands, etc. and even a footrace in which the Olympic star, Jesse Owens, gave an exhibition."[68] The fans fought over seats, as usurpers occupied reserved seats and refused to yield them to their rightful owners.[69] Johnny Vander Meer made the debut memorable by throwing his second consecutive no-hitter. While some observers might have claimed Vander Meer's feat suggested that batters had trouble under the lights, the *Sporting News* brushed this off. "Redheads are lucky. And, in one sense, L. S. MacPhail received a break that few promoters could hope for. The Brooklyn players undoubtedly would have blamed their futility on the lights. They were completely restrained from that alibi by the fact that Vander Meer had proved his ability to pitch no-hitters in the afternoon only four days before."[70]

MacPhail had proved once again that night ball could be lucrative, and this time he did it in a large city with a mediocre team. By season's end the Dodgers had drawn over 27,000 per night game, more than the average for Sunday doubleheaders and more than the Memorial Day game. Alluding to the political climate, a *Sporting News* writer claimed,

"If all that doesn't prove Larry MacPhail's introduction of after-dark ball in Brooklyn is not an outstanding success, it's easier to make Herr Hitler listen to reason than to break down the prejudice of skeptical baseball reactionaries."[71] Night ball continued to be popular at Ebbets Field, so popular that fans repeatedly got into fistfights over seats.[72]

As an answer to Donald Barnes's conundrum, MacPhail used the increased revenue from night games to improve the playing talent. By 1941 he had acquired enough talent for the team to win its first pennant since 1920. While he had been less successful at turning Cincinnati into a winner, the succeeding general manager of the team took the strong financial base MacPhail had created and acquired sufficient talent to win pennants in 1939 and 1940.

Brooklyn's success proved more persuasive than Cincinnati's, as the American League now evinced a renewed interest in night ball. Although such wealthy clubs as the Yankees, Tigers, and Red Sox continued to disdain night ball, league president Will Harridge admitted, "there isn't any question that it would measurably benefit certain clubs, such as St. Louis. . . . I believe that if a club needed night ball to increase its financial position American League owners now would grant permission." Harridge continued by saying that Washington would also be a prime candidate for night ball, given its unbearable heat. He quoted Clark Griffith's belief that "night baseball in Washington would pack them in."[73] The White Sox joined the three wealthy clubs in opposing night ball, but the other American League teams seriously considered it.[74]

Brooklyn's experience with night ball persuaded Connie Mack to change his mind: "[night ball] has its place in the scheme of the Major Leagues just as much as day baseball. Baseball must progress the same as any other sport." Mack waxed nostalgic and recalled the odd (to modern sensibilities) dating patterns of his youth: "Date night, Wednesday, would be a good spot [for night ball]. I remember the days when I was doing a bit of courting. If I could have gone to the baseball game it would have solved quite a few problems of entertainment."[75]

Despite Brooklyn's success, the Giants and Yankees maintained their opposition to night games. Even after the American League approved night ball, with Philadelphia and Cleveland planning to install lights, the Yankees continued to refuse to play at night. However, both New York teams soon wavered in their refusal to play night games on the road. By May 1939, the Yankees and Tigers finally relented and agreed to play night ball on the road, leaving the Giants as the sole holdout. Barrow admitted that he still disliked night ball but relented in order to help other clubs.[76] American League President Harridge hoped that if the league approved night ball, it would "be of a more permanent character so that no club, after a heavy expenditure of installing lights for one season, might find its request denied the following year."[77]

Connie Mack received permission for night ball. The league instituted similar restrictions to those in place in the National League, with no night ball on Sundays or holidays and only seven dates per season. The league also prohibited night games on Saturdays; the National League had recently permitted Saturday night ball. The league's approval was on a year-by-year basis, which created the risk that an owner buying a lighting system might be unable to use it in subsequent seasons.[78] Since the Phillies shared Mack's Shibe Park, there would be fourteen night games played in Philadelphia during the 1939 season. The city would be the first to have two teams with night ball and the first to have so many night games. "Fourteen games under the mazdas make up an unprecedented number in any Major League city, although the total is infinitesimal compared to the many staged in the minors. Only Philadelphia will be confronted with such a situation next season, but the result may go a long way in determining the course followed in St. Louis . . . or in other two-club cities."[79]

In order to get night ball, Mack had to satisfy the Philadelphia zoning board. Foes of night ball in Philadelphia made arguments similar to those raised in Chicago's Wrigleyville decades later when the Cubs wanted to play night games. Certainly some fans disliked night games that were broadcast on the radio, as "every one is awakened, especially now with the windows wide open, and from two to eight radio sets going in one apartment house. Night games are fine in the ball parks—but not on the air."[80]

Cleveland owner Alva Bradley planned to spend between $50,000 and $75,000 for a lighting system for Cleveland's Municipal Stadium. Donald Barnes remained uncommitted. "We are certain night games would increase our attendance figure, but would the increased patronage be great enough to make seven night games a paying proposition? If the Cardinals want to take a chance and put in the lighting system, we will rent it for American League contests. If St. Louis had as great a population as Brooklyn, we would not hesitate to put in the lights."[81] The reader might note that Barnes had now reversed the old argument that night ball might work in the smaller cities but not in the larger ones.

Connie Mack's night ball debut with the Philadelphia Athletics suffered from chilly weather; a disappointing crowd of only 15,000 showed up. He hoped for better results from the second night game. When the Yankees came to Shibe Park for their first night game, both teams' management had reason to be pleased, as the crowd of 33,000 filled the park. Observers noted that a typical day game would have drawn around 3,000.[82] Noticing Mack's success with night ball, Clark Griffith made another about-face regarding the policy. He became enthusiastic about night games, although he still refused to light up his park.

I won't put lights in my park to play seven night games a year. It isn't a good investment, and I have figures to prove it. In the first place, it takes three years to get your money back. That's just for the cost of equipment and doesn't include the juice that's going into those things, maintenance, or anything else. Besides, I've studied this thing pretty thoroughly, and the minor leagues have shown us that you can't play night baseball even as often as one or two nights a week without knocking the heck out of attendance at day games. We'll have to be consistent.[83]

Despite his hesitation, Griffith advocated for two months of night ball, and the *Sporting News* endorsed his idea.[84]

Bradley had to be ecstatic over the initial night game at Cleveland's Municipal Stadium. The game set a record for attendance at a night game with 55,000 fans. The Indians had visions of 70,000 when the Yankees would come to town to face Bob Feller. Despite the large night crowds at Philadelphia and Cleveland the Yankees still resisted night ball at Yankee Stadium.[85]

Even with these encouraging signs, night ball was not foolproof. Although the Yankees attracted 33,000 at Shibe Park, some observers thought Mack erred by scheduling night games too early in the season when the weather was still problematic. The Phillies found their night game crowds disappointing. The club averaged fewer than 14,000 per night game, easily the lowest average of the six teams with night ball. Apparently many of those attending the Phillies' night games came with discounted tickets or free passes, as the team's cash book shows just 62,400 paying customers for the seven night games.[86]

The White Sox also installed lights for the 1939 season, but waited until August before playing any night games. The team claimed the lighting system cost $140,000. Clearly the management was gambling on being allowed to play night games in future seasons, since it scheduled only six games (all in August). The experiment gratified the owners; the six games had a collective 186,000 in attendance.[87]

In the postseason the New York Giants finally succumbed to the turnstile allure of night ball and made plans to start playing such games in 1940, scandalizing the Yankees. The Giants had to build eight steel floodlight towers at a cost of $50,000; the total cost of lighting was estimated to be $125,000. The Giants' first home night game was disappointing, as cold weather blunted the fans' enthusiasm. The good news was that all the reserved and box seats were sold.[88] Horace Stoneham (who took over after his father, Charles, died in 1936) was disappointed with night ball at the Polo Grounds, and wondered whether New York fans were indeed different. The first three games averaged fewer than 22,000 attendees, although poor weather hurt attendance. The fourth game against the Pirates featured ace hurler Carl Hubbell. Only 12,000 people showed up. A *Sporting News* writer thought that New York's crowds were different than those drawn by other ball clubs. "It seems that New York baseball attendance is from 30 to 40 percent transient. These people presumably had tasted night ball at various minor league parks and were more interested in sampling the city's night life, including theatre, opera, the World's Fair, and other entertainment venue."[89]

Across the Harlem River, Ed Barrow dug in his heels against night ball at Yankee Stadium. Part of the reason might have been the much larger expenditure needed to light the stadium adequately. The Giants' lighting system was expected to cost up to $150,000. "If it were a matter of $75,000, the Yankees possibly would pocket their pride and Ed would forget his deadly antipathy toward night ball."[90] Barrow did, in fact, inveigh against the heavy capital investment. "The way I see it, a club which can draw without night baseball is a sucker to go for the lights.... However, I am afraid that the game under lights might turn out a passing fancy. It would be tough to invest $250,000 in lights and then discover that the fad has passed and you are stuck with a white elephant."[91] Sportswriter Frank Graham claimed that Barrow's acumen was proven by Stoneham's disappointing night ball crowds.[92]

Some owners wanted to boost the number of night games, but Larry MacPhail urged restraint. "Club owners who now want to boost the total of night games a season to all sorts of fantastic figures because of the fine crowds the game thus far has been drawing are as wrong as they were when they fought me tooth and nail.... But owners who think they suddenly can draw on this new font of patronage to an unlimited degree are dead wrong." MacPhail feared an over-saturation of night ball would lead to an overall diminution of attendance.[93] It was ironic that his ally in the effort to limit the number of night games was Barrow. The Yankees threatened to withdraw from night games if more than seven per home team were scheduled.[94] Barrow and other anti-night owners were able to maintain the status quo on night ball and to continue the necessity of year-by-year approval.[95]

The American League voted to allow St. Louis and Washington to play night games if they so desired. The St. Louis teams would be the next clubs to host night games. The *Sporting News* stated the obvious when it pointed out that St. Louis, with its muggy, hot weather, would be a prime candidate for lights. In the National League, the Pittsburgh Pirates decided to install lights for the 1940 season. The team hoped to draw 40,000 or more for the first night game.[96]

St. Louis faced construction costs of $150,000, with the Cardinals remaining more enthusiastic about the possibilities of night ball than the Browns. "With a team reputedly about to dash into the pennant zone again, the possibilities for the Cardinals are unlimited. Should they be up in the race, it is probable that they will pack Sportsman's Park on each of the seven night contests. Last year, the Cards drew 411,000 at home. Brooklyn and Cincinnati had nearly half that many patrons at seven nocturnals."[97]

The Browns had a relatively successful night ball debut, drawing the franchise's third-largest crowd ever. The 25,000 paid attendance represented one-fifth as much as the total attendance of the previous season.[98]

The American League, recognizing the Browns' parlous situation, had granted the club fourteen home night games. The Cardinals did not favor special treatment for the Browns, as Breadon feared the extra night games would detract from his club's ability to draw fans. Unfortunately for the Browns, more was not necessarily better. The club's last two home games under the lights attracted a combined 7,000 fans. Despite the poor attendance at some of the Browns' night games, about 11,000 attended each night game; those thirteen games (the season was not finished at the time the source compiled its figures) accounted for roughly half of the team's weak season attendance.[99] The Browns' night game attendance for the 1940 season was greater than its total attendance for 1939. As a comparison, the Cardinals had about the same number of night ball patrons as did the Browns, but in only seven games.

Despite the Browns' lukewarm success with night ball, owner Donald Barnes decided to request permission for at least fourteen night games in 1941. Browns fans soon tired of watching their inept players lose under the lights, and the 1941 night ball attendance fell off.[100]

The American League also granted Connie Mack an additional night game during the 1940 season, as he was plagued by bad weather throughout the season's slate of night games; his night attendance was 15,000 below that of the 1939 season.[101]

Cleveland and Chicago both averaged over 30,000 fans at their night games. The successful night ball results in the American League convinced the Detroit Tigers to consider bringing in lights for the 1941 season, although the team later backed off. Although the *Sporting News* thought the Tigers and Yankees would have had even greater attendance with lights, the Yankees still eschewed the technology.[102] Even Chicago Cubs owner P. K. Wrigley developed plans to install lights at Wrigley Field. "If our fans indicate they want night ball, we will give it to them. If they are satisfied with day games, we may never start a lighting system."[103] The owner also considered playing night games at Comiskey Park but decided against it. His plans to install lights at Wrigley Field ended when he turned over the equipment he had already purchased to the U.S. government for the war effort.[104]

Clark Griffith vacillated over night ball yet again. He decided not to install lights before the 1940 season, blaming the high cost of installation. "I won't be held up on the price like Connie Mack and the rest of those club owners were. The lowest bid we got for installation of lights in my ball park was $124,000, plus about $6,000 more for the engineers' percentage. It's a downright hold-up." A reporter asked Griffith whether he would change his mind if the Major Leagues increased the number of night games beyond the current seven-game limit. His response was, "Never, I don't care much for night ball anyway."[105]

Despite Griffith's reluctance, the successful experiences of the White Sox and the Indians finally persuaded him to ante up $130,000 for a lighting system. Washington's ball park was not well suited for night ball, which added to the expense of installation. "The playing surface is greater than any other big league park and the stands, most of which are 28 years old, are low. Here was presented quite a problem and undoubtedly figured importantly in the $130,000 estimate."[106] In an attempt to recoup his investment Griffith allied himself with Donald Barnes to request a higher limit on the number of night games.

The other American League owners, as well as Breadon of the National League Cardinals, opposed increasing the number of night games from seven to fourteen. These owners also rescinded the Browns' one-year privilege of playing fourteen games, which bitterly disappointed Barnes.[107] Connie Mack did not give up. He requested an increase in night games again during 1941; Barrow of the Yankees was one of the officials who doomed Mack's request. Barrow still loathed night ball: "It's a wart on the nose of the game. Of course, I do not want to see other clubs hampered or harried. I realize they are counting strongly on returns from night games."[108] Commissioner Landis was sympathetic toward the move toward more night games, but he also recognized the potential problem for two-team cities such as St. Louis, in which too many night games might be injurious to one club or the other.[109] Since his club wasn't in financial jeopardy, Cleveland President Bradley could quip in opposition, "Why, I don't think I could stay up so late fourteen nights in the season."[110]

Fortunately for Mack and Barnes, there was a power greater than Ed Barrow: President Franklin Roosevelt. After the attack on Pearl Harbor, baseball owners wondered whether their business would be shut down, as a cogent argument could be made that baseball was nonessential. The president quickly reassured them that he felt baseball was important for maintaining morale. (It also provided that stock character of World War II movies, the private from Brooklyn who was always querying, "How's dem Dodgers doin'?") Because defense plants ran multiple shifts, night baseball was a logical solution to the need for entertainment for defense workers. Roosevelt urged the Major League owners to expand night baseball (not that the Yankees responded): "I hope that night games can be extended because it gives an opportunity for the day shift to see a game occasionally."[111]

Barnes hoped the president's suggestion would help him get more night games: "Now, we can plan on at least 14 games under the lights, and that will mean much to us and I'm sure to the fans tied down to daytime jobs."[112] The National League allied itself with Barnes in seeking an increase in night games. Even a fourteen-game limit was not enough for night-ball convert Griffith; he wanted thirty-five such games. "We want more. My idea of 35 night games for the Senators isn't unreasonable." As the *Sporting News* pointed out, his enthusiasm for an idea he had once scorned was based on an average attendance of 20,000 per night game during 1941, compared with 5,000 for daytime games. For such hefty attendance figures, Griffith probably didn't regret being "held up" for the $130,000 installation cost and, of course, he had Washington all to himself.[113] The New York clubs opposed increasing the number of night games, but were outvoted as other owners acceded to the poorer clubs' financial need for additional night games. While Griffith did not get his exact wish, he did get twenty-one night games. The Athletics, White Sox, Browns, and Indians each got fourteen night games for the 1942 season.[114]

Although the Dodgers, Giants, and Yankees were defeated in their attempts to limit night ball, they now discovered that, due to the German U-boat campaign, the New York police commissioner planned to order the lights turned off at Ebbets Field and the Polo Grounds. Big city lights along the coastlines had silhouetted shipping, providing the German U-boat commanders with easy targets. The Giants and Senators turned to "twi-night" ball, but the Giants discontinued the policy in August 1942.[115] In a patriotic gesture, the Detroit Tigers finally switched on the lights in order to cater to the large defense-plant workforce in the city. "It was pointed out that Detroit must have an attendance of 12,000 to make a profit on a twilight game. Expenses are higher because stadium employees have to be paid at an overtime rate; receipts are lower because the club loses $2,000 that ordinarily is derived from broadcasting rights."[116]

Conclusion

Baseball historians can easily castigate baseball owners for their conservatism in installing lights for night games, especially given night ball's enduring popularity. Few baseball historians have been called upon to gamble $1.5 million in today's dollars (roughly equivalent to $100,000 in 1935) on a risky venture. Yes, night ball was popular in the Minor Leagues, but many Major League owners had drawn sufficiently large crowds with daytime games alone to believe their fan bases differed from those of smaller cities.

Larry MacPhail's initial success with night ball in Cincinnati might have convinced other owners that smaller big-league cities were fertile candidates for night ball, but several of the owners of teams in smaller cities, such as Clark Griffith, Sam Breadon, and Donald Barnes, had most of their wealth tied up in the ballclub and may have been especially reluctant to take risks. Perhaps they also recognized (consciously or subconsciously) that MacPhail was a better promoter. The hesitant owners also hoped that improving economic conditions would restore attendance.

MacPhail's second triumph in Brooklyn washed away some of the arguments against night ball, including the idea that sophisticated New Yorkers (New York readers may dispute my characterization of Brooklyn fans as sophisticated) would disdain it as a gimmick. Because Cincinnati and Brooklyn received increased revenues from night ball and built strong teams, other owners began to realize that investing in night ball and then using the increased funds to improve their teams might be wise.

Despite MacPhail's success, naysayers such as Ed Barrow worried that night ball's popularity might be ephemeral. Such worries were not completely unwarranted, as some owners found that night ball was no panacea. The Browns found that night ball and a poor team did not conjure really large crowds. The team did generate larger crowds, at least temporarily, but night ball did not prevent Donald Barnes from casting about for better venues. Connie Mack, Clark Griffith, and Horace Stoneham, too, found night ball of questionable value, although none of them turned off their lights (aside from wartime restrictions). Once an owner installed lights, the installation costs became "sunk costs." The owner might as well have kept the lights burning if the electrical and maintenance costs were not too high. A better, though hypothetical, question was whether the owners would have made the same decision if they had it to do all over again. After World War II, night ball became an integral part of Major League Baseball, with the sole exception of the Chicago Cubs' Wrigley Field.

We will make a quantitative examination of the effect of night ball and other innovations on attendance and profits in chapter 12.

11. Other Innovations

The owners considered many proposals in addition to radio and electric lighting to lure more fans through the turnstiles. To help the owners, The *Sporting News* was quick to publicize other proposed innovations. The editor wrote, "if the magnates are barren of ideas, The *Sporting News* suggests that they read 'The Voice of the Fan' column in this publication each week."[1] Some ideas proved impractical, while others quickly became an established part of the game. Some of the ideas would be implemented . . . after a few decades.

We Want More . . . No, Less Scoring

During the days of my youth, conventional wisdom held that sports fans wanted scoring and lots of it. With the American League setting records for batting futility in 1968 and professional football capturing the attention of ever-increasing numbers of people, pundits claimed that baseball needed to juice the offense. In reality, the American League experienced greater attendance in 1968 than during the home-run display of 1961. In the 1920s baseball fans witnessed the home-run revolution led, of course, by the incomparable Babe Ruth, who out-homered most American Leagues teams by himself. Eventually other home-run kings such as Hack Wilson, Hank Greenberg, and Jimmie Foxx demonstrated Ruthian abilities to swat the long ball, but they did not seize the public's fancy in the same way. When the National League as a whole, including pitchers, hit .304 for the 1930 season, many people wondered whether things had gone too far. Was there a surfeit of offense? Ty Cobb and John McGraw were two of the reactionaries with regard to the home run, although Cobb himself once belted three in a game and McGraw employed the prolific slugger Mel Ott. Some fans also preferred the old, 1901–19 style of scientific baseball, with its reliance on bunts, clever and daring base running, and place hitting. A poll of big league managers in 1929 showed a large majority were against the home-run craze, although Miller Huggins, Connie Mack, and Joe McCarthy, all possessors of one or two top sluggers, favored the long ball.[2]

The Game on the Field

What was the game on the field like during the 1930s? The National League was the better slugging (or worse pitching) league in 1929–30. Fans of offense could revel in home runs and runs in both leagues, however. As table 34 shows, there was a marked drop in scoring in the National League between 1930 and 1933; the number of home runs was cut almost in half. Thereafter, offense increased in the National League but remained well below the level in the American League. The 1930s continued to be a feast for American League batters, with high on-base percentages and slugging averages.

National League owners claimed that fans tired of the scoring, but historians have suggested another motive: reduced offensive statistics meant lower salaries (for hitters, at least).[3]

There are some conundrums associated with the historians' thesis. First, savvy hitters could argue that they should be paid on the basis of their relative performance and not strictly on absolute performance. The owners' attempt to restrict salaries by reducing batting figures implies that there was a "slugging average illusion" (similar, perhaps, to the "money illusion" in macroeconomics, in which people care about the dollar amount and not the purchasing power of their money).

Second, if batters' figures fell in absolute terms, pitchers' numbers would look better. Why wouldn't the pitchers' better records result in higher pay for them, unless ERA and hits per nine innings didn't matter to owners during salary negotiations? Of course, there were fewer pitchers than hitters. The top batters usually did receive higher salaries than did the top pitchers, and teams usually carried twice as many batters as pitchers; however, given that starting pitchers might work over a thousand plate appearances during a season (roughly twice as many plate appearances as the typical batter) one might argue that pitchers should have earned more than hitters. This wasn't the case, at least for the Yankees.

Third, as the table shows, American League hitters continued their happy times, with runs scored peaking in 1936 at a level just a fraction lower than the National League's figure in 1930. Because of the divergent paths taken by the two leagues, we can test whether fans preferred lower-scoring to higher-scoring games.

The historians making the claim that owners manipulated playing conditions to reduce salaries did not address any of these questions.

Prototype of the Designated Hitter

Before National League owners tampered with baseball in 1931, their president suggested an innovation that would have boosted the offense. John Heydler suggested at the winter meetings in December 1928 that a tenth man be added to the lineup. Almost forty-five years before the American League would introduce the designated hitter, Heydler's proposal went nowhere at the meeting, and he backtracked: "talked about it apologetically, explaining he merely wanted to go on record with the scheme for future consideration."[4] American League owners and managers excoriated the idea. In arguments that would be echoed decades later, Bucky Harris, Detroit Tigers manager, claimed the change would ruin baseball, while his Cleveland counterpart, Roger Peckinpaugh, thought the proposed rule would reduce the manager's importance: "The manager would not have a chance to do any master minding." Chicago White Sox manager Lena Blackburne joked, "My pitchers would assassinate me if they could not take their regular turn at bat." He then made the weak conclusion, "A pitcher lends a doubtful, but interesting angle to the game."⁵ Although American League officials were not interested, John McGraw, New York Giants manager, wanted to experiment with the rule and Pittsburgh owner Barney Dreyfuss said, "Heydler's ten-man team idea is not a bad one at all."⁶

The idea persisted throughout the 1929 season before disappearing. With the almost ridiculous offensive fireworks of 1929 and 1930, owners decided that adding another slugger with gaudy offensive numbers was unnecessary. It is also probable that owners did not want to contend with another slugger at contract time. An observer suggested that even pitchers were feasting on the lively ball, as "a majority of pitchers' hitting, at least this year, is apparently better than has been in preceding years, making less necessary the substitution of a pinch hitter for the pitcher."⁷

National League owners decided to go for less offense rather than more, as would have been the case with Heydler's designated hitter idea.

Resurrecting the Dead Ball

The baseball is the basic tool of the game. One might think it relatively uniform, but, of course, technology and preferences have induced manufacturers to tamper with it. In 1929 the *Scientific American* tested 1924-vintage baseballs versus 1929 balls. The testing found similar resiliency between the balls but found the balls lost liveliness after they had been hit a number of times. If balls were used longer in earlier times than in 1929, this might have accounted for the perceived differences in liveliness.⁸ Interested parties also tested baseballs during and after Roger Maris's pursuit of Babe Ruth's single-season record in 1961.

To curb batting averages after the 1930 season, National League owners first passed a rule eliminating the sacrifice fly. The rule change appeared to affect batting averages by five to ten points. Owners had vacillated on the rule in the past, and the sacrifice fly would later be reinstated.⁹ This change would at most knock only a few points off the robust batting averages and would not directly affect scoring, so the

National League owners ordered the manufacturer of their baseballs to raise the stitching and to use slightly heavier material for the cover. As an experiment, the American League followed in changing the stitching on their ball but maintained the same cover weight.[10]

A quick glance at a baseball encyclopedia reveals the success of the National League's change: offense skidded in 1931 as batting averages fell from .304 to .277 and home runs dropped from 892 to 493. The trend was obvious within the first month of the 1931 season. The National League teams varied in adapting to the new ball, with the Cardinals basing "their attack and defense on it" and winning the pennant.[11] The American League did not experience any dramatic change in its game. National League president John Heydler hailed the change: "the new ball has proved a great success. It has cut down the batting averages to some extent, but it has given us closer and better games. We have enjoyed excellent attendance despite the nation-wide depression."[12]

While National League owners felt good about taming their hitters and some old-time advocates of scientific baseball returned to ball parks, some critics groused about the absurdity of employing two distinct baseballs. For the remainder of the decade, the leagues bickered about employing a uniform ball.[13]

In a surprising development, Jacob Ruppert of the Yankees favored the new, deader ball, believing that it gave the advantage to a team based on speed. He claimed that fans preferred a speedy game to a slugging game, citing Ben Chapman's base stealing as a crowd pleaser. The fact that he had finished behind the Athletics for the third straight year may have dampened his delight in the slugging antics of Ruth and Gehrig.[14] The less lively ball could not completely snuff out the slugging prowess of Chuck Klein and Mel Ott, but National League owners favored continued use of the ball, even though proposals to adopt a uniform ball recurred.[15] The controversy extended to the Minor Leagues; American League president Harridge complained that the differences in balls used in the Minor Leagues distorted batting records and made scouting difficult, a situation akin to today's use of metal bats in college baseball.[16]

In 1933 the leagues finally voted to use a uniform ball, one "patterned almost exactly along the specifications of the American League sphere." Suspicions persisted that the leagues continued to use different balls despite the legislation, as the American League remained the home-run league. Harridge issued a statement in 1936 claiming that the two leagues used the same ball. The leagues chafed under the uniform ball, and the American League modified theirs for the 1938 season. This led to a break with the National League, with the leagues again issuing different balls: a number 3 in the American League and a number 4 in the National League. The American League sphere was livelier, which its owners thought pleased their fans. Some cited an increase in attendance of 1 million between 1936 and 1937 (the official record showed a 600,000 increase). Eventually the leagues agreed again to use a uniform ball, although the one they chose was slower than the 1937 ball.[17] After the 1938 season Clark Griffith wanted an even slower ball to slow down the powerful Yankees offense. The final agreement was truly a hybrid: "the new [ball] will have the American League covering with National League stitching."[18]

Lively or not, the balls themselves were valued by owners seeking to trim expenses. Sometimes owners wanted their baseballs back, and the *Sporting News* encouraged fans to return balls hit into the stands. "The outlay for unreturned balls is a heavy item in all leagues, big and little. Spectators should be honest enough . . . to return them."[19]

Hitters compiled their prodigious offensive numbers with a significant disadvantage relative to today's sluggers, and that disadvantage was not the absence of steroids or weight training. Hitters had to be more macho in the past. They stood in against pitchers wielding dirty, heavily-used balls, (whether those balls were lively or not), in inadequately-lighted stadiums . . . and without batting helmets. A fan wrote to the *New York Times* in 1940 wondering why the players were exposed to such risk. Not until a series of serious beanings, particularly those of Brooklyn Dodgers players Joe Medwick, Dolph Camilli, and Pete Reiser, did the owners begin to consider batting helmets.

The National League resolved to allow clubs to experiment with batting helmets during the 1941 spring training, prompting the *Sporting News* to ask why the helmets weren't made mandatory.[20] Batting helmets were not a panacea, and baseball fans of a certain vintage may recall the ghastly *Sports Illustrated* cover featuring Tony Conigliaro after his near-fatal beaning in August 1967.

Did Altering the Offense Matter?

While National League owners professed pleasure over the effects of the dead ball in 1931, the attendance and profit figures give scant credence to their belief. Both Major Leagues endured significant drops in attendance between 1930 and 1931. The National League had drawn more fans than the American League for every season since 1926 (1926 was essentially a tie). The National League's attendance exceeded the American League's by 16.2 percent in 1930, a margin of 760,000. The National League's attendance fell by 15.8 percent between 1930 and 1931, while the American League fell by 17.1 percent. In absolute numbers, the senior circuit lost 863,000 fans versus 802,000 in the junior league. The numbers worsened in the subsequent years, but the National League suffered larger absolute and relative slumps in 1932 and 1933. The National League also stayed in the doldrums a season longer than the American League. The latter league's attendance jumped by more than 800,000 fans in 1934, while the National League's attendance increased by fewer than 40,000 fans.

If National League owners thought reduced offensive statistics would reduce real payrolls, they were disappointed. Since owners only reported team salaries for 1929, 1933, 1939, and 1943, a direct comparison between 1930 and 1931 is not possible. National League owners paid 10.3 percent more in real team salaries in 1933 than in 1929, while the American League owners saw a mere 0.5 percent increase in their real team salaries. The National League owners would see a smaller increase in such salaries between 1933 and 1939 than their American League brethren, but it is unlikely this can be attributed to the deader ball. The American League began attracting larger crowds than did the National League in 1938 and 1939. American League teams, such as Boston, Cleveland, and Detroit, boosted their real team salaries considerably as the 1930s waned.

According to information reported to Congress in 1951, real profits fell in both leagues in 1931. National League owners might have found comfort in the fact that they still reported a collective net profit for 1931, unlike American League owners. But National League owners witnessed a larger drop in profits: over $1 million. The American League owners saw a drop of $670,000 in their collective profits.[21] Until 1934 National League owners reported smaller collective losses than their fellow owners in the other league.

National League owners found that reducing the offense by deadening the ball was a disappointing way to boost attendance and profits or to cut real payrolls.

The Ballpark Experience

Modern baseball fans sent by time machine to a Major League park circa 1929 would be stunned by the primitive aspects of the experience. Their first question might be, "Who are these guys?" as players did not wear numbers on their uniforms, much less names. The scorecards would list a batting order with numbers, but the players did not wear the numbers. While there would be the usual fan noise—cheering, booing, and epithets against the umpires and rival players—there would be no public address system aside from a man with a megaphone. There would be no organ music whipping the crowd into a frenzy. There would be no big-screen Diamond Vision to show replays. While there were box seats, no team had skyboxes. The concessions stands would have limited menus. The time traveler might hear, "Nachos? We don't need no stinkin' nachos." There would be no sushi or pizza, either. In some parks, there would be no legal beer. In short, a modern fan would find the 1930s-era baseball experience to be roughing it.

Reading through the *Sporting News* and *New York Times*, one can see nascent attempts to improve the ballpark experience by catering to the fans. Rather than assuming that putting a strong team on the field was sufficient, some owners began to explore ways to appeal to the casual fan. Bill Veeck wrote in the 1960s, "If you depend solely on people who know and love the game, you will be out of business by Mother's Day."[22]

Informing the Customers at the Ballpark

The owners were notorious for secrecy regarding attendance, revenue, and profits. They also liked secrecy at the ballpark. Well into the 1930s they were debating whether to list scorers' decisions on hits and errors on the scoreboards. Fans usually had to sit in ignorance of these basic decisions. Sam Breadon and Donald Barnes, owners of the St. Louis teams, installed a new scoreboard for the 1938 season and by mutual consent decided to break the silence regarding hits and errors by flashing the scorer's decision on the scoreboard. Because they feared gamblers, the owners did not announce starting pitchers before the game, although astute fans could probably guess the likely starters.[23]

Fans could get some information by purchasing scorecards, but these varied in quality. While all the teams sold scorecards for a nickel or a dime, many scorecards were of limited use for identifying players. The Cincinnati Reds were an exception; they produced a thirty-two page handbook of information on the players and coaching staff, including pictures and playing statistics.[24]

Baseball fans, especially Yankee fans, revere the numbers 3, 4, and 5 worn by Babe Ruth, Lou Gehrig, and Joe DiMaggio. Ruth almost missed out on uniform number immortality. Only in 1929 did the Yankees begin sewing numbers on the back of the players' uniforms, with the scorecards listing the roster and numbers.[25] Clearly some players did not require numbers, given their unique abilities, but one can imagine that fans might have had difficulty identifying members of the St. Louis Browns, for example. Baseball owners might have shared the fears of early motion picture producers who were wary of identifying their players on the big screen, lest the actors gain some bargaining leverage over salaries.

The *Sporting News* approved of the Yankees' action but could not resist a gibe at baseball owners. "It generally takes the owners about 70 years to grasp an idea that costs nothing and adds to the attractiveness of their bid for the public coin.... The strange feature of the passive resistance in the number scheme was that the adoption would not have cost the clubs the price of a dozen baseballs. Players are numbered on the scorecards for identification on the scoreboards, and the numbers of the regulars are usually permanent for the season."[26]

In an editorial, the periodical took a bow: "For a long time this journal has advocated the plan, feeling that baseball clubs owe it to their supporting public to provide this kind of information and service." The writer hoped that "other Major League clubs will fall into line now that the progressive and successful Yankee officials are about to show the way."[27]

According to baseball historian Peter Morris, the Cleveland Indians quickly realized the value of putting numbers on the uniforms. Although the Yankees were to have been the first American League team with numbers on the back of their uniforms, their 1929 opening day game was rained out. Cleveland played with uniform numbers later that day and became the first American League team to do so.[28]

The St. Louis Cardinals had preceded the Indians and the Yankees in putting numbers on uniforms. The team put six-inch numbers on the uniform sleeves. Branch Rickey explained, "I think we owe it to the patrons.... The fans do not know all the players. Even I, a manager in the same league, when away from home, must often call an usher aside and ask him who this or that player is. And, if I do not know the players, how is any ordinary person to figure it out?"[29] The numbers were too small for the fans to get much value from them, and the experiment was discontinued shortly thereafter.

After the Yankees and Indians put numbers on the back of their players' uniforms, the National League owners responded slowly. The

Boston Braves became the first senior circuit club to attach numbers in 1932, but most of the other National League teams did not act. The league discussed numbers in December 1933. The more radical idea of sewing player names onto uniforms did not germinate until 1960, when Bill Veeck put them on his White Sox uniforms. Until then, players were, in a sense, just numbers and not names.[30]

Between the lack of numbers and loudspeakers, fans often sat in ignorance of who was pitching to whom and the explanation of a bizarre play. "Why club owners believe their patrons should be allowed to remain in such ignorance is difficult to understand, for there can be no logical reason for their failure to supply supplemental aids that other sports have furnished and which help toward enjoyment of the spectacle, or to meet the argument that the radio listener learns more about [the game] than does the spectator." The *Sporting News* editor wondered why owners did not install loudspeakers. "It always have been a mystery why club owners have persisted in keeping their patrons in the dark as to what is occurring on the field, except by such information as they can get through the eyes. It is no wonder that many fans stay at home and listen to the game over the radio—for they rightfully claim they can learn more about what is going on at the ball field in that way than even by sitting in a field box."[31]

The New York Giants introduced a prototype public address system in 1929. "One of the most interesting features at the Polo Grounds yesterday was the operation of the Giants' newly installed amplifying set, which not only broadcasts the batteries and substitution of players but which enables the umpire to call out each ball and strike so all may hear. This he does by standing on two plates behind the catcher and talking into a microphone attached inside his mask."[32]

The Chicago Cubs installed loudspeakers and a new scoreboard for the 1934 season. The Dodgers and Yankees waited until the 1936 and 1937 seasons respectively to do so. The *Sporting News* reported snidely, "For years, an announcer trudged about that huge enclosure [Yankee Stadium], almost vainly shouting, 'For New York, Gomez pitchin',

Dickey catchin'." Still as one columnist remarked, "New York was the last town to do away with hoss cars."[33] An editor did admit that the guy with the megaphone had a second purpose at the ball park: "it is remembered that about all the fellow with a megaphone does is to collect stray balls after he announces the batteries for the game."[34] Sometimes the acoustics within a stadium were poor, creating new complaints as described by a letter complaining about the Polo Grounds' inadequate public address system.[35] Another Giants fan complained about the difficulty in reading the scoreboards from the center-field bleachers, "way out yonder... situated, it seems, somewhere near the Canadian border, the scoreboards barely can be seen with the naked eye."[36]

The *Sporting News* lauded Cincinnati, Pittsburgh, Chicago's Wrigley Field, and the two Boston parks for their good sound systems, while Detroit, Cleveland, and the Philadelphia stadiums had adequate systems. At least the boys in the National League press boxes were kept informed, as the owners installed telephonic communication between the playing field and the boxes.[37]

According to Peter Morris, music piped through the public address system began at Wrigley Field on April 26, 1941.[38]

Owners even seemed timid about announcing their games. Another suggestion for raising revenue at the ball park came from a writer in *Editor & Publisher*, a trade journal for newspapers. The writer asked why baseball owners did not better employ advertising in newspapers. The New York clubs, for instance, placed small ads on game days announcing the time and place (and sometimes ticket prices). These ads were difficult to see unless one was looking for them, although sometimes they were placed next to the league standings. The writer's point may have been valid; a larger ad might have garnered a better response. On the other hand, owners may have experimented with larger ads in the past and settled on the smaller ones as adequate, given the expense. Chris von der Ahe, of the old St. Louis club in the American Association, used larger, bombastic advertisements during the 1880s. His ad copy could have been written by P. T. Barnum, given its use of superlatives: "THE BROWNS ARE HERE! The Hardest Hitters, the Finest Fielders, the Best Base-Runners, The Coming Champions."³⁹

Owners also proved dilatory in letting fans know whether games were canceled or not, and fans had to guess whether the weather was good enough to trek to the stadium. As goofy as German immigrant Von der Ahe's behavior seemed to fans and baseball historians, he did come up with a practical way to inform fans of whether a game was on or was rained out: "displaying a golden ball inscribed 'Game Today' or flew a flag reading 'No Game Today' over [his] Golden Lion saloon, which was located next to the ballpark."⁴⁰

If fans were bemused at the ballpark during the 1930s, at least the games were cheap relative to other sporting events. While baseball fans often bemoan the expense of attending games, a practice that has culminated in the development of modern-day fan cost indices, observers in the 1930s pointed out what a bargain the game was. An editorial in the *Sporting News* pointed out that "if a prize fight between two uncouth principals, and probably a prearranged affair, is valued at $5.00 at the gate, a baseball game is worth $25. But baseball holds its price charge at a minimum figure, while prize fighting, and kindred sports mullet thousands out of thousands."⁴¹

Stadium Construction

Major League Baseball had a construction boom that ended during the First World War. Thereafter, only the Yankees' owners built a new stadium during the 1920s. With one exception, the owners would use existing stadiums until 1953, when the Braves moved into Milwaukee's new facility.

Some of the stadiums built during the prewar boom had inadequate seating capacity for the larger crowds of the prosperous 1920s. Stadium capacity was similar to an inventory problem. For most teams, few games came anywhere close to filling the stadium. There were some games—such as holidays, Sunday doubleheaders, and crucial pennant-race games—that might create an overflow crowd, and an owner would be unable to sell enough tickets to the crowds outside his stadium. Building more seats entailed tying up scarce capital and incurring additional maintenance expenses.

With the strong attendance of the 1920s, some owners, such as Jacob Ruppert and his partner at the time, T. L. Huston, increased the number of seats within their stadiums. By 1928 Yankee Stadium hosted crowds in excess of 80,000. Ruppert was not satisfied and made plans in early 1929 to replace the existing bleachers with a new concrete bleacher section, but he delayed these plans. At the trough of the Depression, Ruppert decided to revive plans to increase the bleacher section at Yankee Stadium: "My confidence in the baseball outlook for 1933 is such that I am reviving my plans to . . . provide at least 10,000 more 50-cent seats. You see, I still believe that we are moving toward the 100,000 crowd in baseball, and when that comes I want to be prepared for it."[42] Ruppert finally awarded a contract for the new construction in late 1936, and reporters speculated that the cost would be as much as $850,000. According to figures in Lowry's *Green Cathedrals*, the stadium temporarily had a capacity of 82,000 in 1927 but held fewer than 70,000 until 1937. The team was probably able to push capacity beyond 70,000 with standing room sections.[43]

Although Ruppert was hoping to build in anticipation of permanently larger crowds, other teams attempted to meet temporary increases in demand. The Chicago Cubs, the attendance pacesetters of the late 1920s, could rival the Yankees in terms of World Series gate receipts for a sellout, despite a much smaller capacity. Wrigley Field had 20,000 box seats, which was four times as many as Yankee Stadium. The club erected temporary wooden bleachers with 8,000 seats for the 1929 series, and also created a temporary standing-room section. The Pittsburgh Pirates, too, considered erecting temporary bleachers in anticipation of a World Series appearance in 1938; that hope was spoiled by Gabby Hartnett's famous home run for the Chicago Cubs.[44] The Cubs eventually made permanent improvements in their park. Wrigley Field had seats of different widths, ranging from 17 to 19 inches. The boxes had folding chairs, while the stands had opera seats. William Wrigley insisted that the stadium be neat and clean: "You can't sell goods in a grimy package." As the sportswriter observed, "No woman ever leaves Wrigley Field with a soiled dress because of dirty seats or railings. The place is immaculate." The writer added that, unlike Comiskey Park, which was near Chicago's infamous stockyards, "[Wrigley Field] is situated in the cleanest part of Chicago, free of soot and smoke of factories."[45] In 1935, Wrigley announced plans for constructing the outfield bleachers beloved by current Cubs fans, even though the club lost money in 1934. Other improvements during the 1930s included installing new seats in the grandstands (18 inches instead of 14 inches). These changes had the effect of reducing the total number of seats from the planned 43,000 to around 38,000. Down the elevated train tracks from Wrigley Field, the White Sox had already double-decked their grandstands in 1926, expanding their capacity to roughly 50,000. Charles Comiskey stated that, "[The capital] isn't my money that I am putting into the park, it was merely loaned to me by the fans and I'm returning it to them in the form of improvements, so that every White Sox rooter can have a comfortable seat."[46]

In cities with two teams, owners sometimes shared a stadium. The Philadelphia Phillies played in the Baker Bowl, which was the epitome of a baseball-style "bandbox" park. The park's short right-field wall made it a paradise for left-handed hitters but a potential nightmare for an owner, as only 20,000 fans could occupy it. The Phillies' only World Series appearance had been in 1915, and National League owners were concerned that if the team ever contended again, the Phillies' owner still would not be able to make much money. In 1930 the league owners encouraged the new ownership of the Phillies to share the Athletics' Shibe Park, which held almost twice as many seats. Eventually the Phillies became renters when owner Gerald Nugent came to terms with Athletics owner Connie Mack on use of Shibe Park.[47]

The Philadelphia teams mirrored the St. Louis teams that had shared Sportsman's Park since 1921. When Browns owner Phil Ball died, the park reverted to his heirs, so the Browns also became renters. The club typically paid just $30,000 per year in rent, since it rarely triggered the attendance clause that would have required them to pay additional sums. Browns fans might have been bemused by the clause, which stipulated: "plus $1,000 per game in the event of world's championship games played at Sportsman's Park."[48] The Browns did reach the World Series in 1944.

Boston's two Major League teams played in relatively small stadiums: Braves Field and Fenway Park. Even today, Fenway Park has a limited number of seats (at premium prices). Braves Field could seat over 40,000, while Fenway Park initially seated fewer than 30,000. Since both teams typically occupied the lower rungs of the league standings as the Depression worsened, seating capacity was not a serious concern. When Thomas Yawkey purchased the Red Sox, he quickly bought several star players and invested money into the park. Part of the stadium improvements included putting steel and concrete grandstands along the third base line to replace wooden bleachers that had burned in 1928.[49]

Because of Fenway's proximity to a church, the club could not host games there on Sundays and used Braves Field instead. The Red Sox rebuffed the Braves' overtures to rent Fenway Park during a brouhaha over dog racing. Eddie Collins, the Bosox general manager, denied them the opportunity, saying, "The Red Sox would be glad to extend the courtesy of their park to the Braves if their own was damaged by a fire or an accident of some sort. But we will not take them in if they move because of dog racing." In the end, the Braves' owner decided not to host dog racing, and the team occupied the park until the end of the 1952 season.[50]

Today's owners have proven adept at getting public financing of new stadiums, replete with skyboxes and other amenities. The Major League building boom early in the twentieth century was privately funded, although city officials sometimes helped owners acquire land or arranged for convenient access to transportation. During the Depression years, only one team enjoyed a new stadium. The Cleveland Indians eagerly awaited the city's new stadium with its vast seating. The club and the city officials sparred over revenue from concessions and from parking: "The [Indians] frankly [are] not interested in a new and municipal home if it cannot install, operate and finance all the concessions that go with the great American ball game, including scorecards, bottle pop, cushions and hot dogs." The Indians offered a twenty-five year contract with the city to lease the park, including a $50,000 per season flat rent (with extra rent for a World Series), 15¢ on each admission above 700,000, parking for 8,000 cars at 25¢ each, and no municipal free list. According to the reporter, "The club owners frankly are skeptical about the city's ability to withstand the temptation to make passes for the ball game one of the most valuable and sinister adjuncts of political patronage." The reporter went on to discuss the possibility that since "free passes" counted towards the 700,000 admission limit, an unscrupulous city government could issue many free passes to boost the attendance above the 700,000 threshold.[51] Cleveland's city council rejected the Indians' terms, so the Indians remained in their League Park during 1931. The Indians would eventually use Municipal Park, as the city's stadium came to be known officially (it was called the "Mistake by the Lake" by less genteel fans), on a sporadic basis. As the years passed, club officials decided that it was too expensive to lease the stadium.[52]

Despite the economic downturn, the Brooklyn Dodgers decided to build new grandstands at Ebbets Field. The Dodgers could only pack 23,000 people into Ebbets Field and hoped to increase the number to 35,000 or more. Frank Yorke, club president, testified that the field's limited capacity meant the team turned away more than 200,000 potential patrons during the 1930 season (one of the club's better years on the field and at the gate during the Depression era), with some Sunday games seeing tens of thousands of frustrated fans. Enlarging the stadium required large sums of capital. If the large crowds of 1930 (over a million) had dissipated permanently in the wake of weaker clubs, the owners might have rued their decision to enlarge the field. The Dodgers later improved the concession stands and added some reserved seats behind home plate in time for the 1938 season.[53]

The author has no scientific data on whether baseball fans today are more rotund than in the past, but stadium seating in the past certainly fit more svelte people. During the new stadium building of the 1950s and 1960s, owners touted the wider seats offered, increasing from 17 or 18 inches up to 21 inches in newer stadiums such as the Los Angeles Dodgers' Chavez Ravine. The Yankees during the Depression era boasted that their seats were more comfortable than those at other parks. Charles McManus, superintendent of the Stadium, explained why the seats ran from 18 to 21 inches: "Well, they ought to be wide enough.... They were measured to fit the seating needs of both Ed Barrow and Cap Huston.... Ed and the Cap were pretty broad-beamed the day we measured 'em."[54]

The Detroit Tigers had signaled a new effort at improving their team on the field by buying Mickey Cochrane from the Philadelphia Athletics. Frank Navin, the team's owner, wanted to expand Navin Field from its 29,000 seats. As the Tigers neared their first pennant in a quarter century in 1934, he sought permission from the city to erect a temporary set of bleachers seating 17,000 (selling for $1.00 per seat). These may have been the temporary bleachers from which fans showered St. Louis Cardinals star Joe Medwick with (presumably rotten) vegetables in Game 7 of the series. The Tigers' success in 1935 inspired Navin to invest $500,000 in enlarging the park by over ten thousand seats. After the 1937 season, in which the club drew over a million patrons, new owner Walter Briggs ordered another round of expansion which cost $600,000 and gave the stadium almost 60,000 seats.[55]

Cincinnati's Redland Field (later renamed Crosley Field) featured a spacious playing field, making home runs rare. The park had 24,000 permanent seats but up to 36,000 people could be crowded in, presumably by allowing fans to stand on the field. When the Reds participated in the 1939 and 1940 World Series, the club considered, but chose not to build, temporary bleachers.[56]

Selling Tickets

If owners were secretive and old-fashioned, at least they paid attention to how to sell tickets more efficiently. Fans disliked waiting in line to buy tickets or seeing "favored customers" receiving preferential treatment at the ticket window. Even worse, some fans found that teams oversold their general admission seats, just as airlines now overbook flights.[57]

The New York Yankees and Giants led the way in arranging for Western Union ticket offices to sell reserved seats. The Chicago Cubs and Brooklyn Dodgers also began selling reserved tickets through the offices. There were 102 Western Union offices throughout Chicago, so presumably fans could find a vendor easily. The Browns came up with a different and perhaps quixotic scheme. They sent mailers to 1,800 civic and business leaders informing them that they could purchase tickets on credit. All the leader had to do was to sign a signature card. At the ticket window, the signatures were matched, and a bill was later sent to the leader's office.[58] The number of civic and business leaders who took advantage of the convenience is not known.

Rowdy Fans

Owners sometimes devised policies to reduce rowdiness at the ballpark. While "Kill the umpire" is a classic American shibboleth, fans occasionally engaged in potentially dangerous activities such as throwing bottles. The *Sporting News* published recurring editorials urging owners to prohibit the sale of bottled beverages. The editorials spanned the Depression era. In 1929 the writer warned, "we do feel that it is dangerous business to have bottles passed around to the spectators... the alternative seems to be soft drinks in soft containers." The following year the editorial page took Brooklyn fans to task and showered contempt upon the rowdy ones among them. "Brooklyn fans have degenerated and at last have returned to the stage of throwing pop bottles, a condition in baseball which is contemporaneous with the hick and the rube. Brooklyn would resent being called a municipality of hicks and rubes, yet it is permitting that element of its population to get the whip hand at its ball games."⁵⁹ Not much progress was made until 1940 when Ford Frick, then president of the National League, endorsed the idea of using paper cups instead of bottles in the wake of two bottle-tossing incidents at Sportsman's Park in St. Louis.⁶⁰ The *Sporting News* editorial writer (who published in the city) did not refer to St. Louis as a town of hicks and rubes, however.

The other libation, beer, may have fueled rowdy behavior but not for much of the era. Beer and baseball, while not quite as American as Mom and apple pie, were not a legal combination between 1919 and 1933. When Prohibition ended, owners in Chicago and New York moved quickly to sell beer at the ball park, while owners of Pittsburgh, Cleveland, Cincinnati, Detroit, and Washington did not turn on the spigots. The reader may note that the teams that did not sell beer were all in single-team cities. Teams in Boston and Philadelphia had not decided, while the St. Louis clubs disagreed. Fans of the Cardinals will be surprised to read that the team did not want to sell beer, while the Browns did. Eventually all the Pennsylvania teams decided to maintain Prohibition in their ballparks. Phillies fans smuggled in alcohol; a 1950s observer wrote that the team had the rowdiest crowds in baseball due, in part, to smuggled liquor. Local politics played a part in the Philadelphia Athletics' inability to sell beer, when the Pennsylvania Superior Court backed the city treasurer who rejected the team's application for a beverage license, "on the ground that Shibe Park was not a bona fide eating place under the terms of the Malt Beverage Act of 1881."⁶¹

On the other end of the beverage wholesomeness spectrum, fans had difficulty slaking their thirst with milk. A fan queried the *Sporting News* as to why milk was unavailable at most parks. "It may sound 'sissified,' but a great many fans no doubt would enjoy a cool drink of milk on a hot afternoon." The editor responded that in parks served by the Stevens concessionaires, fans could buy milk, "but only at the concessions stands and not in the grandstands."⁶²

Occasionally fans were quixotic in their desires. One fan pleaded for an end to booing: "No real follower of sport will ever 'boo' if he thinks for a minute how degrading this vulgar noise is to all concerned."[63]

Fans also differed by the time of the game. "The night fan is a louder rooter than the sun worshipper but less partisan. He apparently goes more for the show with the attitude of a theatergoer plus a chance to yell, throw cushions at the umpire, eat hot dogs and smoke. It is bringing about a great change in baseball, and the old-time enthusiasts mourn."[64]

There were ushers, ostensibly to assist fans and to promote order, but fans were not necessarily well served by them. "[Dodger ushers] thought of themselves as strong armed policemen and, therefore, brought out the same combativeness in the Dodgers' fans." Sportswriter Frank Graham recounted how pre–Andy Frain ushers roughed up a customer who caught and retained a foul ball. The ushers accused the hapless fan of stealing the ball.[65] "Larry [MacPhail] always tried to create an atmosphere of fun, one that would encourage entire family participation. He had seen what Andy Frain had done with Comiskey Park and Wrigley Field in Chicago. . . . Therefore he hired Frain to bring out some of his courteous, uniformed ushers from Chicago to train local recruits to conduct themselves in the same fashion."[66] How embarrassing it must have been for Brooklyn fans that MacPhail had to bring the boys from Chicago to teach manners to the Brooklyn gang.

Having barely survived the Black Sox scandal in the 1919 World Series, team owners combated gambling within their parks. The *Sporting News* reported that several owners ejected gamblers and threatened permanent banishment against repeat offenders. The periodical lauded the Yankees for throwing out more than one hundred "cheap allies of gunmen, some of them little better than gunmen, all of them willing to take pennies from the cup of a blind organ grinder."[67] The Yankees did refund the money the gamblers paid for admission. In Chicago, more violent characters than gamblers, such as mobster Al Capone, frequented Wrigley Field and Comiskey Park. Even after World War II, gamblers remained a worry, and teams continued to publish their ban on gambling in their scorecards.

Women and Children Free!
Women: A Calming Influence?

Owners hoped women might mitigate rowdiness at the ballpark. As early as 1867, baseball pioneer, Henry Chadwick wrote, "The presence of an assemblage of ladies pacifies the moral atmosphere of a base ball gathering, repressing, as it does, all outbursts of intemperate language which the excitement of a contest so frequently induces."[68] As a *New York Times* writer reported, "Ball players and magnates like to have women at the games. They say women draw more men to the game, and their presence gives color to the ball park."[69] The owners' experiences with encouraging women to attend early in the twentieth century were disappointing, however.

William Wrigley Jr., owner of the Chicago Cubs, renewed efforts to encourage women to attend games both at Wrigley Field in Chicago and at his Los Angeles Minor League park. He revived ladies' days. In the postwar era Bill Veeck would be a staunch proponent of wooing women to the ballpark; as the son of Cubs general manager William Veeck Sr., he had seen the game's popularity with women at first hand. Wrigley went much further than did Veeck Jr., at least with his Minor League team, by allowing women in for free at every Los Angeles home game. When he experimented with ladies' days in Chicago, 30,000 showed up; there were so many that they almost displaced all the paying customers.[70]

Other Minor League owners tried other tactics to draw women. To attract female fans, Al Eckert, owner of the Minor League Springfield team in the Western Association, gave "each society editor in town six passes to present to prominent misses and matrons. Then the society writers told of the costumes they wore and various other bits of descriptions peculiar to society page news. On another night Eckert dressed up the city's beauties in clothes of the 80's and 90's, which also drew a banner audience."[71]

Not all Wrigley's fellow minor-league owners approved of his policy, but, as a *Sporting News* editor wrote, "If a man finds that his best girl knows all about baseball, or wants to know, he will discover a greater need of outdoor air during the baseball season than if he must take Arabella to a movie. . . . If there are clubs in the Pacific Coast League that really think they are losing huge sums of money because the Los Angeles club . . . insists on permitting ladies to come out to visit his ball ground daily without cost, we feel sorry for them."[72] The other Pacific Coast League owners voted to require women to pay regular admission prices, but Wrigley refused to obey. During the Cubs' highly-successful 1929 season, Wrigley inaugurated ladies' days in Chicago, regularly attracting up to ten thousand women. Due to his success, the cross-town White Sox, the St. Louis teams, and Cincinnati quickly followed.[73] The Boston Braves had an even more generous policy, offering half-price tickets for women on Monday through Thursday and free tickets on Fridays. Later the Braves would boast in their postwar scorecards that they had revived ladies' days.[74]

Wrigley's ladies' days reflected the growing independence for women. The original ladies' day policy required women to be escorted by a man. "On Ladies' Day now, women may walk right in and help themselves to unreserved seats, or on payment of the fee enter the reserved section."[75]

Postwar owners wondered whether baseball fans of different races could coexist peacefully in the grandstands. During the 1930s, male fans wondered whether they could coexist peacefully with females at the ball park. Some men were so disgruntled by ladies' days that they voiced their opinions publicly. One wrote a letter to the *New York Times* complaining, "Why is it on Ladies Day that so many of the girls believe that the 10-cent tax they pay, if unaccompanied by a male, entitles them to hold four or five adjoining seats for their tardy friends and relatives? . . . Do not make me feel sorry that I voted and spoke for woman suffrage. Please give us mere men a fair break. If you continue in your unfair actions, I will feel compelled to write to my Congressman to advocate a law to deprive you of your powder puffs and lipsticks, than which I can think of no worse punishment."[76]

Another man complained to the *New York Times* that Ladies Day "is destroying one of man's last sanctuaries.... Some [ladies] even want to know personal habits of the players. What's a man going to do about his ball game." The ladies could produce some disconcerting effects. A war veteran who survived a Japanese banzai charge in the Philippines recalled, "They make the weirdest sound as they rush at you, screaming. It sounds like Ladies' Day at Ebbets Field."[77]

Other men liked having women attend games and expressed their support in the same newspaper. A few urged the Yankees, in particular, to hold ladies' days, but the editor wrote sarcastically, "Possibly the Yankee officials are stanch supporters of Equal Rights. No free day for men; no free day for the ladies."[78]

The Yankees finally scheduled ladies' days on Fridays during the 1938 season, with women paying 25¢ to cover the tax and a service charge. About 5,000 women attended the first ladies' day at Yankee Stadium on April 29, 1938.[79]

The Dodgers occasionally had problems with their ladies' days. One fan complained that the club sometimes rescinded the privilege on Fridays (Brooklyn's day for the ladies) if there was a doubleheader or a special day, thereby disappointing many women. On other occasions the team took advantage of its fellow owners by allowing ladies to upgrade their seats upon payment of an additional fee. Since teams did not have to share receipts paid by women on ladies' days with the visiting club, Larry MacPhail could be accused of breaking the spirit of the gate-sharing rules.[80]

A long-term tactic to boost the gate was to "grow fans." The Chicago teams started admitting children for free to some games during the 1929 season. Children paid 25¢ at other games. Cubs owner P. K. Wrigley maintained his father's policy throughout the Depression, and he urged other owners to do the same. His suggestion initially met with little approval, although the Washington Senators had implemented a similar policy earlier in the year. The St. Louis Cardinals created a "Knothole Gang" for the 1931 season.[81]

A *Sporting News* editor discussed a St. Louis fan's lament concerning the cost of attending a ball game with his two sons. The fan constructed his own casual fan cost index by calculating the cost of attending the game (three tickets at $1.10 each), concessions ($1.80 for the three of them), and parking ($0.25). The fan figured it cost him $5.35 to attend the game. He hoped that owners might set special children's prices, as well as lower concession prices for children. In 2007 dollars the fan's costs would be equivalent to roughly $80, which would be relatively cheap for reserved seats and concessions for an adult and two children in today's market. Charging lower prices for children's concessions probably ran into the problem of keeping an adult from "buying one for my little [fictitious] child," and then consuming it himself, but the editor sympathized with the fan. "The same youngster who has to pay ten or fifteen cents for soda, ice cream, peanuts and hot dogs at the ball park can obtain similar refreshments in the vicinity of most movie shows for five cents."[82]

By the 1935 winter meetings the American League owners voted to admit children under 13 years to all parks for 25¢. Larry MacPhail announced that all boys (no age specified) would be admitted free to all Dodger games. These policies appeared to work fairly well, although the *New York Times* occasionally ran letters by fans urging even more liberal policies for boys.[83]

As a variation on letting boys in at discounted prices, father and son days proved popular, first at San Francisco Seals games and then at Chicago White Sox and Cubs games. The Seals began the promotion in the wake of a newspaper poll commissioned by the club.[84]

The St. Louis clubs discovered that women and children had tastes similar to those of adult males: they wanted to see the home team win. The *Sporting News* wrote, "even boys, girls, and women know their baseball. They'll flock to the ball park when their Cardinals and their Browns are putting out a pennant challenge." According to numbers supplied to the *Sporting News* in the same article, more women than boys were admitted to St. Louis Cardinals games between 1932 and 1940, but boys greatly outnumbered girls. Almost 250,000 women and children attended Cardinals games for free in 1937 but the number barely exceeded 100,000 in 1940. Women, like men, apparently eschewed the Gashouse Gang of 1934; their free passes sank to 68,115, the lowest figure until 1940. The Browns typically admitted fewer than 15,000 women for free per season between 1934 and 1940. Boys outnumbered women, and very few girls bothered to attend Browns games.[85]

More Excitement

A *Sporting News* editorial urged baseball owners to create "color" in their games. The writer cited the Notre Dame football team's continued success in generating large crowds, even in the midst of the Depression. "Color, whether manufactured or otherwise, Notre Dame teams have sport followers talking and, in getting them to talk, the Irish are inducing them to come through the turnstiles."[86] The editor's opinion would give scant comfort to Sam Breadon, whose "Gashouse Gang" club of 1934 was the epitome of color, ranking with the John McGraw/Wilbert Robinson Baltimore Orioles of the 1890s and Oakland A's of the early 1970s as most colorful teams of all time. All three colorful clubs boasted mediocre home attendance, however.

The *Sporting News* editor probably did not mean "color" as in the hue of a player's skin. While a *Sporting News* writer lauded Clark Griffith for having "something of a corner on the Latin talent in the big leagues," not many people were advocating "Negro" participation in Major League baseball, except as paying customers or renters of big league stadiums.[87]

Recurring calls to speed up the games appeared in the periodicals of the era (and other eras, too). National League President John Heydler launched a campaign to eliminate time-killing practices (which were unspecified in the article), while his American League counterpart E. S. Barnard wanted umpires to enforce edicts against delay of game tactics. As the *Sporting News* editor pointed out, eliminating slow spots in games was especially important during doubleheaders, lest "fans be compelled to sit through five hours of listless play."[88]

Finding Out What the Fans Wanted

Owners sometimes commissioned polls to ascertain what their patrons wanted. In 1935 the National League hired four surveyors, three men and one woman, to query people on the streets. The surveyors used two sets of questions, one for people who attended games and one for people who did not attend games. The woman pollster was the only one who asked women questions, in accordance with the mores of the time. The *Sporting News* pointed out that this survey was the first of its kind.[89] One of the key questions of interest was why ladies' days at the Polo Grounds failed to attract a larger number of women. The *Sporting News* also dabbled in polls by asking its subscribers (who certainly were not a representative sample) whether they preferred "prolonged, heavy-hitting, high-scoring games" or "faster, closer, more scientific type of contest." Fans of the latter outvoted the slugfest aficionados.[90]

Cubs owner P. K. Wrigley surveyed Pacific Coast League fans in 1937. He discovered that respondents preferred night ball to day ball, and as a portent of postwar desires, they wanted more automobile parking.[91] Wrigley was unique among owners in considering fan comfort when he thinned the number of chairs in the boxes at Wrigley Field. The *Sporting News* pointed out that boxes at Wrigley Field "have always been very congested, if not with customers, certainly with chairs." As the periodical commented, "most clubs operate on the theory of crowding 'em in somehow, and let 'em worry afterwards."[92]

Ideas Ahead of Their Times: Futuristic Ideas

Flying

Today's teams fly constantly, but eighty years ago commercial passenger flight was still largely an unfulfilled potential. Some baseball officials envisioned a future with flight, however. Cleveland General Manager Billy Evans foresaw air travel and the eventual inclusion of Pacific Coast cities in the Major Leagues. John McGraw of the Giants thought that teams would not only fly from city to city but that teams would buy airplanes, although he went too far in suggesting that teams might operate their own airports or use their fields as landing strips.[93] Thomas J. Hickey, president of the American Association, suggested that the Minor Leagues consider air travel as an economy measure in the face of rising rail fares. A few years later, a Texas League official echoed Hickey's idea: "Transportation of baseball teams by air would not be economical but efficient.... It would eliminate conflicts in the playing schedule and be economical in several ways when you consider the savings on hotel bills and other such expenses."[94]

Larry MacPhail inaugurated Major League air travel by transporting most of his Cincinnati Reds team from Cincinnati to Chicago by airplane in 1934. A few players opted for the more familiar railroad. The Reds reportedly played well the next few days after the flight. In 1936, the Boston Red Sox became the first entire team to fly.[95]

Interleague Games

Baseball introduced interleague games in the 1990s. The idea was not new. Your great-grandfather might have heard baseball officials and writers propose various forms of interleague play. At first, some advocates wanted interleague play to answer a simple question: which league was stronger? Heading into the 1930 season, American League president E. S. Barnard boasted that his circuit was 20 percent stronger.[96] Aside from the nonsensical figure of 20 percent, Barnard undoubtedly raised a question that haunted National League fans, who had seen their champions defeated in the previous three World Series (twelve games to one). Of course, two of these series featured the 1927 Yankees and the 1929 Athletics, two of the strongest collections of players ever. The series did not address whether the American League was stronger from top to bottom. Unlike today's college football where all teams play non-conference games that give a strength-of-conference measure, only the pennant winners played interleague games (apart from meaningless spring training or exhibition games).

After years of Yankee dominance in the 1930s, National League inferiority remained a hot topic. Larry MacPhail suggested a postseason interleague series between teams matched by finish in the standings (second-place teams would play second-place teams and so on, down to eighth-place teams). He suggested the American League was a one-team league and that the National League might be stronger overall, and he hoped his series would settle the issue. Most of his fellow big league officials scorned the idea, with Ed Barrow issuing a terse "No comment," in reply. Whether fans of eighth-place teams would bother to come and see the fulfillment of the boast "our last-place team can lick yours" is a question that Giants owner Charles Stoneham pinpointed with his remark, "Who'd want to watch the [last-place] Browns and Phillies in a series? Would you?"[97] The National League later considered MacPhail's idea, putting it on the agenda for the December 1939 winter meetings, but the American League demurred.[98] He was a wonderful promoter, but his brilliance did not preclude questionable ideas. At least his plan might have demonstrated conclusively whether fans preferred relative quality (closely-contested games) or absolute quality in the visiting team.

The declining attendance of 1932–34 inspired other officials to propose a more general interleague system. William Veeck Sr.'s rationale for interleague games differed from MacPhail's. "It is a fact that from July 5 to the middle of August Major League baseball is in the doldrums. These are the game's 'dog days,' so far as public interest is concerned in a sport that runs for so long—too long if I may express another conviction of mine. What then is more natural than to break up this monotony by scheduling a series of games between clubs of rival leagues?"[99]

Sportswriters Fred Lieb and F. C. Lane suggested interleague play as a way to spice up the pennant races and to attract larger audiences. Both recalled that Garry Herrmann, former chairman of the National Commission, and former Pirates owner Barney Dreyfuss had proposed the tactic years earlier.[100] As proponents of interleague play, an idea that wouldn't die, discovered, synchronicity was lacking: usually one league was for the proposal while the other opposed it. In the 1930s, it was the American League's turn to be "agin' it." Clark Griffith argued, "We are not going in for any hippodrome stuff. The American League is a big league. Our business has held up at least as well as any other. We're going on just the way we are. That's all I've got to say."[101] Although some National League owners openly supported Veeck's idea and the leagues discussed it, nothing became of it.[102]

As the All-Star Game became a fixture and gave baseball fans another opportunity to debate the relative strengths of the two leagues, sportswriters and fans continued to beat a drum in support of the concept. Sportswriter J. W. Sloan wrote: "Why, night ball as an incentive to pull fans into a big league ball park, would be nothing compared to interleague games that count in the standings." Sloan continued by predicting that owners would resist the idea at first, but would eventually come around. Only the first half of his statement was accurate.[103]

Another fan retorted that if interleague play began, each team would have to play every one of the other league's teams an equal number of games, lest "one National League team has to play the Yankees two or three games and another team does not have to play them at all."[104] In the current interleague setup, the prescient fan's fear has become reality. Pity the poor New York Mets, who must play six games each season against the Yankees (but to packed stadiums).

Split Season

Some Minor Leagues hoped to boost the gate by playing split seasons. The Major Leagues' unhappy experiences with the concept during the strike-interrupted 1981 season may have justified their predecessors' disavowal of such gimmicks earlier in the twentieth century. In the words of the *Sporting News*, a split season "is not good. It is not sound baseball. It is like an abridged seven-inning game, which is a fraud."[105]

Promotion and Relegation

Another idea whose time has never come was the thoroughly European idea of promotion and relegation (an idea that excites some sports economists). A fan wrote to the *New York Times* that baseball should consider a practice of the English soccer leagues in which the two bottom-finishing teams were relegated to the next highest league while the two top teams in that league were promoted to the higher league.[106] The National League had struggled for decades (a struggle in which they were later joined by their American League peers) to inculcate the belief that their teams were indisputably the best in the game. The idea that a high Minor League team such as the Newark Bears could reasonably displace the St. Louis Browns or Philadelphia Phillies was undoubtedly distasteful to the big-league owners.

Conclusion

Owners tried several innovations to restore prosperity. Ladies' days became a fixture for decades, although it is difficult to tell whether the promotion actually increased profitability. Certainly more women attended games, but the reduced ticket price meant that revenue from women may have fallen. How many men attended because women came to the ballpark also remains unknown.

Owners were conservative about implementing some changes to the game itself, such as the designated hitter, although they were not shy about tampering with the baseball. Most of the owners, though, were content to improve their ballparks or attempt to field better clubs. They appeared willing to wait grimly for fans to return when the economic conditions improved. Since attendance rebounded after 1934, their faith was confirmed.

12. How Effective Were the Innovations?

Baseball owners tried several innovations to boost attendance. In the case of night ball and radio broadcasts, they initiated innovations well after the trough of the economic downturn. Sunday baseball, while not an innovation, was coveted by the five clubs prohibited from playing at home on Sundays before 1929.

How did owners ascertain whether an innovation was worthwhile? What evidence persuaded them? Owners may have examined attendance or gate receipts before and after initiating a change. Such before and after comparisons were accompanied by changing economic conditions, such as changes in the general price level (deflation or, later, a modest inflation) or in their consumers' incomes, changes in the quality of their team as evidenced by win-loss records or finishes in the standings, and other factors. The simple before and after comparison, then, was just the first step. To disentangle the effects, an owner might have resorted to using statistical analysis, including estimating regression equations. During the 1930s few owners would have known of such techniques or had the computing power to calculate such estimates. Today's owners can use spreadsheets and simple regression software and generate a multitude of estimates. Appendix One contains the regression analysis.

I will present the simple before and after comparisons of various innovations with respect to attendance. Since fans could move around the stadium to different classes of seats, all attendance figures are not created equal.[1] Using gate receipts adjusted for changes in the price level would have been preferable, and the owners certainly had such information. Aside from the Yankees' and Phillies' game-by-game and season gate receipts, we have only home gate receipts, net of federal amusement taxes, and visitors' shares for four selected years.

Sunday Baseball

Eleven teams could play home games on Sunday by 1919. The Pennsylvania teams and the Boston teams could not do so until at least a decade later. Table 35 shows the before and after comparisons in attendance, win-loss record, and real consolidated profit/loss. From a six-year comparison, the Boston teams appear to have benefited from their newfound right to stage home games on Sundays, although both teams showed some on-the-field improvement. On a one-year comparison, the Red Sox showed negligible effect from Sunday ball. Judge Fuchs might well have been pleased with the new law, as the Braves' attendance rose substantially (in Braves terms, at least). His club even turned a profit the first two years with Sunday ball. If the judge had truly spent $250,000 to persuade Boston politicians to support him, the payback period might have taken several seasons, as attendance faltered in later seasons.

Sunday ball probably came too late for Connie Mack and his Athletics. The team, already reeling from the loss of several key players, fell below .500 for the first time in several seasons. Sunday ball may have cushioned any decrease in weekday and Saturday attendance, as the team actually increased its attendance by almost 3 percent in 1934. Unfortunately the increased attendance could not stave off a staggering loss of almost $175,000. The Phillies saw modest improvements in attendance and real profits in 1934 compared with 1935, while the Pirates may have fared best of the Pennsylvania teams with respect to Sunday ball. For both Philadelphia teams, the three-year comparisons were discouraging, although Sunday ball may have prevented even worse outcomes.

In all of these cases Sunday ball hardly proved a boon, and even staunch advocate Judge Fuchs eventually had to sell his team after repeated financial embarrassments. As a saving grace, Sunday ball was of dubious value to weak teams. Mack might have gotten more benefit from it had he received such permission in 1929 instead of 1934.

Radio Broadcasts

The Cubs had broadcast their home games since the mid-1920s. Other teams also began doing so, although they occasionally stopped their broadcasts. By 1934 only six teams broadcast their home games, as the two St. Louis teams pulled the plug on broadcasts for the 1934 season. The next season, however, thirteen clubs broadcast their home or road games, including the St. Louis teams whose owners had reconsidered their previous decision.[2] In effect, almost one-third of the Major League teams were conducting an experiment in the broadcasting of home games. Table 36 provides the necessary information for a before and after comparison. The Athletics had the largest change in win-loss record. Connie Mack could not be certain whether his team's growing ineptitude or radio was to blame for the shrinking fan interest in his club. At least he saw significant improvement in his real consolidated profit/loss, but his relatively small loss in 1935 might have been attributed in part to selling some of his remaining star players. The five teams collectively had slightly greater attendance and transformed collective losses into profits in 1935.[3]

The eleven teams that maintained the status quo on radio had experiences similar to those of the teams that began (or reinstated) radio broadcasts in 1935. As table 36 shows, both sets of teams had increases in attendance, although the five teams initiating home broadcasts had a larger percentage increase than teams that refused radio (including Pittsburgh and Washington). Both groups had improved consolidated profit/loss figures in 1935. These results, of course, may be the effects of improvement in the general economy. The simple comparison fails to yield any definitive answer as to the effects of broadcasts of home games.[4] I will later combine all of the innovations in equations spanning the period between 1929 and 1941.

Teams started to collect revenue from radio stations. In 1933 only four teams received any revenue from radio, a combined $18,000; by 1939, every one of the sixteen Major League teams received at least $27,500 from radio. The total radio revenue for Major League Baseball approached $900,000 in 1939.[5] Attendance at big league games was almost three million more in 1939 than in 1933.

Night Baseball

Perhaps Larry MacPhail had to conjure his night baseball success twice to convince wary owners. MacPhail was a rare combination of visionary and competent promoter. In the cases of Sunday ball and radio, an owner did not have to invest any capital (except, perhaps, as a means of persuading recalcitrant local politicians), but night ball required capital. As table 37 shows, MacPhail's gift for promotion and good fortune with regard to weather demonstrated the potential of night ball. He also proved night ball to be a tool for boosting the gate over many seasons, thereby encouraging owners to invest capital in order to capture the long-run benefits, and he showed night ball's appeal to fans in both small and large cities (Cincinnati and Brooklyn). Night ball's long-term effects are perhaps magnified in the simple before and after comparisons due to the two teams' improvement on the field.

The simple before and after comparisons show that night ball was not a success everywhere and at every time. The next four teams to use lights had mixed experiences. The White Sox saw a large gain in attendance, but they also fielded a much stronger team in their first season with night ball. Cleveland had a lagged effect, with attendance and real profits falling in their first year with the lights. The Phillies might have had a burst of success, but they and the Athletics had reason to be disappointed in night ball. According to the Phillies' financial records, the team had 62,411 in paid attendance for its seven night games in 1939.[6] The remaining games attracted 215,901. The night games averaged almost 7,000 fans, while the remaining playing dates struggled to attract more than 4,000 on average. The night game attendance boost was accompanied by an increase in the purchase of more expensive seats. The team sold fewer than 12,000 box seats during the season, but over half of these were for the night games. The percent of bleacher seats sold was 26.5 percent for day games and just 20.0 percent for night games. The team got 96.6¢ per paid attendee for night games and 91.9¢ for day games. Whether other teams got similar effects from night games is not known.

Because owners had an initial start-up cost for installing lights, the way in which they expensed the cost is important in analyzing night ball's effects upon profits. The drop in Cleveland's profits mentioned above may have been an example. Under modern accounting practices, the cost of installing a lighting system would be amortized (spread out) across several years, as an owner was not using it up immediately. It is not clear whether owners in the 1930s amortized the cost of their new systems. Certainly the sportswriters acted as though the cost would be applied solely to the present season's profit/loss statement. If owners did not amortize the cost, then a drop in profits the first year lights were used would be misleading.

The next group of teams to light up, in 1940, also had varying results. The Browns' attendance more than doubled in 1940, giving credence to Donald Barnes's plea for more night games. Concurrent with the doubling of attendance (admittedly from a very small base—109,000 in 1939), the Browns moved from the pathetic to the mediocre by winning twenty-four more games. The hoopla evaporated in 1941 as attendance decreased by over one-fourth despite a slight improvement in win-loss record. The Senators, Giants, and Pirates probably felt bemused by their night ball efforts, and Horace Stoneham was publicly disappointed.

Clark Griffith had vacillated on night ball for years. When he finally took the plunge in 1941, he could have been disillusioned by the modest increase in attendance, despite a somewhat improved record. He reported a negative swing of $80,000 in profitability (possibly because he might have "expensed" the entire cost in 1941), yet he became a chief advocate of raising the limit on the number of night games. With the influx of government workers during the war, perhaps he felt the times were propitious for his club.

Conclusion

The available evidence shows that owners faced uncertain outcomes with regard to Sunday and night games and broadcasting home games. The owners, of course, had more data to form their conclusions, so perhaps the best gauge of the costs and benefits of these innovations was that none of the owners stopped using lights or petitioned for fewer Sunday games. The Yankees, Cardinals, and Browns did, on occasion, halt broadcasts of their home games. During the 1950s some owners initially chose to telecast home games, but they later stopped doing so. For franchises in smaller markets, aside from Cincinnati, these innovations were not sufficient to transform them into contenders or make them highly profitable: Mack and Griffith could not restore their franchises to their former glory, while Barnes desperately sought a way out of St. Louis.

13. The Inept and the Restless
Franchise Relocation

Major League baseball's lineup of teams had remained stable and had been limited to the northeast quadrant of the continental United States since 1903. The populations of the ten cities with Major League Baseball, however, had changed both absolutely and relatively. The economic downturn of the 1930s further revealed the inability of some of the cities with two teams to sustain both clubs. St. Louis, Philadelphia, and Boston were declining in population relative to New York and Chicago. Detroit was growing rapidly. With Minor League teams and entire leagues folding in 1931 and 1932, observers called for the consolidation of teams and the relocation of teams in geographically sensible leagues.[1] The Major Leagues were not immune to such suggestions.

The *Sporting News* editorial page began hinting that some Major League franchises might move to other cities. An editorial examined the existing rules pertaining to relocation, mindful that no relocations had occurred since the American League's Baltimore team moved to New York and became the Yankees (after being the Highlanders for a while). An owner could move his franchise if he could convince a supermajority of his fellow owners to approve the move and if he could offer sufficient payment for invading someone's Minor League territory. At the winter meetings in December 1939 both leagues made the rules covering relocation more restrictive by requiring a unanimous vote in favor. At the same meetings some owners tried to establish a fixed $100,000 compensation for any Minor League team whose territory was invaded, but the plan failed.[2]

Because of travel expenses and other matters, league constitutions always contained a section governing such movement. An owner could not transfer a franchise unilaterally. As law professor Jeffrey Glick pointed out, an owner trying to move his franchise to (for example) San Francisco during the 1930s would have increased transportation costs for all of the teams.[3] Therefore the other owners had an interest in any proposed franchise relocation.

Fans, too, recognized that it was futile for the three smaller two-team cities to continue their efforts to support six ball clubs. One fan suggested moving the Cardinals to Detroit and the Athletics to Brooklyn, while another touted Baltimore, then the eighth-largest city in the country, as a better home for the Phillies or Athletics. The interesting thing about the latter letter was its author: William Shea of Jackson Heights, Long Island.[4] Two decades later a William Shea would be at the center of New York's efforts to get a National League team to replace the dearly departed Brooklyn Dodgers and New York Giants. Whether this was the same William Shea is unknown to this author. Arguing in a different vein, another fan wondered why the owners did not expand and make the Major Leagues truly a national pastime.[5]

There were some attractive sites. Some Los Angeles investors decided to entice the Major League owners into relocating to their burgeoning city. According to the *New York Times*, a group of them offered $5 million for a Major League franchise, specifically targeting the Browns, Phillies, and Braves. A spokesman for the group said that the airline industry had advanced sufficiently to alleviate any worries about transportation, although Harridge disputed the feasibility of air travel. While Donald Barnes said his team was not for sale, he did admit that, "for $5,000,000 I could do a lot of listening."[6]

Candidates for New Homes

A reader might think owning a downtrodden club such as the Braves or the Browns was a dreary prospect. One of the property rights embedded in owning a sad-sack franchise was the potential of moving to a better venue (if you could convince your fellow owners). Buying the Browns on the cheap and then moving the team to Los Angeles or San Francisco might have been extremely lucrative. Which teams were candidates for relocation?

Philadelphia Phillies

The National League had two teams in extremis: Philadelphia and Boston. The Philadelphia Phillies were threatening to become permanent occupants of the league's basement. Between 1936 and 1945 the Phillies finished last eight times, an exceptional number even for a club for which finishing last was not a novel experience.

Gerald Nugent survived the depression by selling many of his best players and by getting a loan from the National League. At the winter meetings in late 1941, National League president Ford Frick denied that the league had loaned the beleaguered club additional funds; "the league last summer offered to lend the Phils some money to operate in deals at the World Series draft meeting, but Gerry Nugent never took up the offer." He also denied stories that the league had threatened foreclosure on its previous loan to the Phillies.[7] By 1941, despite the team's terrible record, there was no shortage of alleged suitors for the team, including such worthies as Branch Rickey. As a reporter joked, "Everyone has been mentioned as a potential buyer, except Joseph Stalin, and you must admit that he has troubles of his own."[8] John B. Kelly was a more serious potential buyer. He claimed his group was willing to assume the club's obligation to pay $20,000 a year rental for the Baker Bowl, even though the team now played in Shibe Park. Nugent had agreed to make five $20,000 payments in order to break a ninety-nine year lease on the Baker Bowl. Kelly's reputed $500,000 bid for the club failed. It was later reported as $750,000.[9]

The team even became the butt of a fan's letter to the *New York Times*. The fan wrote that a buddy of his traveled to Philadelphia on business and decided to attend a Dodgers-Phillies game at Shibe Park.

The buddy discovered that a general admission ticket cost $1.14 instead of the $1.10 he usually paid in Brooklyn. He examined the ticket and found that the city of Philadelphia assessed an extra 4¢ for an amusement tax. He quipped, "I didn't know the Phillies were that amusing."[10]

The Phillies continued to stagger. After the 1942 season National League owners sought new ownership for the team. Nugent sang his usual song of woe that he'd have to sell his "three aces"—Rube Melton, Danny Litwhiler, and Tommy Hughes—if his finances did not improve. The reader may note that "aces" were not the same in all Major League cities. In one intriguing scenario, the Phillies might have become the first twentieth-century Major League club to integrate . . . en masse. Bill Veeck Jr. claimed (and other sources accepted the story), that he had a group of buyers ready. If they gained control Veeck planned to hire a group of Negro League stars. Veeck claims that he made the mistake of sharing his intention with Judge Landis, an avowed racist, and the commissioner quickly nixed the plan. The National League took over the team.[11] How the baseball world would have reacted is interesting to contemplate. At the time, however, reporters simply stated that rumors circulated to the effect that Veeck was interested in buying. One reporter joked, "Veeck stopped in to see me on his way to the World's Series and did not mention buying or even being interested in the club. When he got back home I saw a clipping from a Milwaukee paper that quoted Veeck as saying he had stopped in to see me because he had read that he was interested in buying the club—and he wanted to see what it was all about."[12] Some researchers believe Veeck was grandstanding.[13]

In the end the National League bought 4,685 of the team's 5,000 shares, paying $10 a share and, presumably, absorbing the previous loans.[14] Ford Frick eventually induced William Cox to purchase the team. Branch Rickey enthused to the prospective buyers that the Phillies, at $230,000 in cash, represented "the most alluring buy in the history of the Major Leagues." He admitted that, "You will lose around $100,000 the first year. You will lose $100,000 the second season. But once you get around the corner, you will be able to build this club on profits... I'd rather buy the Phillies than the Yankees, any day."[15] Cox had sufficient wealth to stop the player sales, but he also had a penchant for betting on the team. Landis blacklisted the wayward owner. The team's fortunes changed for the better when Robert Carpenter Sr. bought the team, allegedly so his son Robert Jr. would have something to do. Oh, the travails of the young and wealthy! Robert Jr. hired Herb Pennock and poured money into a farm system. Phillies fans were rewarded for thirty-five years of waiting for a second pennant when the Whiz Kids won the 1950 National League title.[16]

Boston Braves

The Boston Braves struggled during Judge Emil Fuchs's ownership. At times Braves fans may have felt their team was literally going to the dogs. The franchise had won just one National League pennant since 1903, and that club was dubbed the "Miracle Braves." While the club never quite sank to the level of the Philadelphia Phillies, a not-so-genteel mediocrity was its fate. The team played .500 or better ball between 1932 and 1934, but then it collapsed. Despite a winning record in 1934, the team lost $44,000. Fuchs claimed that the club had made money during a recent three-year period but that it had expended the profits in purchasing new players, most of whom proved disappointing.[17]

Trouble began when the team surrendered its long-term lease to the newly-formed Boston Kennel Club, which planned to stage dog races at Braves Field. Since few people ventured to dog races merely to see which dog was the fastest, the prevalence of gambling troubled organized baseball. The logical solution was for the Braves to lease Fenway Park, but Red Sox owner Tom Yawkey refused to lease his stadium, given the circumstances surrounding the Braves' departure from Braves Field. Eventually the National League itself signed an eleven-year lease on Braves Field, thereby preventing the kennel club from using Braves Field for its races. The league guaranteed payment of the annual rent, although the Braves were supposed to pay the rent.[18]

The team's stadium trouble was just one symptom of the financial weakness demonstrated by Judge Fuchs and his co-owners. The First National Bank of Boston held outstanding loans made to the Braves and wanted to divest its interests in the club. The National League also promised to help the team financially. Fuchs needed $50,000 to keep the club going through spring training. The team sold $43,400 worth of tickets by early February, giving it enough cash to begin the season. Fuchs revealed that the club's cash woes could have been alleviated, if only briefly, had he sold the team's best players, Dutch Brandt and Wally Berger.[19]

At least Fuchs was imaginative and daring. He decided that getting Babe Ruth for one season would jump-start the lethargic crowds at Braves Field. Because Ruth aspired to manager Joe McCarthy's job, Jacob Ruppert was happy to let him go to Boston. National League president Ford Frick was enthusiastic about Ruth's National League debut, and he gushed that "Ruth will draw a half million additional fans through National League turnstiles." Teams in the league were planning gala receptions for the slugger's first visit to each city. At first Fuchs's experiment worked, as Ruth pulled in thousands of extra patrons for exhibition games. One club official said the Babe's popularity might account for enough extra attendees to cover his $25,000 salary as well as paying the team's training expenses.[20] Alas! Ruth's legs were shot, and though he could still belt home runs, he was a liability on the field. (Perhaps Fuchs should have pressed for Heydler's designated hitter proposal.) He quit in May, before all of the National League teams could honor him with gala celebrations. According to club stockholder Charles Adams, the club was actually showing a profit through July 1, thanks largely to Ruth's drawing power.[21]

The Braves endured a collapse of historic proportions in 1935. The team retained most of its key personnel from 1934, when it had won 78 games. Somehow these players lost their prowess, as the club won 40 fewer games in 1935, finishing 38-115. Modern teams would have jettisoned stars Wally Berger and Dutch Brandt by midseason, but Fuchs refused to sell them to the Dodgers, saying, "When I leave Boston I want to leave a club with some good players still on the payroll." The *Sporting News* thought his statement indicated his intention to divest himself of the team. A reporter stated that the team currently did not owe any money to the National League and had only one note outstanding (for more than $100,000), so Fuchs was in a good position to sell.[22] Charles F. Adams, who had financial interests in the team, was ambivalent about Fuchs's efforts to sell the club. He was tired of the chronic turmoil and even offered his shares of stock to the National League, but eventually he acquired Fuchs's shares and became a majority owner. Readers should not shed any tears for the judge, who had enlisted Adams to bail out the club years before. Some observers thought the judge had only invested $35,000 of his own money while withdrawing $300,000 in salary and expenses![23] If this is true, there should be a place in a Hall of Fame for such financial wizardry. Adams offered all the shares at $30 each, but any prospective buyer would have to assume a $200,000 note held by a bank.

Adams tried to get the remaining stockholders to invest more in the club, but by November the National League stepped in and declared the franchise forfeited to the league (shades of the Montreal Expos). Ford Frick announced that the owners' decision was based upon the Braves' failure to fulfill contractual obligations. The Braves' debts amounted to $325,000.[24] The *New York Times* expressed surprise that the Braves floundered so badly, claiming that Boston was one of the three best baseball cities: "Only the mildest sort of pennant threat is sufficient to toss the city into a baseball frenzy."[25]

For some reason, several parties were reputed to be interesting in buying the Braves/Bees. At times reporters identified former Giants standout Bill Terry and Larry MacPhail as potential buyers. For a few days Albert Powell, a retired coal dealer, negotiated with Adams, but nothing came of this. Frick later reassured stockholders and Braves fans that the team would continue to play and that whatever residual funds remained after the liquidation of debts would be disbursed to stockholders. Robert Quinn eventually formed a group to buy out Adams's shares.[26] Manager Casey Stengel was part of the syndicate that Quinn put together. The most important member, though, was Lou Perini, who would eventually own the team with two other construction-industry entrepreneurs. Perini's group became the first to succeed in persuading the other owners to countenance transferring a franchise to another city. They moved the team to Milwaukee in 1953. Quinn reorganized the club in December by agreeing to take care of the $325,000 debt and to put in enough capital to restore the team.[27] The other National League owners were undoubtedly relieved that the team's finances were stabilized, if only temporarily. One of Quinn's first acts was to bestow a new nickname upon the team: the Bees. At least the new nickname was economical in terms of letters.

The (Dis)Spirit of St. Louis

By now the reader is familiar with the woes of the St. Louis Browns. The Cardinals also failed to attract large crowds during the 1930s. Cardinals owner Sam Breadon addressed rumors that the club was thinking of moving to Detroit and leasing the Tigers' stadium. At first he admitted he would move the club if Tigers owner Frank Navin would agree, but he quickly changed his story and denied that the club had discussed any such transfer: "The Cardinal franchise is in no danger of being moved to Detroit."[28] Since the Cardinals had just defeated the Tigers in a hotly-contested World Series, the idea of their moving in as tenants was quite bizarre. Then again, the Cardinals remained profitable primarily by selling surplus players and not because of lucrative gate receipts. The *Sporting News* editorial page found the rumors credible, especially since many observers felt that St. Louis could no longer support two teams. Because the Cardinals were tenants at Sportsman's Park, most observers figured they were the likely candidates for relocation. A few months later, though, rumors surfaced that the Browns might be transferred to an unnamed location.[29]

A more outlandish rumor arose in early 1936. The *Sporting News* discussed a proposed switch of the Cardinals and the Brooklyn Dodgers. It would have been natural for Breadon to prefer Brooklyn's drawing power, though the attraction to the Dodgers was left unstated. The editorial admitted that the rumor started as a jest but that there was a serious undercurrent. Breadon remained dissatisfied with fan support in St. Louis.[30] Neither the Browns or Cardinals left St. Louis during the Depression, but owners of both teams admitted during the war that St. Louis was a one-team city. Barnes stated, "St. Louis simply can't support two Major League clubs, and there isn't any use kidding yourself otherwise. The increased night games should help us, but will not entirely solve our situation."[31]

The Perils of the Browns

There cannot be very many St. Louis Browns fans left. It has been over fifty years since the club moved to Baltimore and became the Orioles. Their half century in St. Louis was marked by futility. The club's closest pennant race before World War II, in 1922, ended on a controversial note when a Browns fan tossed a bottle at Yankees outfielder Whitey Witt, knocking him unconscious and unsettling the Browns players.[32]

During the 1920s and early 1930s Philip Ball owned the club. He claimed publicly to have lost money almost every season, but he had enough capital to absorb any such losses (and in reality he did not suffer the losses he claimed). Once Ball died, the team's precarious finances made its existence resemble a movie serial with frequent cliffhangers. Every season American League fans and owners wondered whether the club could hang on. Even before Ball died in October 1933, rumors circulated that he would relocate the team; there were more such rumors after his death. This time an exotic element was added, as some of the rumors suggested the club would move to Canada. American League president William Harridge stated that the club would not move.[33]

Ball's heirs sought buyers for the club. The *New York Times* estimated that the heirs were seeking $400,000 for the franchise, but the *Sporting News* cited a lower figure of $300,000. Club officials denied the

$400,000 price, which was based on the par value of the club's stock. The officials admitted they had no offers at that point. Meanwhile the club needed cash for the upcoming 1934 season, but a fortuitous probate court ruling freed up $276,000. Ball had borrowed money from the club two years previously. The club officials remained optimistic well into 1935, even turning down an offer of $325,000.[34]

While club officials continued to profess optimism, the club's continued woes at the gate prompted fellow American League owners to pressure them to sell out. Detroit played two games with the Browns and found their visitor's share amounted to less than $250, which did not cover the expenses of visiting St. Louis. The Browns drew fewer than 100,000 patrons at home, but did reasonably well on the road, thereby earning a small profit. After the 1935 season club officials still waxed enthusiastic, although they admitted the team could not afford to bid for established stars and would continue to depend upon young players.[35]

Another group of potential investors hoped to scrape together $325,000, but the club officials now wanted $375,000. The $325,000 would buy the franchise's San Antonio Minor League team but not Sportsman's Park, which the group would lease for $35,000 per year. The parties failed to consummate a deal. The team struggled to draw even 5,000 for afternoon games. At one point, after fifty-two home games, the club had attracted only 76,000 paying customers.[36]

Enter Donald Barnes. Barnes was the president of a St. Louis investment company. This time Ball's estate asked for about $350,000 for the club. The parties delayed completing the deal when Barnes and his associates balked at paying $35,000 rental on Sportsman's Park. He had examined the attendance figures for 1935 and 1936 and discovered that fewer than 200,000 paying fans attended games in those two years combined. The estate eventually agreed to reduce the yearly rent, and Barnes took over the club. Barnes had put together enough capital to buy the franchise, but his group had scant capital left to improve it. Almost immediately, Harridge had to deny reports that the new owners asked the American League to "dig into its surplus fund to assist in financing the Browns."[37]

An interesting facet of the sale was Branch Rickey's involvement. Rickey acted as an intermediary bringing Barnes and the Ball estate together. He may also have wanted to help William DeWitt, who became the Browns' general manager. In any event, the Ball estate reportedly paid Rickey $25,000 for his services.[38]

Barnes still needed to gain the assent of the other American League owners. In his argument seeking approval for his purchase, he stated that the Cardinals wanted night ball, so the Browns needed permission to stage night games, lest the Cardinals corner even more of the St. Louis market.[39]

Seeking new capital, Barnes invited St. Louis fans to invest in the club, thereby making them "feel that the Browns belonged to them, as well as to the men who were furnishing the bulk of the financial backing." He was aggressive in seeking new players; since he lacked large sums of money, he failed to obtain stars. William DeWitt pointed out that Tom Yawkey of the Red Sox had spent hundreds of thousands of dollars on star players but had failed to win a pennant. DeWitt asked Browns fans to be patient as the team developed a farm system capable of producing quality players.[40]

The club reported a loss of $75,000 for 1937, although Barnes claimed that some of this loss was actually an investment in their farm system. He stated that had the team sold Beau Bell and Harlond Clift, two of their better players, it could have reported a profit for the year. His summary: "The club is in good financial condition. There is no discord among the directors over the 1937 deficit."[41] The era of good feeling was drawing to a close, however.

The Browns lost money again in 1938, but Barnes again attributed this to the farm club losses. "We can't write off farm club losses as actual deficits, if these clubs produce players who will fit into the Brownie picture. If we had to go out and buy players, they would cost us big money."[42] There was an air of unreality in Barnes's statements to the press. Given that the club's attendance was just 132,000 in 1938, his continued optimism seems misplaced: "We all are solidly in the Browns to bring out a successful and interesting team that will attract fans to Sportsman's Park."[43]

The St. Louis fans did not share Barnes's enthusiasm. While the early attendance in 1939 ran slightly ahead of the 1938 pace, a sportswriter wrote a pessimistic article on the club. "The game [between the Athletics and Browns with 487 in attendance] came as close to being a private performance as one would care to see in a big league park. Some wag said that it was so quiet at Sportsman's Park that day that you could hear the curves of the pitchers bend." The writer also mentioned that the Cardinals had not drawn particularly well, even though the team was popular with people across the border in Illinois. He pointed out that Barnes and Breadon could not agree on financing a lighting system that might boost attendance at a risk of $150,000 in scarce capital.[44]

In June 1939 the stockholders of the Browns agreed to ante up another $100,000 in capital. The club's ten directors each put up $5,000, while Barnes provided the remaining $50,000. The American League may have been involved, too, as it allegedly guaranteed the return of the $100,000 out of its common fund if the team failed to reach a certain attendance level. After a delay, Barnes purchased an outfielder, Joe Gallagher, from the Yankees' Minor League system. At first the Yankees refused to sell the youngster. Other American League owners, seeing the Yankees running away with a fourth straight pennant, bemoaned that club's surfeit of talent in the Minor Leagues. The Cleveland Indians, in particular, were still aggrieved at the Yankees' signing of Tommy Henrich in 1937. The Browns wanted to sign the free agent (freed from Cleveland's farm system due to violations of the major-minor agreement), but the Yankees swooped in and offered more money.[45]

Gallagher was no miracle worker. The Browns continued to flounder, losing 111 games. Some members of the team's board of directors were beginning to get impatient, and two of them withdrew from the board. Breadon of the Cardinals wasn't feeling much better, as he had declared during the season that St. Louis wasn't, to use a western movie cliché, big enough for the two of them and that "either the Browns will have to get out, or arrangements must be made to move the Cards."[46] Barnes managed to contain the insurrection, but Breadon continued to hope that he would be allowed to relocate. Detroit surfaced again as a likely destination, with sportswriter James Gould stating on good source that Navin might countenance such a situation if Breadon would sell out to Detroit investors. Breadon, of course, had no intention of selling his team.[47]

Whether or not the American League loaned the Browns money, it was not passive. Harridge persuaded the other owners to help the Browns but in ways that would not smack of syndicating. Clark Griffith of the Senators was not sympathetic to the Browns, as he was having difficulties of his own. The wealthier teams in the league, however, recognized that it might be in their own interests to offer the Browns some discreet help, as increased crowds at Sportsman's Park would generate visitors' shares that would cover transportation and lodging costs. The Yankees sold Walt Judnich to the Browns at a bargain price of $12,000, although both clubs denied that the deal was a relief effort. The Detroit Tigers also sent pitcher George "Slick" Coffman to the Browns in a trade.[48] The Red Sox sent pitcher Eldon Auker to the Browns. The league also granted the Browns additional night games in 1940.[49] Night games attracted large crowds, at least by Browns standards. To further bolster the team, other American League rivals offered the Browns some players at $7,500 each. The Browns purchased one from the Yankees and one from the Tigers: Myril Hoag and Chet Laabs. The various transactions helped the team win 24 more games in 1940. These sales were not mere charity. Since the Browns were so inept, they tended to kill the gate at the other parks. It would take the combined efforts of the Germans, Italians, and Japanese to make the Browns' win-loss records respectable, as the World War II–inspired military draft of talented Yankees, Tigers, Indians, and Red Sox players strengthened the Browns in a relative, if not in an absolute, sense.

Even with these sops, Barnes had to deny stories that he and his fellow American League owners were trying to move the Browns to some more viable city. Concurrent with the stories about a Browns transfer, Sam Breadon cast a roving eye upon his Minor League franchise in Columbus, Ohio. He owned both the ball club and the stadium in that city. The eight-year-old stadium had a lighting plant and seated 17,500. Columbus would have been the smallest city in the Major Leagues with just more than 300,000 residents. Because Barnes was hesitant to install lights at Sportsman's Park, Breadon was becoming frustrated with the situation in St. Louis. The difficulty in moving his Major League franchise to Columbus was the question of how to placate the American Association Minor League for the invasion of its territory. The problem of territorial rights loomed large in discussions of any potential relocations. All the cities capable of supporting a Major League team had an existing Minor League club. American League president William Harridge tried to quell talk of an impending transfer. He stated that the compensation to Minor League interests and other expenses would probably amount to more than $1 million and there would be no guarantee that the prospects would be greener in another stadium than they had been in the original stadium.[50]

Unfortunately the rebound in the Browns' fortunes evaporated, although the team won three more games in 1941 than in 1940. Attendance fell off again as the novelty of night ball wore off. While sports economists may argue that fans prefer tightly contested games, which they dub "relative quality," they would have found few adherents in St. Louis. Certainly St. Louis fans disdained games between the Browns and Athletics or Senators; fewer than 500 would show up for some of these lackluster contests. The Yankees were the best draws for the Browns. The club's weakness extended to its Minor League franchise, as San Antonio was hard-pressed to draw 50,000. Observers anticipated that the club would lose over $75,000 in 1941.[51]

By season's end Barnes and his beleaguered stockholders were desperate. He pleaded with his fellow owners for permission to continue playing more night games, even though he knew the games would not be a panacea. The Browns' night games did in fact attract more fans than their weekday afternoon games, but the average attendance at them was less than 7,000, a figure a reporter attributed partly to bad weather. The league did not permit the team to have fourteen night games, as they had done in 1940. The Browns requested a financial bailout from the league, claiming to have lost hundreds of thousands of dollars over five years. The club might have raised some capital by selling its top players, and the Yankees were interested in first baseman George McQuinn, but Barnes and the stockholders knew that such short-term palliatives would only delay the disastrous financial denouement: no quality players, no sizable crowds.[52]

Barnes wanted to move the team from St. Louis to Los Angeles after the 1941 season. Since Mondays were frequently off days, teams playing in Chicago could take a train such as the *Zephyr* across the country after a Sunday game and be able to play on a Tuesday without scrambling the schedules. He thought that other clubs might have to fly only once or twice during the season. The Japanese attack on Pearl Harbor and his fellow owners' reluctance thwarted him. His fellow owners weren't ready for such a radical departure, war or no war, although they thought the idea might be feasible after the war.[53]

The Browns later wanted to move to Detroit and share the Tigers' stadium, but that team's ownership wanted no such thing. The Browns' financial woes continued after Pearl Harbor. Barnes told stockholders that the team "had no working capital for 1942," and that he was looking for loans from directors and banks. Barnes dismissed the team's four full-time scouts and its publicity man. While DeWitt was buying shares of the club for as little as $2.00 per share (the shares originally cost $5), Barnes was hoping to persuade directors and banks to loan the club additional funds. According to attendance figures, the Browns played before 176,000 at home and 486,000 on the road during 1941. These figures were lower than those of 1940, which saw numbers of 240,000 at home and 577,000 on the road. Barnes hoped to force the league either to loan the team another $100,000 or to grant it fourteen night games.[54]

Because of the war and the President Roosevelt's insistence that baseball was good for morale, the owners finally decided to increase the number of night games. The increased limit was good news for Barnes. The league also agreed to loan the club additional funds. Barnes also succeeded in finding investors for a new issue of stock in the club, which may have been his most impressive feat. In any event, the Browns would "go into the 1942 American League season debt-free and with a surplus of working capital."[55] Just as the war reduced the disparity between incomes of Americans, it also denuded the playing rosters of stronger teams over time; in 1944, the Browns actually won a pennant and appeared in their only World Series. For Barnes and Browns fans, it was indeed an ill war that bred some good. After the war the Browns reverted to their precarious existence.

Barnes was nothing if not persistent. As early as October 1942 an item in the *Sporting News* noted, "Don't be surprised if Don Barnes takes another shot at transferring his franchise to Los Angeles."[56]

Conclusion

Although economic conditions had improved by 1941, some Major League Baseball teams were struggling to remain solvent. The Browns, Athletics, and Senators received loans from the American League during 1940, while the Phillies and Braves continued to pay interest on their outstanding loans to the National League.[57]

The rumors and loans swirling around woebegone franchises during the 1930s and early 1940s presaged the tumultuous 1950s, when the Braves, Browns, and Athletics relocated. Later in that decade, the Dodgers, Giants, and Senators would move from the East Coast to Midwest and West Coast locations. Although all found improved attendance, at least in the short run, the National League transfers were far more successful than those of their American League peers. Had World War II not intervened, Barnes might well have received his wish and moved to Los Angeles.

Epilogue
The End of an Era

I end with Donald Barnes' dramatic bid to relocate his team to Los Angeles. Although the Japanese attack on Pearl Harbor may not have been the sole reason he was unable to effect the relocation, the attack began another round of upheaval for Major League Baseball. Uncle Sam drafted many big-name stars, including Hank Greenberg, Ted Williams, Bob Feller, and Joe DiMaggio. Travel restrictions affected playing schedules. Fans were preoccupied by more serious matters, and, of course, having millions of young men serving around the world at military bases shrank the game's fan base (although this may have been partially offset by the increased number of workers with money in their pockets at industrial plants). President Roosevelt supported baseball, so the owners did not have to shut down for the duration. Baseball's first two wartime summers were not particularly profitable ones, but as the Allies became paramount, profits rose and presaged the stunning 1946–49 boom.

For the owners, having the crowds return even though the talent level was diluted meant increasing revenues against stagnant or even falling payrolls. After the war, team payrolls would comprise a significantly smaller proportion of either total revenue or total expenses.

In the absence of the war, one can imagine that television would have developed years ahead of its postwar boom. The owners quickly embraced the new technology during the late 1940s, but it is an open question whether they would have done so in the early 1940s when controversy concerning radio broadcasts' effects upon the gate lingered. The war accelerated the trend towards more night baseball. Had the war not occurred, the 1940s might have shown many of the developments that occurred in the 1950s.

The war may have proved an accelerant in one case. The war forced Caucasian Americans to reexamine their attitudes towards African Americans. Whether this reexamination was a necessary precursor for integration remains an unanswered question.

Barnes's bold bid to relocate his franchise, whether inspired by desperation or vision, tickles the imagination. If the Browns had approximated the success of the Dodgers' later move, would the franchise have become one of the "haves" in the American League? With sufficient funding, would Barnes have been able to compete against the Yankees, Red Sox, and Tigers? It is ironic that later owners of the Browns succeeded in moving the team to Baltimore, which, while not as lucrative as Los Angeles, afforded sufficient support to build the league's next dominant team after the Yankees went through a decade-long funk. While I come not to shed tears for Barnes, his proposal remains an intriguing "might have been" of baseball history.

On the other end of the baseball spectrum, the Yankees' management faced difficult decisions in responding to the economic downturn of the early 1930s, although the team's viability was never threatened. Ruppert and Barrow proved cautious with regard to lowering ticket prices, cutting player salaries, or implementing innovations to bolster the gate. Ruppert made a belated response to the (temporarily) increased demand for bleacher seats and ladies' days. However, he rejected broadcasting games on the radio and night baseball. The team later adapted both of these tactics. One could paraphrase Isaac Newton's law and claim that Ruppert tended to remain at rest, even when disturbed by a Depression. His main response was to improve and increase the bleacher section at Yankee Stadium, and, ironically, he did so just as the cheap seats began receding in popularity. There is little evidence to suggest that he exercised superior management skills in operating the Yankees, despite the team's return to profitability in the later years of the Great Depression. He seems to have relied upon the fans' support of a championship team to restore attendance and profits. Barrow's acumen in signing promising players, such as Joe DiMaggio, restored the team's success on the field and a rebound in the ledgers in 1936.

Another way to think about the Yankees' profitability is to view per-capita attendance (table 38). The New York City teams, including Brooklyn, did attract large crowds. On a per-capita basis, though, the city's support of its ball clubs was not impressive, ranking last among the ten cities with Major League Baseball. The Chicago teams also had low per-capita attendance. Boston and Cincinnati had impressive per-capita attendance, especially considering the many years of lackluster teams. Exacerbating the city's low per-capita attendance, the New York teams also had lower games at home revenue per attendee than their league averages. After the war the Yankees would boast the highest average ticket price (basically the same as the games at home revenue per attendee) in the American League, even though the city's per-capita attendance remained unimpressive.[1] New York City certainly offered an unmatched set of entertainment options that competed with baseball. Years later, Bill Veeck Jr. criticized the Yankees' management for their lackadaisical promotions.[2] Were Ruppert and Barrow adept at drawing crowds? That question remains unanswered. The mere fact that the team won a disproportionate number of pennants is not definitive evidence of their management's skill.

Ruppert's conservatism was like that of most of his fellow owners. Although they slashed nominal salaries of top stars, trimmed player rosters by two players, and reduced coaching staffs, owners struggled to cut their real payrolls. Real payrolls did not fall in general between 1929 and 1933. Most owners also hesitated to reduce nominal ticket prices, allowing real ticket prices to jump coincident with their customers' diminishing real incomes, although they may have counted on their patrons shifting to cheaper seats. Few owners offered even temporary discounts from their listed ticket prices. A few owners or general managers, such as Leland "Larry" MacPhail, were more aggressive in finding ways to bolster their gate, including radio broadcasts, ladies' days, and night baseball.

For Cubs fans, the deaths of William Wrigley and William Veeck Sr. appear, in retrospect, to be more of a calamity than any irate restaurateur and his smelly goat invoking a curse. While the Cubs would win occasional pennants through 1945, the club never regained its preeminence at the gate as it did in 1929 and 1930.

At least P. K. Wrigley had sufficiently deep pockets to maintain respectability. The 1930s revealed the inability of players-turned-owners Connie Mack and Clark Griffith to compete with the wealthier teams. These owners would never again get within ten games of first place, except once during the war. They became baseball's version of the "Flying Dutchman," forever searching the baseball seas for the star that would rejuvenate their franchises. In some respects, the Senators' decline during the 1930s is difficult to explain. Washington DC was the fastest-growing city with Major League Baseball, although it still remained the second-smallest Major League city in 1940. The capital's residents suffered smaller decreases in per-capita income than did the nation as a whole. These favorable trends should have sustained the club.

The baseball world would remain starkly divided into haves and have-nots during the postwar years, and the three New York teams would dominate the World Series between 1947 and 1957. The Yankees would win fourteen pennants in sixteen years between 1947 and 1964, but the George Weiss clubs rarely blew away their competition in the same fashion as did the 1927, 1932, 1936–39, and 1941–43 clubs.

Baseball owners gradually implemented innovations and policies during the 1930s that pushed the game towards its modern version. The owners finally broke the secrecy surrounding their games by numbering players, providing loudspeakers, and other information. They made no moves toward integrating the game, and they maintained the traditional way of playing by eschewing such "gimmicks" as the designated hitter and interleague play.

Surviving the decade intact may have been the owners' biggest achievement.

Appendix 1
Radio and Sunday Ball's Effect on Attendance

In the cases of radio, Sunday ball, and night ball, the benefits were varied and enmeshed with other factors. To help sort out the effects for radio and Sunday, I ran regression equations covering the seasons between 1929 and 1941. There were 208 observations, one for each year for each of the sixteen teams. I looked at each team's win-loss record, whether a team shared a city with another club, whether a team had night ball, whether a team had Sunday ball, estimated city population, and real per-capita Gross National Product (GNP). The estimated city population variable uses the 1930 and 1940 census figures. The population figures for the intervening years were derived by a simple adjustment of one-tenth of the decade's change per year. Obviously this is a crude estimate of a city's population for non-census years. I tried using real spectator sports spending as an indicator of the economic conditions but the real per capita GNP variable was a better explanatory variable.

For the dependent variables I used attendance (or its natural-log transformation) and real profit/loss. Given the potential "noise" in the profit/loss figures from player sales/purchases (which were not amortized) and from installing lights or other stadium improvements, the relatively weak explanatory power of the equations is not surprising.

A dummy variable for radio broadcasts (1 if the team broadcast home games during a given season; 0 if not) was not definitive, given the ambiguity concerning Detroit and Cleveland's broadcasting of home games before 1935. In equations where the natural-log transformed attendance was the dependent variable and where Detroit and Cleveland are assumed to have broadcast home games early during the 1930s (1929–34 for Detroit and 1930–32 for Cleveland), the dummy variable was statistically significant. The coefficient was positive. If Detroit did not broadcast games in 1934 or if Cleveland's dummy variable is altered, the radio dummy variable was not significantly significant. For equations using real profit as the dependent variable, the radio broadcast dummy variable was never statistically significant. There is some evidence, therefore, that radio broadcasts of home games might have had a positive effect, but this result depends largely upon the status of broadcasting in Detroit and Cleveland, and I do not include the radio dummy in the following discussion.

On a game-by-game basis, night games were statistically significant in the Philadelphia Phillies' regression equations.[1] However, equations using game-by-game data could not address the issue of whether night games merely rearranged attendance or augmented it. In the current cross-team seasonal equations, the night baseball dummy variable (1 if by night; 0 if no night) was frequently *not* statistically significant. These results may arise from the relatively high correlation between the night dummy variable and real per-capita GNP—.53. Owners installed lights after the economic conditions improved.[2]

In the equations using real profit/loss as the dependent variable, the Sunday and night dummy variables were not statistically significant. Although there was a win-loss percentage variable, including a dummy variable for pennant winner increased the equation's explanatory power, but the pennant-winner variable had a relatively high correlation coefficient of .55 with win-loss percentage.

The evidence that Sunday and night ball improved a typical team's profit or loss is slender. MacPhail's Reds and Dodgers appear to have been the prime beneficiaries of night ball. Sunday ball could not reverse the Athletics' slide into mediocrity under Connie Mack.

Appendix 2
Dramatis Personae

Phil Ball: Owner of the St. Louis Browns until his death in 1932. He claimed he rarely turned a profit on the club.

E. S. Barnard: American League president from 1928–31.

Donald Barnes: Owner of the St. Louis Browns. Barnes wanted to relocate the hapless Browns to Los Angeles but was thwarted by the Japanese Navy's attack on Pearl Harbor.

Edward Barrow: General manager of the New York Yankees. He presaged Billy Beane and other modern general managers who emphasized getting patient sluggers.

Sam Breadon: Owner of the St. Louis Cardinals until 1947.

Walter Briggs: Owner of the Detroit Tigers from 1920 to 1952.

Ty Cobb: Greatest hitter and base runner of the "Dead Ball Era." He was a savvy investor who died rich and a known curmudgeon. He was more fortunate than Babe Ruth in the actors chosen to portray him (Tommy Lee Jones played Cobb, while William Bendix and John Goodman played Ruth).

Mickey Cochrane: Star catcher for the Philadelphia Athletics and Detroit Tigers. He became the player-manager for the Tigers and helped the team to pennants in 1934 and 1935 before a severe beaning and emotional problems derailed his career.

Eddie Collins: Star infielder with the Philadelphia Athletics and Chicago White Sox. He was one of the "Black Sox," but was not involved in the conspiracy to throw the World Series, although he had a poor series. He was Tom Yawkey's right-hand man between 1932 and 1951.

Charles Comiskey: Former star pitcher turned Chicago White Sox owner. The movie *Eight Men Out* portrays him as a tight-fisted jerk. It is said that he infuriated his players into throwing the 1919 World Series. Upon his death in 1931, his son Lou Comiskey took over.

Powel Crosley Jr. (sometimes spelled Powell): Owner of the Cincinnati Reds.

Dizzy Dean: St. Louis Cardinals star pitcher and colorful character. Dean was brash on the field and at the negotiating table. He later mangled the English language as a radio broadcaster.

Joseph "Joe" DiMaggio: Talented New York Yankees slugging outfielder. He scandalized fans and owners by holding out for more money as a second-year player. Shame on you, Joe, for wanting $25,000 after hitting .346 with 46 home runs and 167 RBIs. He was later immortalized in a Simon and Garfunkel song, "Mrs. Robinson"—"Where have you gone, Joe DiMaggio?"—before becoming Mr. Coffee.

Barney Dreyfuss: Owner of the Pittsburgh Pirates until his death in 1932.

Jimmie Foxx: Philadelphia Athletics and Boston Red Sox slugger.

Ford Frick: National League president after John Heydler died in 1934 and eventual Commissioner of Baseball. He was excoriated by Bill Veeck Jr. for being Babe Ruth's drinking buddy and ghost writer and for using his position as Commissioner to belittle Roger Maris' pursuit of Ruth's single-season home-run record, though the insult was inadvertent.

Judge Emil Fuchs: Owner of the sad-sack Boston Braves until he was forced out in 1935.

Lou Gehrig: New York Yankees slugger eclipsed only by Babe Ruth.

He later became the subject of a wonderful baseball movie. His final speech makes grown men cry.

Clark Griffith: Former ballplayer turned longtime Washington Senators owner. He was prone to making conservative statements and then doing a volte-face. He eventually embraced most of the innovators' ideas. He pioneered signing players from the Caribbean.

Robert "Lefty" Grove: Dominant pitcher in the American League during the era, also the recipient of one of the highest salaries in baseball.

William Harridge: American League president after E. S. Barnard died in 1931.

John Heydler: National League president from 1918 until 1934.

William Hulbert: Pioneer of the National League in 1876.

Lee Keyser: Owner of minor league team in Des Moines and early proponent of night baseball.

Chuck Klein: The greatest Phillies player of the 1930s.

Judge Kenesaw Mountain Landis: Commissioner of Major League Baseball between 1920 and 1944.

Connie Mack: Mediocre catcher turned manager who eventually owned the Philadelphia Athletics. Not a man of deep pockets, he twice dismantled dynasties, thereby anticipating Charles O. Finley, a later owner of the Athletics.

Leland Stanford (Larry) MacPhail: General manager of the Cincinnati Reds and Brooklyn Dodgers. He demonstrated twice that night baseball was viable.

Joe McCarthy: Manager of the New York Yankees during the 1930s and 1940s. After a slow start, he piloted the 1936–39 clubs that thrashed the American League.

John McGraw: Longtime New York Giants manager.

Steve McKeever: President of the Brooklyn Dodgers.

Frank Navin: Owner of the Detroit Tigers.

Branch Rickey: General manager of the St. Louis Cardinals and pioneer of the farm system, a form of vertical integration. He later integrated baseball in the twentieth century by signing Jackie Robinson.

Jacob Ruppert: Owner of the New York Yankees until his death in 1939. In an astute move, he hired Ed Barrow from the Boston Red Sox. Barrow eventually brought most of the talented Red Sox to join him in New York.

George Herman "Babe" Ruth: New York Yankees slugger and gate attraction. Ruth was one of the first players to employ an agent.

Tris Speaker: Boston Red Sox and Cleveland Indians outfielder.

Charles Stoneham: Owner of the New York Giants. He was conservative, but eventually seized upon innovations after others had demonstrated their value.

George Trautman: President of the American Association and later head of the Minor Leagues.

William Veeck Sr.: Innovator and president of the Chicago Cubs until 1933.

William Veeck Jr.: Later owner of the Cleveland Indians, St. Louis Browns, and Chicago White Sox. He was a more flamboyant innovator than his father. He transformed Cleveland and Chicago into the main postwar rivals of the New York Yankees.

George Weiss: Ed Barrow's heir apparent, Weiss eventually became the General Manager of the New York Yankees. He began as farm director for the club and later built rather bland pennant-winning teams during the postwar era. His genius came to an end when he signed on as general manager for the expansion New York Mets.

Hack Wilson: Longtime holder of National League single-season home-run record and all-time Major League single-season RBI leader. His career plummeted in 1931 with the introduction of the dead ball and the loss of manager Joe McCarthy to New York Yankees.

William Wrigley: Owner of the Chicago Cubs when the team was arguably the most successful franchise in the game (1929–32). His death in 1932, along with that of general manager William Veeck Sr., began the Cubs' decline into irrelevance.

Thomas Yawkey: Bought the moribund Boston Red Sox in 1933. He poured hundreds of thousands of dollars into his franchise by buying Hall of Fame players Lefty Grove, Jimmie Foxx, and Joe Cronin, as well as refurbishing Fenway Park.

Appendix of Tables

Table 1: Economic Indicators, 1929–1943

	In $Billions						In $Millions			
	GNP	RGNP	PCE	RPCE	REC	RREC	SPS	RSPS	MOP	RMOP
1929	103.1	100.5	77.2	75.3	4.3	4.2	66	64	720	702
1930	90.4	90.4	69.9	69.9	4.0	4.0	65	65	732	732
1931	75.8	83.4	60.4	66.3	3.3	3.6	57	63	719	788
1932	58.0	71.1	48.6	59.4	2.4	3.0	47	57	527	644
1933	55.6	69.7	45.8	59.0	2.2	2.8	50	64	482	621
1934	65.1	76.1	51.3	64.0	2.4	3.0	65	81	518	646
1935	72.2	83.6	55.7	67.8	2.6	3.2	72	88	556	676
1936	82.5	95.3	61.9	74.6	3.0	3.6	83	100	626	754
1937	90.4	100.2	66.5	77.3	3.4	3.9	89	103	676	786
1938	84.7	95.1	63.9	75.7	3.2	3.8	95	113	663	786
1939	90.5	103.3	66.8	80.3	3.5	4.1	98	118	659	792
1940	99.7	112.0	70.8	84.3	3.8	4.5	98	117	735	875
1941	124.5	130.0	80.6	91.4	4.2	4.8	107	121	809	917
1942	157.9	146.9	88.5	90.7	4.7	4.8	90	92	1022	1047
1943	191.6	166.3	99.3	95.9	5.0	4.8	62	60	1275	1231

GNP: Gross National Product, in $billions
RGNP: Gross National Product, in 1930 dollars (deflated by implicit price deflator)
PCE: Personal Consumption Expenditures, in $billions
RPCE: Real Personal Consumption Expenditures, deflated by CPI "all items" (1930 = 100)
REC: Recreation expenditures, in $billions
RREC: Real recreation expenditures, deflated by CPI "all items" (1930 = 100)
SPS: Spectator sports expenditures, in $millions
RSPS: Real spectator sports expenditures, deflated by CPI "all items" (1930 = 100)
MOP: Motion pictures expenditures, in $millions
RMOP: Real motion pictures expenditures deflated by CPI "all items" (1930 = 100)

Note: GDP for 1929–1941 was slightly higher than GNP (http://www.bea.gov/national/index.html, September 12, 2009). The two series began to diverge by as much as 1.8% in 1941, but the rates of changes in both series were very similar. The divergence between the two series accelerated in 1942 and 1943.

Source: U.S. Department of Commerce, *Historical Statistics* 1: 210–11, 224, and 318–19.

Table 2: Index Numbers for Various Indicators (1930 = 1)

	RGNP	RSPS	RMOP	ALAT	NLAT	MLAT	ALP	NLP	CPI*
1929	1.11	0.98	0.96	1.00	0.90	0.95	1.13	0.50	1.03
1930	1.00	1.00	1.00	1.00	1.00	1.00	1.00	1.00	1.00
1931	0.92	0.97	1.08	0.83	0.84	0.84	-0.34	0.28	0.91
1932	0.79	0.88	0.88	0.67	0.71	0.69	-1.75	-0.40	0.82
1933	0.77	0.98	0.84	0.62	0.58	0.60	-2.72	-0.52	0.78
1934	0.84	1.25	0.88	0.80	0.59	0.69	-0.11	-0.21	0.80
1935	0.92	1.35	0.92	0.79	0.67	0.72	0.66	0.24	0.82
1936	1.05	1.54	1.03	0.89	0.72	0.80	0.48	0.44	0.83
1937	1.11	1.58	1.07	1.01	0.77	0.88	0.31	0.33	0.86
1938	1.05	1.74	1.07	0.95	0.84	0.89	0.70	0.25	0.84
1939	1.14	1.82	1.08	0.91	0.86	0.89	0.66	0.46	0.83
1940	1.24	1.80	1.20	1.16	0.81	0.97	1.15	0.13	0.84
1941	1.44	1.86	1.25	1.05	0.88	0.96	0.60	0.16	0.88

RGNP: Real Gross National Product
RSPS: Real spectator sports spending
RMOP: Real motion picture spending
ALAT: American League attendance
NLAT: National League attendance
MLAT: Major League attendance
ALP: Real American League consolidated profit/loss
NLP: Real National League consolidated profit/loss
CPI*: CPI "all items" (1930 = 100)

Source: U.S. Department of Commerce, *Historical Statistics* 1: 210–11, 224, and 401; Thorn, Palmer, and Gershman, *Total Baseball*, 75–76; U.S. Congress, *Organized Baseball: Hearings*, 1599–1600.

Table 3: Major League Attendance, 1925–1941

	American League games			National League games		
Year	Pennant winner	Ahead	Attendance	Pennant winner	Ahead	Attendance
1925	Washington	8.5	5,186,851	Pittsburgh	8.5	4,353,704
1926	New York	3.0	4,912,583	St. Louis	2.0	4,920,399
1927	New York	19.0	4,612,951	Pittsburgh	1.5	5,309,917
1928	New York	2.5	4,221,188	St. Louis	2.0	4,881,097
1929	Philadelphia	18.0	4,662,470	Chicago	10.5	4,925,713
1930	Philadelphia	8.0	4,685,730	St. Louis	2.0	5,446,532
1931	Philadelphia	13.5	3,883,292	St. Louis	13.0	4,583,815
1932	New York	13.0	3,133,232	Chicago	4.0	3,841,334
1933	Washington	7.0	2,926,210	New York	5.0	3,162,821
1934	Detroit	7.0	3,763,606	St. Louis	2.0	3,200,105
1935	Detroit	3.0	3,688,007	Chicago	4.0	3,657,309
1936	New York	19.5	4,178,922	New York	5.0	3,903,691
1937	New York	13.0	4,735,835	New York	3.0	4,204,228
1938	New York	9.5	4,445,684	Chicago	2.0	4,560,827
1939	New York	17.0	4,270,602	Cincinnati	4.5	4,707,177
1940	Detroit	1.0	5,433,791	Cincinnati	12.0	4,389,693
1941	New York	17.0	4,911,956	Brooklyn	2.5	4,777,647

Source: Thorn, Palmer, and Gershman, *Total Baseball*, 75–76 and 2134–67.

Table 4: Consolidated Real Net Income after Income Taxes, 1929–1941

American League Clubs, 1929–1941 (in $000s)

YEAR	BOS	CHI	CLE	DET	NY	PHI	STL	WAS	LEA
1929	-34	10	-22	120	264	269	5	-43	570
1930	8	15	28	75	244	16	-87	57	503
1931	-79	0	-42	-46	28	112	-113	-31	-172
1932	-102	-299	-148	-75	-39	12	-134	-94	-878
1933	-692	-201	-171	-109	-126	-27	-43	-1	-1,371
1934	-142	-260	42	472	46	-174	-69	25	-58
1935	-249	11	43	634	-126	-5	1	22	331
1936	-277	-6	86	247	396	-50	-192	36	239
1937	-293	10	122	211	332	-2	-126	-99	155
1938	-196	-105	175	137	433	-60	-142	112	354
1939	-128	20	115	69	460	-52	-150	-2	332
1940	-100	49	202	231	163	-67	33	67	577
1941	65	72	69	-7	269	6	-161	-13	300
Total	-2,220	-684	500	1,958	2,343	126	-1,177	37	883

National League Clubs, 1929–1941 (in $000s)

YEAR	BOS	BKN	CHI	CIN	NY	PHI	PIT	STL	LEA
1929	19	121	418	-198	157	24	144	49	734
1930	22	427	524	-17	151	29	95	231	1,462
1931	-18	-6	197	-177	-22	-42	98	379	409
1932	17	-196	69	-142	-263	122	-106	-90	-588
1933	-155	-63	-319	-73	77	4	-124	-103	-757
1934	-51	-172	-212	-78	127	17	-71	136	-304
1935	-58	-181	165	58	242	2	55	75	358
1936	-24	-51	73	127	364	26	45	82	641
1937	-16	-150	116	35	385	-20	68	62	480
1938	-18	-4	39	186	34	-53	198	-18	364
1939	27	173	-26	403	114	-83	-48	108	667
1940	8	149	-217	322	-83	-48	-18	81	196
1941	-69	166	-179	139	52	-69	22	175	238
Total	-315	213	648	585	1,336	-91	358	1,166	3,900

Note: Base year 1930 = 100.

Source: U.S. Congress, *Organized Baseball: Hearings*, 1600; U.S. Department of Commerce, *Historical Statistics* 1: 210.

Table 5: Nominal and Real Net Operating Income (in $000s)

	Nominal Net Operating Income			Real Net Operating Income		
	1929	1933	1939	1929	1933	1939
American League						
Boston	-38	-130	-14	-37	-168	-17
Chicago	n/a	n/a	34	n/a	n/a	41
Cleveland	129	-93	123	126	-120	148
Detroit	279	-51	189	272	-65	228
New York	336	-12	276	328	-16	331
Philadelphia	337	-166	-10	329	-214	-12
St. Louis	16	-113	-97	15	-145	-117
Washington	-28	71	18	-28	92	21
League Total	1,031	-494	519	1,005	-637	623
Less Chicago			484			582
National League						
Boston	-24	47	-4	-23	61	-4
Brooklyn	210	-32	391	204	-41	470
Chicago	819	-36	100	798	-46	120
Cincinnati	-95	-64	652	-93	-83	783
New York	249	139	163	243	180	196
Philadelphia	39	-129	-19	38	-166	-23
Pittsburgh	226	-23	69	220	-30	83
St. Louis	92	-37	73	90	-48	88
League Total	1,516	-135	1,426	1,478	-173	1,714

Net operating income: Gross operating income - gross operating expenses
n/a: not available

Note: Base year 1930 = 100.
Source: U.S. Congress, *Organized Baseball: Hearings*, 1602–3 and 1606–7; U.S. Department of Commerce, *Historical Statistics* 1: 210–11.

Table 6: Sources of Revenue and Expenses across All Major League Baseball Teams (by Percent of Gross Operating Income)

Sources of revenue	1929		1933		1939	
Home games	62.4		57.2		55.9	
Road games	21.1		23.1		19.2	
Exhibition games	4.1		5.1		4.6	
Baseball games		87.6		85.4		79.7
Radio and television		0.0		0.3		7.3
Concessions (net)		5.5		6.4		7.0
Other		6.9		7.9		6.0
Gross income		100.0		100.0		100.0

Sources of expenses	1929		1933		1939	
Team salaries	31.2		44.2		30.2	
Other operating expenses	46.4		65.6		53.7	
Gross operating expenses		77.6		109.8		83.9
Purchase of contracts	7.9		8.2		9.0	
Farms' operating losses	1.2		5.2		-2.0	
Minor League subsidization		9.1		13.4		7.0
Income taxes		1.6		0.0		2.2
Total expenses		88.3		123.2		93.1
Net income		11.7		-23.2		6.9

Note: Chicago White Sox not included in 1929 and 1933.
Source: U.S. Congress, *Organized Baseball: Hearings*, 1610–11.

Table 7: Nominal and Real Games at Home Revenue per Attendee

	Nominal Games at Home Revenue per Attendee			Real Games at Home Revenue per Attendee		
	1929	1933	1939	1929	1933	1939
American League						
Boston	0.612	0.522	0.634	0.596	0.673	0.762
Chicago	n/a	n/a	0.700	n/a	n/a	0.841
Cleveland	0.774	0.612	0.753	0.755	0.789	0.905
Detroit	0.723	0.653	0.788	0.705	0.842	0.947
New York	0.699	0.567	0.655	0.681	0.731	0.787
Philadelphia	0.711	0.596	0.632	0.693	0.767	0.760
St. Louis	0.678	0.574	0.693	0.661	0.740	0.833
Washington	0.725	0.641	0.635	0.707	0.826	0.763
League Total			0.695			0.835
Less Chicago	0.708	0.597	0.694	0.691	0.769	0.834
National League						
Boston	0.680	0.618	0.667	0.663	0.797	0.802
Brooklyn	0.788	0.660	0.787	0.768	0.850	0.946
Chicago	0.866	0.781	0.774	0.844	1.007	0.930
Cincinnati	0.816	0.719	0.933	0.795	0.927	1.121
New York	0.806	0.658	0.772	0.785	0.848	0.928
Philadelphia	0.645	0.588	0.666	0.628	0.758	0.801
Pittsburgh	n/a	0.797	0.930	n/a	1.027	1.117
St. Louis	0.801	0.672	0.753	0.781	0.866	0.905
League Total		0.690	0.807		0.889	0.970
Less Pittsburgh	0.802	0.679	0.797	0.782	0.875	0.958

Nominal and real "games at home" = revenue/attendance
n/a: not available

Note: Per attendee, American League teams paid about 28¢ to the visiting team and National League teams paid about 24¢ to the visiting team, accounting for part of the difference between the league totals. Base year 1930 = 100.

Source: U.S. Congress, *Organized Baseball: Hearings*, 1602–3 and 1606–7; U.S. Department of Commerce, *Historical Statistics* 1: 210–11; Thorn, Palmer, and Gershman, *Total Baseball*, 75–76.

Table 8: Nominal and Real Gross Operating Income (in $000s)

	Nominal Operating Income			Real Operating Income		
	1929	1933	1939	1929	1933	1939
American League						
Boston	428	257	665	417	331	800
Chicago	n/a	n/a	699	n/a	n/a	840
Cleveland	603	347	710	588	447	854
Detroit	834	312	1,004	812	402	1,207
New York	1,281	753	1,355	1,249	971	1,629
Philadelphia	967	311	442	942	401	531
St. Louis	537	228	249	523	293	300
Washington	458	534	451	446	689	542
League	5,107	2,743	5,576	4,978	3,535	6,702
Less Chicago			4,878			5,863
National League						
Boston	462	434	409	450	558	491
Brooklyn	796	493	1,159	776	635	1,393
Chicago	1,669	671	911	1,626	864	1,095
Cincinnati	449	284	1,346	438	366	1,617
New York	1,078	783	1,067	1,050	1,009	1,283
Philadelphia	358	203	348	349	261	419
Pittsburgh	855	445	661	834	574	794
St. Louis	601	399	636	586	514	765
League Total	6,267	3,710	6,537	6,109	4,781	7,857

n/a: not available

Note: Base year 1930 = 100.
Source: U.S. Congress, *Organized Baseball: Hearings*, 1602–3, 1606–7, and 1610; U.S. Department of Commerce, *Historical Statistics* 1: 210–11.

Table 9: Real Games at Home and Games Away Revenue (in $000s)

	Real Revenue Games at Home			Real Revenue Games Away		
	1929	1933	1939	1929	1933	1939
American League						
Boston	235	181	437	118	98	182
Chicago	n/a	n/a	500	n/a	n/a	167
Cleveland	405	306	511	132	106	211
Detroit	613	270	792	118	91	179
New York	654	532	677	284	230	322
Philadelphia	581	228	300	234	161	114
St. Louis	185	65	91	165	88	130
Washington	251	361	259	137	169	140
League	2,925	1,944	3,566	1,188	943	1,444
Less Chicago			3,066			1,278
National League						
Boston	247	413	229	121	92	155
Brooklyn	562	448	904	106	79	161
Chicago	1,253	598	676	162	112	173
Cincinnati	235	202	1,100	135	105	220
New York	682	513	652	144	178	171
Philadelphia	177	119	223	143	113	116
Pittsburgh	n/a	297	421	n/a	146	166
St. Louis	312	222	362	166	153	182
League	3,468	2,811	4,567	977	977	1,344
Less Pittsburgh		2,514	4,146		831	1,178

n/a: not available

Note: Base year 1930 = 100.
Source: U.S. Congress, *Organized Baseball: Hearings*, 1602–3, 1606–7, and 1610; U.S. Department of Commerce, *Historical Statistics* 1: 210–11.

Table 10: Real Exhibition Games and Real Concessions (Net) Revenue

	Real Exhibition Games Revenue			Real Concessions (net) Revenue		
	1929	1933	1939	1929	1933	1939
American League						
Boston	9,109	7,952	30,240	20,922	20,976	49,844
Chicago	n/a	n/a	61,484	n/a	n/a	47,121
Cleveland	0	4,030	23,244	21,972	20,241	33,293
Detroit	11,260	6,976	0	37,962	32,860	81,986
New York	71,282	38,076	125,732	88,739	76,080	127,337
Philadelphia	76,037	6,089	8,180	2,924	3,866	6,010
St. Louis	0	0	20,434	27,484	15,236	10,563
Washington	17,096	88,405	11,972	14,932	19,156	24,554
League	184,785	151,527	281,287	214,935	188,414	380,707
Less Chicago			156,803			333,585
National League						
Boston	2,400	5,255	18,406	12,978	32,648	27,511
Brooklyn	4,631	21,948	51,764	44,870	45,103	88,821
Chicago	60,450	43,450	60,645	128,813	65,536	92,024
Cincinnati	10,811	9,656	131,994	36,062	28,903	131,011
New York	30,675	103,187	29,740	85,357	78,793	109,578
Philadelphia	21,628	10,800	9,544	4,873	9,021	13,143
Pittsburgh	n/a	16,143	6,986	n/a	28,341	92,833
St. Louis	18,507	20,137	29,520	40,156	54,933	86,484
League	149,101	230,576	338,601	353,109	343,278	641,405

n/a: not available

Note: Base year 1930 = 100.
Source: U.S. Congress, *Organized Baseball: Hearings*, 1602–3 and 1606–7, and 1610; U.S. Department of Commerce, *Historical Statistics* 1: 210–11.

Table 11: Nominal and Real Concessions (Net) Revenue per Attendee (Official Attendance)

	Nominal Net Concessions Revenue per Attendee			Real Net Concessions Revenue per Attendee		
	1929	1933	1939	1929	1933	1939
American League						
Boston	0.054	0.061	0.072	0.053	0.078	0.087
Chicago	n/a	n/a	0.066	n/a	n/a	0.079
Cleveland	0.042	0.040	0.049	0.041	0.052	0.059
Detroit	0.045	0.079	0.082	0.044	0.102	0.098
New York	0.095	0.081	0.123	0.092	0.105	0.148
Philadelphia	0.004	0.010	0.013	0.003	0.013	0.015
St. Louis	0.100	0.134	0.081	0.098	0.173	0.097
Washington	0.043	0.034	0.060	0.042	0.044	0.072
League			0.074			0.089
Less Chicago	0.052	0.058	0.075	0.051	0.075	0.091
National League						
Boston	0.036	0.049	0.080	0.035	0.063	0.096
Brooklyn	0.063	0.066	0.077	0.061	0.086	0.093
Chicago	0.089	0.086	0.105	0.087	0.110	0.127
Cincinnati	0.125	0.103	0.111	0.122	0.132	0.133
New York	0.101	0.101	0.130	0.098	0.130	0.156
Philadelphia	0.018	0.045	0.039	0.017	0.058	0.047
Pittsburgh	n/a	0.076	0.205	n/a	0.098	0.246
St. Louis	0.103	0.166	0.180	0.100	0.214	0.216
League		0.084	0.113		0.109	0.136
Less Pittsburgh	0.082	0.085	0.105	0.080	0.110	0.127

Nominal and real net concessions = revenue/attendance
n/a: not available

Note: Base year 1930 = 100.
Source: U.S. Congress, *Organized Baseball: Hearings*, 1602–3 and 1606–7; U.S. Department of Commerce, *Historical Statistics* 1: 210–11; Thorn, Palmer, and Gershman, *Total Baseball*, 75–76.

Table 12: Nominal and Real Radio Revenue

	Nominal Radio Revenue			Real Radio Revenue		
	1929	1933	1939	1929	1933	1939
American League						
Boston	0	5,000	45,000	0	6,443	54,087
Chicago	n/a	n/a	41,000	n/a	n/a	49,279
Cleveland	0	0	44,500	0	0	53,486
Detroit	0	0	70,000	0	0	84,135
New York	0	0	110,000	0	0	132,212
Philadelphia	0	0	45,000	0	0	54,087
St. Louis	0	6,000	42,500	0	7,732	51,082
Washington	0	0	30,000	0	0	36,058
League	0	11,000	428,000	0	14,175	514,423
Less Chicago			387,000			465,144
National League						
Boston	0	5,000	45,000	0	6,443	54,087
Brooklyn	0	0	87,500	0	0	105,168
Chicago	0	0	41,000	0	0	49,279
Cincinnati	0	2,000	27,500	0	2,577	33,053
New York	0	0	110,000	0	0	132,212
Philadelphia	0	0	46,500	0	0	55,889
Pittsburgh	n/a	0	66,000	n/a	0	79,327
St. Louis	0	0	33,000	0	0	39,663
League	0	7,000	456,500	0	9,021	548,678

n/a: not available

Note: Base year 1930 = 100.

Source: U.S. Congress, *Organized Baseball: Hearings*, 1602–3, 1606–7, and 1610; U.S. Department of Commerce, *Historical Statistics* 1: 210–11.

Table 13: New York Yankees on the Field and on the Ledger, 1926–1941

	Finish	Win-Loss	W-L%	Games Ahead	Attendance	Real Net Income
1926	1	91-63	0.591	+3.0	1,027,095	449,641
1927	1	110-44	0.714	+19.0	1,164,015	511,140
1928	1	101-53	0.656	+2.5	1,072,132	286,479
1929	2	88-66	0.571	-18.0	960,148	264,160
1930	3	86-68	0.558	-16.0	1,169,230	244,374
1931	2	94-59	0.614	-13.5	912,437	27,913
1932	1	107-47	0.695	+13.0	962,320	-38,542
1933	2	91-59	0.607	-7.0	728,014	-126,451
1934	2	94-60	0.610	-7.0	854,682	45,898
1935	2	89-60	0.597	-3.0	657,508	-126,046
1936	1	102-51	0.667	+19.5	976,913	395,569
1937	1	102-52	0.662	+13.0	998,148	331,681
1938	1	99-53	0.651	+9.5	970,916	432,739
1939	1	106-45	0.702	+17.0	859,785	459,727
1940	3	88-66	0.571	-2.0	988,971	162,557
1941	1	101-53	0.656	+17.0	964,722	269,417

n/a: not available

Note: Base year 1930 = 100.

Source: Thorn, Palmer, and Gershman, *Total Baseball*, for all data except "consolidated net income after taxes"; U.S. Congress, *Organized Baseball: Hearings*, 1599, "consolidated net income after taxes"; U.S. Department of Commerce, *Historical Statistics* 1: 210, CPI deflator.

Table 14: New York Yankees' Revenue Sources, 1926–1939 (in $000s)

	Nominal					Real				
	Net rec	Away rec	Train exh	Conc rec	Total rev	Net rec	Away rec	Train exh	Conc rec	Total rev
1926	719	243	58	109	1,130	678	229	55	103	1,066
1927	786	285	69	115	1,255	756	274	66	110	1,207
1928	731	260	86	127	1,205	713	254	84	124	1,174
1929	671	291	85	92	1,139	654	284	83	90	1,111
1930	788	220	88	108	1,204	788	220	88	108	1,204
1931	585	195	55	93	927	641	213	60	102	1,016
1932	585	143	38	62	829	716	175	47	76	1,013
1933	412	178	34	69	692	531	230	43	88	892
1934	512	189	48	75	824	639	236	59	94	1,028
1935	387	156	16	72	632	471	190	20	88	768
1936	624	220	14	96	955	752	266	17	116	1,150
1937	663	282	47	101	1,092	771	328	54	117	1,270
1938	633	252	49	105	1,038	750	298	58	124	1,230
1939	556	267	63	108	1,105	669	322	76	129	1,328
1940	665	278	50	95	1,163	792	331	60	113	1,385
1941	660	289	55	116	1,120	748	328	62	131	1,270

Net rec: Net receipts = total gate receipts - visiting share - league share - war tax
Train exh: Training game receipts + exhibition game receipts
Conc rec: Concessions receipts
Away rec: Receipts from away games
Total rev: Total revenue = net receipts + training receipts + exhibition receipts + away receipts + concession receipts + broadcasting receipts

Note: Real broadcasting receipts include $132,211 in 1939; $89,286 in 1940; and $0 in 1941. Deflated by CPI "All Items." Base year 1930 = 100.
Source: U.S. Department of Commerce, *Historical Statistics* 1: 210.

Table 15: New York Yankees' Total Gate Receipts, 1926–1939

	Attendance	Nominal Total Gate Receipts	Nominal Total Gate/ Attendance	Real Total Gate Receipts	Real Total Gate/ Attendance	Percent Cheap Seats
1926	1,027,675	$1,039,387	$1.01	$ 980,554	$ 0.95	n/a
1927	1,164,015	$1,139,871	$0.98	$1,096,030	$ 0.94	26.0
1928	1,072,132	$1,057,465	$0.99	$1,030,668	$ 0.96	25.7
1929	960,148	$ 964,684	$1.00	$ 940,238	$ 0.98	23.9
1930	1,169,230	$1,141,660	$0.98	$1,141,660	$ 0.98	27.4
1931	912,437	$ 857,661	$0.94	$ 940,418	$ 1.03	31.1
1932	962,320	$ 868,822	$0.90	$1,061,130	$ 1.10	35.4
1933	728,014	$ 639,266	$0.88	$ 823,797	$ 1.13	37.7
1934	854,682	$ 763,641	$0.89	$ 952,171	$ 1.11	36.0
1935	657,508	$ 577,996	$0.88	$ 703,159	$ 1.07	39.6
1936	976,913	$ 916,915	$0.94	$1,104,717	$ 1.13	30.3
1937	998,148	$ 964,089	$0.97	$1,121,034	$ 1.12	28.0
1938	970,916	$ 924,838	$0.95	$1,095,780	$ 1.13	29.5
1939	859,785	$ 834,876	$0.97	$1,003,456	$ 1.17	25.9
1940	988,975	$ 985,985	$1.00	$1,173,792	$ 1.19	25.5
1941	964,722	$ 974,631	$1.01	$1,105,023	$ 1.15	24.0

Total gate receipts = home receipts + season sales + rain checks + advance sales + other - war tax (1925–1944)

Note: Base year 1930 = 100.

Source: Thorn, Palmer, and Gershman, *Total Baseball*, 75–76, for attendance; New York Yankees Base Ball Club cash books and general ledger for all other data, deflated by CPI "all items"; U.S. Department of Commerce, *Historical Statistics* 1: 210.

Table 16: New York Yankees' Visiting Share Divided by Attendance

	Season attendance	Season average	Lowest attendance	Lowest series average	Highest attendance	Highest series average
1929	960,148	$0.2761	10,168	$0.2637	157,329	$0.2817
1933	728,014	$0.2623	13,320	$0.2473	70,671	$0.2753
1939	859,785	$0.2741	12,767	$0.2558	76,328	$0.2821
1943	618,330	$0.2832	13,659	$0.2741	45,280	$0.2873

Season average = Visiting share/attendance
Lowest series average = Series with the lowest visiting share/attendance
Lowest attendance: Attendance at the series with the lowest average
Highest series average = Series with the highest visiting share/attendance
1929: High series included 5 games, low series 1 game
1933: High and low series both included 2 games
1939: High series included 5 games, low series 2 games
1943: High series included 4 games, low series 2 games

Source: New York Yankees Base Ball Club cash books.

Table 17: Real Team Salaries 1929, 1933, and 1939

American League

	1929	1933	1939
Boston	$ 166,920	$ 188,010	$ 273,121
Chicago	$ 214,425	$ 193,299	$ 292,117
Cleveland	$ 210,061	$ 230,152	$ 327,355
Detroit	$ 181,063	$ 178,812	$ 357,156
New York	$ 356,473	$ 380,131	$ 434,460
Philadelphia	$ 248,763	$ 214,604	$ 198,627
St. Louis	$ 195,236	$ 181,429	$ 192,218
Washington	$ 225,749	$ 241,055	$ 199,338
Total	$1,798,690	$1,807,494	$2,274,392

National League

	1929	1933	1939
Boston	$ 232,222	$ 281,928	$ 205,720
Brooklyn	$ 239,093	$ 231,575	$ 245,249
Chicago	$ 302,436	$ 343,339	$ 351,176
Cincinnati	$ 218,962	$ 207,201	$ 278,112
New York	$ 283,984	$ 271,450	$ 350,298
Philadelphia	$ 243,665	$ 254,514	$ 281,420
Pittsburgh	$ 136,864	$ 220,776	$ 173,383
St. Louis	$ 214,245	$ 254,210	$ 230,871
Total	$1,871,470	$2,064,992	$2,116,228

Note: Team salaries include players, coaches, and managers' salaries.

Source: U.S. Congress, *Organized Baseball: Hearings*, 1610, and U.S. Department of Commerce *Historical Statistics* 1: 210–11 for CPI "all items" (1930 = 100).

Table 18: Nominal and Real Revenue Compared to New York Yankees' Player Payrolls, 1926–1939 (in $000s)

	Nominal				Real			
	Rev	Pay	Diff	% Pay	Rev	Pay	Diff	% Pay
1926	1,130	210	920	0.186	1,066	198	868	0.186
1927	1,255	253	1,002	0.201	1,207	243	964	0.201
1928	1,205	288	916	0.239	1,174	281	893	0.239
1929	1,139	290	850	0.254	1,111	282	828	0.254
1930	1,204	284	920	0.236	1,204	284	920	0.236
1931	927	281	646	0.303	1,016	308	708	0.303
1932	829	277	552	0.334	1,013	339	675	0.334
1933	692	242	450	0.349	892	312	580	0.349
1934	824	215	609	0.261	1,028	268	759	0.261
1935	632	202	430	0.320	768	246	523	0.320
1936	955	218	737	0.228	1,150	263	887	0.228
1937	1,092	247	845	0.226	1,270	287	982	0.226
1938	1,038	282	756	0.272	1,230	334	896	0.272
1939	1,105	297	808	0.269	1,328	357	971	0.269

Rev: Total revenue = total gate receipts - visiting share - league share - war tax + training receipts + exhibition receipts + abroad revenue + concessions revenue + broadcasting revenue
Pay: Player payrolls for only the players appearing in a game; includes bonus payments
Diff = Total revenue - player payrolls
% Pay: Player payroll/total revenue

Note: Numbers may not add up due to rounding.
Source: Deflated by CPI, "All Items." 1930 = 100. U.S. Department of Commerce, Historical Statistics 1: 210.

Table 19: Adjusting the New York Yankees' Payroll, 1930–1934

	Babe Ruth's pay	Payroll w/o Ruth	Total payroll
Nominal			
1930	$ 83,335	$ 200,862	$ 284,197
1931	$ 82,000	$ 198,696	$ 280,696
1932	$ 77,184	$ 199,724	$ 276,908
1933	$ 56,652	$ 185,336	$ 241,987
1934	$ 35,711	$ 179,622	$ 215,333
Real			
1930	$ 83,335	$ 200,862	$ 284,197
1931	$ 89,913	$ 217,862	$ 307,781
1932	$ 94,357	$ 244,162	$ 338,519
1933	$ 73,005	$ 238,835	$ 311,839
1934	$ 44,528	$ 223,967	$ 268,495

Note: Base year 1930 = 100.
Source: New York Yankees Base Ball Club cash books and general ledger.

Table 20: New York Yankees' Core Player Nominal Salaries, 1930–1934

	1930	1931	1932	1933	1934
Gehrig	25,000	25,000	25,000	23,000	23,000
Lazzeri	16,000	16,000	12,000	12,000	12,000
Lary	7,500	9,000	9,000	8,000	7,500
Ruth	80,000	80,000	75,000	52,000	35,000
Chapman	4,500	7,500	12,000	11,000	11,000
Combs	13,500	13,500	12,500	11,500	10,000
Dickey	10,000	12,500	12,500	12,500	14,500
Byrd	6,000	6,000	6,500	6,000	6,000
Ruffing	6,750	9,000	8,000	10,000	7,500
Pipgras	12,000	12,000	8,000	9,000	gone
Pennock	15,000	12,500	10,000	9,000	gone
Gomez	2,700	4,000	7,500	12,000	12,000
Total	198,950	207,000	198,000	176,000	

Note: Only players who played all four seasons (100+ at bats or 50+ innings) are included. The amounts listed are contract amounts. Chapman was paid $750 per month in 1930; Gomez was paid $450 per month in 1930. Ruth also got 25 percent of exhibition money from 1931–1934. Pipgras was traded during 1933.
Source: New York Yankees Base Ball Club cash books.

Table 21: Real Gross Operating Expenses and "Other Expenses" (in $000s)

	Real Gross Operating Expenses			Real Other Expenses		
	1929	1933	1939	1929	1933	1939
American League						
Boston	454	499	817	287	311	544
Chicago	n/a	n/a	798	n/a	n/a	506
Cleveland	462	568	706	252	338	379
Detroit	541	468	979	360	289	622
New York	921	986	1,298	564	606	863
Philadelphia	614	615	543	365	401	344
St. Louis	508	439	416	313	257	224
Washington	474	596	521	248	355	322
League	3,973	4,171	6,079	2,389	2,557	3,805
Less Chicago			5,280			3,298
National League						
Boston	473	498	496	241	216	290
Brooklyn	572	675	923	333	444	678
Chicago	828	910	974	526	567	623
Cincinnati	530	449	834	321	241	556
New York	808	829	1,086	524	557	736
Philadelphia	310	428	442	67	173	161
Pittsburgh	614	604	711	477	383	537
St. Louis	496	562	677	282	308	446
League	4,631	4,955	6,143	2,769	2,890	4,027

Other expenses: Gross operating expenses – team salaries
n/a = not available

Note: Base year 1930 = 100.
Source: U.S. Congress, *Organized Baseball: Hearings*, 1602–3, 1606–7, and 1610; U.S. Department of Commerce, *Historical Statistics* 1: 210–11.

Table 22: Selected "Other Expenses" Incurred by the New York Yankees (in $000s)

	Nominal			Real		
	1929	1933	1939	1929	1933	1939
Transportation	25	20	21	24	26	26
Hotels	18	14	17	17	18	20
Baseballs	9	12	9	9	16	11
Baseball uniforms	4	2	5	4	3	7
Baseball bats	0	0	1	0	0	1
Cabs/baggage	1	1	1	1	1	1
Miscellaneous road expenses	4	3	1	3	4	1
Scouting expenses	18	37	57	18	48	69
Scouting salaries	30	28	42	29	36	50
Office salaries	20	15	19	19	19	23
Officer salaries	33	39	53	32	50	64
Total	161	172	227	157	222	272

Note: The team spent $349, $364, and $613 for bats in 1929, 1933, and 1939. Base year 1930 = 100.

Source: New York Yankees Base Ball Club general ledger; U.S. Department of Commerce, *Historical Statistics* 1: 210–11.

Table 23: Real Cost of Player Contracts and Farm Losses

	Real Cost of Player Contracts			Real Farm Losses		
	1929	1933	1939	1929	1933	1939
American League						
Boston	-3,021	515,077	194,031	0	0	-82,700
Chicago	n/a	n/a	17,788	n/a	n/a	0
Cleveland	96,199	46,456	-45,127	51,895	3,802	55,166
Detroit	147,100	35,857	130,289	0	7,941	12,518
New York	35,181	70,550	33,834	0	40,135	-274,370
Philadelphia	15,070	-325,258	40,024	10,712	138,177	0
St. Louis	10,234	-102,076	20,072	0	0	13,096
Washington	15,241	12,649	-17,698	0	80,124	41,077
League	316,004	253,256	373,213	62,606	270,178	-235,213
Less Chicago			355,424			-235,213
National League						
Boston	-41,910	197,036	-61,719	0	18,899	23,181
Brooklyn	74,951	29,840	278,906	0	0	17,588
Chicago	293,957	152,191	146,319	32,066	120,857	0
Cincinnati	105,409	-9,924	201,022	0	0	72,993
New York	69,490	94,633	160,838	0	6,897	-96,875
Philadelphia	14,230	-170,425	60,036	0	0	0
Pittsburgh	58,333	88,821	125,962	0	0	0
St. Louis	-17,349	49,369	23,137	43,834	6,277	-67,544
League	557,112	431,540	934,500	75,901	152,930	-50,657

n/a: not available

Note: Base year 1930 = 100.

Source: U.S. Congress, *Organized Baseball: Hearings*, 1602–3 and 1606–7; U.S. Department of Commerce, *Historical Statistics* 1: 210–11.

Table 24: Measures of Competitive Balance in Major League Baseball, 1929–1941

	American League					National League				
	Games ahead	GB last	W-L pct	StDev	$Real profit	Games ahead	GB last	W-L pct	StDev	$Real profit
1929	18.0	48.0	0.693	0.103	570	10.5	43.0	0.645	0.090	734
1930	8.0	50.0	0.662	0.110	503	2.0	40.0	0.597	0.097	1,462
1931	13.5	51.5	0.704	0.125	-172	13.0	43.0	0.656	0.092	409
1932	13.0	64.0	0.695	0.148	-878	4.0	30.0	0.584	0.060	-588
1933	7.0	43.5	0.651	0.094	-1,371	5.0	33.0	0.599	0.085	-757
1934	7.0	47.0	0.656	0.101	-58	2.0	42.0	0.621	0.102	-304
1935	3.0	34.0	0.616	0.081	331	4.0	61.5	0.649	0.134	358
1936	19.5	49.0	0.667	0.101	239	5.0	38.0	0.597	0.083	641
1937	13.0	56.0	0.662	0.119	155	3.0	40.0	0.625	0.099	480
1938	9.5	46.0	0.651	0.109	354	2.0	43.0	0.586	0.093	365
1939	17.0	64.5	0.702	0.136	332	4.5	50.5	0.630	0.109	667
1940	1.0	36.0	0.584	0.088	577	12.0	50.0	0.654	0.098	196
1941	17.0	37.0	0.656	0.073	300	2.5	57.0	0.649	0.123	238
Ave.	11.3	48.2	0.661		68	5.3	43.9	0.622		300

Games ahead: Games ahead of runner-up
GB last: Games ahead of last-place team
W-L pct: Win-loss percentage of pennant winner
StDev: Standard deviation of win-loss percentage of all eight teams
$Real Profit: Consolidated profit/loss for the league in $000's, deflated by U.S. CPI (1930=100)

Source: Thorn, Palmer, and Gershman, *Total Baseball*, and U.S. Congress, *Organized Baseball: Hearings*, 1599–1600.

Appendix of Tables

Table 25: Records of Major League Baseball Teams, 1929–1941

	Wins	Losses	W-L Pct	Attendance	Profit	Real Profit
American League						
Boston	929	1,053	.469	6,651	-$ 1,819	-$2,220
Chicago	896	1,083	.453	5,874	-$ 538	-$ 684
Cleveland	1,069	923	.537	7,123	$ 433	$ 500
Detroit	1,053	943	.528	10,007	$ 1,656	$ 1,958
New York	1,247	739	.628	12,004	$2,080	$2,343
Philadelphia	945	1,031	.478	5,887	$ 199	$ 126
St. Louis	794	1,195	.399	1,881	-$1,008	-$ 1,177
Washington	1,011	977	.509	5,292	$ 28	$ 37
Total	7,944	7,944	.500	54,719	$ 1,031	$ 883
Std. Dev.			.068			
National League						
Boston	883	1,106	.444	4,772	-$ 250	-$ 315
Brooklyn	992	995	.499	9,477	$ 291	$ 213
Chicago	1,132	863	.567	11,357	$ 739	$ 648
Cincinnati	918	1,073	.461	6,235	$ 452	$ 585
New York	1,098	883	.554	9,897	$ 1,171	$ 1,336
Philadelphia	745	1,239	.376	3,010	-$ 77	-$ 91
Pittsburgh	1,059	932	.532	5,201	$ 365	$ 358
St. Louis	1,128	864	.566	5,412	$1,062	$ 1,166
Total	7,955	7,955	.500	55,361	$ 3,751	$3,900
St. Dev.			.069			

Attendance: 000's for the thirteen seasons
Profit: Consolidated profit/loss in $000's for the thirteen seasons
Real Profit: Deflated by CPI "All Items," with 1930 = 100
STD. DEV.: Standard deviation of win-loss pct.

Source: Thorn, Palmer, and Gershman, *Total Baseball*; U.S. Congress, *Organized Baseball: Hearings*, 1599–1600; U.S. Department of Commerce, *Historical Statistics*, Vol. I, 210, for deflator.

Table 26: Records of Major League Baseball Teams' Highs and Lows, 1929–1941

	P	W-L pct High	W-L pct Low	Attendance High	Attendance Low	Real Profits High	Real Profits Low
American League							
Boston	0	.591	.279	718	182	$ 65	-$692
Chicago	0	.558	.325	677	233	$ 72	-$299
Cleveland	0	.578	.487	903	388	$201	-$171
Detroit	3	.656	.396	1,113	321	$634	-$109
New York	6	.702	.558	1,169	658	$460	-$126
Philadelphia	3	.704	.346	839	233	$269	-$174
St. Louis	0	.520	.279	281	81	$ 33	-$192
Washington	1	.651	.416	614	255	$112	-$ 99
National League							
Boston	0	.539	.248	518	233	$ 27	-$155
Brooklyn	1	.649	.405	1,215	434	$427	-$196
Chicago	4	.649	.455	1,485	535	$524	-$319
Cincinnati	2	.654	.344	981	207	$403	-$198
New York	3	.608	.468	927	485	$385	-$263
Philadelphia	0	.506	.279	299	156	$122	-$ 83
Pittsburgh	0	.575	.444	641	260	$198	-$124
St. Louis	3	.656	.468	634	256	$379	-$103

P: Pennants won
W-L pct high: Highest win-loss percentage
W-L pct low: Lowest win-loss percentage
Attendance high: Highest attendance
Attendance low: Lowest attendance
Real profits high: Highest consolidated real profit in $000's (1930 = 100)
Real profits low: Lowest consolidated real profit in $000's (1930 = 100)

Source: Thorn, Palmer, and Gershman, *Total Baseball*; U.S. Congress, *Organized Baseball: Profits*, 1599–1600.

Table 27: Population of Cities With and Without Major League Baseball (in 000s)

	1900	1920	1930	1940	1950	Growth*	1930 NY
With Major League Baseball							
Boston	561	748	781	771	801	0.99	8.87
Chicago	1,699	2,702	3,376	3,397	3,621	1.01	2.05
Cincinnati	326	401	451	456	504	1.01	15.36
Cleveland	382	797	900	878	915	0.98	7.70
Detroit	286	994	1,569	1,623	1,850	1.03	4.42
New York	3,437	5,620	6,930	7,455	7,892	1.08	1.00
Philadelphia	1,294	1,824	1,951	1,931	2,072	0.99	3.55
Pittsburgh	322	588	670	672	677	1.00	10.35
St. Louis	575	773	822	816	857	0.99	8.43
Washington	279	438	487	663	802	1.36	14.23
Without Major League Baseball							
Baltimore	509	734	805	859	950	1.07	8.61
Buffalo	352	507	573	576	580	1.00	12.09
Los Angeles	102	577	1,238	1,504	1,970	1.22	5.60
Milwaukee	285	457	578	587	637	1.02	11.99
New Orleans	287	387	459	495	570	1.08	15.11
San Francisco	343	507	634	635	775	1.00	10.92

Growth*: 1940:1930 population ratio
1930 NY: 1930 New York population/city population

Source: Dodd, Historical Statistics of the States.

Table 28: Introduction and Movement of Top Players, 1919–1941

	Number	Total Rating	All	All but 2	% All	% All but 2
Boston Braves	2	29.8	0	0	0.0	0.0
Boston Red Sox	7	194.4	4	4	57.1	57.1
Brooklyn Dodgers	6	99.7	1	1	16.7	16.7
Chicago Cubs	7	159.4	1	2	14.3	28.3
Chicago White Sox	3	91.0	2	2	66.7	66.7
Cincinnati Reds	3	30.2	0	0	0.0	0.0
Cleveland Indians	14	274.7	2	4	14.3	28.6
Detroit Tigers	11	264.2	3	6	27.3	54.5
New York Giants	11	289.4	5	5	45.5	45.5
New York Yankees	19	379.9	8	11	42.1	57.9
Philadelphia Athletics	8	261.7	1	0	12.5	12.5
Philadelphia Phillies	5	89.1	1	1	20.0	20.0
Pittsburgh Pirates	10	244.6	1	1	10.0	10.0
St. Louis Browns	5	71.8	0	0	0.0	0.0
St. Louis Cardinals	13	292.5	2	4	15.4	30.8
Washington Senators	5	76.1	1	1	20.0	20.0
Total	129	2848.5	32	43	24.8	33.3

Number: Number of hitters with TBR of 7.1 or higher or pitchers with TBR of 8.9 or higher (roughly top 800 players of all time), making major league debut with the team

Total Rating: Combined ratings of players

All: Played entire major league career with the team

All but 2: Played entire major league career except the last one or two years with the team

% All: Percentage of players spending entire major league career with the team

% All but 2: Percentage of players spending all but last one or two years with the team

Source: Thorn, Palmer, and Pietrusza, *Total Baseball.*

Table 29: Main Players of the St. Louis Cardinals' Pennant-Winning Teams

	1926	1928	1930	1934
1b	Bottomley*	Bottomley*	Bottomley*	Collins*
2b	Hornsby*	Frisch	Frisch	Frisch
Ss	Thevenow*	Maranville	Gelbert*	Durocher
3b	Bell*	Holm*	Adams	Martin*
RF	Southworth	Harper	Watkins*	Rothrock
CF	Douthit*	Douthit*	Douthit*	Orsatti*
LF	Blades*	Hafey*	Hafey*	Medwick*
C	O'Farrell	Wilson	Wilson	Davis
UT	Hafey*	High	Fisher	Whitehead*
UT	Mueller*	Roettger*	Mancuso*	Delancey*
UT	Holm*	Thevenow*	High	Fullis
UT			Blades*	
P	Rhem*	Sherdel*	Hallahan*	D. Dean*
P	Sherdel*	Alexander	Johnson	Carleton*
P	Haines	Haines	Haines	P. Dean*
P	Keen	Rhem*	Grimes	Hallahan*
P	Alexander	Mitchell	Rhem*	Walker
P	Reinhart*	Johnson	Bell*	
P	Bell*	Reinhart*	Grabowski*	
P			Lindsey	

* Debuted with Cardinals

Note: Pitchers are listed in descending order of innings pitched.
Source: *Macmillan Baseball Encyclopedia*, 10th ed.

Table 30: Estimated Redistribution Due to Revenue Sharing in 1929, 1933, and 1939 (in $000s)

	1929	1933	1939	1939*
American League				
Boston	$ 10	$ 2	-$ 10	-$ 11
Chicago	n/a	n/a	-$ 28	-$ 17
Cleveland	-$ 15	-$ 25	$ 17	-$ 8
Detroit	-$122	-$ 17	-$ 87	-$ 85
New York	$ 22	-$ 22	$ 26	-$ 92
Philadelphia	$ 5	$ 43	-$ 16	$ 39
St. Louis	$ 90	$ 44	$ 77	$119
Washington	$ 41	$ 11	$ 21	$ 55
National League				
Boston	$ 35	-$ 53	$ 61	$ 72
Brooklyn	-$ 67	-$ 65	-$ 93	-$ 87
Chicago	-$190	-$ 55	-$ 29	-$ 33
Cincinnati	$ 67	$ 29	-$ 50	-$ 93
New York	-$ 61	-$ 7	-$ 25	-$ 27
Philadelphia	$ 79	$ 50	$ 1	$ 74
Pittsburgh	n/a	$ 44	$ 49	$ 50
St. Louis	$ 74	$ 57	$ 56	$ 45

Nominal "games away" revenue — estimated paid to visiting team (home attendance x average gate share per attendee)

American League paid to visiting team: Used 0.28 for 1929 (est.); 0.275 for 1933 (est.); and 0.28137 for 1939

National League paid to visiting team: Used 0.24 for 1929 (est.); 0.239788 for 1933; and 0.237638 for 1939

1939*: Estimated redistribution under a common-pool sharing arrangement

n/a: not available

Note: Chicago (American League) did not report "games away" revenue for 1929 and 1933; Pittsburgh did not report "games away" revenue for 1929. Columns may not add, due to rounding.

Source: "Games away" revenue from U.S. Congress, *Organized Baseball: Hearings*, 1602–3 and 1606–7.

Table 31: Nominal Games Away Revenue and Win-Loss Percentages in the Major Leagues (in $000s)

	Games Away Revenue	W-L Pct	Games Away Revenue	W-L Pct	Games Away Revenue	W-L Pct
	1929		1933		1939	
American League						
Boston	$121	0.377	$ 76	0.423	$151	0.589
Chicago	—	0.388	—	0.447	$139	0.552
Cleveland	$136	0.533	$ 82	0.497	$176	0.565
Detroit	$121	0.455	$ 71	0.487	$149	0.526
New York	$291	0.571	$178	0.607	$267	0.702
Philadelphia	$240	0.693	$125	0.523	$ 95	0.362
St. Louis	$169	0.520	$ 68	0.364	$108	0.279
Washington	$141	0.467	$131	0.651	$116	0.428
National League						
Boston	$124	0.364	$ 71	0.539	$129	0.417
Brooklyn	$109	0.458	$ 61	0.425	$134	0.549
Chicago	$167	0.645	$ 87	0.558	$144	0.545
Cincinnati	$138	0.429	$ 81	0.382	$183	0.630
New York	$147	0.556	$138	0.599	$142	0.510
Philadelphia	$146	0.464	$ 87	0.395	$ 97	0.298
Pittsburgh	—	0.575	$114	0.565	$138	0.444
St. Louis	$170	0.513	$119	0.536	$151	0.601

Note: Chicago (AL) 1929, 1933, and Pittsburgh 1929 did not report "games away" revenue
Source: U.S. Congress, *Organized Baseball: Hearings*, 1602–3 and 1606–7.

Table 32: Visiting Teams' and League's Shares, Road Receipts, and Revenue Sharing at Yankee Stadium Nominal Amounts,* 1926–1939

	League share	League per att	Visiting share	Visiting per att	Road receipts	Nominal revenue share	Real revenue share
1926	$ 30,830	$0.030	$289,421	$ 0.2818	$ 243,147	-$ 46,274	-$ 43,655
1927	$ 34,920	$0.030	$ 318,998	$ 0.2741	$ 285,343	-$ 33,655	-$ 32,361
1928	$ 32,166	$0.030	$294,039	$ 0.2743	$260,290	-$ 33,749	-$32,894
1929	$28,804	$0.030	$ 265,051	$ 0.2761	$ 291,159	$26,108	$ 25,446
1930	$ 35,077	$0.030	$ 318,708	$ 0.2726	$ 220,112	-$ 98,596	-$ 98,596
1931	$ 27,373	$0.030	$ 245,384	$0.2689	$ 194,588	-$ 50,796	-$ 55,697
1932	$28,870	$0.030	$ 254,589	$ 0.2646	$ 143,399	-$111,190	-$135,930
1933	$ 36,401	$0.050	$190,990	$ 0.2623	$ 178,233	-$ 12,756	-$ 16,439
1934	$ 25,640	$0.030	$ 225,658	$0.2640	$ 188,896	-$ 36,762	-$ 45,838
1935	$ 19,725	$0.030	$ 171,184	$0.2604	$ 155,969	-$ 15,215	-$ 18,509
1936	$ 29,307	$0.030	$263,504	$ 0.2697	$ 220,378	-$ 43,126	-$ 51,960
1937	$ 29,944	$0.030	$ 271,485	$ 0.2720	$ 282,369	$10,884	$ 12,655
1938	$ 29,127	$0.030	$ 262,635	$ 0.2705	$ 251,715	-$ 10,919	-$ 12,927
1939	$ 42,989	$0.050	$ 235,639	$ 0.2741	$2 67,499	$31,809	$ 38,232

League per att = League share/attendance
Visiting per att = Visiting share/attendance
Revenue sharing = Road receipts - visiting share
* except where noted

Source: New York Yankees Base Ball Club cash books; Thorn, Palmer, and Gershman, *Total Baseball*, 75–76, for attendance. Deflated by CPI "All Items." 1930 = 100 (U.S. Department of Commerce, *Historical Statistics* 1: 210).

Table 33: Average Attendance at American League Holiday Doubleheaders, 1946–1953

	At Home			On the Road		
	Dates	Attendance	Average	Dates	Attendance	Average
Boston	11	345,747	31,432	12	398,741	33,228
Chicago	10	341,821	34,182	13	339,929	26,148
Cleveland	13	436,244	33,557	11	374,224	34,020
Detroit	13	527,385	40,568	10	300,487	30,049
New York	12	642,686	53,557	11	338,517	30,774
Philadelphia	11	233,452	21,223	11	386,686	35,153
St. Louis	11	113,860	10,351	13	404,670	31,128
Washington	12	266,645	22,220	12	364,587	30,382
League	93	2,907,841	31,267	93	2,907,841	31,267

Note: Three doubleheaders were rained out (Detroit at Chicago, New York at Philadelphia, and Philadelphia at Boston).

Source: New York Times, 1946–1953.

Table 34: Offensive and Pitching Statistics, 1929–1941

	American League						National League					
	RUNS	HR	BAVE	SAVE	OBP	ERA	RUNS	HR	BAVE	SAVE	OBP	ERA
1929	10.01	0.97	.284	.408	.350	4.24	10.73	1.22	.295	.426	.357	4.72
1930	10.83	1.09	.288	.421	.351	4.65	11.37	1.44	.304	.448	.361	4.98
1931	10.28	0.93	.279	.398	.345	4.38	8.96	0.80	.277	.387	.335	3.87
1932	10.47	1.15	.277	.405	.346	4.48	9.19	1.05	.277	.397	.328	3.88
1933	10.00	1.00	.273	.391	.343	4.29	7.94	0.74	.267	.363	.318	3.34
1934	10.25	1.12	.279	.400	.351	4.50	9.37	1.08	.280	.395	.333	4.07
1935	10.18	1.09	.280	.402	.352	4.46	9.41	1.07	.278	.392	.332	4.02
1936	11.34	1.23	.290	.422	.363	5.04	9.41	0.98	.279	.387	.336	4.02
1937	10.45	1.30	.282	.415	.355	4.63	9.02	1.01	.272	.383	.332	3.92
1938	10.74	1.41	.281	.415	.358	4.79	8.83	1.00	.268	.377	.329	3.79
1939	10.41	1.29	.279	.408	.352	4.62	8.88	1.05	.273	.386	.336	3.92
1940	9.93	1.43	.272	.408	.343	4.39	8.79	1.12	.264	.376	.327	3.85
1941	9.49	1.18	.269	.390	.342	4.15	8.47	0.96	.259	.362	.327	3.64

RUNS: Runs per game (both teams)
HR: Home runs per game (both teams)
BAVE: Batting average
SAVE: Slugging average
OBP: League on-base percentage
ERA: Earned Run Average

Source: Thorn, Palmer, and Gershman, *Total Baseball.*

Table 35: Effects of Sunday Ball: Three Years Before and Three Years After

		Before Sunday ball			After Sunday ball		
		Att	W-L	P/L	Att	W-L	P/L
Boston Red Sox	1926–31	987	0.335	-150	1,190	0.374	-105
Boston Braves	1926–31	819	0.383	-119	1,352	0.411	24
Philadelphia Athletics	1931–36	1,330	0.613	97	824	0.396	-229
Philadelphia Phillies	1931–36	710	0.443	84	625	0.382	44
Pittsburgh Pirates	1931–36	836	0.537	-132	1,048	0.534	29

Att: Attendance in 000's for three seasons
W-L: Win-loss percentage for three seasons
P/L: Real consolidated profit/loss for three seasons

Note: Boston teams played Sunday games beginning in 1929. Pennsylvania teams played Sunday games beginning in 1934.

Source: U.S. Congress, *Organized Baseball: Hearings*, 1602–7, for Consolidated Profit/Loss; U.S. Department of Commerce, *Historical Statistics* 1: 210–11 for price deflator (1930=100); Thorn, Palmer, and Gershman, *Total Baseball* for attendance and win-loss records.

Table 36: Effects of Radio Broadcasts of Home Games, 1934–1935

	Before Radio (1934)			After Radio (1935)		
	Att	W-L	P/L	Att	W-L	P/L
Cleveland Indians	391	0.552	42	398	0.536	43
Phil. Athletics	306	0.453	-174	233	0.389	-5
Phil. Phillies	170	0.376	17	205	0.418	2
St. Louis Browns	115	0.441	-69	81	0.428	1
St. Louis Cardinals	325	0.621	136	506	0.623	75
Total	1,307	0.489	-46	1,423	0.480	116

Teams Maintaining Status Quo on Radio between 1934 and 1935

	1934			1935		
	Att.	W-L	P/L	Att.	W-L	P/L
Boston Braves	303	0.517	-51	233	0.248	-58
Boston Red Sox	610	0.500	-142	559	0.510	-249
Brooklyn Dodgers	434	0.467	-172	471	0.458	-181
Chicago Cubs	708	0.570	-212	693	0.649	165
Chicago White Sox	237	0.349	-260	470	0.487	11
Cincinnati Reds	207	0.344	-78	448	0.444	58
Detroit Tigers	919	0.656	472	1,035	0.616	634
New York Giants	731	0.608	127	749	0.595	242
New York Yankees	855	0.610	46	658	0.597	-126
Pittsburgh Pirates	323	0.493	-71	353	0.562	55
Washington Senators	330	0.434	25	255	0.438	22
Total	5,656	0.505	-315	5,922	0.509	572

Att.: Attendance in 000's for the season
W-L: Win-loss percentage for the season
P/L: Real consolidated profit/loss for the season

Note: Only the Boston, Chicago, Cincinnati, and Detroit teams broadcast home games in 1934. In 1935, the Cleveland, Philadelphia, and St. Louis teams began broadcasting home games (Cleveland had done so in 1932; St. Louis teams had done so up to 1933). Teams in Pittsburgh and Washington DC joined the New York Giants in broadcasting road games.

Source: U.S. Congress, *Organized Baseball: Hearings*, 1602-7 for Consolidated Profit/Loss; U.S. Department of Commerce, *Historical Statistics* 1: 210-11 for price deflator (1930 = 100); Thorn, Palmer, and Gershman, *Total Baseball*, for attendance and win-loss records. See "Where They Broadcast," *TSN*, May 4, 1933, 4, and Jonathan Light, *Cultural History of Baseball*, 602. Light appears to be incorrect about Detroit not broadcasting home games in 1934.

Table 37: Effects of Night Baseball: Three Years Before and Three Years After

		Before Night Ball			After Night Ball		
		Att	W-L	P/L	Att	W-L	P/L
Cincinnati Reds	1932–37	782	0.372	-293	1,326	0.430	219
Brooklyn Dodgers	1935–40	1,443	0.433	-382	2,595	0.530	317
Phil. Athletics	1936–41	1,101	0.351	-112	1,356	0.376	-113
Phil. Phillies	1936–41	628	0.350	-47	717	0.301	-200
Cleveland Indians	1936–41	1,717	0.541	383	2,212	0.543	386
Chicago White Sox	1936–41	1,368	0.512	-102	1,932	0.528	141
St. Louis Browns	1937–42	363	0.313	-417	671	0.477	-45
St. Louis Cardinals	1937–42	1,122	0.533	152	1,511	0.624	322
New York Giants	1937–42	2,429	0.563	533	2,291	0.505	25
Pittsburgh Pirates	1937–42	1,477	0.526	218	1,439	0.495	-30
Washington Senators	1938–43	1,243	0.446	177	1,394	0.472	76

Att.: Attendance in 000's for three seasons
W-L: Win-loss percentage for three seasons
P/L: Real consolidated profit/loss for three seasons

Note: Cincinnati began night ball in 1935. Brooklyn began night ball in 1938. Philadelphia Athletics, Philadelphia Phillies, Cleveland, and Chicago began night ball in 1939. St. Louis Browns, St. Louis Cardinals, New York Giants, and Pittsburgh Pirates began night ball in 1940. Washington Senators began night ball in 1941.

Source: U.S. Congress, *Organized Baseball: Hearings*, 1602–7 for Consolidated Profit/Loss; U.S. Department of Commerce, *Historical Statistics* 1: 210–11, for price deflator (1930=100); Thorn, Palmer, and Gershman, *Total Baseball*, for attendance and win-loss records.

Table 38: Per Capita Attendance by City, 1929–1941 (in 000s)

	1930 Population	1940 Population	Attendance	Per-Capita
Boston	781	771	11,422	14.72
Chicago	3,376	3,397	17,231	5.09
Cincinnati	451	456	6,235	13.75
Cleveland	900	878	7,123	8.01
Detroit	1,569	1,623	10,007	6.27
New York	6,903	7,455	31,378	4.36
Philadelphia	1,951	1,931	8,898	4.58
Pittsburgh	670	672	5,201	7.75
St. Louis	822	816	7,292	8.90
Washington	487	663	5,293	9.21
Total	17,938	18,662	110,080	6.02

Attendance: 1929–1941 total for all teams in each city
Per-Capita = Attendance/average population (1930 and 1940)

Source: Thorn, Palmer, and Gershman, *Total Baseball*, 75–76; U.S. Department of Commerce, Bureau of the Census, *Population* 1: 32.

Notes

Abbreviations

BM: *Baseball Magazine*
NYT: *New York Times*
TSN: *The Sporting News*

Introduction

1. There were some similarities between the 1930s and baseball's "Golden Age" of the postwar era. Baseball adapted to new technologies: radio and electric lights during the 1930s and television during the postwar period. Some franchises proved spectacularly inept, such as the Philadelphia Phillies in the 1930s and Pittsburgh Pirates in the 1950s. There were maverick owners: Larry MacPhail in the 1930s and Bill Veeck in the postwar era. Some teams reported persistent losses both during the Great Depression and in the postwar era. These losses were large enough that some clubs tried to relocate, especially the St. Louis teams, who made the attempt before and after World War II.
2. Burk, *Never Just a Game* and *Much More Than a Game*.
3. National League and American Association, *Annual Meeting*, 92.
4. National League and American Association, *Annual Meeting*, 104.
5. Fort, *Sports Economics*, 1st ed., 130.
6. "Baseball Owners Assailed as Trust," NYT, April 3, 1937.
7. "Baseball Inquiry Refused," NYT, April 15, 1937; "Cummings Orders Study on Baseball," NYT, April 8, 1937; "Decision by Holmes Nips Baseball Case: Monopoly Charge," NYT, April 10, 1937.
8. Researchers of demand for baseball games try to use a single ticket price, but the price-setting baseball owners offered a range of ticket prices. During the 1930s, most teams had three or four categories of seats, ranging from cheap bleacher seats to expensive box seats. The multiplicity of prices may have accounted for the counterintuitive findings of some researchers listed above, as they struggled to define *the* price variable. Fort, "Inelastic Sports Pricing," reviews many of the key studies.
9. Craig, "Organized Baseball," vii.
10. Haupert and Winter, "Pay Ball."

11. Zimbalist, *Baseball and Billions*, 62–63.
12. U.S. Congress, *Organized Baseball: Hearings*.
13. Levitt, *Ed Barrow*, 304.

Prologue: Clash of Titans

1. New York Yankees Base Ball Club, cash books.
2. "Crowd of 85,265, Baseball Record, Sees Yanks Win Two," NYT, September 10, 1928; Richard Vidmer, "Bishop's Homerun in 9th Beats Yanks," NYT, September 13, 1928.
3. "'The Same Old A's,' Chant the Yankees," NYT, September 10, 1928.

1. American Economy and Baseball Profits

1. "Attendance Marks Bettered," TSN, June 19, 1930, 4.
2. U.S. Department of Commerce, *Historical Statistics* 1: 224.
3. U.S. Department of Commerce, *Historical Statistics* 1: 137.
4. Motion picture theater operators had long believed that women comprised the bulk of the audience, or at least made the decision regarding which movie to attend. Movie historian Thomas Doherty relates how pollster George Gallup presented information contradicting this shibboleth. "He presented figures revealing that men actually slightly edged out women as frequent moviegoers . . . although women did seem to choose the film when moviegoers attended in couples, 'men attend the theater *alone* [italics in quote] much more often than do women. The net result is that in 51 cases out of every 100 the picture is chosen by the male.'" The theater owners were skeptical of Gallup's findings and chose to rely on their traditional beliefs. One movie official said that, even if women didn't make the decision on which movie to attend, they made the decision on whether to attend a film in the first place. He also disparaged the finding that single men attended movies more frequently by stating these congregated "in congested downtown centers of larger cities where there are enough male drifters and time-killers to keep a grind spot running on a diet of gangster, adventurer and rawer sex fare" (Doherty, *Projections of War*, 150–53; see also Doherty, *Pre-Code Hollywood*, 125–26). The obvious result of the movie moguls' belief was their production of romances and other genres featuring handsome men. One can only wonder how Major League Baseball owners would have reacted to carefully conducted market research showing that women were a larger segment of their audience than anticipated.
5. They did not deflate these numbers because of a lack of city-based consumer price indices.
6. Garrett and Wheelock, "Income Growth Across States," 465.
7. U.S. Department of Commerce, "State Personal Income 1929–99;" U.S. Department of Commerce, *Statistical Abstract 1941*, 452.
8. U.S. Department of Commerce, *Historical Statistics* 1: 224 and 319.
9. U.S. Department of Commerce, *Historical Statistics* 1: 319.
10. U.S. Department of Commerce, *Historical Statistics* 1: 401.
11. Baseball, of course, did not operate in a vacuum. Baseball teams responded to the growing need for charity events to help the unemployed. Fred Van Ness, "Teams Will Play for Charity Today," NYT, September 24, 1931; William Brandt, "Polo Grounds Crowd Pays $48,135 to Mayor's Relief Fund," NYT, September 25, 1931; "Jobless Fund

Gets $8,528," NYT, September 29, 1931; "Giant-Yankee Series for Jobless Urged," NYT, September 30, 1934.

12. U.S. Congress, *Organized Baseball: Hearings*, 1636.
13. U.S. Congress, *Organized Baseball: Hearings*, 1599–1600; Surdam, "Yankees Cope With the Great Depression."
14. "Pull Down the Dollar Sign," TSN, January 31, 1935, 4.
15. L. D. Robins, "New York Giants' Club Finances," NYT, March 8, 1941.
16. James Gould, "Fans or Just Business Men?" BM, June 1937, 299–300.
17. J. G. Taylor Spink, "Ruppert of the Hard Head and Soft Heart," TSN, January 19, 1939, 4.
18. "Rules AAA Payments Subject to Taxation," NYT, July 31, 1936.
19. New York Yankees Base Ball Club, cash books and Philadelphia Phillies, cash books.
20. Jack Malaney, "Deficit of Red Sox Shows Yawkey Grit," TSN, June 29, 1939, 3.
21. F. C. Lane, "Hard Times Are Baseball's Golden Opportunity," BM, September 1933, 426.
22. F. C. Lane, "Baseball Problems of the Winter Meetings," BM, December 1933, 292.
23. Harry Brundidge, "Phil Ball Has Lost Money on Browns All but One Year of Ownership," TSN, October 20, 1932, 5; an earlier article claimed Ball lost $250,000 per year on the team (Dan Daniel, "Phil Ball, Despite Huge Cost of His Hobby, Still Pursues Pennant," TSN, February 11, 1932, 7).
24. U.S. Congress, *Organized Baseball: Hearings*, 1599.
25. "Breadon and Barnes Optimistic Over Chances of St. Louis," NYT, January 3, 1938; Dick Farrington, "Barnes At Bat Again for 14 Night Games," TSN, October 23, 1941, 1 and 5.
26. "Cards Declare Dividend," NYT, October 17, 1928; "Dividend of 20 Per Cent Is Declared by Cardinals," NYT, August 19, 1931.
27. Dick Farrington, "Breadon Glad He Didn't Sell Out," TSN, December 13, 1934, 1.
28. Dick Farrington, "Flagless Cards Earn Big Coin, Dividend Nets Breadon $80,657," TSN, October 17, 1935, 1.
29. "Cards Vote $8 Dividend," NYT, October 28, 1937.
30. "No First Division, No Dividends," TSN, February 23, 1939, 4. Another writer stated that some teams needed 300,000 paid admissions just to cover player salaries ("What Spectators Mean," TSN, February 25, 1932, 4).
31. Dick Farrington, "Cards Pay Dividend Out of Cash Deals," TSN, January 2, 1941, 1 and 6; Dick Farrington, "Barnes at Bat Again for 14 Night Games," TSN, October 23, 1941, 1 and 5.
32. Dick Farrington, "Card Farm Losses Far Over $100,000," TSN, October 15, 1942, 1 and 13.
33. Frederick Lieb, "Card Profit Doubled to $100,000," TSN, October 21, 1943, 1 and 2; Dick Farrington, "Card Dividend of $2 Smallest in Years," TSN, December 17, 1942, 3.
34. Tom Swope, "Reds Dip Into the Red," TSN, November 15, 1934, 1; "Reds Finished in Black," NYT, October 15, 1935; Tom Swope, "Reds Finish in Black with $105,000 Profit," TSN, November 26, 1936, 1 and 2; "Powel Crosley Reports on 1939 Profits and Attendance," NYT, October 27, 1939.
35. "Reds' Profit Decreases Despite World Series," NYT, October 11, 1940; Tom Swope, "Pair of Flags Gives Cincinnati Gate of 2,019,591 For Two Years," TSN, October 17, 1940, 2; "Reds Pay $12 a Share," NYT, November 19, 1940.

36. Tom Swope, "Dollar Token Dividend Declared on Red Stock," TSN, October 29, 1942, 7; Tom Swope, "Reds in Black for 1943, Show $18,000 Profit," TSN, November 18, 1943, 4; U.S. Congress, *Organized Baseball: Hearings*, 1600.

37. Denman Thompson, "Nats Allow Boys to See Games for 25 Cents," TSN, January 11, 1934, 1.

38. Paul Shannon, "Braves Loss in 1939 Ran Above $150,000," TSN, December 13, 1934, 1; U.S. Congress, *Organized Baseball: Hearings*, 1600.

39. "Phil Directors Pass Dividend," TSN, December 2, 1943, 4; U.S. Congress, *Organized Baseball: Hearings*, 1600.

40. Ralph Davis, "Majors Scheduled to Open on April 15," TSN, November 21, 1929, 5; U.S. Congress, *Organized Baseball: Hearings*, 1600.

41. Joe Vila, "Hoyt and Reese Dissatisfied with Terms of Yankees and Hold Out," TSN, January 30, 1930, 1.

42. Dan Daniel, "'Game Will Surpass '27-'28 This Year'—Ruppert," TSN, January 7, 1937, 1."

43. "Cubs Report Loss of $600,000 in 3 Years; Balanced Payroll," NYT, January 10, 1935; U.S. Congress, *Organized Ball: Hearings*, 1600.

44. Ed Burns, "Wrigley Spreads Holiday Cheer, Reveals Substantial Cub Profit," TSN, December 26, 1935, 1; U.S. Congress, *Organized Baseball: Hearings*, 1600.

45. "Yawkey's Deficit Nearly $2,000,000," NYT, April 28, 1937; U.S. Congress, *Organized Baseball: Hearings*, 1599.

46. Jack Malaney, "Deficit of Red Sox Shows Yawkey Grit," TSN, June 29, 1939, 3; U.S. Congress, *Organized Baseball: Hearings*, 1599.

47. U.S. Congress, *Organized Baseball: Hearings*, 1599–1611.

48. Quirk and Fort, *Pay Dirt*, quote on 55, charts on 49–57 and 391–408.

49. James Dawson, "Barrow Is Elected President of Yankees," NYT, January 18, 1939.

50. Dan Daniel, "Sale of Yankees to Group Headed by Jim Farley Reported to be Near," TSN, May 9, 1940, 1; Dan Daniel, "No Serious Bid Yet Made for Yankees," TSN, May 9, 1940, 11.

51. J. G. Taylor Spink, "Here's Why Yanks Are Being Sold—And Why Deal Is Delayed," TSN, May 16, 1940, 4.

52. "Contracts Drawn, Money Up, for Sale of Yankees to Farley," TSN, July 11, 1940, 1; "$4,000,000 Price in Contract to Buy Yankees," NYT, July 16, 1940; Dan Daniel, "Yankee-Farley Deal Nearing Showdown," TSN, November 21, 1940; John Drebinger, "Farley Expects Deal for Yankees Shortly," NYT, January 10, 1941.

2. Why Did Profits Collapse? Revenue Side

1. "Attendance Marks Bettered," TSN, June 19, 1930, 4.

2. Irving Sanborn, "Does Football Threaten Baseball's Supremacy?" BM, February 1928, 392–93.

3. "Keeping the Crowds Away," TSN, July 16, 1936, 4; "Baseball Crowds Showed Big Gains," NYT, October 6, 1937.

4. George Bennie, "Major League Baseball Attendance Reports," NYT, July 8, 1939.

5. "Yankees Drew 2,500,000 Fans Last Season," NYT, January 4, 1928.

6. Irving Vaughan, "Chicago Will Retain Place as Best Fan Center in National,"

Notes to pages 30–33

TSN, September 20, 1928, 1; John Drebinger, "Ten-Man Baseball Advocated by Heydler," NYT, December 12, 1928.

7. "Decline in Crowds Worries Magnates," NYT, August 24, 1929; "Barnard Sees Gain of 1,000,000 at Games," NYT, July 7, 1929.

8. A sportswriter claimed that because the Cubs' park contained four times the number of box seats as did Yankee Stadium, the Chicago team could get more gate receipts than the Yankees. The World Series receipts for 1928 and 1929 reported in *The Sporting News* disputed the sportswriter's claim. Two games at Yankee Stadium brought in $467,000 in receipts, while two games at Chicago's Wrigley Field had just $281,000 in receipts. John Drebinger, "Cubs Expect to Top Yanks' Best Gate," NYT, September 21, 1929; "Athletics' Tickets Ready for Fans," NYT, October 2, 1929; "Facts and Figures of the Big Classic," TSN, October 18, 1928, 3; "Facts and Figures on World's Series," TSN, October 17, 1929, 3.

9. "Major Leagues Put Off Radio Problem," NYT, December 9, 1931.

10. "250,000 Free Passes Here Bring Curb on Free List," NYT, February 5, 1932; "AL Attendance Shows Big Drop; NL Keeps Pace with 1930–31," NYT, April 20, 1932.

11. "Real Fan Sentiment," TSN, May 5, 1932, 4. Using game-by-game data from http://www.Retrosheet.org, I examined how many games were decided by one run in the National League in 1930 and 1931. The reduction in scoring in 1931 did not lead to an increase in the number of such games. There were 190 games decided by a single run in 1930 and 185 in 1931, after the National League deadened the baseball to curtail offense. There were fewer such games in the American League: 176 in 1930 and 166 in 1931.

12. "Better Baseball," TSN, May 12, 1932, 4.

13. "NL Will Number Its Players; Decrease in Gate: Bad Weather," NYT, June 23, 1932.

14. "Cleveland in New Stadium," TSN, August 4, 1932, 4; "80,285 See Indians Bow to Athletics," NYT, August 1, 1932; Ed Bang, "Cleveland Sets All-Time Mark with Stadium Crowd of 80,284," TSN, August 4, 1932, 1.

15. Ed Bang, "93,000 Is Cleveland 'Dream Game' Goal," TSN, December 20, 1934, 5.

16. Dan Daniel, "Big Leagues Indulge Wholesale Trading of Players—Curb Landis: Commissioner Will Find Farms Posted," TSN, December 22, 1932, 3 and 6.

17. "Baseball in Depression," NYT, October 9, 1932.

18. "Attendance Drops 20% in Football," NYT, October 20, 1932.

19. "Survey Shows 1932 Football Receipts Off 5 to 50% on Price Cuts and Attendance Drop," NYT, December 14, 1932.

20. The Chicago White Sox, proud owners of three of Connie Mack's former stars, boosted the gate by 165,000 in 1933. "Gain in White Sox Fans," NYT, November 30, 1933.

21. "Landis Predicts Baseball Revival," NYT, November 14, 1933.

22. The *Sporting News* stated that only two teams in the American League (Washington and Chicago) had lower attendance in 1934 and that only one team lost money during the season. H. G. Salsinger, "Why Attendance Increased in '34," TSN, December 6, 1934, 3; U.S. Congress, *Organized Baseball: Hearings*, 1599.

23. "Baseball Upturn Seen by Harridge," NYT, December 23, 1934.

24. Dick Farrington, "Sale Talk Reveals Cardinals Drew 334,000," TSN, November 22, 1934, 1.

25. "Something to Think About," TSN, November 22, 1934, 4.

26. Dan Daniel, a reporter for the *Sporting News*, reported that the New York teams

drew a combined 500,000 more fans in 1934, although he admitted that much of the Yankees' attendance was in the stadium's large bleacher section, some 22,000 seats. Dan Daniel, "N.Y. Attendance Jumps 500,000 Despite Absence of Flag Winner," TSN, November 22, 1934, 1.

27. Tom Swope, "Reds Draw 152,276 at 18 Home Games," TSN, May 30, 1935, 3; "Cincinnati Ends the Argument," TSN, July 9, 1936, 4.

28. "Financial Records Created in Series," NYT, October 7, 1936; "All Reserved Seats for Giants' Twin Bill Gone," NYT, September 9, 1936.

29. "Cards Popular on the Road," NYT, October 27, 1936; "Browns Show Patronage Gain," NYT, July 20, 1937.

30. The *New York Times* was impressed that a Sunday crowd of 62,000 came to watch the Indians defeat the Yankees. The newspaper cited how Cleveland had been "confronted with the gravest relief problem in the nation," with 87,000 families on relief. "If we in New York did as well by a baseball game we should have to turn out a crowd of 450,000 spectators." "Baseball Draws Cleveland," NYT, May 25, 1938.

31. The paper reported a total attendance of 10 million, an increase of 600,000. The figures shown by Thorn, Palmer, and Gershman in Total Baseball, 76 showed 9 million and an increase of less than 100,000. "Good Season Financially," NYT, October 3, 1938.

32. "Brooklyn Season Attendance Record," NYT, September 12, 1939; "Cincinnati Reds: Comment on Attendance," NYT, June 1, 1939; see also John Drebinger, "Yanks to Play 3 Twin Bills in 4 Days," NYT, September 28, 1939; Tommy Holmes, "A Million or Bust, MacPhail's Slogan," TSN, September 28, 1939, 3; James Isaminger, "Improved Gait at Gate Shown by Philly Clubs," TSN, October 12, 1939, 14 for MacPhail's attempt to reach 1 million in attendance.

33. The Tigers' pennant in 1940 pushed attendance higher by over a quarter-million, but the team's on-the-field woes in 1941 triggered a collapse in attendance, as 430,000 fewer fans paid admission. "Major League Attendance for 1941," NYT, October 28, 1941.

34. Ed Burns, "Figures Show Cubs No Bears as Draws," TSN, November 6, 1941, 2.

35. Edgar Brands, "Breadon, with 23 Farms, 13 More Than Any Rival," TSN, November 19, 1942, 1 and 8.

36. "Major Leagues: 1942 Attendance Report," NYT, October 3, 1942. The *Sporting News* thought the New York clubs' combined drop of about 200,000 was not too bad, considering that the city was "without the wartime financial advantages which have come to so many other cities, especially in the Middle West. New York virtually has been ignored in the allotment of war works contracts. There are 400,000 idle men in this city, while in other cities there is a shortage of labor." Dan Daniel, "Draw of N.Y. Clubs Nearing 2,000,000," TSN, August 6, 1942, 3; Dan Daniel, "Giants' Turnstiles Keep Hot with Ott," TSN, June 4, 1942, 16.

37. "ML Will Not Cut Ticket Prices, Because They Were Not Raised," NYT, January 16, 1932.

38. Joe Vila, "N.L. Economy Plans Explained by President Heydler," TSN, December 24, 1931.

39. "ML Will Not Cut Ticket Prices, Because They Were Not Raised," NYT, January 16, 1932; see Ford Frick's comments in "Frick to Oppose Cuts," NYT, March 15, 1935.

40. "Opportunity of the Majors," TSN, December 7, 1933, 4.

41. "Indians Reduce Admission Prices," NYT, February 5, 1933.

42. James Isaminger, "Philly Fans Watch Extremes in Pilots," *TSN*, April 19, 1934, 2.

43. "Reds Cut Admissions," *NYT*, April 13, 1934. Given the owners' conservative approach to ticket pricing, the idea of varying ticket prices on the basis of desirability of a playing date or opponent may have been too exotic for them. In addition, the ticket-price system based on multiples of fifty cents was easy to handle at the box office, whereas changing prices, by ten or twenty cents might have proven a headache with a large crowd. Why the owners resisted a form of today's differential pricing remains an intriguing question.

44. "Four Half-Price Days, One Free for Women at Braves' Games," *NYT*, April 7, 1932; "Night Lights Burning Low in the Majors," *TSN*, December 5, 1935, 1.

45. "Paying the Freight," *TSN*, January 28, 1932, 2; "It All Depends," *TSN*, July 7, 1932, 4.

46. "The Pass Evil," *TSN*, February 18, 1932, 4.

47. Joe Vila, "Gotham Clubs Put Lid on Pass Addicts," *TSN*, March 17, 1932, 2; James Harrison, "Schedule for 1928 Is Adopted by National League," *NYT*, February 4, 1928.

48. "Ticket Tax Cut Starts Tomorrow," *NYT*, June 28, 1928; "Admissions Tax Begins on June 21," *NYT*, June 4, 1932; "That Tax," *TSN*, April 7, 1932, 4; "Admission Tickets Tax-Free to June 21," *NYT*, June 21, 1932.

49. "Not the Same Law," *TSN*, June 23, 1932, 4; "Federal Tax Will Cost Game About $2,000,000," *TSN*, April 7, 1932, 4.

50. The burden of the tax depends on relative elasticities of demand and supply. If supply is perfectly elastic (horizontal) and the tax reduces demand, market price stays constant but you get a large decrease in quantity; with relatively inelastic demand, a tax on suppliers results in a relatively large increase in price.

51. "Something for Nothing," *TSN*, May 24, 1934, 4.

52. "Modify the Admission Tax," *TSN*, November 17, 1932, 4.

53. "Heydler Farewell a Warning on Taxes," *TSN*, December 20, 1934, 3; "Tax Gougers Threaten," *TSN*, August 3, 1933, 4; "Defeating the Tax Grabbers," *TSN*, May 3, 1934, 4.

54. James Isaminger, "New State Tax Adds More Woe in Philly," *TSN*, August 1, 1935, 5.

55. "Sensible," *TSN*, May 19, 1932, 4; "Admission Prices," *TSN*, April 14, 1932, 4.

56. A. R., "A Baseball Complaint," *NYT*, July 24, 1937.

57. J. F. X. C., "Problem in Price-Fixing," *NYT*, July 31, 1937.

58. Louis Burt, "Wants Lower Admission Prices," *NYT*, July 29, 1939.

59. John McDonald, "Prices at Ebbets Field," *NYT*, June 22, 1940; E. J. Marchese, "Ebbets Field Bleacher Seats," *NYT*, April 29, 1939; Dale Zysman, "Dodger Ticket Prices," *NYT*, June 15, 1940.

60. "Ticket Speculation," *TSN*, May 12, 1932, 4.

61. Years ago the Art Institute of Chicago held a wildly successful Monet exhibit. Ticket arbitragers bought up blocks of tickets for the show's conclusion, but overestimated demand. These speculators took an impressionistic bath (one might say they should have "taken the Monet and run").

62. Kahneman, Knetsch, and Thaler, "Fairness as a Constraint on Profit Seeking."

63. "Yanks Ready for Applications for World Series Tickets," *NYT*, September 14, 1932; John Simmons, "World Series Seats," *NYT*, September 25, 1937; "Mail Orders Necessary for Yankees World Series Tickets," *NYT*, September 27, 1939.

64. James Dawson, "Series Sale Points to $1,000,000 Gate," *NYT*, September 26, 1936; James Dawson, "Sale of Tickets for Series Spurts," *NYT*, October 3, 1933.

65. "Speculators Ask $12," NYT, October 6, 1937.
66. "MacPhail Is Quizzed on Ticket Charges," NYT, September 18, 1941
67. Richard Vidmer, "Yankee-Athletic Ticket Rush Brings Police," NYT, September 7, 1928.
68. "75,000 Requests Rejected," NYT, October 3, 1928.
69. James Harrison, "Record World's Series Crowd," NYT, October 5, 1928; "St. Louis Fans Gay as They Storm Park," NYT, October 8, 1928; James Harrison, "Yankees Win Series, Total Receipts $277,290," NYT, October 10, 1928; "U.S. to Get $80,000 Tax," NYT, October 10, 1928.
70. "Landis to Pick Dodgers' Home Site for World Series," NYT, September 3, 1941; Louis Effrat, "World Series Start Set Officially for the Yankee Stadium," NYT, September 4, 1941.
71. "Record Baseball Throng Paid $91,610 at Stadium," NYT, May 31, 1938. The Yankees' cash book listed $90,909.50 in home receipts, but there were some advance sales, too. The team paid almost $25,000 to the visiting Bosox for the entire series.
72. Dan Daniel, "It Is Not All Gravy," BM, August 1940, 391.
73. Daniel also discussed the Brooklyn club. Because Ebbets Field had fewer than four thousand bleacher seats out of over thirty thousand seats, the club's per-attendee figure was close to 99¢, which was higher than the Yankees' per-attendee figure. Dan Daniel, "It Is Not All Gravy," BM, August 1940, 392.
74. L. D. Robins, "New York Giants' Club Finances," NYT, March 8, 1941.
75. Dan Daniel, "Peanuts, Pop and Popcorn!," BM, April 1937, 489; Robert Coughlan, "Baseball: Nine Men," *Sports Illustrated*, February 27, 1956, 23.
76. New York Yankees scorecards, 1934–42; New York Giants scorecards 1938–39; Brooklyn Dodgers scorecards 1934–41.
77. Meyer Berger, "In the Ball Park Every Man's a King," NYT, April 14, 1935; Arthur Patterson, "Stevens Family Sold First Hot Dog at Polo Grounds, 40 Years Ago," TSN, November 23, 1939, 3.
78. J. G. Taylor Spink, "Feeding the Fans in Stevens Family Style," TSN, February 13, 1941, 4 and 7.
79. T. W. McNiel, "Hot Dogs, Peanuts and Popcorn!" BM, July 1938, 358; Veeck, *Veeck—As In Wreck*, 119.
80. "Putting on the Dog for the Hot Dog," TSN, January 23, 1941, 4.
81. Boston Red Sox scorecards 1935–36; Philadelphia Athletics scorecards 1938; Boston Braves scorecards 1941; Chicago Cubs scorecards 1935–40; Philadelphia Phillies scorecards 1944.
82. Veeck, *Veeck—As In Wreck*, 121 and 127.
83. Joe Vila, "Stadium Panic Has Kickback in Court," TSN, November 14, 1929, 3.
84. Haupert and Winter, "Pay Ball."
85. "Giants and Yanks Complete Arrangements for Broadcasting," NYT, January 26, 1939; W. A. McWade, "Ball Games on the Air: Reader Scolds Giants and Yank for Stand on Broadcasts," NYT, May 8 1943.
86. U.S. Congress, *Organized Baseball: Hearings*, 1113 and 1119.
87. I examined the *New York Times* archives from June 1932 to see whether any articles referred to the resumption of the amusement tax and ticket prices at Yankee Stadium but found no mention of the tax in any baseball stories.

88. U.S. Congress, *Organized Baseball: Hearings*, 1119 and Dan Daniel, "'Game Coming Back Bigger Than Ever,' Says Ruppert, Park Enlarged," TSN, January 19, 1933, 3.
89. National Baseball Hall of Fame & Museum collection.
90. http://www.cgi.ebay.com/x-1929-New-York-Yankees-Babe-Ruth-2-Home-Run and cgi.ebay.com/x-1934-Yankees-Game-Ticket-Stub-Ruth-HR.
91. New York Yankees Base Ball Club, Cash Book, November 10, 1939.
92. "Ads for today's game," NYT, July 1, 1931; June 1, 1932; July 1, 1932; July 1, 1933; and July 13, 1934.
93. "Fans to Pay Tax," NYT, June 16, 1932.
94. F. C. Lane, "Big Business in a Ball Park," BM, April 1929, 516.
95. U.S. Congress, *Organized Baseball: Hearings*, 1107; U.S. Congress, *Organized Professional Team Sports*, 1448.
96. "Ladies' Day Announced for Yankee Stadium," NYT, March 23, 1938.
97. Surdam, "Yankees Cope with the Great Depression," 824.
98. Surdam, "Yankees Cope with the Great Depression," 828–29; Surdam, "What Brings Fans to the Ball Park," 42–43.
99. "Yankees Will Enlarge Stadium to Seat 84,000," NYT, February 5, 1936; see also "Yankees Plan New Stand," NYT, March 4, 1933; Joe Vila, "Ruppert Looks Out for Bleacher Fans," TSN, March 16, 1933.
100. "Dodgers Plan New Bleachers to Give 6,500 55-Cent Seats," NYT, March 8, 1933; Joe Vila, "Ruppert Looks Out for Bleacher Fans," TSN, March 16, 1933, 1; "Cubs to Enlarge Park," NYT, October 12, 1935.
101. "What About Bleachers?" TSN, December 22, 1932, 4.
102. "Ladies' Day Announced for Yankee Stadium," NYT, March 23, 1938.

3. Why Did Profits Collapse? Player Salaries

1. U.S. Congress, *Organized Baseball: Hearings*, 1602–11; U.S. Congress, *Organized Professional Team Sports*, 2048–52; Surdam, *Postwar Yankees*, 72.
2. Levin, Mitchell, Volcker, and Will, *Report*, 61, 65, 69, 73, and 77.
3. Rottenberg, "Baseball Player's Market," 248.
4. Helyar, *Lords of the Realm*; Burk, *Never Just a Game*; Burk, *Much More than a Game*; U.S. Congress, *Organized Baseball: Report*.
5. "Profitable 'Bondage,'" TSN, February 8, 1940, 4.
6. "Why Tie Them Up?" TSN, January 22, 1931, 4.
7. "This Matter of Salaries," TSN, January 23, 1930, 4; "Players and Contracts," TSN, March 6, 1930, 4.
8. U.S. Congress, *Organized Baseball: Hearings*, 1611.
9. Years later, Lou Comiskey of the White Sox maintained that when the club drew over 500,000 at home he was willing to "split a good portion of the gravy among deserving employees." Unfortunately for Sox players, the team only attained the 500,000 figure once between 1928 and 1938 (in 1937), so there wasn't much gravy to share. Irving Vaughan, "Half-Million Attendance Chisox' Salary Yardstick," TSN, February 9, 1939, 1; "Valuation of a Player," TSN, January 1, 1931, 4.
10. "Players and Automobiles," TSN, April 18, 1929, 4.
11. "Why Player Unions Fail," TSN, February 18, 1937, 4.
12. "Players' Union," TSN, August 4, 1932, 4.

13. "Pensions for Players," TSN, November 11, 1937, 4.
14. Surdam, *Postwar Yankees*, 220 and 229.
15. "The Players' Salaries," TSN, June 27, 1929, 4; "Players' Salaries," TSN, August 22, 1929, 4.
16. F. C. Lane, "Serious Problems Which Confront Baseball," BM, January 1933, 340.
17. Bill Dooly, "Connie Mack Spent $700,000 to Produce a Winning Club," TSN, January 30, 1930, 3.
18. A reporter thought Simmons made just $18,000 in 1930 but correctly reported the three-year contract for $100,000. Ed Burns, "Simmons Clouts Near $28,000 Mark," TSN, January 11, 1934, 5.
19. "The Fortunate Ball Player," TSN, February 5, 1931, 4.
20. "Signing Players," TSN, March 5, 1931, 4.
21. "The Valuation of Labor," TSN, March 19, 1931, 4.
22. "Sad Plight of Heroes," NYT, January 14, 1932.
23. "The Unnecessary Surplus," TSN, November 7, 1929, 4.
24. John Drebinger, "Majors to Reduce Squads on May 15," NYT, December 14, 1932; "Ban on Radio or High Fee for Broadcasting Games Looms," NYT, December 8, 1931; "Salary Cuts and Reduction of Player Limit Voted by ML," NYT, December 11, 1931; "The Cut in Players," TSN, December 17, 1931, 14.
25. "The Player Limit," TSN, July 28, 1932, 4.
26. "The Player Reduction," TSN, June 23, 1932, 4.
27. Dan Daniel, "Majors Expected to Return to Old 25-Player Limit," TSN, December 8, 1938, 1; John Drebinger, "Big Leagues Ready to Adopt One Ball; Restore 25 Man Roster," NYT, December 11, 1938; Edgar Brands, "Major Leagues Split on Changing Ball and Increasing Player Limit," TSN, December 16, 1937, 3 and 10; Dan Daniel, "Barrow to Put Up Battle for Player Limit of 28 to 30," TSN, November 26, 1942, 1.
28. Denman Thompson, "Senators Force Cuts in Salary for 1932," TSN, September 10, 1931, 3; "The Question of Salary," TSN, October 22, 1931, 4; Edgar Brands, "Economy Made Watchword of Majors at Meetings," TSN, December 17, 1931, 3; "Conforming to National Conditions," TSN, December 17, 1931, 4.
29. "Ban on Radio or High Fee for Broadcasting Games Looms," NYT, December 8, 1931; "Salary Cuts and Reduction of Player Limit Voted by ML," NYT, December 11, 1931; "Trades Imminent; Ruppert Against Salary Limits," NYT, December 5, 1931.
30. "Ruth and $50,000," TSN, January 26, 1933, 4.
31. "Ruth, Relenting, Would Accept 15% Pay Cut," NYT, January 20, 1933.
32. Burk, *Much More than a Game*, 308.
33. Levin, Mitchell, Volcker, and Will, *Report*, 61, 65, 69, 73, and 77.
34. "Salary Lists of Major Leagues to be Cut $1,000,000," NYT, January 13, 1932; F. C. Lane, "Slashing Baseball Salaries," BM, February 1932, 402; "Reductions in Salaries," TSN, September 8, 1932, 4.
35. Gregory, *Baseball Player*, 96.
36. "Majors Put Off Consideration of Contracts Till After Parley," TSN, November 10, 1932, 1; "The Players," TSN, October 27, 1932, 4; "Big League Salaries Are Due for a Slashing, Fuchs Says," NYT, December 6, 1932; "Indians to Cut Salaries," NYT, January 20, 1933.
37. Dick Farrington, "Majors Likely to Shelve Move for Horizontal Cut in Salaries," TSN, December 8, 1932, 1.

38. William Brandt, "Meal Money," *BM*, July 1933, 343.
39. "Where Economy Won't Hurt," *TSN*, October 13, 1932, 4; "Wave of Economy Washing Away Major Leagues' Coaching Staffs," *TSN*, November 24, 1932, 1; "Ten Umpires for Staff; AL Drops One Umpire," *NYT*, January 5, 1932.
40. Lewis, *Cleveland Indians*, 178.
41. "The Commissioner Takes a Cut," *TSN*, January 12, 1933, 4; "Landis Cuts His Own Pay $10,000 to $40,000," *NYT*, January 8, 1933; "Landis Voluntarily Cuts Salary 40 Per Cent," *TSN*, January 12, 1933, 1; "Up to the Commissioner," *TSN*, January 5, 1933, 4.
42. "The Boys Fall in Line," *TSN*, February 2, 1933, 4; "Breadon to Slash Cardinals $60,000," *TSN*, January 19, 1933, 5; Ed Bang, "General Reduction in Pay of Tribesmen," *TSN*, January 19, 1933, 2; Tom Swope, "Further Cut Made in Payroll of Reds," *TSN*, August 17, 1933, 2; "Exceeding Salary Limits," *TSN*, June 22, 1933, 4.
43. F. C. Lane, "What's Wrong with Baseball, Anyway?" *BM*, April 1933, 384; "Harridge Sees Pay Cut," *NYT*, October 11, 1933.
44. Tommy Holmes, "Dodgers Planning Blanket Salary Cut," *TSN*, January 11, 1934, 8; Denman Thompson, "Senators to be Cut in Spite of Triumph," *TSN*, November 2, 1933, 6.
45. "Yankees' Success in Signing Ruth Early," *NYT*, January 17, 1934.
46. Bill Dooly, "Grove Drawing $25,000 Salary, Ranks as Best Paid Moundsman," *TSN*, March 10, 1932, 1.
47. "Salaries on the Rebound," *TSN*, January 23, 1936, 4; Ed Bang, "Payroll of Indians Due to Rise $30,000," *TSN*, January 24, 1935, 6.
48. "Peak Baseball Salaries of 1931 Not Approached by Today's," *NYT*, February 11, 1936.
49. Paul Shannon, "Depression Sets in On Millionaires," *TSN*, January 28, 1937, 2; "No Cuts for Red Sox; Several to Get Good Increases," *NYT*, January 19, 1939; U.S. Congress, *Organized Baseball, Hearings*, 1610.
50. "Baseball Payroll Biggest on Record," *NYT*, March 25, 1937; "$3,000,000 Big League Payroll Fails to Cut Holdout Ranks," *NYT*, January 24, 1937; Dan Daniel, "Payroll of Yanks May Run $300,000," *TSN*, March 11, 1937, 5; Dan Daniel, "N.Y. Players' Pay Close to $700,000," *TSN*, January 28, 1937, 5.
51. "Cuts in View Despite Pennant," *NYT*, January 27, 1939.
52. Dan Daniel, "Yankee 'Board' Reorganizing Under Barrow," *TSN*, January 19, 1939, 1; Dan Daniel, "Generous Contract Policy for Yankees," *TSN*, December 1, 1938, 3.
53. Dick Farrington, "Pay Roll of Cards Close to $200,000," *TSN*, February 2, 1939, 3; Dick Farrington, "Cards Payroll Rises 15 Pct. Along with Flag Prospects," *TSN*, February 22, 1940, 1 and 7.
54. Tom Swope, "Red Payroll to Top 1939 All-Time High," *TSN*, January 18, 1940, 1.
55. Stan Baumgartner, "Mack Shares Gate Increase," *TSN*, January 2, 1941, 10.
56. Dick Farrington, "Owl Ball Hurdles Cleared in St. Louis," *TSN*, February 1, 1940, 3.
57. John Drebinger, "10% of Players' Salaries to be Voluntarily Diverted," *NYT*, February 3, 1942; John Drebinger, "New York Club Seeks Ruling on Player Salary Freezing," *NYT*, November 28, 1942; "New York Club Player Contracts Unaffected by Salary Freeze," *NYT*, December 16, 1942.
58. U.S. Congress, *Professional Sports Antitrust Bill—1965*, 144.
59. Joe Vila, "Gehrig Heads for Yankee Camp After Quitting Holdout Ranks," *TSN*, February 19, 1931, 1.

60. James Harrison, "Yanks Sign Gehrig to 3-Year Contract," NYT, January 7, 1928; Eig, *Luckiest Man*, discusses Gehrig's failings as a negotiator, 192–95.

61. Dan Daniel, "Gehrig in Line for $7,000 Raise as Yankees Cut Payroll $50,000," TSN, February 7, 1935, 1; Roscoe McGowen, "Gehrig Expected to Ask $35,000 Salary from Yanks," NYT, February 14, 1935; James Dawson, "Yanks Sign Gehrig for One Year; Salary Reported $30,000," NYT, February 20, 1935.

62. Eig, *Luckiest Man*, 195, cites Eleanor Gehrig's scrapbooks.

63. "$31,000 Received by Gehrig in 1935," NYT, January 12, 1937; Roscoe McGowen, "Gehrig and Ruppert Fail to Reach Salary Accord," NYT, January 29, 1937; John Drebinger, "Gehrig Signed by Yanks at Estimated Salary of $35,000," NYT, January 26, 1939; New York Yankees Base Ball Club, Player Contract Books.

64. Dan Daniel, "Gehrig's Weak Legs Worry Joe M'Carthy," TSN, March 30, 1939, 3.

65. Dan Daniel, "DiMaggio Asks for $40,000," TSN, January 27, 1938, 1; Dan Daniel, "Yanks Ready to 'Up' DiMag's Pay $7,000," TSN, January 20, 1938, 1; "Ruppert Favors Ban on Post-Season Play," NYT, November 22, 1935.

66. Dan Daniel, "Year 'Round Monthly Salaries, Ruppert Idea to Curb Hold-Outs," TSN March 31, 1938, 1.

67. Dan Daniel, "Hoag Takes a Load Off Yanks, Places It on Joe DiMaggio," TSN, April 7, 1938, 1; Cramer, *Joe DiMaggio*, 114–19; Dan Daniel, "Col. Ruppert Blasts Yank Break-Up Idea," TSN, January 13, 1938, 3.

68. Dan Daniel, "DiMag Gives Laugh to Training Theory," TSN, May 12, 1938, 2.

69. "Braves Will Pay Hornsby $121,800," NYT, March 2, 1928.

70. "Terry Cuts Demand to $25,000 for Year," NYT, March 11, 1931; John Drebinger, "Terry Accepts Giants' Terms," NYT, March 13, 1931.

71. John Drebinger, "$9000 Salary Cut Spurned by Terry," NYT, January 12, 1932; "Terry Is Signed at $40,000 Salary," NYT, October 10, 1933.

72. John Drebinger, "Terry Announces Giants Will Grant Some Increases in Pay," NYT, January 11, 1936.

73. John Drebinger, "Robins Sign Vance at $20,000 for Year," NYT, March 7, 1928; Roscoe McGowen, "$25,000 For Vance; His Terms Are Met," NYT, March 15, 1929; "Vance Agreeable to $17,000 Salary," NYT, February 22, 1932; Tommy Holmes, "Pay Cut of $5,000 Waiting for Vance," TSN, January 19, 1933, 3.

74. Fred Van Ness, "Gomez of Yankees Wins $20,000 Pay," NYT, March 3, 1935; Dan Daniel, "Gehrig in Line for $7,000 Raise as Yankees Cut Payroll $50,000," TSN, February 7, 1935, 1; "$31,000 Received by Gehrig in 1935," NYT, January 12, 1937.

75. "Ruppert and Barrow Off on Mission to Sign Ruth, Seeks $85K," NYT, November 15, 1929; John Drebinger, "Yanks Refuse Ruth $85,000 a Year; Offer $75,000," NYT, January 8, 1930; Joe Vila, "Babe Seeks $85,000 Per For Three Years," TSN, January 16, 1930, 1; William Brandt, "Babe Ruth Rejects $85,000 for 1930," NYT, March 8, 1930.

76. Maikovich and Brown, *Sports Quotations*, 19; DeVito, *Ultimate Dictionary of Sports Quotations*, 221.

77. Joe Vila, "Yanks Stand Pat After Offering Ruth $75,000 Per for Two Years," TSN, January 23, 1930, 1; Haupert and Winter, "Pay Ball."

78. Joe Vila, "Shawkey Indicates Ruth May Soon Sign," TSN, February 6, 1930, 1; William Brandt, "Babe Ruth Accepts $160,000 for 2 Years," NYT, March 9, 1930; "Ruth's Salary Cut $10,246 Each Year by U.S. Income Tax," NYT, March 11, 1930; Joe Vila, "Ruth

Notes to pages 77–81

and Ruppert Compromise When Ruth Signs for Two Years," TSN, March 13, 1930, 1; "The Agony Is Over," TSN, March 13, 1930, 4.

79. No one got more than Ruth's $80,000 salary until Joe DiMaggio got $100,000 in 1949. Of course, dollars had much less purchasing power in 1949 than in 1930. "Ruppert to Slash Ruth's $80,000 Salary," NYT, December 5, 1931; "Ruppert to Cut Ruth's Pay—Babe Not So Sure," TSN, December 10, 1931, 10.

80. John Drebinger, "Ruth Spurns Cut of $15,000 in Pay," NYT, January 17, 1933; Joe Vila, "Ruth's Pay May be Reduced to $50,000," TSN, December 17, 1931, 1.

81. Joe Vila, "Babe Ruth Expected to Agree on $60,000 Pay for 1933 Season," TSN, January 26, 1933, 1; John Drebinger, "Ruth Says $50,000 Was Yanks' Offer," NYT, January 18, 1933; Joe Vila, "Yankee Fans Think Only a Flag Will Justify Ruth's Big Salary," TSN, March 24, 1932, 1.

82. Joe Vila, "Yankee Fans Think Only a Flag Will Justify Ruth's Big Salary," TSN, March 24, 1932, 1.

83. Joe Vila, "Ruppert Looks Out for Bleacher Fans," TSN, March 16, 1933, 1.

84. "Babe Ruth Signs Up," TSN, March 31, 1932, 4.

85. James Dawson, "Ruth and Ruppert Agree on $52,000," NYT, March 23, 1933.

86. "Shorn, But Still King," TSN, March 30, 1933, 4.

87. According to the Haupert Database, Lefty Grove earned $45,000 in 1934, supplanting Ruth as the highest-paid player. John Drebinger, "One-Year Contract with the Yankees Signed by Ruth," NYT, January 16, 1934; John Drebinger, "Contract to Be Signed by Ruth at Reported $37,500," NYT, January 13, 1934.

88. "Coast Club Seeks Ruth," NYT, February 14, 1934.

89. "Ruth Pondering Over Problem of 'To Play or Not to Play,'" NYT, May 7, 1935.

90. Joe Vila, "$100,000 to Get Ruth As Pilot Is Price Tag Facing White Sox," TSN, August 10, 1933, 1 and 4.

91. The *New York Times* chronicled Wilson's travails throughout the 1932 pre-season: "Hack Wilson Balks at $25,000 Pay Cut," January 9, 1932; John Drebinger, "Hack Wilson Sold to Robins by Cards," January 24, 1932; "Hack Wilson, After Conference with Carey, Plans to Sign," February 1, 1932; John Drebinger, "One-Year Contract with Robins for Wilson," February 2, 1932.

92. "Klein of Phillies Goes to the Cubs," NYT, November 22, 1933.

93. James Isaminger, "Foxx' Salary Talk," TSN, February 15, 1934, 1; "Foxx Is Dissatisfied with $11,000 Offer," NYT, February 21, 1934; "Foxx Will Stand Pat on $25,000 Pay Demand," NYT, March 6, 1934; "Foxx Signs for One Year for $20,000," NYT, March 10, 1934.

94. James Isaminger, "Mack Hints He'll Play Lower-Priced Players," TSN, March 8, 1934, 1.

95. Gregory, *Story of Dizzy Dean*; Heidenry, *Gashouse Gang*.

96. Dick Farrington, "Dean to Demand $25,000," TSN, November 1, 1934, 1; "Dean Threatens to Quit," NYT, December 2, 1934; "Cardinals and Dean Come to Terms," NYT, December 6, 1934; "Cardinals' Terms for 1935 Campaign Accepted by Dizzy Dean," NYT, February 8, 1935; John Drebinger, "Past Series Stars in Cast of Cards," NYT, October 1, 1934.

97. "Dean Warns Cards He's Ready to Quit," NYT, February 29, 1936.

98. Red Byrd, "Dizzy Dean's $24,000 Pay Pact Carries Clause on Attendance," TSN, March 26, 1936, 1.

99. "Dean Will Demand $50,000 From Cards," NYT, October 29, 1936.

100. Dick Farrington, "Dean, Offered $22,500 Ready to Bolt Cards," TSN, February 25, 1937, 1.

101. Dean blamed the team for rushing him back too soon after his injury. Edgar Brands, "National Splits with American Over Radio, Landis Denied," TSN, July 14, 1938, 1 and 3.

102. "Branch Rickey's Salary Topped All in Game, Congress Reports," TSN, January 16, 1936, 1; "Rickey Drops to Third in Game's Salary List," TSN, January 14, 1937, 1; "Mickey Cochrane Top Next to Landis in '36 Salary," TSN, January 13, 1938, 1; "Detroit's Salary List Highest in '37, Federal Report Shows," TSN, April 13, 1939, 7.

103. Haupert, "Bonus Clauses".

104. "Bonus Contracts," TSN, February 27, 1930, 4; see also "The Bonus System," TSN, August 20, 1931, 4 for a slightly different criticism of bonus payments.

105. Paul Eaton, "Senators Wonder How Goslin Will View New Bonus System," TSN, January 30, 1930, 1.

106. Denman Thompson, "Griff Will Continue His Bonus Clauses," TSN, January 1, 1931, 7.

107. "Browns Give Up Bonus System, Finding It to be Impracticable," TSN, February 4, 1932, 1. Wes Ferrell was another top pitcher who balked at a salary cut, albeit one with a bonus clause if he won twenty games or more. Ed Bang, "Ferrell Offered $700/Game Bonus," TSN, March 8, 1934, 1; see also Ed Bang, "$18,000 or No Play, Wes Ferrell Insists," TSN, March 2, 1933, 1.

108. "Bonus System Started by Yawkey of Red Sox," NYT, May 5, 1934; Paul Shannon, "Red Sox Bonus," TSN, May 17, 1934, 3; "Briggs Withdraws Tiger Bonus Offer," NYT, March 15, 1936.

109. Warfield, *Roaring Redhead*, 60.

110. "Evils of Bonuses," TSN, November 29, 1934, 4.

111. "Bonus System Comes Home to Roost," TSN, August 27, 1936, 4; Tom Swope, "Cincy Turns Skeptical of Radio," TSN, May 28, 1936, 1.

112. Shaver, "The Cubs," 842.

113. Irving Vaughan, "Wrigley Dangles Spot Bonuses As Reward for Cubs Who Hustle," TSN, February 28, 1935, 1.

114. "Briggs Withdraws Tiger Bonus Offer," NYT, March 15, 1936.

115. "Briggs and the Bonus," TSN, March 26, 1936, 4.

116. Tommy Holmes, "MacPhail 'Share Wealth' Plan," TSN, November 16, 1939, 1; "Brooklyn: Bonuses Paid," NYT, November 9, 1939.

117. "St. Louis Browns: Fred Haney Signed as Manager," NYT, July 19, 1939; Dick Farrington, "Basement Browns Find Bonus No Boon," TSN, July 27, 1939, 5; "Good Purpose, Wrong Principle," TSN, July 27, 1939, 4.

118. Herbert Simons, "The Days of Victory Bonuses Are Over," BM, April 1943, 531–32.

119. An Ordinary Least Squares regression equation for 1920–1944 had a reasonably strong explanatory power; if information on consolidated net income *before* taxes had been available, the correlation coefficient and regression equation's adjusted R^2 might have been higher:

Consolidated Real Net Income = -484,091.1
$$(-3.27)$$

+ 0.8599(Real Difference)
(4.81)

$N = 24$ $\qquad$ $R^2 = 0.502$ $\qquad$ Adjusted $R^2 = 0.480$.

Both the intercept and the "Real Difference in $000's" variable were statistically significant at the 1% level.

120. Joe Vila, "Ruppert Belittles Suggestion Yanks Should Aid Weak Clubs," TSN, November 10, 1932, 1.

121. Joe Vila, "M'Carthy Hits Peak for Manager's Pay," TSN, October 20, 1932, 3; Roscoe McGowen, "Brooklyn Rewards Stengel; Barrow Talks With Gehrig," NYT, February 15, 1935.

122. Brown, Gabriel, and Surdam, "Pay Structure of the New York Yankees," 3. The Ordinary Least Squares regression equation was:

Ln(Real Payroll, 1920-41) = 4.713 + 0.529(Previous W-L Pct.)
$\qquad\qquad\qquad\qquad\qquad$ (13.59) (1.61)
$\qquad\qquad\qquad$ + 0.00038(Previous Total Revenue)
$\qquad\qquad\qquad\qquad\qquad$ (2.52)

$N = 22$ $\qquad$ R-squared = 0.873

The coefficents on total revenue were significant at the 5 percent level, but the previous W-L Pct. was not significant.

123. Brown, Gabriel, and Surdam, "Pay Structure of the New York Yankees"; Scully, "Pay and Performance."

124. An Ordinary Least Squares regression equation tying real total revenue to the team's win-loss record casts doubts on the possibility.

Real Total Revenue = -563,171 + 1,380,269(W-L Pct.)
$\qquad\qquad\qquad\qquad\qquad$ (-1.11) (2.05)
+ 1,268,939(Previous W-L Pct.)
(2.07)

$N = 23$ Adjusted R-squared = 0.279.

Both variables were significant at the 10% level (falling just outside the 5% level).

125. Hanes, "Nominal Wage Rigidity," 1432.

126. Bewley, *Why Wages Don't Fall*, 5–6.

127. "Union for Players," TSN, April 2, 1936, 4.

128. Joe Vila, "N.L. Economy Plans Explained by President Heydler," TSN, December 24, 1931, 7. Sportswriter John Drebinger described some "other expenses," including the cost of printing tickets and spring training expenses. John Drebinger, "Turning the Turnstiles," BM, November 1940, 541; "The Training Season," TSN, November 3, 1932, 4.

129. New York Yankees Base Ball Club, General Ledger.

130. Philadelphia Phillies 1939 scorecard; Philadelphia Phillies, cash books; Mary Nugent quote from Westcott and Bilovsky, *New Phillies Encyclopedia*, 477; *Baseball Blue Book for 1939*, 16.

131. The Ordinary Least Squares regression equation for the American League Real Gross Operating Expenses was:

Real Gross Op. Expenses = 56,860 + 922,483(Current W-L Pct.)
$\qquad\qquad\qquad\qquad\qquad$ (0.58)(4.79)
+ 195,394(1939 Dummy Variable)
(5.11)

+ 368,199(New York Dummy Variable)
(6.17)
N = 22 $R^2 = 0.879$ Adjusted $R^2 = 0.858$
For the National League, the equation was:
Real Gross Op. Expenses = 128,799 + 735,851(Current W-L Pct.)
                                        (1.21)(3.34)
+ 173,334(1939 Dummy Variable)
(4.79)
+ 185,505(Brooklyn Dummy Variable)
(3.53)
+ 288,838(Chicago Dummy Variable)
(4.97)
+ 312,670(New York Dummy Variable)
(5.60)
N = 23 $R^2 = 0.877$ Adjusted $R^2 = 0.841$.

In both equations, all of the independent variables were significant at the 1% level.

Given the panel nature of the data (there might be correlation within each team's observations), I also ran fixed-effects panel regression equations. Because of that, I was unable to use a dummy variable for New York City teams. The remaining variables had similar coefficients.

American League R.G.O.E. = 95,028 + 949,616(Current W-L Pct.)
                                     (1.31) (7.94)
+ 190,621(1939 Dummy Variable)
(4.20)
N = 22   Within $R^2 = 0.767$
National League R.G.O.E. = 364,711 + 470,032(Current W-L Pct.)
                                      (4.10) (2.73)
+ 169,740(1939 Dummy Variable)
(5.05)
N = 23   Within $R^2 = 0.720$

All of the variables were significant at the 1% level, except for the National League Current W-L Pct. Variable which was significant at the 5% level.

4. Farm Systems

1. J. Newton Colver, "The Future Keystone of the Yankee's Infield," BM, April 1928, 499.
2. Levitt, *Ed Barrow*, 244 and 388–90.
3. Donald Anderson's dissertation examines Rickey and the Cardinals' farm system. Dick Farrington, "Branch Rickey, Defending Farms, Says Stark Necessity Forced System," TSN, December 1, 1932, 3; Anderson, *Branch Rickey and the St. Louis Cardinal Farm System*.
4. "By Way of Contrast," TSN, August 27, 1931, 4.
5. Jim Nasium, "Shift of Minors to Major Control Silent but Sure," TSN, January 12, 1928, 5.
6. Roy Terrell, "Doom around the Corner," *Sports Illustrated*, December 16, 1957, 36.
7. J. G. Taylor Spink, "Mass Productions of Pitchers Behind Card Rise," TSN, May 29, 1941, 1 and 16.

8. Dick Farrington, "Backing Up on Chain Store," *TSN*, March 2, 1939, 3.
9. Roy Terrell, "Doom around the Corner," *Sports Illustrated*, December 16, 1957, 36.
10. Francis Powers, "Chain Store Plan Appeals to Bradley," *TSN*, January 5, 1928, 3; Levitt, *Ed Barrow*, 264.
11. "Yanks May Buy Club," *NYT*, June 7, 1928; Joe Vila, "Ruppert Makes First Real Move in Baseball Agricultural Field," *TSN*, January 17, 1929, 1; Graham, *New York Yankees*, 187–88; Barrow, *Fifty Years in Baseball*, 179.
12. Joe Vila, "Yankees Ask Landis for Ruling in Fight to Keep $75,000 Beauty," *TSN*, June 26, 1930, 1; Steve George, "Yanks Get Hoag in Compromise Deal with Sacs," *TSN*, July 3, 1930, 3; "Some Baseball Evolution," *TSN*, February 18, 1932, 4; Joe Vila, "Yanks Lay Out Nearly $500,000 to Get Class AA Proving Ground," *TSN*, November 19, 1931, 1; "Yankees Purchase Springfield Club," *NYT*, February 24, 1932.
13. "Paternalism," *TSN*, November 24, 1932, 4.
14. Graham, *New York Yankees*, 190–91; John Drebinger, "Yankees Acquire Two More Clubs," *NYT*, January 3, 1935; "Yankees Increase Chain," *NYT*, February 27, 1936; "Yanks Get Farm Club," *NYT*, July 25, 1937.
15. "Growing Arm of Farm System," *TSN*, April 18, 1935, 4; Barrow, *Fifty Years in Baseball*, 178–79.
16. Michael Gaven, "No Charlie Kellers in Sight, But Over-Supply of Talent Is Barrow's Chief 'Worry,'" *TSN*, October 19, 1939, 1 and 7.
17. "Indians Get Toledo Club," *NYT*, January 8, 1932; "Red Sox Buy Reading Club in Second Step of Rebuilding Team," *NYT*, August 1, 1933; "Giants Not After Clubs," *NYT*, November 3, 1933.
18. John Drebinger, "New York Plans Farm System," *NYT*, December 3, 1936.
19. John Drebinger, "Dodgers Enlarge Farm Team List," *NYT*, January 14, 1937; "Dodgers Extend Chain," *NYT*, January 28, 1938; "Dodgers Add to Chain," *NYT*, January 14, 1939; "Dodgers Seek New Farm," *NYT*, February 1, 1940.
20. "Yankees Acquire Two More Clubs," *NYT*, January 3, 1935.
21. "Talent, How to Get It," *TSN*, November 7, 1935, 4.
22. Paul Eaton, "Chain Store Curb Likely to Be Asked," *TSN*, April 4, 1929, 1; "To Talk It Over," *TSN*, April 4, 1929, 4.
23. Dan Daniel, "Barrow Unmoved by Trade Ban, Calls Slap at Chains a Mistake," *TSN*, December 14, 1939, 1 and 12; John Drebinger, "Reaction of Yankees and Giants to Dodgers' Radio Broadcast," *NYT*, December 13, 1938.
24. "Major League Ownership," *TSN*, May 23, 1929, 4; "Senators Buy Atlanta Club, Valued by Owner at $750,000," *NYT*, June 6, 1929.
25. Bill Bryon, "One-Third of Big League Talent Discovered by Three Clubs!" *Baseball Digest*, May 1958, 71.
26. "Baseball Season to End Week Later," *NYT*, December 14, 1928.
27. "Landis Swings the Big Stick," *TSN*, March 21, 1929, 4.
28. H. A. L., "Rickey Denies Farm Players Are Kept Down," *TSN*, April 19, 1934, 1.
29. Lieb, *Baltimore Orioles*, 147–48.
30. Irving Sanborn, "Baseball's Biggest Problem—The Draft," *BM*, March 1928, 439–40.
31. "Then, What?" *TSN*, July 17, 1930, 4.
32. "Landis Puts Ban on Drafting by Clubs From Own Farms," *NYT*, October 23, 1930.
33. Lewis, *Cleveland Indians*, 195–97; "Landis Defers Ruling in Henrich Dispute," *NYT*, April 2, 1937; "Claim to Henrich Denied Cleveland," *NYT*, April 15, 1937; "Henrich Accepts Yankees' Terms; Outfielder Will Sign Here," *NYT*, April 19, 1937.

34. "Major Leagues Set Position on Draft," NYT, July 10, 1930.

35. John Drebinger, "Club Owners Back Chain-Store Plan; No Action on Radio," NYT, December 16, 1932.

36. "Rickey Is Advised to Make No Reply," NYT, March 25, 1938; "Landis Rules Against Cards," NYT, March 24, 1938; "73 Players Named in Cardinals Case," NYT, April 2, 1938; "Decision of Landis Voids 91 Contracts," TSN, April 7, 1938, 10.

37. Dick Farrington, "Landis Gets Blame," TSN, September 22, 1938, 1.

38. "Landis Fines Tigers for Concealing Player Contracts," NYT, November 30, 1939; "Detroit Tigers: Farm System Investigated," NYT, May 17, 1939; "Landis Grants Free Agency to Five Tigers and 87 Others," NYT, January 15, 1940; "Baseball Talent Worth $500,000 Lost to Detroit by Landis," NYT, January 15, 1940; "Baseball World Awaits Another Blast by Landis Today," NYT, January 16, 1940; Sam Greene, "Tigers' Loss Through Decision by Landis Estimated at $500,000," TSN, January 18, 1940, 1 and 9; "Landis Lays Down Law for Farms, Working Agreements," TSN, January 18, 1940, 1 and 6.

39. "Landis Announces Code for Baseball Clubs in Dealing," NYT, January 17, 1940; "Yanks Must Revise Seven Agreements," NYT, January 23, 1940; "Indians Drop Farm Club," NYT, April 17, 1938.

40. "International League Voices Opposition to Landis Plan," NYT, February 4, 1940.

41. "Landis and Leagues Agree," NYT, March 5, 1940.

42. Thomas Connery, "Chain-Made Changes," BM, February 1940, 403.

43. U.S. Congress, *Organized Baseball: Hearings*, 1611.

44. U.S. Congress, *Organized Baseball: Hearings*, 1602–3 and 1601–7.

45. U.S. Congress, *Organized Baseball: Hearings*, 1604–5 and 1606–7.

5. Competitive Balance

1. Fort, *Sports Economics*, 2nd ed., 17.

2. Quirk and Fort, *Pay Dirt*, 247.

3. Cubs fans have often failed to note that even before the fateful 1945 World Series, the team had lost in its six previous World Series appearances. One could argue that the goat was merely kicking the club when it was already down.

4. Sporting News, *Complete Baseball Record Book 2003*, 135 and 138.

5. F. C. Lane, "The Yankee Peril," BM, January 1929, 339.

6. Joe Vila, "Fans View Yankees Dubiously As They Fail to Take Mackmen," TSN, June 27, 1929, 1; Joe Vila, "Huggins Prepares to Renovate Yanks," TSN, September 12, 1929, 3.

7. Joe Vila, "Look for New York Meetings of Majors to Build Up Club," TSN, December 1, 1932, 1.

8. "Consolidating Territory," TSN, June 16, 1932, 4.

9. A. B. C. "Lament for Boston Fans," NYT, August 22, 1936.

10. "Some Day," TSN, June 23, 1932, 4.

11. "Returning Equal Opportunity," TSN, August 12, 1937, 4.

12. Joe Vila, "Ruppert Belittles Suggestion Yanks Should Aid Weak Clubs," TSN, November 10, 1932, 1.

13. Barrow, *Fifty Years in Baseball*, 56.

14. "Renaissance at Boston," TSN, May 3, 1934, 4; "Gain in White Sox Fans," NYT, November 30, 1933.

15. "Stabilising the Leagues," TSN, November 8, 1934, 4.

16. "How to Help Lowly Clubs," TSN, September 26, 1935, 4; "Grimes for Closer Races: Suggest Giving Weak Teams Players," NYT, January 1, 1937.
17. Yankee Hater, "Boycott of Yankees Proposed," NYT, October 8, 1938.
18. Vincent Woodburn, "Resents Extravagant Claims," NYT, October 15, 1938.
19. William Rock, "Monopoly Injurious to Game," NYT, October 15, 1938.
20. Robert Singleton, "Baseball Trust-Busting," NYT, March 23, 1940.
21. Dan Daniel, "Yanks Now Concern A.L. as Much as N.L.," TSN, October 19, 1939, 3.
22. Dan Daniel, "Col. Ruppert Blasts Yank Break-Up Idea," TSN, January 13, 1938, 3.
23. Frederick Lieb, "Col. Ruppert Ridicules Idea of 'Weakening Yankees,'" TSN, October 6, 1938, 3.
24. Dan Daniel, "A.L. Growing Panicky Over Yankee Domination," TSN, September 1, 1938, 1.
25. Denman Thompson, "Griffith Gives Out His Formula to End Flag Monopolies," TSN, July 27, 1939, 1.
26. Dan Daniel, "'Curb-Yankees' Movement Dies Down, But Barrow's Resentment Flares," TSN, August 17, 1939, 1 and 2.
27. Dan Daniel, "If We Can Improve Yanks, We'll Do It," TSN, October 12, 1939, 1 and 10.
28. Carl Peterson and Edward Wolf, "Break Up Yankees," NYT, October 14, 1939.
29. Dan Daniel, "Yanks Would Stand Pat, Give A.L. Break," TSN, December 7, 1939, 3.
30. Dan Daniel, "New York Clubs Air Broadcasting Views," TSN, December 21, 1939, 3; John Drebinger, "American League Bars Champion's Trades with Rival Clubs," NYT, December 8, 1939; Edgar Brands, "Minors Stymied by Landis' Adverse Action," TSN, December 14, 1939, 3 and 6.
31. Dan Daniel, "Move Afoot to Lift Ban on Yank Deals," TSN, January 4, 1940, 5.
32. Dan Daniel, "Barrow Unmoved by Trade Ban, Calls Slap at Chains a Mistake," TSN, December 14, 1939, 1 and 12.
33. Dick Farrington, "Rickey Hangs Label of Socialism on A.L.," TSN, December 14, 1939, 12.
34. Dan Daniel, "Move Afoot to Lift Ban on Yank Deals," TSN, January 4, 1940, 5.
35. Dan Daniel, "Move Afoot to Lift Ban on Yank Deals," TSN, January 4, 1940, 5.
36. "Yankees Find Way to Detour," TSN, January 11, 1940, 4; Dan Daniel, "Yankees Laugh at Trading Ban in Slipping Over Grissom Deal," TSN, January 11, 1940, 1 and 2.
37. Sam Greene, "Trading Ban to Hit Tigers Hard," TSN, October 10, 1940, 1.
38. "American League May Lift Trading Ban," NYT, June 6, 1941; James Dawson, "American League Lifts Trading Ban," NYT, July 8, 1941; "American League Kills No-Trading Regulation," TSN, July 10, 1941, 1; Leonard Gettleson, "'41 Yanks Earliest Clinchers," TSN, September 11, 1941, 6.
39. Dan Daniel, "What Makes Those Yankees Tick? Explanation Makes It Seem Simple," BM, October 1942, 526.
40. Halberstam, *Summer of '49*.
41. "No Lease-Lend to Phils," TSN, February 18, 1943, 1.
42. "No Lease-Lend to Phils," TSN, February 18, 1943, 1.

6. Player Movement

1. "An Equitable Decision," TSN, September 20, 1934, 4; "Clarifies Club's Tax Problems," TSN, February 14, 1935, 4.

2. There was probably a lag between a player's debut and his effect upon the team, so using 1919–41 has some defects but would cover almost all of the most productive players playing between 1929 and 1941 except Babe Ruth, who started his career in 1915.

3. New York Yankees Base Ball Club, Cash Book, August 23, 1928; August 24, 1928; and September 4, 1928.

4. James Harrison, "Yankees Purchase Zachary, Southpaw," NYT, August 24, 1928; "Yanks Buy Bill (Rosey) Ryan, Ex-Giant," NYT, August 25, 1928; "Yankees Buy Wells, Ex-Detroit Southpaw," NYT, August 29, 1928; "Yanks Buy Fay Thomas," NYT, September 8, 1928; "Jorgens Sold to Yankees," NYT, August 25, 1928.

5. Burt Whitman, "Red Sox Refuse to Deal with Yankees," TSN, February 13, 1930, 6; "Ruffing of Red Sox Obtained By Yanks in Trade for Durst," NYT, May 7, 1930; New York Yankees, Financial Records, Cash Book, May 6, 1930.

6. Some observers felt the Yankees bought the two Minor League players partly as insurance in case incumbents Mark Koenig and Tony Lazzeri got injured and also to prevent other teams from acquiring them. James Harrison, "Lary and Reese Are Bought by Yankees," NYT, January 5, 1928; Richard Vidmer, "What Strategy Prompted Yanks to Purchase Lary," NYT, January 8, 1928.

7. Barrow, *Fifty Years in Baseball*, 181–82.

8. Dan Daniel, "$35,000 Hang-Over on DiMaggio Option," TSN, November 29, 1934, 7; "Yanks Buy Selkirk from Jersey City," NYT, November 5, 1931.

9. "Athletics Give Orioles $50,000 for Earnshaw," NYT, May 29, 1928.

10. "Ruppert Says He Would Have Paid $150,000 for Grove," NYT, February 7, 1934; "Says Ruth Will Stay," NYT, August 18, 1934.

11. Dan Daniel, "Sky's the Limit: Rich Clubs Still Pay Highly for Men They Want," TSN, February 15, 1934, 5.

12. Joe Vila, "Ruppert Belittles Suggestion Yanks Should Aid Weak Clubs," TSN, November 10, 1932, 1.

13. While modern fans may debate the merits of the emphasis placed on statistics by current general managers such as Billy Beane and Theo Epstein, especially their concern with the on-base percentage, Barrow anticipated them. The team also frequently led the league in OPS, the ill-advised marriage of on-base percentage and slugging, but this author eschews the statistic, finding it a needless hybrid. Statistically, it is better to use the on-base and slugging figures separately than to combine them artificially. The combination literally adds base runners to bases.

14. George Weiss, Yankees farm director and later general manager, apparently did not share Barrow's enthusiasm for patient hitters who drew a lot of walks, and his postwar Yankees rarely led the league in either walks or on-base percentage.

15. John Drebinger, "Pipgras, Werber Sold to Red Sox," NYT, May 13, 1933; "Yankees Sell Lary to Red Sox," NYT, May 16, 1934; Joe Vila, "Hand of Joe M'Carthy Visible in Sale of Pipgras to Red Sox," TSN, May 25, 1933, 3.

16. "Griffith Is Ready to Let Speaker Go," NYT, January 24, 1928; "Speaker Released by the Senators," NYT, January 26, 1928.

17. "Simmons and Haas Sold to White Sox," NYT, September 29, 1932.

18. "Sale of 3 Players Explained by Mack," NYT, October 5, 1932; Bill Dooly, "New Mack Policy Limits Deals to Last Three Clubs in Race," TSN, October 13, 1932, 1. Mack later broke his promise by selling Jimmie Foxx to fourth-place Boston.

19. "Sale of Simmons, Dykes, and Haas," TSN, October 6, 1932, 4.

20. "Mack Lays Deals to Wage Demands," NYT, December 19, 1933; "Mack Sells Grove and 4 Other Stars," NYT, December 13, 1933; "Mack Again Startles Baseball World by Disposing of Five Stars," *Washington Post*, December 13, 1933; "Pay Demands Forced A's Shake-Up," *Washington Post*, December 19, 1933; "Connie Mack Starts Over," TSN, December 21, 1933, 4; James Isaminger, "A's Remain Strong Except in Pitching," TSN, December 21, 1933, 1; James Isaminger, "Mack Denies Bankers Closed In, Says Payroll Had to be Reduced," TSN, December 28, 1933, 1. See "Fans Voice Regret," NYT, December 13, 1933 and Ford Sawyer, "Boston Fans Vision Renaissance of Red Sox in Deals by Yawkey," TSN, December 21, 1933, 1 on the dashed hopes that Philadelphia's approval of Sunday ball would keep Mack from selling more players.

21. "Gain in White Sox Fans," NYT, November 30, 1933.

22. Paul Eaton, "Griffith Balances Books and Finds New Men Cost $154,750," TSN, January 16, 1930, 1; U.S. Congress, *Organized Baseball: Hearings*, 1599.

23. Deveaux, *Washington Senators*, 128–29.

24. "Griff Delays Choice of Cronin Successor After $200,000 Sale," *Washington Post*, October 27, 1934; Shirley Povich, "This Morning... with Shirley Povich," *Washington Post*, October 27, 1934; Richard Vidmer, "Red Sox Buy Joe Cronin From Senators for $150,000 to be Player-Manager for Five Years," *New York Herald Tribune*, October 27, 1934; "Cronin to Red Sox in a Record Deal," NYT, October 27, 1934.

25. "Deal Sends Yawkey's Investment in Red Sox Over $2,000,000 Mark," *New York Herald Tribune*, October 27, 1934; for another perspective on the likely reaction of Senators' fans, see Denman Thompson, "Cronin Deal Irks Capital Fans, Who Feel Griff Sold Them Out," TSN, November 1, 1934, 1.

26. "Connie Mack Willing to Sell Most of Team," NYT, November 1, 1939.

27. "Red Sox Not to Bid $200,000 for Foxx," NYT, October 3, 1935.

28. "Rumors Regarding Selling Jimmie Foxx Denied," NYT, December 1, 1935; Bill Dooly, "Mack Sale Parade Thins, But Goes On," TSN, November 21, 1935, 2.

29. "Foxx Asks Higher Salary and New Contract If Sold by A's," NYT, December 3, 1935.

30. On the same day, Mack's former star, Al Simmons, was sold yet again, this time by the Chicago White Sox to the Detroit Tigers for $75,000. John Drebinger, "Deals for Foxx and Simmons; Braves Sale to Quinn," NYT, December 11, 1935; "11 of 16 Clubs Get New Faces in Deals," TSN, December 19, 1935, 3.

31. "Estimated Yawkey Has Spent $3,500,000," NYT, December 11, 1935; "Owner Has Put $3,000,000 Into Sox," *Washington Post*, October 27, 1934; "Yawkey's Total Outlay Set at $2,160,000," *New York Herald Tribune*, October 27, 1934; "Yawkey Spent $3,000,000," NYT, October 27, 1934; "Cronin Sale Recalls Other Big Deals," NYT, October 27, 1934.

32. The White Sox were another club that scavenged Mack's Athletics.

33. "The Cubs Get Klein," TSN, November 30, 1933, 4; "Klein of Phillies Goes to the Cubs," NYT, November 22, 1933; *MacMillan Baseball Encyclopedia*, 2614 lists three players and $65,000 in exchange for Klein, while the reporters used $100,000 and $125,000 figures. Dick Farrington, "Klein Deal Leaves $125,000 Hangover," TSN, November 30, 1933, 5.

34. John Drebinger, "Terry Moves to Rebuild Giants by Getting Bartell," NYT, November 1, 1934.

35. Roscoe McGowen, "Purchase of Camilli Ends Brooklyn's Search for Power Hitter," NYT, March 7, 1938.

36. Herbert Friedman, "Hurtful Trading Tactics," NYT, April 8, 1939.
37. Bill Dooly, "Nugent Rang Up $500,000 in Ten-Year Deals for Phils," TSN, February 18, 1943, 1 and 7.
38. Tommy Holmes, "Arcs Light the Way in Build-Up of Dodgers," TSN, August 18, 1938, 1; Tom Swope, "Fans Share Payoff from Cincy Lights," TSN, January 4, 1940, 3; J. G. Taylor Spink and Larry MacPhail, "A Million Fans a Year Can't be Wrong," TSN, June 5, 1941, 1; "Hats Off to Leland Stanford MacPhail," TSN, October 2, 1941, 4.
39. Dick Farrington, "Rajah Raps Selfish Rich Clubs, Demands 'Square Deal' Trades," TSN, December 7, 1933.
40. Dick Farrington, "M'Quinn to Yankees Deal On, St.L. Hears," TSN, May 29, 1941, 3.
41. "Browns Buy Auker of Red Sox," NYT, February 9, 1940; "Judnich of Yanks Is Sold to Browns," NYT, January 31, 1940.
42. Dick Farrington, "Had to Get Cash, Breadon Declares of Big-Money Deals," TSN, December 12, 1940, 1 and 11; Dan Daniel, "Giants Bid $250,000 for Medwick, Mize," TSN, November 24, 1938, 2; Dick Farrington, "Cards Pay Dividend Out of Cash Deals," TSN, January 2, 1941, 1 and 6; John Drebinger, "Barrow Denies Club Plans Night Games/Mize Traded to Giants," NYT, January 24, 1942.
43. "Hornsby Is Traded 'For Good of Giants,'" NYT, January 11, 1928; John Drebinger, "Hornsby Deal made 'To Avoid Conflict,'" NYT, January 12, 1928; James Harrison, "Hornsby Traded by Stoneham Alone," NYT, January 13, 1928.
44. Bill Dooly, "Connie Mack Spent $700,000 to Produce a Winning Club," TSN, January 30, 1930, 3; Alexander, *Ty Cobb*, 194–95.
45. "Landis's Order Makes Nine Men Free Agents," NYT, March 17, 1929.
46. "Feller Stays with Indians Under Landis Decision," NYT, December 11, 1936; "Feller, Losing $100,000 Chance, Is 'Glad;' Demands $20K," NYT, December 11, 1936; Dan Daniel, "Deadening of Ball Put Off Until '38; Landis Decision on Feller," TSN, December 17, 1936, 3 and 8; Ed Bang, "Schoolboy Bob Feller Leans to Add," TSN, January 14, 1937, 1; Lewis, *Cleveland Indians*, 195–97.
47. "Claim to Henrich Denied Cleveland," NYT, April 15, 1937; "Henrich Accepts Yankees' Terms, Outfielder Will Sign Here," NYT, April 19, 1937; "Landis Defers Ruling in Henrich Dispute," NYT, April 2, 1937.
48. "Landis Rules Against Cards," NYT, March 24, 1938; "Rickey Is Advised to Make No Reply," NYT, March 25, 1938; "73 Players Named in Cardinals' Case," NYT, April 2, 1938.
49. The Tigers had to pay almost $50,000 to players who were now outside their organization but who would have been declared free agents. "Athletics Get McCoy for $45,000 Bonus," NYT, January 30, 1940; "Landis Grants Free Agency to Five Tigers and 87 Others," NYT, January 15, 1940; "Baseball Talent Worth $500,000 Lost to Detroit by Landis," NYT, January 15, 1940; "Baseball World Awaits Another Blast by Landis Today," NYT, January 16, 1940; James Isaminger, "Real M'Coy Deal Swung by Mack," TSN, February 1, 1940, 1; "McCoy Chooses Wisely," TSN, February 8, 1940, 4; "Detroit Tigers: Farm System Investigated," NYT, May 17, 1939.
50. Tommy Holmes, "Brooklyn Forced by Browns to Go High for Cullenbine," TSN, February 8, 1940, 1.
51. Harold Burr, "The Free Agents Go to Market," BM, April 1940, 485–86 and 523.
52. If you are a fan of tabloid journalism and are looking for a Yankees third baseman with marital problems, Dugan is your man. His wife eventually sued him and won $25

per week in alimony and legal fees. The couple was separated, and she accused him of "carousing and disappearing for indefinite periods." Joe was a big spender during the couple's "five years of marital harmony, spending $400 weekly." But "he began spending money on drinking, gambling, associating with other women and refus[ing] to pay her hospital bills when his conduct made her ill." Former teammate Waite Hoyt's wife also accused him of similar shenanigans. Dugan's claim that his wife did the carousing apparently was not compelling ("Wife Sues Ball Player," NYT, July 23, 1931). How Dugan could spend $400 a week on a $12,000 per year baseball salary was not explained.

53. Dan Daniel, "Braves Get Dugan; Deal Is Surprise," NYT, December 25, 1928; Dan Daniel, "Yanks Turn Reese Back to Oakland," NYT, December 27, 1928.

54. Ira Irving, "The Mysteries of the Baseball 'Waiver' Rule," BM, September 1928, 448.

55. Paul Shannon, "$800,000 Purchase Bid for Braves Fail," TSN, November 23, 1934, 1.

56. Alexander, *John McGraw*, 75–76.

57. Shirley Povich, "This Morning... With Shirley Povich," *Washington Post*, April 7, 1939; Gregory, *Story of Dizzy Dean*, 242.

58. "Filibuster Fails in Youth Session," NYT, January 31, 1938.

59. E. J. Marchess, "Taking a New Tack," NYT, August 13, 1938.

60. "Major Leagues: Perry Resolution Condemning Discrimination," NYT, May 17, 1939; "Senator Perry Champions Negro Stars," NYT, January 23, 1940; "Fight Ban on Negroes," NYT, April 14, 1940.

61. Harry Pesin, "Negroes in Baseball," NYT, May 18, 1940. Since it took a dozen years for all Major League teams to integrate, they must have been falling over one another in slow motion.

62. "No Good from Raising Race Issue," TSN, August 6, 1942, 4.

63. "Pittsburgh Club to Give Negro Players Tryouts," NYT, July 29, 1942; "Cleveland Club to Give Negro Players Tryouts Before 1943," NYT, September 2, 1942; "Negroes Picked for Pittsburgh Club Tryouts," NYT, August 21, 1942; Carl Peterson, "Letter Urging Acceptance of Negro Players," NYT, April 11, 1942; Lorenzo White, "Letter Urging Acceptance of Negro Players," NYT, May 16, 1942; "Citizens Committee to End Discrimination in Baseball," NYT, October 13, 1942; John Drebinger, "CIO Hearing on Negro Discrimination; Night Game Limit," NYT, December 4, 1942; "NY CIO Council Acts to Get Negro Players in League," NYT, July 30, 1942; Edgar Brands, "Majors' Plans for 1943 Streamlined Into War Effort," TSN, December 10, 1942, 3 and 10.

64. Tygiel, *Baseball's Great Experiment*.

7. Helping the Indigent

1. Seymour, *Baseball: Golden Age*, 8.
2. Seymour, *Baseball: Early Years*, 209.
3. "Financing Minor Leagues," TSN, November 13, 1930, 4.
4. Leifer, *Making the Majors*, 103.
5. "Business in Minor Leagues," TSN, January 2, 1930, 4.
6. Scully, *Business of Major League Baseball*, 80; see also Scully, *Market Structure of Sports*, 68–70; Quirk and Fort, *Pay Dirt*, 287–92.
7. Fort and Quirk, "Cross-subsidization, Incentives, and Outcomes," 1287. Other sports economists have come to slightly different conclusions. See Surdam, "Tale of Two Gate-Sharing Plans," 932–34, for a discussion of the literature.

8. Rottenberg, "Baseball Players' Market"; Quirk and Fort, *Pay Dirt*.

9. Canes, "Social Benefits of Restrictions," 92, 94, and 95.

10. National League, *Constitution*, 1933 and 1936, no page numbers.

11. John Drebinger, "Turning the Turnstiles," BM, November 1940, 541; U.S. Congress, *Organized Professional Team Sports*, 1448. The constitutions had sections covering turnstiles. As researcher Peter Morris points out, before the invention of turnstiles, visiting teams negotiated for guarantees, since "there was no way for the visitors to be certain of the attendance count. . . . The guarantee system eliminated the disputes but created an equally serious problem. The visiting club had no direct financial incentive to place a competitive team on the field. The National League's use of turnstiles in its first season solved the problem of basing the visitor's share on attendance." Morris, *Game Behind the Scenes*, 85.

12. U.S. Congress, *Organized Baseball: Hearings*, 1119 and *Organized Professional Team Sports*, 1447. *Baseball Magazine* articles claim that only bleacher seats paid the twenty cents in gate sharing, while all other seats paid thirty cents (Dan Daniel, "It Is Not All Gravy," BM, August 1940, 392; John Drebinger, "Turning the Turnstiles," BM, November 1940, 541).

13. Because of the panel nature of the data, I ran fixed-effects panel regression. These equations did not include data for Chicago (AL in 1929 and 1933 and Pittsburgh in 1929). The American League equation was:

Games Away Revenue = 13,199 + 320,587(W-L Pct.)
$$(0.59) \quad (7.43)$$
$$-42,321(1933 \text{ Dummy})$$
$$(-6.24)$$

$N = 22$ \qquad Within $R_2 = 0.814$

The National League equation was:

Games Away Revenue = 44,433 + 223,647(W-L Pct.)
$$(1.13) \quad (2.93)$$
$$-34,743(1933 \text{ Dummy})$$
$$(-3.63)$$

$N = 23$ \qquad Within $R_2 = 0.639$ \qquad Between $R_2 = 0.485$

All variables were significant at the 1% level, except for the National League Win-Loss Pct. which was significant at the 5% level. Ordinary Least Squares regression equations generated similar results to the fixed-effects panel equations. The equations, aside from the 1933 dummy variable, were similar to those for the decade following World War II.

14. U.S. Congress, *Organized Baseball: Hearings*, 1113.

15. Francis Stann, "It's 'Buy the Browns' Time Again," *Baseball Digest*, March 1951, 35–36.

16. Gordon Cobbledick, "Why Browns Get Fantastic Prices," *Baseball Digest*, February 1949, 59–60.

17. Surdam, "Tale of Two Gate-Sharing Plans."

8. Manipulating the Schedule

1. National League and American Association of Professional Baseball Clubs, *Annual Meeting*, 104.

2. Fort, *Sports Economics*, 1st ed., 129, cites NFL Report 1999.
3. Peterson, *Pigskin: Early Years of Football*, 70.
4. "National League Schedule For 1932," TSN, February 4, 1932, 8.
5. "Schedule Change Planned," NYT, December 11, 1935; "N.L. Schedule Adds to Mileage, But Spices Up Menu for Fans," TSN, February 6, 1936, 8; "Plan Cut in 1943 Road Trips," NYT, October 8, 1942.
6. Ford Sawyer, "Red Sox Seek Changes in Schedule for 1933," TSN, November 17, 1932, 1; "American League to Shift Schedule," NYT, January 19, 1933; J. C., "Radical Changes Made in Major Schedules," TSN, February 9, 1933, 1.
7. "New Schedules Meeting Test," TSN, April 30, 1936, 4; "Western Clubs Go East Earlier Under Frick-Traband Schedule," TSN, February 7, 1935, 6; "A.L. Schedule for '35 Moves Up Intersection Play Two Weeks," TSN, February 14, 1935, 6.
8. "Arcs Give NL More Sunday Twin Bills," TSN, February 9, 1939, 2.
9. "Frick Favors Breadon 6 Day Week Plan," NYT, November 11, 1939; "Breadon to Propose Regular 6-day Week with Sunday DHs," NYT, November 8, 1939; Dick Farrington, "Breadon Comes Out for a Six-Day Week," TSN, November 9, 1939, 1 and 2.
10. "16 Sabbath 'Twins' Scheduled by A.L.," TSN, January 30, 1941, 2; "25 Sabbath Bargains on N.L. Date Chart," TSN, February 6, 1941, 2.
11. Joe Vila, "Major Leaguers Prepare for New York Meetings," TSN, December 5, 1929, 5; Denman Thompson, "Football Kicks Up Annual Griff Worry," TSN, September 5, 1940, 5.
12. John Drebinger, "Less Lively Ball Adopted by National League to Decrease Homeruns," NYT, February 4, 1931; see also John D. Martin, "The Annual Battle of the Schedule Makers," BM, May 1933, 549–50 and 566–67 for the travails of scheduling in a minor league.
13. "Switch Game to Aid Bout," NYT, May 5, 1933; "Sticking to the Schedule," TSN, June 6, 1935, 4.
14. "Unavoidable Doubleheaders," TSN, May 2, 1929, 4.
15. U.S. Congress, *Organized Baseball: Hearings*, 1120.
16. "Elias Digs Up Data on Early Weather," TSN, April 4, 1929, 5; "American League to Shorten 1930 Schedule," NYT, September 22, 1929; Ralph Davis, "Majors Scheduled to Open on April 15," TSN, November 21, 1929, 5; Ford Sawyer, "Extension of Playing Schedule to 168 Games Favored by Fuchs," TSN, December 14, 1933, 1. Many readers may recall those early World Series night games played in mid- to late-October in the 1970s, including one chilly evening when commissioner Bowie Kuhn foolishly insisted on wearing a short-sleeved shirt and no jacket.
17. "Major League Schedules," TSN, May 16, 1929, 4.
18. "Synthetic Doubleheaders," TSN, July 16, 1931, 4.
19. "The Synthetics End," TSN, December 17, 1931, 4; "Stabilizing Doubleheaders," TSN, December 3, 1936, 4.
20. "Snubbing Rainy-Day Friends," TSN, July 7, 1938, 4.
21. "Synthetic Doubleheaders," TSN, May 25, 1933, 4.
22. "Major Leagues Put Off Radio Problem," NYT, December 9, 1931; "The Synthetics End," TSN, December 17, 1931, 4; "Salary Cuts and Reduction of Player Limit Voted by ML," NYT, December 11, 1931.
23. "Doubleheader Craze," TSN, September 21, 1933, 4.

24. "Synthetic Doubleheaders," TSN, May 26, 1932, 4; "Synthetic Doubleheaders," TSN, May 25, 1933, 4.

25. "Big Leagues Vote for Uniform Ball," NYT, December 15, 1933; Edgar Brands, "Majors Clear Decks for '34 Campaign; Uniform Ball to be Used," TSN, December 21, 1933, 5; "Night Ball One of Three A.L. Problems," TSN, November 14, 1935, 1; "Action at Joint Confab Bars Early Twin Bills," TSN, December 19, 1935, 3.

26. "Early Season Doubleheaders," TSN, June 25, 1936, 4; "Stabilizing Doubleheaders," TSN, December 3, 1936, 4.

27. Stan Baumgartner, "Mack to Double Up on Doubleheaders," TSN, January 1, 1942, 2.

28. U.S. Congress, *Organized Baseball: Hearings*, 1119.

29. U.S. Congress, *Organized Baseball: Hearings*, 1105.

30. U.S. Congress, *Organized Baseball: Hearings*, 1119.

31. U.S. Congress, *Organized Baseball: Hearings*, 1106.

32. Surdam, "What Brings Fans to the Ball Park."

33. The advantage of holiday doubleheaders dissipated in the immediate postwar era, probably due to increasing numbers of midweek night games.

34. Seymour, *Baseball: Early Years*, 67–68 and 139; U.S. Congress, *Organized Baseball: Hearings*, 1119; U.S. Congress, *Organized Professional Team Sports*, 1447.

35. John Martin, "Annual Battle of the Schedule Makers," BM, May 1933, 549–50.

36. Surdam, "The American 'Not-So-Socialist' League," 278–79.

37. Ironically, the gains from swapping holiday home dates are greater when the visiting team's record negatively affects its drawing power on the road. For instance, as St. Louis gets worse its drawing power at home decreases while its attractiveness on the road increases.

38. We note in passing that increased revenues might spur the demand for top players.

39. The $1.07 and 97¢ are net of the 5¢ per-customer league fee and federal taxes.

40. The teams would have also had to work out a way to split concessions revenue. Both clubs averaged 8¢ per admission in net revenue from concessions. A holiday doubleheader in Detroit with 30,000 in attendance would have created $2,400 in net concessions revenue, while a similar doubleheader in St. Louis would have brought in just $800.

41. Because of the other teams' limited stadium capacities, the Yankees' ability to draw on the road for holidays was muted. Despite this, the team frequently led the league in road attendance.

42. Such potential gains persisted after World War II, as St. Louis continued to attract the smallest crowds in the American League. In the east, the Yankees also continued to face poor paydays when venturing to Boston, Philadelphia, and Washington for the holidays. The Yankees averaged 23,000 more fans per holiday doubleheader at the Stadium than on the road. The gains from transferring holiday playing dates were strongest before 1951, but continued through 1953. Thereafter, the transfer of the Browns and Athletics to Baltimore and Kansas City assuaged the situation.

43. New York Yankees Base Ball Club, cash books, April 28, 1939 and May 16, 1939.

44. The league stood to gain financially from such trades, as it received 3¢ to 5¢ for each attendee who bought a ticket at the regular price.

45. New York Yankees Base Ball Club, cash books, September 24, 1935.

46. "No at Home Holiday Dates for Browns," TSN, January 25, 1940, 2.

47. Voigt, *Gentleman's Sport*, 212–14.

48. "The Conflicting Elements Opposed to Sunday Ball," *Sporting Life*, February 13, 1897, 4; see also Bevis, *Sunday Baseball*, 66 and 121.

49. "Plans Drive to End All Sunday Sports," NYT, December 11, 1928.

50. James Isaminger, "Sunday Ball for Pennsylvania May Result from Fall Election," NYT, October 30, 1930; Harold Burr, "Brooklyn to Lose Some Extra Dates," TSN, November 15, 1928, 2.

51. Burt Whitman, "Sunday Ball Gains Point in Bay State," TSN, February 23, 1928, 1.

52. Harold Burr, "Brooklyn to Lose Some Extra Dates," TSN, November 15, 1928, 2.

53. Bevis, *Sunday Baseball*, 239.

54. Burt Whitman, "Wild Charges Flung as Boston Adopts Sunday Baseball Bill," TSN, January 3, 1929, 1.

55. "Fuchs Pays Fee of $2,500 For Sunday Baseball Permit," NYT, February 3, 1929; "Sunday Baseball Jangle Had Been On for Six Weeks," TSN, February 14, 1929, 2.

56. "Braves Permit Plea Tabled for Week," NYT, February 5, 1929; "Braves Get Permit for Sunday Games," NYT, February 12, 1929.

57. "Braves Pay $1,000 in Sunday Law Case," NYT, May 14, 1929.

58. Burt Whitman, "Boston Council Plays Politics, Delaying Sunday Sports Law," TSN, December 27, 1928, 1; Surdam, *Postwar Yankees*, 118–19; Brooklyn Dodger scorecards 1950–55; Cincinnati Reds scorecards 1950.

59. Bevis, *Sunday Baseball*, 237.

60. Burt Whitman, "Sunday Ball Strife at End in Boston," TSN, February 14, 1929, 1; "Red Sox to Play Sunday Games at Braves Field This Season," NYT, February 20, 1929.

61. Daniel M. Daniel, "Bright Prospects of Sunday Baseball," BM, January 1934, 343–44 and 381–82.

62. Bevis, *Sunday Baseball*, 207.

63. "Sees Struggle for Athletics," NYT, March 15, 1933.

64. "Clergy Fight Shibe in Ball Park Move," NYT, March 29, 1931; "Schedule Includes Sundays in Philly," TSN, February 9, 1933, 1; Ralph Davis, "Sunday Ball Ballots Exceeded Repeal Votes in Pennsylvania," TSN, November 16, 1933, 1; "Sunday Baseball Loses By 2 Votes," NYT, March 15, 1933.

65. Daniel M. Daniel, "Bright Prospects of Sunday Baseball," BM, January 1934, 343–44 and 381–82.

66. Ford Sawyer, "Red Sox Lose Hope of Deals with A's," TSN, November 16, 1933, 2.

67. Bevis, *Sunday Baseball*, 204.

68. Tommy Holmes, "Dodgers Lose Juicy Dates on N.L. Card," TSN, November 16, 1933, 7.

9. Radio and Baseball

1. Harry Hartman, "In Defense of Baseball by Radio," BM, October 1930, 506.

2. "The Radio and Baseball," TSN, December 17, 1931, 4.

3. John Drebinger, "Draft Is Discussed in National League," NYT, December 11, 1928; N. J. Abodaher, "Baseball via the Ether Waves," BM, November 1929, 551–52.

4. "Baseball Broadcasts Are No Longer Banned," NYT, September 14, 1930; "Baseball Programs Approved for 1932," *Broadcasting*, December 15, 1931, 16.

5. "Southern Bans Broadcasting," TSN, May 16, 1929, 4.

6. "Radio and Baseball," TSN, October 17, 1929, 4.
7. "Barnard Favors $50,000 Broadcasting Charge," TSN, December 5, 1929, 5.
8. "The Radio Again," TSN, May 5, 1932, 4; "Want Radio to Help the Minor Leagues," NYT, December 1, 1931; Surdam, Postwar Yankees, 126–62.
9. "Ban on Broadcasting," TSN, August 16, 1934, 4.
10. "Stretching Territorial Rights," TSN, May 9, 1935, 4.
11. John Connolly, "L.A. Drops Radio, Free Games May be Cut," TSN, May 9, 1935, 1; Lloyd Gregory, "Texas League to Ban Broadcast of Games," TSN, January 16, 1930, 6.
12. "Minors Seek Check on Radio Baseball," NYT, April 28, 1936.
13. "Landis Seeks Curb on Broadcasting," NYT, April 29, 1936.
14. "Regulating Radio," TSN, May 7, 1936, 4.
15. "Southern Bans Broadcasting," TSN, May 16, 1929, 4.
16. "Big Leagues Will Not Ban Baseball Broadcasts," Broadcast Advertising, December 1929, 12 and 22.
17. N. J. Abodaher, "Baseball via the Ether Waves," BM, November 1929, 551.
18. John Drebinger, "Landis Peace Plea to Robins Fails," NYT, December 12, 1929.
19. "Baseball Broadcasts Are No Longer Banned," NYT, September 14, 1930; see also "For Better Broadcasts," TSN, October 29, 1931, 4.
20. David Driscoll Jr., "Should Baseball Ban Broadcasting?" Broadcasting, February 1, 1933, 27.
21. Hal Tate, "General Mills to Use 75 for Baseball," Broadcasting, April 15, 1938, 16–17 and 72; Val Adams, "Red Barber Dismissed after 13 Years as Yankee Broadcaster," NYT, September 27, 1966.
22. "Ban on Broadcasts of Football and Fight Ruling Start Furore [sic]," Broadcasting, July 15, 1932, 12 and 24.
23. "What Price Sports," Broadcasting, July 15, 1932, 16.
24. "Eastern Collegiate Lifts Football Ban," Broadcasting, September 15, 1932, 12; "Recovering a Fumble," Broadcasting, September 15, 1932, 16.
25. "Colleges Split on Football Sponsorship," Broadcasting, September 15, 1936, 9; "Oil Companies Main Football Sponsors," Broadcasting, September 1, 1936, 13.
26. "Broadcasting of Games," TSN, September 29, 1932, 4.
27. David Driscoll Jr., "Should Baseball Ban Broadcasting?" Broadcasting, February 1, 1933, 26–27.
28. Dick Farrington, "Majors Likely to Shelve Move for Horizontal Cut in Salaries," TSN, December 8, 1932, 1.
29. F. P. Wagner, "Consistency Pays Prima Beer," Broadcasting, April 1, 1934, 16; "Beer Advertising," Broadcasting, February 15, 1933, 8.
30. "Sponsor Takes Baseball Games on Yankee Net," Broadcasting, May 1, 1934, 15.
31. "Baseball Openings Attract Sponsors," Broadcasting, April 15, 1936, 20.
32. "Support of Chicago May Save the Radio," TSN, November 17, 1932, 1; David Driscoll Jr., "Should Baseball Banish the Radio?" BM, January 1933, 351–52 and 373.
33. "Radio Ban Expected by American League," NYT, October 20, 1932.
34. Joe Vila, "Ruppert Belittles Suggestion Yanks Should Aid Weak Clubs," TSN, November 10, 1932, 1; "Colonel Ruppert Objects," TSN, November 10, 1932, 4.
35. "Radio Broadcasts," TSN, October 20, 1932, 4.
36. "Broadcasting of Games," TSN, October 19, 1933, 4; see also "Position on Ra-

dio," *TSN*, January 4, 1934, 4 for another discussion of radio providing free advertising for baseball.

37. "Major Leagues Put Off Radio Problem," *NYT*, December 9, 1931; "Ban on Radio or High Fee for Broadcasting Games Looms," *NYT*, December 8, 1931; Dan Daniel, "Commissioner Will Find Farms Posted/Radio," *TSN*, December 22, 1932, 3 and 6; John Drebinger, "Revamped Giants Seek More Trades," *NYT*, December 17, 1932; John Drebinger, "Majors to Reduce Squads on May 15," *NYT*, December 14, 1932.

38. "Where They Broadcast," *TSN*, May 4, 1933, 4; "Press Predicts Decline in Baseball Attendance," *Broadcasting*, January 1, 1933, 15.

39. "Opportunity of the Majors," *TSN*, December 7, 1933, 4; Edgar Brands, "Majors Clear Decks for '34 Campaign; Uniform Ball to be Used," *TSN*, December 21, 1933, 5; "Baseball Broadcast Ban Proclaimed in St. Louis," *Broadcasting*, February 15, 1934, 10; "Radio Broadcast of St. Louis Cardinals," *NYT*, February 4, 1934.

40. Dick Farrington, "St. Louis Club Signs Off on Radio," *TSN*, February 8, 1934, 1.

41. "Radio Staging Comeback," *TSN*, February 28, 1935, 4; "St. Louis Halts Broadcasts," *TSN*, February 8, 1934, 4.

42. Edgar Brands, "Broadcasts of Games," *TSN*, April 23, 1936, 2; "Night Lights Burning Low in the Majors," *TSN*, December 5, 1935, 1.

43. Tom Swope, "Cincy Turns Skeptical of Radio," *TSN*, May 28, 1936, 1.

44. J. F. Hopkins, "Baseball vs. Radio Again," *Broadcasting*, June 1, 1936, 18.

45. "Baseball in Detroit," *Broadcasting*, April 15, 1937, 79. Another source claimed that the Tigers did not broadcast in 1934, but Smith suggests that the team had, in the past, broadcast games (Smith, *Baseless Fears*, 39).

46. Smith, *Baseless Fears*, 36.

47. "Chicago Baseball Teams to Add Talent Charges for Broadcasts in 1937," *Broadcasting*, November 15, 1936, 36; "Broadcasting Fees Set," *NYT*, January 1, 1937; Irving Vaughan, "Sox Pay-Hike Hopes Better than Cubs; Four Chicago Radio Stations Sign Up with Cubs," *TSN*, January 7, 1937, 5; "A.L. Sits Down on Radio," *TSN*, November 19, 1936, 10; "Bringing Radio and Game in Tune," *TSN*, November 19, 1936, 4.

48. Paul Shannon, "Both Boston Clubs Stand Pat on 'Mike,'" *TSN*, December 3, 1936, 1.

49. "Sponsors Sign for Baseball Season," *Broadcasting*, April 1, 1937, 15 and 104; "Airing of Game Climbs to New High," *TSN*, April 22, 1937, 5.

50. "Baseball Coverage Left to Each Club," *Broadcasting*, December 15, 1937, 44; Don Basenfelder, "Radio Broadens Baseball Broadcasts," *TSN*, April 21, 1938, 5; "To Broadcast Pirates' Games," *NYT*, July 15, 1938.

51. Hal Tate, "General Mills Spends Million on Baseball," *Broadcasting*, April 15, 1937, 13 and 72.

52. Hal Tate, "General Mills to Use 75 for Baseball," *Broadcasting*, April 15, 1938, 16–17.

53. "Kellogg Sponsoring Baseball on 60 Stations This Season," *Broadcasting*, May 1, 1938, 23; "Sponsors Arrange for Baseball Time," *Broadcasting*, January 1, 1938, 67.

54. Walter Ford, "Radio as Baseball Boon," *NYT*, July 30, 1938.

55. "Dodger Baseball to Be Broadcast," *NYT*, December 7, 1938.

56. "Dodger Baseball to Be Broadcast," *NYT*, December 7, 1938; Roscoe McGowen, "Giants Will Sell Radio Rights to Polo Ground Games," *NYT*, December 17, 1938.

57. "Yankees Will Broadcast Their Contests in 1939," *NYT*, December 23, 1938; U.S.

Congress, *Organized Baseball: Hearings*, 1602–3 and 1606–7; Edgar Brands, "New Player Limit, Uniform Ball for Majors," TSN, December 22, 1938, 3 and 7.

58. New York Yankees Baseball Club, Yankees Baseball Collection, "Minutes of a Special Meeting of the Board of Directors, October 24, 1939" and "Minutes of February 20, 1941 Meeting."

59. "Radio in Full Partnership with Game," TSN, January 5, 1939, 4.

60. "Giants and Yanks Complete Arrangements for Broadcasting," NYT, January 26, 1939; "P & G to Expand Baseball Activity," *Broadcasting*, February 15, 1939, 18.

61. James Dawson, "'Tampering' Discussion Enlivens NL Schedule Meeting," NYT, February 8, 1939; "Summer Baseball Schedules Being Completed by Sponsors," *Broadcasting*, March 1, 1939, 16.

62. Dan Daniel, "Washington, Early Radio Booster, to Lead Trek from Air," TSN, July 20, 1939, 1 and 14.

63. "Radio and the Game," TSN, May 4, 1939, 4.

64. "Radio in Full Partnership with Game," TSN, January 5, 1939, 4.

65. "Summer Baseball Sponsorship Doubled by Atlantic Refining," *Broadcasting*, March 15, 1939, 14; "General Mills Baseball on 67 Stations," *Broadcasting*, April 1, 1939, 14; "Pro Grid Signed by General Mills," *Broadcasting*, June 1, 1939, 14; Don Basenfelder, "Broadcasts at All Major Parks Put Radio at New Peak," TSN, May 4, 1939, 5 and 14.

66. "Three Chicago Stations Pay More for Baseball as WBBM Drops Out," *Broadcasting*, February 24, 1941, 54; "Big League Games Shifted to WPEN," *Broadcasting*, February 24, 1941, 54.

67. Dan Daniel, "New York Clubs Air Broadcasting Views," TSN, December 21, 1939, 3; "Camels, Gen. Mills Get N.Y. Baseball," *Broadcasting*, February 1, 1940, 81.

68. "163 Radio Stations Give Play-by-Play Reports of Games," TSN, May 15, 1941, 2.

69. Dan Daniel, "New York Clubs Air Broadcasting Views," TSN, December 21, 1939, 3; John Drebinger, "New York Clubs Discuss 1940 Radio Plans," NYT, December 16, 1939.

70. "Sports Broadcasting Clarified in Ruling," *Broadcasting*, March 1, 1936, 10.

71. "More Static in Radio Problem," TSN, March 12, 1936, 4.

72. "FCC Requested to Rule on Off-Scene Drama of Baseball," NYT, July 26, 1936; "Baseball Clubs Charge Game Pirating by WMCA in Complaint Filed with FCC," *Broadcasting*, July 15, 1936, 66.

73. "Rebroadcast of Play-by-Play Baseball Without Permission Criticized/FCC," *Broadcasting*, March 15, 1937, 68.

74. "FCC Gets League Baseball Complaint," *Broadcasting*, August 1, 1937, 24; "KQV's Broadcasts of Pirates Games Enjoined by Court," *Broadcasting*, April 15, 1938, 82.

75. "World's Series on Radio," NYT, September 24, 1933; "Radio Plans Settled," NYT, September 27, 1934; "Ford to Link Nets for World Series," *Broadcasting*, October 1, 1934, 14; "World Series on Big Hook-Up," NYT, September 27, 1936.

76. "Ford Declined to Broadcast World Series After Paying $100K," NYT, November 4, 1937; "Series to be Broadcast," NYT, October 2, 1937.

77. "Ready for the Kick-Off," NYT, September 4, 1938; "World Series Games to be Broadcast," NYT, October 4, 1938.

78. The Cincinnati Reds' owner, Powel Crosley Jr., owned a number of radio stations; ironically, he was unable to broadcast any World Series games on them as "permission to carry the World Series broadcasts on WSAI was denied, even though we

offered to make no charge to the Gillette Razor Company or Mutual Broadcasting System." "Baseball Carried by 238 Stations," *Broadcasting*, October 15, 1939, 16; "World Series Broadcast Plans," NYT, August 18, 1939; "Mutual Broadcasting System's Exclusive Rights to be Investigated," NYT, November 6, 1939.

79. "Radio and the Game," TSN, October 31, 1940, 4; "Landis Sets Radio Plans for World Series," NYT, July 23, 1940.

80. "Radio 'Eye' Favors Baseball," NYT, May 16, 1937.

81. "Telecast of Major League Game Discussed," NYT, September 3, 1939; "Television: First Major League Game Televised," NYT, August 27, 1939.

82. "Radio and the Game," TSN, May 4, 1939, 4; "Telecast of Major League Game Discussed," NYT, September 3, 1939.

83. Surdam, *Postwar Yankees*, 126–62.

84. Blayne R. Butcher, "Sports! Sports! Sports!—and Results!" *Broadcasting*, August 15, 1935, 11.

85. Surdam, *Postwar Yankees*, 126–62.

10. Baseball Under the Lights

1. "Night Baseball Is Proposed by Western League Club Head," NYT, December 5, 1929.

2. Sec Taylor, "Park Floodlights Provide Rays for Western League's Optimism," TSN, March 13, 1930, 7.

3. "Night Baseball," TSN, January 16, 1930, 4.

4. "Night Baseball Games on Pacific Coast Draw Three Times," NYT, September 7, 1930; Irving Gutterman, "Night Baseball Winning Its Way," NYT, August 10, 1930.

5. "Night Baseball to Be Staged at Des Moines Park This Year," NYT, February 6, 1930.

6. Leonard J. McAdams, "Why Not Twilight Big League Baseball?" BM, July 1930, 361.

7. "12,000 Fans See Night Ball Game," NYT, May 3, 1930. An article in the *Sporting News* claimed 10,000 fans: Sec Taylor, "Test at Des Moines Regarded as Success," TSN, May 8, 1930, 2.

8. "Baseball by Artificial Light," TSN, May 8, 1930, 4; Sec Taylor, "Average Night Crowd at Des Moines is 2,300," TSN, May 22, 1930, 3.

9. "Night Baseball Idea Spreads; Springfield, IL Will Try It," NYT, June 3, 1930; "Indianapolis Night Games Triple Attendance Figures," NYT, July 20, 1930; Irving Gutterman, "Night Baseball Winning Its Way," NYT, August 10, 1930.

10. "Reds to Try Baseball at Night," NYT, June 26, 1930.

11. "First Night Baseball in Metro Area, When Newark Plays Jersey City," NYT, July 22, 1930.

12. "First Night Football Game in New York at Polo Grounds," NYT, July 25, 1930; "Night Baseball Edging Nearer the Majors; Giants in Bridgeport," NYT, July 27, 1930; John Drebinger, "Giants Lose to White Sox in First Nocturnal Contest," NYT, March 22, 1931; "Night Baseball Tried at the Polo Grounds," NYT, August 2, 1930.

13. J. Roy Stockton, "The Pros and Cons of Night Baseball," BM, August 1930, 391.

14. "Night Ball for N.L. Aim of Sam Breadon," TSN, August 28, 1930, 3.

15. Sec Taylor, "Banner Year in Western League Brightened by Night Arclights," TSN, November 13, 1930, 6; "Ad for Giant Floodlights Now Claim 600% Increase in Attendance," TSN, February 12, 1931, 8; see also ad in TSN, February 5, 1931, 8.

16. "Curtails Night Baseball," NYT, July 10, 1931; "Jersey City Abandons Night Ball," TSN, February 26, 1931, 4.
17. John Foster, "What of Night Ball's Trend?" TSN, June 25, 1931, 4.
18. "Night and Day Comparisons," TSN, December 3, 1936, 4.
19. "Los Angeles People Take to Night Sports," NYT, September 7, 1930.
20. "Revised Rules Lift Majors' Ban on Night Games," TSN, April 9, 1931, 2; "Night Games Will be Played in Parks of 16 Minor League Teams," TSN, April 2, 1931, 5.
21. The manufacturer also stated that Independence Club of Washington, Kansas of the Western Association was the first professional team to play night ball (April 18, 1930), a statement later baseball researchers appear to have accepted. Clyde Harding, "Manufacturers Anticipate that 80 Per Cent of Minors Will Play Night Ball," TSN, April 16, 1931, 8; Warfield, *Roaring Redhead*, 57; Light, *Cultural History of Baseball*, 510.
22. Tom Laird, "Lights Treble Attendance in San Francisco," TSN, June 11, 1931, 3; "End Night Baseball," NYT, May 24, 1932; "The Shades of Night Cease," TSN, June 2, 1932, 4.
23. "'Night Ball Savior of Small Leagues, No Limit to Possibilities,'" TSN, November 19, 1931, 6; Damon Kerby, "Night Game Dying in Minors, Novelty Wearing Off, Claims Leifield," TSN, November 12, 1931, 5.
24. F. C. Lane, "The Sweeping Success of Night Baseball in the Minors," BM, January 1937, 369–70; Pietrusza, *Lights On!*, 122.
25. Walter N. Harper, "The Battle of the Arc-Lights," BM, February 1940, 428; see also Arthur O. Anderson, "What Do the Fans Prefer?" BM, June 1942, 315–16 and 329–30.
26. F. C. Lane, "The Romance of Night Baseball," BM, October 1930, 483–85.
27. "Night Ball 'Fad' Says Mack," NYT, February 16, 1935; "M'Carthy Opposed to Night Baseball," NYT, February 17, 1935.
28. "Night Ball Wearing Off," TSN, June 16, 1932, 4.
29. "Night Baseball," TSN, January 26, 1933, 4; "Is It Taps for Night Ball?" TSN, February 8, 1934, 4.
30. "Night Ball for Majors," TSN, August 23, 1934, 4.
31. Edgar Brands, "Minors, Night Game Experience Lights Way for Majors," TSN, January 24, 1935, 5.
32. MacPhail later claimed that Commissioner Landis told him at the 1934 winter meetings, "Young man, you can write this down. Not in my lifetime or yours will you ever see a baseball game played at night in the majors." Warfield, *Roaring Redhead*, 58.
33. Tom Swope, "MacPhail Lights On A.L. Critics as Reds Light Way for Night Ball," TSN, December 20, 1934, 1; John Drebinger, "Night Baseball on Limited Scale Adopted by National League," NYT, December 13, 1934.
34. Tom Swope, "Cincinnati Lights the Way in Big League Style," TSN, May 23, 1935, 3.
35. Warfield, *Roaring Redhead*, 58; Dan Daniel, "Reds Likely to be Alone in Experiment with Night Ball," TSN, December 20, 1934, 3; John Drebinger, "Rule Permitting Night Baseball Passed by National League," NYT, February 6, 1935; "Night Game Rules," TSN, February 14, 1935, 7.
36. Dan Daniel, "Night Ball Dangers Steer Giants Away," TSN, December 27, 1934, 1; Dan Daniel, "Night Baseball Nothing New," BM, February 1935, 390.
37. Dan Daniel, "Night Baseball Nothing New," BM, February 1935, 390.
38. "Turning on the Lights," TSN, May 16, 1935, 4.
39. Warfield, *Roaring Redhead*, 58–59; Tom Swope, "Seven Cincy Games Draw 77,695

Fans," TSN, May 2, 1935, 3; John J. Ward, "When the Arc Lights Blazed at Cincinnati," BM, July 1935, 351.

    40. Dick Farrington, "Cardinals in Dark on Nocturnal Play," TSN, December 20, 1934, 2; "Venturing Out After Dark," TSN, December 20, 1934, 4; "No Night Ball in St. Louis," NYT, April 29, 1935.

    41. "More Light on the Subject," TSN, May 9, 1935, 4.

    42. Tom Swope, "Seven Cincy Games Draw 77,695 Fans," TSN, May 2, 1935, 3.

    43. Edgar Brands, "Initial Test of Nocturnal Game at Cincinnati Proves Itself as Added Feature for Major Leagues," TSN, May 30, 1935, 2.

    44. "The Cincinnati Experiment," TSN, May 30, 1935, 4.

    45. "Nocturnal Opponents Die Hard," TSN, June 6, 1935, 4.

    46. "More Light on a Dark Subject," TSN, July 11, 1935, 4.

    47. Larry MacPhail, "The Triumph of the Arc Lights," BM, September 1936, 445.

    48. Tom Swope, "Cincy Night Games Draw 130,337," TSN, September 5, 1935, 3.

    49. "Night Ball at the Bar," TSN, September 12, 1935, 4.

    50. F. C. Lane, "Will the Major Leagues Adopt Night Baseball?" BM, October 1935, 522.

    51. Larry MacPhail, "The Triumph of the Arc Lights," BM, September 1936, 445.

    52. Tom Swope, "Fans Share Payoff from Cincy Lights," TSN, January 4, 1940, 3.

    53. Larry MacPhail, "The Triumph of the Arc Lights," BM, September 1936, 445.

    54. Ford Frick, "Sees Boon in Night Ball," NYT, July 16, 1935.

    55. F. C. Lane, "Will the Major Leagues Adopt Night Baseball?" BM, October 1935, 487–89.

    56. Denman Thompson, "Griff Favorable to Night Ball, But Against It for Own Park," TSN, November 7, 1935, 1; "Night Ball One of Three A.L. Problems," TSN, November 14, 1935, 1; Denman Thompson, "A.L. Lines Break on Night Ball, Griffith Counts on Two Allies," TSN, August 22, 1935, 1.

    57. Dan Daniel, "Sentiment on Arcs Grows in National," TSN, February 13, 1936, 5.

    58. "Night Ball at Dead Center," TSN, December 26, 1935, 4; "Night Lights Burning Low in the Majors," TSN, December 5, 1935, 1; Edgar Brands, "American Thumbs Down on Night Games," TSN, December 19, 1935, 3.

    59. "League Approves Sale of Browns; Permits Night Ball," NYT, November 13, 1936; "Browns' Deal Delayed," NYT, November 17, 1936; Red Smith, "Connie Sees Light, May Play at Night," TSN, November 19, 1936, 3; "No Night Baseball in St. Louis," NYT, February 16, 1937; "Sale of Browns Complicated," NYT, November 21, 1936; "No St. Louis Lights in '37," TSN, February 18, 1937, 7; "Night Ball Plan Fails," NYT, October 21, 1937.

    60. F. C. Lane, "Selling Baseball to the Public," BM, December 1936, 332.

    61. Frederick Lieb, "Lights or Players? Browns' Problem," TSN, August 11, 1938, 3.

    62. John Drebinger, "Yankees Follow Lead of Giants and Bar Night Games," NYT, December 1, 1936; John Drebinger, "Major Leagues Split on Type of Ball and Night Contests," NYT, December 8, 1937.

    63. Dan Daniel, "American League Turns Down Tribe on Night Ball," TSN, December 9, 1937, 1.

    64. In the same article, some of the other National League owners enthused about MacPhail's return to the league, with Breadon gushing, "our share of the receipts for our games at Brooklyn probably will be $10,000 more than they would be without him." Roscoe McGowen, "Full Control Over Operation of Dodgers Goes to MacPhail," NYT, January 20, 1938.

65. "Night Game Soon for Ebbets Field," NYT, May 23, 1938.
66. Warfield, *Roaring Redhead*, 76.
67. "MacPhail Lights the Way Again," TSN, June 2, 1938, 4.
68. Warfield, *Roaring Redhead*, 77.
69. Graham, *Brooklyn Dodgers*, 164.
70. Tommy Holmes, "Everybody Follows the Ball but Dodgers as MacPhail Sells Night Game," TSN, June 23, 1938, 5; Roscoe McGowen, "Dodgers Bow in Night Inaugural," NYT, June 16, 1938.
71. Tommy Holmes, "Lights Shed Bright Ray on 700,000 Dodger Gate," TSN, September 15, 1938, 2; Tommy Holmes, "153,498 At Five Dodger Games Make Owl Ball Critics Blink," TSN, August 11, 1938, 3.
72. "Brooklyn: Sheriff Threatens Night Game Ban If Rows Occur," NYT, June 6, 1939.
73. "Night Baseball Trend Is Seen by Harridge in Major Leagues," NYT, July 3, 1938.
74. James Isaminger, "Athletics Weighing Arc Ball," TSN, July 14, 1938, 3.
75. "Mack for Night Baseball," NYT, October 19, 1938.
76. Roscoe McGowen, "Yanks and Giants Shun Night Games," NYT, December 8, 1938; Dan Daniel, "Yankees-Giants Put Dimmers on Lights," TSN, December 22, 1938, 2; John Drebinger, "Big Leagues Ready to Adopt One Ball; Restore 25 Man Roster," NYT, December 11, 1938; James Isaminger, "Yankees and Giants Weakening in Objections to Night Ball," NYT, December 15, 1938; Dan Daniel, "Yankees Yield on Night Ball to Aid Other Clubs," TSN, May 25, 1939, 1; "Detroit Tigers: Night Games Planned; Yankees Road Night," NYT, May 18, 1939.
77. John Drebinger, "Harridge Elected for 10-Year Term," NYT, December 14, 1938.
78. Edgar Brands, "New Player Limit, Uniform Ball for Majors," TSN, December 22, 1938, 3 and 7.
79. "Night Ball/Radio," TSN, January 5, 1939, 4; James Isaminger, "Mack to See 'Uncle' in Installing Lights," TSN, December 22, 1938, 1 and 5.
80. Louis Elfin, "Attacks Night Game Broadcast," NYT, August 2, 1939; "Will Permit Night Ball," NYT, February 9, 1939.
81. Edgar Brands, "New Player Limit, Uniform Ball for Majors," TSN, December 22, 1938, 3 and 7; "Bradley Nails 'Tight Purse' Charge," TSN, January 26, 1939, 1.
82. Louis Effrat, "Yankees Reaction to Night Game with Philadelphia," NYT, June 28, 1939; Stoney McLinn, "Connie Mack, Linking Birth of American with Present, First to Light Up in Loop," TSN, May 25, 1939, 2.
83. Denman Thompson, "Griffith Advocates Two Months of Continuous Night Play in Majors," TSN, June 29, 1939, 1 and 2.
84. "Let There Be More Light," TSN, July 6, 1939, 4.
85. Dan Daniel, "Yanks in Last-Ditch Stand Against Arcs," TSN, July 6, 1939, 3; Ed McAuley, "Fans Won Over by Arcs, Order Tickets for Future Nocturnals," TSN, July 6, 1939 2.
86. James Isaminger, "A's Average 18,014 at Five Night Tilts," TSN, July 6, 1939, 5; "Night Ball's Pulling Power," TSN, August 31, 1939, 10; Philadelphia Phillies Baseball Club, cash books.
87. Ed Burns, "Sox Play to 186,000 in Six Owl Tilts," TSN, September 7, 1939, 5; "White Sox Plan Night Games," NYT, August 1, 1939.
88. Joseph Nichols, "MacPhail Suggests Interleague Games; NL Night Games," NYT,

October 27, 1939; "To Light Polo Grounds," NYT, January 27, 1940; John Drebinger, "Night Baseball Inaugural at Polo Grounds," NYT, May 25, 1940.

89. Dan Daniel, "Arclights Add Only to Gloom of Giants," TSN, August 1, 1940, 2.

90. Dan Daniel, "'Never at Stadium,' Bellows Barrow, As Giants Prepare for Night Play in '40," TSN, November 2, 1939, 1 and 7; John Drebinger, "Polo Grounds Being Equipped with Lights for 1940," NYT, November 15, 1939.

91. Dan Daniel, "Night Ball Irresistible," BM, January 1940, 347; see also Dan Daniel, "Majors Going Sour on Broadcasting as Harmful to Attendance; Washington, Early Radio Booster, to Lead Trek from Air," TSN, July 20, 1939, 1 and 14. Years later, Barrow related an anecdote in his autobiography. He had agreed to a night game at the turn of the century that ended badly; that experience soured him on the innovation. Barrow, *My Fifty Years in Baseball*, 35–36.

92. Graham, *New York Yankees*, 288–89.

93. "Warning is Issued by MacPhail Against Night Ball Overloading," NYT, July 16, 1939.

94. Barrow took a patronizing attitude: "Your child hollers for candy and you know it's going to get a stomachache, but the holler gets so loud and insistent that it annoys the company, so you give the kid the candy, and stay up the rest of the night, feeding it paregoric and telling your wife, 'I told you so.' If the fans want the candy, we may have to do something about it. But personally I say nix." Dan Daniels, "Barrow Warns American League He'll Bolt Move to Increase Arc Tilts," TSN, November 23, 1939, 1 and 5.

95. Ed Burns, "A.L. Required to Act on Arcs Each Year," TSN, November 30, 1939, 5.

96. "Arc Light Ball Open to All AL Clubs," TSN, January 25, 1940, 5; "Letting in More Light," TSN, January 25, 1940, 4; Charles Doyle, "Buc Arcs Cast Rays toward Box Office," TSN, February 8, 1940, 1.

97. Dick Farrington, "Owl Ball Hurdles Cleared in St. Louis," TSN, February 1, 1940, 3; "Games Under Lights Assured in St. Louis," NYT, February 1, 1940.

98. Edgar Brands, "St. Louis Greets Nocturnal Ball With Third Largest Attendance," TSN, May 30, 1940, 5.

99. "Night Games Seen by 1,558,021 in Major League Parks," NYT, September 7, 1940; "Hot Teams Draw to Cool of Evenings," TSN, August 22, 1940, 4; "Night Game Figures Tell the Story," TSN, September 19, 1940, 4.

100. Dick Farrington, "'Better Days Ahead for Browns'—Haney," TSN, September 26, 1940, 2; Dick Farrington, "Barnes All Abubble on Hot Springs Visit," TSN, November 28, 1940, 2; Dick Farrington, "Browns' Dark Look Due to Light Limit," TSN, December 19, 1940, 3; "Browns' Head Hits Night Game Limit," NYT, December 14, 1940; "Night Crowds Hold Up," TSN, August 7, 1941, 2.

101. James Isaminger, "A's Twin-Bill Chart Fouled Up by Rain," TSN, September 5, 1940, 5.

102. "Night Game Figures Tell the Story," TSN, September 19, 1940, 4; "No Lights for Tigers," NYT, December 18, 1940; Hal Borland, "Night Baseball Packs 'em In," NYT, June 9, 1940; "5,433,791 Saw Games in American League," NYT, October 15, 1940.

103. "Chicago Night Games Depend on Demand," NYT, March 21, 1942.

104. "Chicago Cubs to Drop Comiskey Park Night Game Plans," NYT, February 13, 1942.

105. Francis Stan, "Griff Turns Down Lights 'Due to Costs,'" TSN, March 14, 1940, 1 and 9.

106. Denman Thompson, "Griffith May Urge Bigger Light Bills," TSN, November 14, 1940, 10.

107. Dick Farrington, "Browns' Dark Look Due to Light Limit," TSN, December 19, 1940, 3; Edgar Brands, "Organized Ball, In Harmony Move," TSN, December 19, 1940, 5 and 6.

108. Dan Daniel, "'Arc Ball War on Nose of the Game'—Barrow," TSN, January 1, 1942, 1 and 5; see also "Comments on Macks' Proposal to Increase Night Games," NYT, May 17, 1941.

109. Shirley Povich, "'Let Any Club Play 14 Arc Tilts'—Griff," TSN, November 6, 1941, 1 and 5.

110. "Opposes More Night Ball," NYT, November 8, 1941.

111. "For the Day Shift," TSN, January 29, 1942, 4.

112. Dick Farrington, "Barnes See Bright Days on Night Ball," TSN, January 22, 1942, 7.

113. Dan Daniel, "N.L. Setting Aside 7-Game Limit Rule, Seeks Limit of 14," TSN, January 22, 1942, 1; Shirley Povich, "Griffith to Demand at Least 35 Night Games," TSN, January 29, 1942, 1.

114. Dan Daniel, "Arc Date Conflict New York Problem," TSN, February 12, 1942, 7; see John Drebinger for a recap of night ball in the majors, "The Increase in Major League Night Baseball," BM, April 1942, 497–98 and 523–24; "American League Schedule for 1942," NYT, March 3, 1942; Dan Daniel, "Giants May Stick to Seven Arc Tilts," TSN, January 29, 1942, 1 and 12.

115. "Night Games Banned for War Duration," NYT, May 19, 1942; James Dawson, "Stoneham Announces New York Giants Will Stop Twilight Games," NYT, August 4, 1942; Shirley Povich, "Defiant Griff Turns to 'Twi-Night' Ball," TSN, July 16, 1942, 1.

116. Sam Greene, "Tiger Twilight Tilt Ticks at Turnstiles," TSN, July 2, 1942, 5a.

11. Other Innovations

1. "Hearken to the Fans," TSN, March 16, 1933, 4.

2. "Survey Condemns Home-Run Epidemic," NYT, July 14, 1929.

3. Burk, *Never Just a Game*, 246.

4. "Baseball Season to End Week Later," NYT, December 14, 1928; Robert Kelley, "'Sports of the Times,' Refusal of Ten Man Plan," NYT, December 13, 1928; John Drebinger, "Ten-Man Baseball Advocated by Heydler," NYT, December 12, 1928.

5. All quotes from "American League Hits Heydler Plan," NYT, December 12, 1928.

6. "Dreyfuss of Pirates Favors 10-Man Teams," NYT, December 28, 1928; John Drebinger, "Giants Adopt the Chain-Store Idea," NYT, December 18, 1928.

7. "Hitting Ability of Pitchers Is Closely Watched by Fans," NYT, September 8, 1929. Pitchers who had the most innings pitched in the National League hit .222 in 1930 but slumped, along with hitters, to .193 in 1931 (compiled from pitchers' hitting records in the *Macmillan Baseball Encyclopedia*).

8. "Says Tests Reveal Ball Is Not Lively," NYT, August 28, 1929.

9. Herman Wecke, "Rule Makers Hit Sluggers Hard Blow, Eliminate Sacrifice Fly," TSN, December 31, 1931, 6; John Drebinger, "Big Leagues Change Sacrifice Fly Rule," NYT, December 13, 1930.

10. John Drebinger, "Less Lively Ball Adopted by National League to Decrease Homeruns," NYT, February 4, 1931; "American League to Alter Inside of Ball," NYT, February 6, 1931.

Notes to pages 251–257

11. "The National League Ball," TSN, October 22, 1931, 4.
12. "Better Games and Bigger Crowds Seen by Heydler," TSN, May 7, 1931, 1; "Less Lively Baseball Is Having Livelier Habits Than Old," NYT, May 21, 1931; "'Dead' Ball Is Called a Success by NL Club Owners," NYT, June 25, 1931.
13. "328 Fewer Homeruns Hit in Major Leagues," NYT, July 31, 1931; "Standardize the Ball," TSN, August 13, 1931, 4; "Old-Time Fan Coming Back," TSN, August 13, 1931, 4; Clifford Bloodgood, "Expert Opinions on the New Ball," BM, October 1931, 499–500.
14. Joe Vila, "Yank Owner Favors Less Lively Sphere," TSN, October 29, 1931, 7.
15. Klein's impressive hitting marks of the early 1930s were aided by the Baker Bowl's tiny size; however, after the 1931 season, a reporter mentioned that there were more home runs hit in four other Major League parks, including two parks used by National League batters (Herman Wecke, "Four Other Major League Parks Saw More Homeruns than Baker Bowl," TSN, December 24, 1931, 3).
16. "Lively Ball Not Sought," NYT, June 11, 1929; "Harridge Favors Uniform Baseball; Owners Fooled by BAVE," NYT, December 6, 1933; "Opportunity of the Majors," TSN, December 7, 1933, 4.
17. "Big Leagues Vote for Uniform Ball," NYT, December 15, 1933; Edgar Brands, "Majors Clear Decks for '34 Campaign; Uniform Ball to be Used," TSN, December 21, 1933, 5; "Same Ball in Both Leagues," NYT, July 30, 1936; "Expert to Seek Slower Ball," NYT, October 27, 1937; John Drebinger, "Major Leagues Split on Type of Ball and Night Contests," NYT, December 8, 1937; Edgar Brands, "Major Leagues Split on Changing Ball and Increasing Player Limit," TSN, December 16, 1937, 3 and 10.
18. John Drebinger, "Indians and Athletics to Introduce Night Ball; Uniform Ball," NYT, December 15, 1938; John Drebinger, "Big Leagues Ready to Adopt One Ball, Restore 25-Man Roster," NYT, December 11, 1938; John Drebinger, "Harridge Elected for 10-Year Term," NYT, December 14, 1938.
19. "Returning Balls Hit Into Stands," TSN, August 16, 1934, 4.
20. C. Throckmorton, "Favors Baseball Helmet," NYT, June 22, 1940; James Dawson, "National League Annual Meeting; Schedule Approved," NYT, February 5, 1941; "Helmets Should be Compulsory," TSN, August 21, 1941, 4.
21. U.S. Congress, *Organized Baseball: Hearings*, 1599–1600.
22. Veeck and Linn, *Veeck—As In Wreck*, 119.
23. "Giving Needed Information," TSN, April 20, 1939, 4; "So the Fans May Know," TSN, May 9, 1935, 4; Dick Farrington, "Head of Browns to Demand A.L. Liberalize Views on Giving Fans Info," TSN, June 16, 1938, 1; "Advertise the Pitchers," TSN, May 11, 1933, 4.
24. "Real Handbook of Information," TSN, April 19, 1934, 4; see "Keeping the Public Informed," TSN, May 17, 1934, 4 for Cubs' efforts to publicize player information.
25. "Yankees to Wear Numbers This Year," NYT, January 23, 1929.
26. Thomas Rice, "Yanks Adopt Numbering System," TSN, January 31, 1929, 2.
27. "Numbering the Players," TSN, January 31, 1929, 4.
28. Morris, *Game on the Field*, 466.
29. Morris, *Game on the Field*, 465–66
30. "Satisfying the Customer," TSN, June 9, 1932, 4; "National Should Number Players," TSN, November 26, 1931, 4; Morris, *Game on the Field*, 266.
31. "Why Not Loud Speakers," TSN, September 28, 1933, 4.

32. "Giants' Amplifying Set Makes Umpire's Voice Audible to All," *NYT*, August 26, 1929.

33. "Making the Customer Happy," *TSN*, April 29, 1937, 4; "Amplifier for Ebbets Field," *NYT*, March 24, 1936; "To Keep Chicago Fans Informed," *TSN*, March 22, 1934, 4; "Keeping the Public Informed," *TSN*, May 17, 1934, 4.

34. "Keeping the Fans Informed," *TSN*, June 15, 1933, 4.

35. T. W. Buckley, "Problems of Bleacherites," *NYT*, May 9, 1936.

36. D. Phillips, "Polo Grounds Problems," *NYT*, August 20, 1938.

37. Edgar Brands, "Many Major Parks Lag in Giving Needed Information," *TSN*, January 17, 1935, 5; John Drebinger, "Draft Is Discussed in National League," *NYT*, December 11, 1928.

38. Morris, *Game Behind the Scenes*, 92; "Organ Music to Soothe Cubs Fans," *TSN*, May 1, 1941, 4.

39. Seymour, *Baseball: Early Years*, 196; "Display Advertising," *TSN*, September 22, 1932, 4.

40. J. X. O'Melia, "Information System for Fans Wanted," *NYT*, April 25, 1936; Seymour, *Baseball: Early Years*, 196. The Cleveland Indians used a similar mechanism to indicate whether the game was to be played. According to the team's scorecards, "This baseball flag will fly from the top of the Terminal Tower every day on which a game is scheduled in Cleveland. If flag is not flying it will indicate the game has been postponed" (Cleveland Indians scorecards 1929, 1932–35).

41. "The Fans Sun Themselves," *TSN*, July 23, 1931, 4.

42. Dan Daniel, "'Game Coming Back Bigger Than Ever,' Says Ruppert, Park Enlarged," *TSN*, January 19, 1933, 3; "Yankees Plan New Stand," *NYT*, March 4, 1933; "Change in Subway Sought by Ruppert," *NYT*, February 2, 1929.

43. "Yankees Will Enlarge Stadium to Seat 84,000," *NYT*, February 5, 1936; "Contract for Yankee Stadium Enlargement Awarded," *NYT*, December 31, 1936; Lowry, *Green Cathedrals*, 60.

44. John Drebinger, "Cubs Expect to Top Yanks' Best Gate," *NYT*, September 21, 1929; "Pirates Add New Seats," *NYT*, September 19, 1938.

45. Harry Neily, "Visiting Major League Parks: Wrigley Field," *TSN*, January 11, 1934, 5.

46. "Visiting Major League Parks: Comiskey Park," *TSN*, December 7, 1933, 5; "Cubs to Enlarge Park," *NYT*, October 12, 1935; Ed Burns, "Wrigley Orders $150,000 Start on Half-Million Park Program," *TSN*, February 20, 1936, 1.

47. James Isaminger, "Many Ready to Bid for Baker Holdings," *TSN*, December 11, 1930, 1; "Phils Set to Close Deal For Use of Shibe Park," *NYT*, June 26, 1938; "Phils Quit Old Field," *NYT*, July 2, 1938.

48. Dick Farrington, "Browns Lease, Has a 'Believe-It-or-Not,'" *TSN*, December 10, 1936, 2; Dick Farrington, "Visiting Major League Parks: Sportsman's Park," *TSN*, March 1, 1934, 7.

49. Ford Sawyer, "Visiting Major League Parks: Braves' Field," *TSN*, March 15, 1934, 5; Ford Sawyer, "Yawkey to Put $300,000 in Fenway," *TSN*, September 28, 1933, 1; Ford Sawyer, "Visiting Major League Parks: Fenway Park," *TSN*, February 15, 1934, 7.

50. "Collins Explains Stand of Red Sox," *NYT*, January 15, 1935; John Drebinger, "National League Meeting Discuss Boston Braves," *NYT*, January 15, 1935; John Drebinger, "National League Reaffirms Ban on Dog Racing; Braves Problem," *NYT*, January 19, 1935.

51. N. R. Howard, "Cleveland Seeking City Baseball Deal," NYT, January 4, 1931; "Cleveland Indians to Have New Home," NYT, April 17, 1928.

52. "Indians Will Not Move," NYT, July 15, 1931; "Use of City Stadium by Indians Halted," NYT, July 14, 1931; "Indians to Use Old Park; Stadium Is Too Costly," NYT, October 15, 1933; Ed Bang, "Visiting Major League Parks: Cleveland's League Park," TSN, February 1, 1934, 6; see also "A Lesson for Cleveland," TSN, August 6, 1931, 4 on the perils of municipal funding of stadiums.

53. "Plans to Enlarge Ebbets Field Made," NYT, February 12, 1931; "Brooklyn Improvements," TSN, February 19, 1931, 4; "Ebbets Field Improved," NYT, April 11, 1938.

54. Arthur Patterson, "Yankee Stadium, World's Largest Privately-Owned Park, Grew Out of Club's Eviction from Polo Grounds," TSN, April 17, 1941, 4.

55. Sam Greene, "Visiting Major League Parks: Navin Field," TSN, March 22, 1934, 6; "Tigers Seek New Stands," NYT, September 5, 1934; "Detroit Will Add 10,000 Seats," NYT, October 9, 1935; "Detroit Loyalty Pays Dividends," TSN, October 17, 1935, 4; "No Retreat, Game Moves Ahead," TSN, February 13, 1936, 4; "Tigers' Park to Seat 60,000," NYT, October 22, 1937; Sam Greene, "Tigers Making Park Fit 1,181,000 Draw," TSN, October 28, 1937, 1.

56. Tom Swope, "Visiting Major League Parks: Cincinnati," TSN, February 8, 1934, 7; "Cincinnati Hotel to Give Yanks Cots," NYT, September 30, 1939.

57. "The Fan Has the Final Say," TSN, February 20, 1936, 4; Warren Milius, "Ticket Sale Criticized," NYT, June 29, 1940.

58. "Cubs' New Plan Aims Blow at Scalpers," NYT, April 5, 1936; "Baseball Fans Now May Reserve Seats for Games by Wire," NYT, April 26, 1931; "Dodgers Try New Plan for Selling Tickets at Western Union," NYT, May 13, 1938; "Charge Account for Fans," NYT, June 23, 1937.

59. "Throw Out the Pop Bottles," TSN, May 16, 1929, 4; "Very Bad Manners," TSN, September 25, 1930, 4; see also "The Deadly Bottle Must Go," TSN, July 30, 1936, 4.

60. "Ban the Bottle," TSN, June 20, 1940, 4.

61. "No Beer in Shibe Park," NYT, March 2, 1935; "32 Pages of Scouting Reports," Sports Illustrated, April 15, 1957, 47–83; "Pirates Ban Beer in Park," NYT, April 1, 1933.

62. Harry Sokol, "Wants Milk Sold at Ball Parks," NYT, July 15, 1939.

63. Lee Rourke, "A Bronx Cheer for 'Booers,'" NYT, February 19, 1938.

64. "Los Angeles People Take to Night Sports," NYT, September 7, 1930.

65. Graham, Brooklyn Dodgers, 160. One can only shiver at the thought of Dodger-style ushers facing Cubs fan Steve Bartman after his ill-fated catch of a foul ball in a recent National League Championship Series game.

66. Warfield, Roaring Redhead, 74.

67. "Move Against the Gamblers," TSN, August 20, 1931, 4; "Halting the Gamblers," TSN, August 13, 1931, 4.

68. Morris, Game Behind the Scenes, 121.

69. "Ladies' Days at Ball Games Found Successful in West," NYT, August 4, 1929.

70. "Ladies Days at Ball Game Found Successful in West," NYT, August 4, 1929; "Women Jam Park, Cash Fans Outside," TSN, July 31 1930, 1.

71. "Shows How to Put Click in Turnstiles," TSN, July 14, 1932, 4.

72. "The Ladies, God Bless 'Em," TSN, May 23, 1929, 4.

73. "Bars Free Admission of Women to Games," NYT, July 6, 1929; "Ladies' Days at

Ball Games Found Successful in West," NYT, August 4, 1929; see also Tom Swope, "Free Days a Plenty for Cincy's Fair Sex," TSN, February 27, 1930, 6.

74. "Four Half-Price Days, One Free for Women at Braves' Games," NYT, April 7, 1932; Boston Braves scorecard, 1946.

75. "Ladies' Days at Ball Games Found Successful in West," NYT, August 4, 1929.

76. Lester Goodkind, "Wail of a Harried Male," NYT, July 9, 1938.

77. Edgar Millis, "Ladies for a Day," NYT, July 24, 1937; Graham, *Brooklyn Dodgers*, 179.

78. Mrs. Bernard Weiss, "More on Ladies' Day," NYT, February 26, 1938; Minerve Matzkowitz, Shirley Taub, Dorothy Brink, Edith Washington, "Fair Play for Fair Fans," NYT, February 19, 1938.

79. "Ladies' Day Announced for Yankee Stadium," NYT, March 23, 1938; James Dawson, "Yankees' First Ladies' Day," NYT, April 30, 1938.

80. F. U. L., "Asks Fair Deal for Fair Fans," NYT, April 8, 1939; "Major League Attendance Report," NYT, May 10, 1941.

81. "School Children to See Chicago Ball Games Free," NYT, December 13, 1929; "Wrigley Goes It Alone: Knothole Prices," TSN, December 20, 1934, 4; Denman Thompson, "Nats Allow Boys to see Games for 25 Cents," TSN, January 11, 1934, 1; "Making New Fans," TSN, June 11, 1931, 4.

82. Making comparisons between the cost of attending games during the 1930s and today is difficult. "Supersizing" makes the comparison treacherous. While sodas may have gone for a dime during the 1930s (roughly $1.50 in today's dollars), the cup sizes are undoubtedly larger today. Fans may be getting larger and better hot dogs, too. The seats and overall ballpark maintenance are also better today. The modern "Fan Cost Index" published by the Team Marketing Report (http://teammarketing.com.ismmediacom) assumes that fans want more than just beverages and hot dogs. They also want a fancier program and baseball caps. In addition, they have to pay for parking. "Helping the Fans' Budget," TSN, February 7, 1935, 4.

83. "Schedule Change Planned," NYT, December 11, 1935; John Drebinger, "MacPhail Considering Admitting Boys for Free," NYT, January 20, 1939; Dwight Franklin, "Wants Lower Baseball Prices," NYT, March 11, 1939; Stanley French, "Half Price for Boys," NYT, April 27, 1940; Slim Dorney, "A Better Break for Boys," NYT, June 15, 1940.

84. "Making the Public a Partner," TSN, June 7, 1934, 4; "Father & Son Day," TSN, June 14, 1934, 4.

85. Sid Keener, "Does Game Need Extra Stimulant?" TSN, January 23, 1941, 4.

86. "Lessons from Other Sports," TSN, January 5, 1933, 4.

87. Shirley Povich, "Griff Talking Latin Over Nats' Outlook," TSN, February 5, 1942, 5.

88. "Speed Up the Game," TSN, July 7, 1932, 4; "Speeding Up Games," TSN, August 9, 1934, 4; Irving E. Sanborn, "President Barnard Holds the Stop Watch," BM, June 1928, 301–3 and 326–27.

89. Dan Daniel, "N.L. Sounds Out Fans on Streets for Suggestions to Help Game," TSN, October 31, 1935, 1.

90. "The Fan Speaks Out," TSN, August 27, 1936, 4; "Fans Vote 8 to 5 for Curb on Heavy Hitting," TSN, September 3, 1936, 5.

91. "Surveying the Fans' Wants," TSN, March 25, 1937, 4.

92. Warren Brown, "Wrigley Puts Fans' Comfort First," TSN, February 14, 1935, 5.

93. "Future Ball Teams to Fly, Play Coast Cities," NYT, October 4, 1929; "McGraw Sees Planes Revolutionizing Game," NYT, December 31, 1932.

94. "League Goes Air-Minded," NYT, January 28, 1940; "American Association Owners to Discuss Use of Airplanes," NYT, January 16, 1932.

95. "MacPhail Starts Something," TSN, June 21, 1934, 4; "Red Sox Travel by Plane," NYT, July 31, 1936.

96. "Schedule-maker Would Have Major Teams Play Interleague Contests on Open Dates," TSN, February 6, 1930, 6.

97. Roscoe McGowen, "MacPhail Suggests Post-Season Series Between NL and AL," NYT, October 26, 1939; Joseph Nichols, "MacPhail Suggests Interleague Games, NL Night Games," NYT, October 27, 1939; Dick Farrington, "MacPhail's 16-Club Playoff Plan Causes Stir," TSN, November 2, 1939, 5; "MacPhail Pulls Out Another Rabbit," TSN, November 2, 1939, 4; W. C. Durand, "Interleague Warfare," NYT, March 19, 1938.

98. John Drebinger, "American League Bars Champion's Trade with Rival Clubs," NYT, December 8, 1939.

99. "Veeck Urges Interleague Games to Revive Interest," NYT, August 23, 1933.

100. F. C. Lane, "Hard Times Are Baseball's Golden Opportunity," BM, September 1933, 435–36 and 472; "Spicing Up the Schedules," TSN, July 20, 1933, 4.

101. "Griffith Opposes Interleague Plan," NYT, August 24, 1933.

102. F. C. Lane, "Baseball Problems of the Winter Meetings," BM, December 1933, 291–92 and 333–34.

103. J. W. Sloan, "Regularly Scheduled, Non-Exhibition, Interleague Games," BM, February 1939, 408 and 430; see also William Fowler, "Interleague Baseball," NYT, December 18, 1937; Solon Gartenlaur, "Letter Urging Interleague Games," NYT, August 9, 1941.

104. R. W. Hayes, "Reply to Letter Urging Interleague Games," NYT, August 23, 1941.

105. "Split Seasons," TSN, July 9, 1931, 4.

106. Arnold James, "Demoting Cellar Clubs," NYT, March 26, 1938; see also A. R. Oestricher, "Cure for Last-Place Teams," NYT, November 18, 1939.

12. How Effective Were the Innovations?

1. Surdam, "Do the Cheap Seats Go First?"

2. "Where They Broadcast," TSN, May 4, 1933, 4 lists the Boston, Chicago, Cincinnati, Detroit, and St. Louis teams broadcasting home games in 1933, with the Giants broadcasting road games; Light suggests that only five teams broadcast home games in 1934, but the Tigers broadcast such games in 1933 and the Indians did so in 1932. The Indians apparently stopped, but I could find no evidence that the Tigers suspended broadcasts. Of the teams Light lists as having initiated broadcasts in 1935, Pittsburgh and Washington only broadcast road games. The Giants also broadcast road games briefly in the early 1930s. Light, *Cultural History of Baseball*, 602.

3. U.S. Congress, *Organized Baseball: Hearings*, 1599–1600; Thorn, Palmer, and Gershman, *Total Baseball*, 7th ed., 76.

4. The teams that instituted radio broadcasts of home games were no different than teams that maintained the status quo in 1935 according to regression estimations. Using either the percentage change in attendance, the absolute change in attendance, or change in real profit/loss as the dependent variable with the change in Win-Loss percent-

age and a dummy variable for maintaining the status quo as the independent variables generated equations with very low explanatory variables as measured by the adjusted R^2. The status quo dummy variable was not significant in any of the three equations, although the change in Win-Loss percentage was significant with respect to either using the percentage change in attendance or using absolute change in attendance variables.

    5. U.S. Congress, *Organized Baseball: Hearings*, 1602–3 and 1606–7.
    6. Philadelphia Phillies Baseball Club, cash books.

13. The Inept and the Restless

    1. "The Lessons of 1932," TSN, July 28, 1932, 4.
    2. "Moving a Major League Franchise," TSN, November 2, 1933, 4; "Moving a Franchise Not Easy," TSN, July 20, 1939, 4; Edgar Brands, "Landis Dynamites Interlocking Farm System," TSN, December 14, 1939, 1; Edgar Brands, "Minors Stymied by Landis' Adverse Action," TSN, December 14, 1939, 3 and 6.
    3. Glick, "Professional Sports Franchise Movements."
    4. William Shea, "Baseball's Big Problem," NYT, July 16, 1938; Charles Best, "Another Team for Brooklyn," NYT, May 14, 1938.
    5. Alvin Stein, "Enlarging the Big Leagues," NYT, September 10, 1938.
    6. "Big Leagues Spurn Los Angeles Offer," NYT, March 24, 1940.
    7. John Drebinger, "Frick Calls Special Meeting to Consider More Night Games," NYT, January 18, 1942.
    8. Stan Baumgartner, "Nugent Gets News—Phils 'Sold' Twice," TSN, September 4, 1941, 3.
    9. "Kelly Reported Head of Syndicate Seeking to Buy Phillies," NYT, September 18, 1941; "Kelly Reports Plan Dropped to Buy Phillies," NYT, September 24, 1941; Stan Baumgartner, "'I'll Sell, But Find Me Buyer'—Nugent," TSN, November 19, 1942, 1 and 7.
    10. Douglas Kingston, "Letter on Philadelphia Phillies Ticket Prices," NYT, September 27, 1941.
    11. Veeck, *Veeck—As In Wreck*, 171.
    12. Stan Baumgartner, "'I'll Sell, But Find Me Buyer'—Nugent," TSN, November 19, 1942, 1 and 7.
    13. Jordan, Gerlach, and Rossi, "Truth About Bill Veeck."
    14. "Terry May Run Phils for N.L. If Purchaser Cannot Be Found," TSN, February 18, 1943, 1.
    15. Dan Daniel, "Philly Fans Envision Brighter Life as Cox-Harris Regime Takes Hold," BM, April 1943, 514.
    16. Dewey and Acocella, *Ball Clubs: Every Franchise*, 427–29.
    17. Paul Shannon, "Public Ticket Sale Gives Braves Lift," TSN, February 7, 1935, 7; "Braves' 1934 Loss $44,308," NYT, June 5, 1935.
    18. Paul Shannon, "Dogs Chase Braves Out of Park, As Yawkey Bars Use of Fenway," TSN, January 17, 1935, 1; John Drebinger, "Rule Permitting Night Baseball Passed by National League," NYT, February 6, 1935.
    19. Paul Shannon, "N.L. Seeks Private Capital in Curing Ills of Braves," TSN, January 24, 1935, 1; Paul Shannon, "Adams Put Stock on Market in Braves' Reorganization Plan," TSN, January 31, 1935, 1; "Ticket Plan Promising," NYT, January 31, 1935; John Drebinger, "Rule Permitting Night Baseball Passed by National League," NYT, February 6, 1935.

20. "Ruth Will Draw 500,000 Fans to National League, Frick," NYT, March 17, 1935; "Ruth Has Drawn 20,000 at Gate for Braves," NYT, March 22, 1935.

21. "Adams Accepts Marshall's Terms on New Corporation," NYT, August 7, 935.

22. Paul Shannon, "$80,000 Bait Fails to Jar Fuchs Loose," TSN, June 13, 1935, 1.

23. Paul Shannon, "Braves to be Sold to Local Syndicate," TSN, July 11, 1935, 3; "Fuchs Quits as Head of Braves," NYT, August 1, 1935; Paul Shannon, "Brave Buyers Still Strangers to Fuchs," TSN, July 4, 1935, 1; "Fuchs Quits as Head of Braves," NYT, August 1, 1935.

24. John Drebinger, "National League Takes Over Affairs of Braves," NYT, November 27, 1935; Paul Shannon, "Shareholders Dig Up $175,000, Promise More, to Float Braves," TSN, November 14, 1935, 1.

25. John Drebinger, "Prospective Purchase Seen Expedited by Forfeit of Boston," NYT, November 28, 1935.

26. "Rumor of Bill Terry Buying Boston Bees," NYT, August 16, 1940; John Drebinger, "MacPhail Denies Interest in Bees," NYT, November 1, 1940; "Sale of Bees Near, Owner Announces," NYT, December 9, 1940; Jack Malaney, "$350,000 Reported Sale Price of Bees," TSN, December 12, 1940, 8; "Clarify the Boston Situation," TSN, December 5, 1935, 4; "Boston Bees May Be Sold to Syndicate Headed by Bob Quinn," NYT, April 20, 1941; "Bob Quinn Reports Deal Completed for Boston Bees," NYT, April 21, 1941; Howell Stevens, "Big Money Support for Bees," TSN, April 24, 1941, 1.

27. "Offer by Quinn to Buy Braves with Adams's Backing Reported," NYT, December 7, 1935; "Braves' Case Statements," NYT, December 11, 1935.

28. "Shifting of Cards to Detroit Remote," NYT, March 29, 1935.

29. "Moving a Franchise," TSN, April 4, 1935, 4; "Waiver Price Raised in American League," NYT, July 8, 1935.

30. "Robbing Peter to Pay Paul," TSN, January 9, 1936, 4.

31. Frederick Lieb, "Both Clubs Call St. Louis Only One-Team City," TSN, December 22, 1943, 7.

32. Steinberg, "Little World Series of 1922," 7–14.

33. Fred Scheiffele, "Behind the Scenes in Big League Baseball," BM, September 1933, 449; "Thinks Browns Will Stay," NYT, October 26, 1933.

34. "Sale of Browns Looms," NYT, January 6, 1934; Dick Farrington, "$300,000 for Browns," TSN, January 11, 1934, 1; Dick Farrington, "Browns Move Into Financial King Row," TSN, April 19, 1934, 2; Dick Farrington, "Browns Entrenched with Ample Funds to Operate," TSN, January 3, 1935, 1; Dick Farrington, "Browns to Use Cash in Bolstering Club," TSN, January 24, 1935, 3.

35. Dick Farrington, "Future of Browns Is Waiting at Gate," TSN, May 9, 1935, 3; Dick Farrington, "A.L. Club Owners May Attempt to Force New Deal on St. Louis," TSN, July 4, 1935, 1; Dick Farrington, "Browns Well Fixed Financially, But Won't Bid for Costly Stars," TSN, November 14, 1935, 1.

36. Dick Farrington, "Syndicate Being Formed to Buy Browns, Plans $325,000 Offer," TSN, December 5, 1935, 1 and 2; Dick Farrington, "Browns Home Gate 76,000 at 52 Games," TSN, August 6, 1936, 2.

37. "St. Louis Group Seeks to Purchase Browns," NYT, October 23, 1936; Dick Farrington, "Browns' Sale Near; Hornsby to Remain," TSN, October 29, 1936, 1 and 2; Dick Farrington, "Deal for Purchase of Browns Delayed by $35,000 Park Rent," TSN, November 5, 1936, 1 and 8; "Plans to Rebuild Browns Are Made," NYT, November 9, 1936.

38. "Blue Skies for Browns," TSN, November 19, 1936, 4.
39. Dick Farrington, "Rog Hornsby Fair Haired Boy Again Under New Ownership," TSN, November 19, 1936, 1 and 3; "Sale of Browns Impends," NYT, November 8, 1936.
40. "Revitalized Browns," TSN, February 11, 1937, 4; "Browns Making Hay in 'Farm' Expansion," TSN, February 18, 1937, 1 and 7.
41. Dick Farrington, "Brownies' Deficit in '37 Tops $75,000," TSN, January 20, 1938, 7.
42. Dick Farrington, "Deficit of Browns to Drop Below 1937," TSN, September 1, 1938, 3; "Browns Report 1938 Loss," NYT, January 11, 1939.
43. Dick Farrington, "Brownie Directors Flash Green Signal," TSN, February 23, 1939, 1 and 8.
44. Dick Farrington, "Weekday Attendance Puts St. Louis on Spot as Two-Club City," TSN, June 8, 1939, 1 and 2.
45. Dick Farrington, "Directors Toss $100,000 More into Brownies' Treasury," TSN, June 15, 1939, 1 and 2; "Browns Get $100,000," NYT, June 15, 1939; Dick Farrington, "Strife Among Browns Directors," TSN, October 12, 1939, 1 and 8; Dick Farrington, "Donald Barnes Increases Holdings of Shares in Club," TSN, October 19, 1939, 1 and 10.
46. Dick Farrington, "Two-Club Situation at St. Louis Nears 'Can't-Go-On' Stage," TSN, July 6, 1939, 1; Dick Farrington, "Strife Among Browns Directors," TSN, October 12, 1939, 1 and 8; "St. Louis Browns: Board Meeting Gives Vote of Confidence," NYT, October 14, 1939.
47. James Gould, "Is St. Louis a One-Team Town?" BM, September 1939, 474; Dick Farrington, "Donald Barnes Increases Holdings of Shares in Club," TSN, October 19, 1939, 1 and 10.
48. Dick Farrington, "Co-Operative Move Under Way in A.L. to Give Brownies Lift," TSN, January 11, 1940, 1; Dick Farrington, "Judnich a $12,000 'Gift' From Yankees," TSN, February 8, 1940, 9.
49. Dick Farrington, "Light Construction Begins in St. Louis," TSN, February 15, 1940, 5; "Night Games Seen by 1,558,021 in Major League Parks," NYT, September 7, 1940.
50. "Donald Barnes Denies Rumor of Planned Move of Club," NYT, July 17, 1939; Dick Farrington, "Cards' Shift to Columbus Considered; Breadon Owns Park," TSN, July 20, 1939, 1 and 5; "Browns Not Moving Harridge Says," NYT, August 3, 1939.
51. Dick Farrington, "Stockholders Hold on as Browns Rally," TSN, July 24, 1941, 3; Dick Farrington, "Browns May Finish $100,000 in the Red," TSN, August 14, 1941, 2.
52. Dick Farrington, "Barnes at Bat Again for 14 Night Games," TSN, October 23, 1941, 1 and 5; Dick Farrington, "Brownies Backers Bolt; 5-Year Loss Close to $500,000," TSN, December 25, 1941, 1 and 2.
53. Edgar Brands, "Majors Gird to Carry on During U.S. Emergency," TSN, December 18, 1941, 7.
54. "Browns Seeking Capital—1941 Deficit $100,000," NYT, March 3, 1942; Dick Farrington, "Hapless Brownies Now Are Scoutless," TSN, January 1, 1942; Dick Farrington, "Browns and League at 'Your Move' Stage," TSN, January 8, 1942, 10; "St. Louis Browns Club Stockholders Meeting—Needs Capital," NYT, January 14, 1942.
55. Dick Farrington, "Browns Refinanced by New Stock Issue," TSN, March 12, 1942, 5; Dick Farrington, "Barnes Sees Bright Days on Night Ball," TSN, January 22, 1942, 7; Dick Farrington, "Frowns of Browns Drowned by Smiles," TSN, February 12, 1942, 7.

56. Dick Farrington, "Card Farm Losses Far Over $100,000," TSN, October 15, 1942, 1 and 13.

57. U.S. Congress, *Organized Baseball: Hearings*, 1333–34 and 1414.

Epilogue: The End of an Era

1. Surdam, *Postwar Yankees*, 316.
2. Veeck, *Veeck—As In Wreck*, 264.

Appendix 1: Radio and Sunday Ball's Effect

1. Surdam, "What Brings Fans to the Ball Park?"
2. Ln(Attendance) = 6.49 + 3.41(W-L Pct.) + 0.29(Sunday Dummy)
   (16.40) (14.40)   (3.39)
-0.32(Shared City Dummy) + 0.29Ln(Estimated Population)
(-5.53)   (9.88)
+ 0.001(Real Per-Capita GNP)
(5.11)
N = 208   Adjusted R^2 = 0.704
All of the variables were significant at the 1% level.

I also ran a fixed-effect panel regression, given that there might be correlation within each individual team's experiences. Because of the nature of fixed-effect panel regression, the Shared City dummy variable dropped out of the model. Sunday and Estimated Population were no longer significant at even the 10% level. The W-L Pct. and Real Per-Capita GNP figures remained statistically significant at the 1% level.

Ln(Attendance) = 14.580 + 2.798(W-L Pct.)
                 (2.09) (12.93)
+ 0.105(Sunday Dummy)
(1.15)
-0.263Ln(Estimated Population)
(-0.54)
+ 0.001(Real Per-Capita GNP)
(5.16)
N = 208   Within R^2 = 0.583

3. Real Profit/Loss = -844,356.4 + 461,600(W-L Pct.)
                      (-5.12) (4.10)
-29,934(Sunday Dummy) -77,549(Shared City Dummy)
(-0.87)   (-3.34)
+ 31,474Ln(Estimated Population) + 324(Real Per-Capita GNP)
(2.66)   (4.10)
+ 188,460(Pennant Winner Dummy) -3,664(Night Dummy)
(5.96)   (-0.13)
N = 208   Adjusted R^2 = 0.451

The Sunday and night dummies were not statistically significant, even at the 10% level.

Again, because of probable correlation within individual team panel data, I ran a fixed-effect (panel) regression. The Shared City dummy variable dropped out. The Sunday and night dummy variables continued to be statistically insignificant as was the Population variable. The other three variables were statistically significant at the 1% or 5% levels.

Real Profit/Loss = -1,250,241 + 576,729(W-L Pct.)
(-0.46) (2.54)
-4,799(Sunday Dummy) + 50,058Ln(Estimated Population)
(-0.15)   (0.26)
+ 340(Real Per-Capita GNP) + 163,357(Pennant Winner Dummy)
(3.77)   (4.74)
-21,573(Night Dummy)
(-0.58)
N = 208   Within R^2 = 0.381

Bibliography

Archives

Hesburgh Library, Joyce Sports Collection, Notre Dame University, South Bend, Indiana. Team scorecards and Philadelphia Phillies Baseball Club cash books, 1935–1939.

National Baseball Hall of Fame, Cooperstown, New York. New York Yankees Base Ball Club. Cash books and general ledger, 1915–1944.

National Oceanic and Atmospheric Administration. "Record of Climatological Observations: New York Central Park Observation," 1929, 1933, 1939, and 1943.

New York Public Library. New York Yankees Baseball Club Collection, 1913–1950.

Published Works

Alexander, Charles. *Ty Cobb*. New York: Oxford University Press, 1984.

———. *John McGraw*. Lincoln NE: University of Nebraska Press, 1995.

———. *Breaking the Slump: Baseball in the Depression Era*. New York: Columbia University Press, 2002.

Anderson, Donald R. "Branch Rickey and the St. Louis Cardinal Farm System: The Growth of an Idea." Ph.D. Diss., University of Wisconsin–Madison, 1975.

Asinof, Eliot. *Eight Men Out: The Black Sox and the 1919 World Series*. New York: Holt, Rinehart and Winston, 1963.

Barrow, Edward G., and James M. Kahn. *My Fifty Years in Baseball*. New York: Coward-McCann, 1951.

Baseball Blue Book for 1939. Fort Wayne IN: Robert Heilbroner, 1939.

Bevis, Charlie. *Sunday Baseball: The Major Leagues' Struggle to Play Baseball on the Lord's Day, 1876–1934*. Jefferson NC: McFarland, 2003.

Bewley, Truman F. *Why Wages Don't Fall During a Recession*. Cambridge MA: Harvard University Press, 1999.

Brown, Kenneth H., Paul E. Gabriel, and David G. Surdam. "An Inquiry into the Pay Structure of the New York Yankees: 1919–1941." *Eastern Economic Journal*, forthcoming.

Burk, Robert F. *Much More than a Game: Players, Owners, and American Baseball Since 1921*. Chapel Hill NC: University of North Carolina Press, 2001.

———. *Never Just a Game: Players, Owners, and American Baseball to 1920*. Chapel Hill NC: University of North Carolina Press, 1994.
Canes, Michael. "The Social Benefits of Restrictions on Team Quality." In *Government and the Sports Business*, ed. Roger G. Noll, 81–113. Washington DC: Brookings Institution, 1974.
Cobbledick, Gordon. "Why Browns Get Fantastic Prices." *Baseball Digest* (February 1949): 59–60.
Craig, Peter S. "Organized Baseball: An Industry Study of a $100 Million Spectator Sport." Bachelor's thesis, Oberlin College, 1950.
Cramer, Richard B. *Joe DiMaggio: The Hero's Life*. New York: Simon & Schuster, 2000.
Deveaux, Tom. *The Washington Senators*. Jefferson NC: McFarland, 2001.
DeVito, Carlo, ed. *The Ultimate Dictionary of Sports Quotations*. New York: Checkmark, 2001.
Dewey, Donald, and Nicholas Acocella. *The Ball Clubs: Every Franchise, Past and Present, Officially Recognized by Major League Baseball*. New York: HarperPerennial, 1996.
Dodd, Donald, ed. *Historical Statistics of the States of the United States: Two Centuries of the Census, 1790–1990*. Westport CT: Greenwood, 1993.
Doherty, Thomas. *Pre-Code Hollywood: Sex, Immorality, and Insurrection in American Cinema, 1930–1934*. New York: Columbia University Press, 1999.
———. *Projections of War: Hollywood, American Culture, and World War II*. New York: Columbia University Press, 1993.
Eig, Jonathan. *Luckiest Man: The Life and Death of Lou Gehrig*. New York: Simon & Schuster, 2005.
Fetter, Henry. *Taking on the Yankees: Winning and Losing in the Business of Baseball, 1903 to 2003*. New York: W. W. Norton, 2003.
Fort, Rodney. "Inelastic Sports Pricing." *Managerial and Decision Economics* 25, no. 2 (March 2004): 87–94.
———. *Sports Economics*. 1st ed. Upper Saddle River NJ: Prentice Hall, 2003.
———. *Sports Economics*. 2nd ed. Upper Saddle River NJ: Pearson Prentice Hall, 2006.
Fort, Rodney D., and James Quirk. "Cross-subsidization, Incentives, and Outcomes in Professional Team Sports Leagues." *Journal of Economic Literature* 33, no. 3 (September 1995): 1265–99.
Garrett, Thomas and David C. Wheelock. "Why Did Income Growth Vary Across States During the Great Depression?" *Journal of Economic History* 66, no. 2 (June 2006): 456–66.
Glick, Jeffrey. "Professional Sports Franchise Movements and the Sherman Act: When and Where Teams Should Be Able to Move." *Santa Clara Law Review* 231, no. 1 (Winter 1983): 55–94.
Graham, Frank. *The New York Yankees: An Informal History*. New York: G. P. Putnam's Sons, 1943.
———. *The Brooklyn Dodgers: An Informal History*. New York: G. P. Putnam's Sons, 1945.
Gregory, Paul M. *The Baseball Player*. Washington DC: Public Affairs Press, 1956.
Gregory, Robert. *Diz: The Story of Dizzy Dean and Baseball during the Great Depression*. New York: Penguin, 1992.
Halberstam, David. *Summer of '49*. New York: Avon, 1990.
Hanes, Christopher. "Nominal Wage Rigidity and Industry Characteristics in the

Downturns of 1893, 1929, and 1981." *American Economic Review* 90, no. 5 (December 2000): 1432–46.

Haupert, Michael. "Bonus Clauses and the Standard Player Contract," *The Baseball Research Journal* 36 (2007): 109–15.

Haupert, Michael, and Ken Winter. "Pay Ball: Estimating the Profitability of the New York Yankees, 1915–1937." *Essays in Economics and Business History* 21 (Spring 2003): 89–102.

Heidenry, John. *The Gashouse Gang: How Dizzy Dean, Leo Durocher, Branch Rickey, Pepper Martin, and Their Colorful, Come-from-Behind Ball Club Won the World Series—and America's Heart—During the Great Depression.* New York: Public Affairs, 2007.

Helyar, John. *Lords of the Realm: The Real History of Baseball.* New York: Villard, 1994.

Honig, Donald. *Baseball When the Grass Was Real.* New York: Berkley Medallion, 1975.

Jordan, David M., Larry R. Gerlach, and John P. Rossi. "The Truth about Bill Veeck and the '43 Phillies." *The National Pastime* 6 (1995): 3–13.

Kahneman, Daniel, Jack Knetsch, and Richard Thaler. "Fairness as a Constraint on Profit Seeking: Entitlements in the Market." *American Economic Review* 76, no. 4 (September 1986): 728–41.

Leifer, Eric. *Making the Majors: The Transformation of Team Sports in America.* Cambridge MA: Harvard University Press, 1995.

Levin, Richard C., George J. Mitchell, Paul A. Volcker, and George F. Will. *The Report of the Independent Members of the Commissioner's Blue Ribbon Panel on Baseball Economics.* July 2000, http://www.mlb.com/mlb/downloads/blue_ribbon.pdf.

Levitt, Daniel R. *Ed Barrow: The Bulldog Who Built the Yankees' First Dynasty.* Lincoln NE: University of Nebraska Press, 2008.

Lewis, Franklin. *The Cleveland Indians.* New York: G. P. Putnam's Sons, 1949.

Lieb, Frederick G. *The Baltimore Orioles: The History of a Colorful Team in Baltimore and St. Louis.* New York: G. P. Putnam's Sons, 1955.

Light, Jonathan Fraser. *The Cultural History of Baseball.* Jefferson NC: McFarland, 1997.

Lowry, Philip J. *Green Cathedrals: The Ultimate Celebration of All 271 Major League and Negro League Ballparks Past and Present.* Reading MA: Addison-Wesley, 1992.

The Macmillan Baseball Encyclopedia. 10th ed. New York: Macmillan, 1996.

Maikovich, Andrew J., and Michele D. Brown, eds. *Sports Quotations: Maxims, Quips, and Pronouncements for Writers and Fans.* Jefferson NC: McFarland, 2000.

Morris, Peter. *A Game of Inches: The Game on the Field.* Chicago: Ivan Dee, 2006.

———. *A Game of Inches: The Game Behind the Scenes.* Chicago: Ivan Dee, 2006.

National League and American Association of Professional Baseball Clubs. *Annual Meeting of the National League and American Association of Professional Baseball Clubs, December 10 to 14, 1901.* N.p., 1901.

National League of Professional Base Ball Clubs. *Constitution and Playing Rules of the National League of Professional Baseball Clubs.* New York: American Sports Publishing Company, 1933 and 1936.

Peterson, Robert W. *Pigskin: The Early Years of Pro Football.* New York: Oxford University Press, 1997.

Pietrusza, David. *Lights On! The Wild Century-Long Saga of Night Baseball.* Lanham MD: Scarecrow, 1997.

Power, Albert Theodore. *The Business of Baseball*. Jefferson NC: McFarland, 2003.
Quirk, James, and Rodney D. Fort. *Pay Dirt: The Business of Professional Team Sports*. Princeton NJ: Princeton University Press, 1992.
Rottenberg, Simon. "The Baseball Players' Market." *Journal of Political Economy* 64, no. 3 (April 1956): 242–258.
Scully, Gerald W. "Pay and Performance in Major League Baseball." *American Economic Review* 64, no. 6 (December 1974): 915–930.
———. *The Business of Major League Baseball*. Chicago: University of Chicago Press, 1989.
———. *The Market Structure of Sports*. Chicago: University of Chicago Press, 1995.
Seymour, Harold. *Baseball: The Early Years*. New York: Oxford University Press, 1960.
———. *Baseball: The Golden Age*. New York: Oxford University Press, 1971.
Shaver, John W. "The Cubs: Baseball's Contribution to Successful Management." *Factory and Industrial Management* 78, no. 4 (October 1929): 840–842.
Smith, Lowell D. "Baseless Fears: Professional Baseball's Wary Relationship with Radio, 1921–1934." Master's thesis, University of Nebraska–Lincoln, 1995.
Spalding Official Base Ball Guides. New York: American Sports Publishing, 1929, 1930, 1934, 1939, 1940, and 1944.
Sporting News, *Complete Baseball Record Book, 2003*. St. Louis: Sporting News Books, 2003.
Steinberg, Steve. "The 'Little World Series' of 1922." *National Pastime* 28 (2008): 7–14.
Surdam, David G. "The American 'Not-So-Socialist' League in the Postwar Era." *Journal of Sports Economics* 3, no. 3 (August 2002): 264–90.
———. "Do the Cheap Seats Go First?" Unpublished paper, 2009.
———. "The New York Yankees Cope with the Great Depression: An Examination of Team Financial Records, 1929–39." *Enterprise & Society* 9 (December 2008): 816–40.
———. *The Postwar Yankees: Baseball's Golden Age Revisited*. Lincoln NE: University of Nebraska Press, 2008.
———. "A Tale of Two Gate-Sharing Plans: The National Football League and the National League, 1952–56." *Southern Economic Journal* 73, no. 4 (April 2007): 931–46.
———. "What Brings Fans to the Ball Park: Evidence from New York Yankees' and Philadelphia Phillies' Financial Records." *Journal of Economics* 35, no. 1 (2009): 35–48.
Thorn, John, Pete Palmer, and David Pietrusza. *Total Baseball: The Official Encyclopedia of Major League Baseball*. 6th ed. New York: Total Sports, 1999.
Thorn, John, Pete Palmer, and Michael Gershman, eds. *Total Baseball: The Official Encyclopedia of Major League Baseball*. 7th ed. Kingston RI: Total Sports, 2001.
Tygiel, Jules. *Baseball's Great Experiment: Jackie Robinson and His Legacy*. New York: Oxford University Press, 1983.
U.S. Congress. House. Committee on the Judiciary. *Organized Baseball: Hearings before the Subcommittee on Study of Monopoly Power of the Committee on the Judiciary*. Serial no. 1, pt. 6. 82nd Cong., 1st Sess. Washington DC: Government Printing Office, 1952.
———. Committee on the Judiciary. *Organized Professional Team Sports: Hearings before the Antitrust Subcommittee of the Committee on the Judiciary*. Serial no. 8. 85th Cong., 1st Sess. Washington DC: Government Printing Office, 1957.
———. Committee on the Judiciary. *Organized Baseball: Report of the Subcommittee on*

the *Study of Monopoly Power of the Committee of the Judiciary*. House Report no. 2002. 82nd Cong., 1st Sess. Washington DC: Government Printing Office, 1952.
U.S. Congress. Senate. Committee on the Judiciary. *Professional Sports Antitrust Bill—1965: Hearings before the Subcommittee on Antitrust and Monopoly of the Committee on the Judiciary*. 89th Cong., 1st Sess. Washington DC: Government Printing Office, 1965.
U.S. Department of Commerce. Bureau of the Census. *Historical Statistics of the United States: Colonial Times to 1970*. 2 vols. Washington DC: Government Printing Office, 1975.
———. *Population*, vol. 1. Washington DC: Government Printing Office, 1942.
———. *Statistical Abstract of the United States, 1941*. Washington DC: Government Printing Office, 1942.
U.S. Congress. Bureau of Economic Analysis. "State Personal Income 1929–99." CD-ROM.
Veeck, Bill and Ed Linn. *Veeck—As in Wreck*. New York: Putnam, 1962.
Voigt, David. *American Baseball: From Gentleman's Sport to The Commissioner System*. Norman OK: University of Oklahoma Press, 1966.
Warfield, Don. *The Roaring Redhead: Larry MacPhail—Baseball's Great Innovator*. South Bend IN: Diamond, 1987.
Westcott, Rich and Frank Bilovsky, eds. *The New Phillies Encyclopedia*. Philadelphia PA: Temple University Press.
Zimbalist, Andrew. *Baseball and Billions: A Probing Look Inside the Big Business of Our National Pastime*. New York: Basic, 1992.

Index

Adams, Charles, 290, 291–92
advertising, 258–59; radio sponsorships, 203–4, 207, 208, 209, 211, 212, 213, 214–15
Alexander, Charles, xxii, 151
Alexander, Dale, 120
Alexander, Grover, 148
Allyn, A. C., Jr., 72
American Association, 39, 179, 224, 274. *See also* Minor Leagues
American League: and antitrust laws, xiii–xiv, xvi, xix; and attendance, 11, 29, 31, 32, 33, 34, 50–51, 121, 123, 179, 253–54, 317, 340, 347, 357n22, 378n42; competitive balance in the, xvii, 113, 115–17, 118–19, 120–21, 123–26, 128, 129, 138, 139, 140, 192, 338; and expenses (gross operating), 91–92, 335, 367n131; and farm system, 106, 107, 125–27, 337; and interleague games, 274–76; and Minor League players, 96; and night baseball, 231–32, 233, 235–36, 240, 241, 242; and profitability, 11, 21–22, 66, 119, 121, 123, 127–28, 129, 340
American League revenue: from away games, 323, 345, 376n13; from concessions, 46, 48, 324, 325; from home games, 44, 321, 323; from radio, 208, 326; and real gross operating income,
43–44, 322; and real net income, 318, 319; and revenue sharing, 51, 162–63, 164, 165–66, 167, 344; and salaries, 66, 70, 91–92, 331; and scheduling, xviii, 172–73, 177–78, 179, 186–88, 192, 194; and scoring, 247, 248–49, 251–52, 254, 357n11; and ticket prices, 51–52, 56; and umpires, 68; and win-loss percentages, 339, 340. *See also* National League; National League revenue
American Professional Football Association, 171–72
amusement tax. *See* taxes
Andrews, Ivy, 143
antitrust laws, xiii–xiv, xvi, xix
Asinof, Eliot, 82
attendance, 317; American League, 11, 29, 31, 32, 33, 34, 50–51, 121, 123, 179, 253–54, 317, 340, 347, 357n22, 378n42; college football, 31–32; decreases in, 11, 27, 30–33, 34–35, 39, 50–51, 57, 253, 275, 358n36; and free passes, 30; holiday doubleheader, 181, 347; increases in, 34, 121; and ladies' days, 56–57; measuring, 28–29, 279–80, 376n11; Minor League, 199–200, 221, 222, 225; National League, 11, 29, 31, 32, 33, 34, 253–54, 317, 340; night baseball, 221, 226, 229–30, 234, 237, 238–39, 240–41, 282–84, 298–300, 351; and pennant

attendance (*cont.*)
races, 29–30, 31, 33, 34; per capita, 303, 352; and profitability, 16, 17, 22, 27, 35, 50, 57; and radio broadcasts, 199–201, 203, 204, 206–8, 211, 212–13, 217, 282, 350; and revenue sharing, 164–65, 166–67, 378n41; and salary bonuses, 83–84, 85–86, 361n9; and scoring, 253–54; World Series, 28–29, 30, 33, 358n36; and World War II, 34–35. *See also* ticket prices

Auker, Eldon, 142, 148, 297

Baker Bowl, 261, 287, 389n15. *See also* stadiums

Ball, Phil, 24, 261–62, 293–94, 309; and night baseball, 227–28; and profitability, 16; and salary bonuses, 83

ballpark experience, 277; and alcohol sales, 266; and fan rowdiness, 265–68; and interleague games, 274–75; and public address systems, 257–58; and speed of game, 272; and ticket selling, 265; and uniform numbers, 255–57; for women and children, 268–72. *See also* fans; stadiums

Bancroft, Dave, 145

Barber, Red, 202

Barnard, E. S., 199, 272, 274, 309

Barnes, Donald, 109, 255, 293, 309; and franchise relocation, 284, 286, 299–300, 302; and night baseball, 232–33, 237, 241, 242, 243, 244–45, 283, 298–99; players purchased by, 148; and profitability, 16; and purchase of St. Louis Browns, 24, 294–97; and salary bonuses, 85

Barrow, Edward, xxi, 25, 120, 309, 312; and farm system, 99, 100, 101, 125–27; and night baseball, 236, 239–40, 242, 244, 387n91, 387n94; and payroll, 70–71; players purchased by, 135–36, 137–38, 303; and profitability, xxiv, 302; and radio broadcasts, 210, 212–13; and statistics, 372n13

Bartell, Richard "Rowdy," 145

baseballs, 250–55. *See also* scoring

batting helmets, 252–53

Beggs, Joe, 127

Bell, Beau, 295

Bengough, Benny, 88

Benswanger, William, 193

Berger, Wally, 146, 290

Berra, Yogi, 102, 128

Bevis, Charlie, 190–91

Bewley, Truman, 90

Bishop, Max, 137, 143

Blackburne, Lena, 249–50

Borowy, Hank, 152

Boston Braves, 78, 146, 257; and ladies' days, 269; and profitability, 18, 22, 23–24, 289–91; and radio broadcasts, 206; relocation of, 289–92, 300; and revenue sharing, 163, 164; and salaries, 74; and Sunday baseball, 190–91, 280; and ticket prices, 37

Boston Red Sox, 94, 121; and attendance, 22, 121; and farm system, 100, 107; and home game revenue, 164; and player movement, 137, 138, 140, 141, 142–44; and profitability, xx, 21, 109; and radio broadcasts, 206; and revenue sharing, 164; and salaries, 69, 70, 83; and Sunday baseball, 186–87, 190–92, 280

Bottomley, Jim, 61

Bradley, Alva, 206, 237, 238, 242

Brandt, Dutch, 290

Brandt, William, 67–68

Braves Field, 46, 47, 191, 262, 289. *See also* stadiums

Breadon, Sam, 24, 34, 104, 149–50, 255, 272, 309; and farm system, 97; and franchise relocation, 292–93, 297, 298; and night baseball, 222, 232, 240, 244, 296; and payroll, 71, 80; and profitability, 16, 17, 385n64; and Sunday baseball, 173–74, 177

Bridges, Tommy, 81

Briggs, Walter, 264, 309

broadcasting rights, 198–99, 203, 208, 211–12, 217, 320, 326; and the Cleve-

Index 407

land Indians, 205; and the New York Yankees, 48, 50, 210; percentage of, as revenue, 48. *See also* radio broadcasts
Brooklyn Dodgers, 45, 56, 88, 94, 106, 257, 263–64, 265; and attendance, 34, 187, 193; and concessions, 47; and fan rowdiness, 265–66; and farm system, 98, 100, 105; and ladies' days, 270; and night baseball, 231, 233–35, 244, 308; pennant wins, 147, 235; and player movement, 145, 146, 147; and profitability, 22; and radio broadcasts, 210–11, 212; and revenue sharing, 164; and road attendance, 34, 164; and salaries, 69, 75, 79, 85; and scheduling, 187, 193; and ticket prices, 40, 42–43, 52, 191
Burk, Robert, xxiii, 60–61, 66

Cain, Sugar, 139, 140
Camilli, Dolph, 145, 147, 252
Cannon, Raymond, xix
Carpenter, Robert, Jr., 289
Carpenter, Robert, Sr., 289
Casey, Hugh, 147
Chadwick, Henry, 268
Chapman, Ben, 251
charity events, 354n11
Chicago Cubs, 56, 257, 265, 304, 370n3; and attendance, 29, 33, 34, 204, 260, 357n20, 361n9; and concessions, 46; and ladies' days, 269; and night baseball, 236, 241; and pennant wins, 20; and profitability, 19, 20, 22, 109; and radio broadcasts, 198, 204, 206, 208, 209, 212, 281; and revenue sharing, 164; and salaries, 69, 70, 78, 81, 84; and win-loss percentage, 117
Chicago White Sox, 101, 121, 257; and night baseball, 238, 282; and radio broadcasts, 198, 206, 208, 209, 212; and revenue sharing, 163; and salaries, 82; and win-loss percentage, 115–16
churning, 116–17, 129. *See also* competitive balance

Cicotte, Ed, 82
Cincinnati Reds, 24, 94, 127, 255, 264, 274; and attendance, 17, 34, 207, 226, 228, 229–30; and concessions, 229; and night baseball, 226–30, 244, 308; and pennant wins, 71, 146; and player movement, 145, 146; and profitability, 17–18, 22; and radio broadcasts, 48, 206; and revenue sharing, 163; and salaries, 68, 69, 71, 83–84; and ticket prices, 36–37
Cincinnati Red Stockings, 171
Clayton Antitrust Act (1914), xiii–xiv
Cleveland Indians, 24, 103–4, 151–52, 263, 296, 390n40; and attendance, 30–31, 33, 238, 358n30; and farm system, 100; and home game revenue, 164; and night baseball, 238, 282; and radio broadcasts, 205, 393n12; and salaries, 66, 68, 69; and ticket prices, 36; and uniform numbers, 256; and win-loss percentage, 115
Clift, Harlond, 295
Coase, Ronald, 102
Coase Theorem, 169, 177, 183, 194
Cobb, Ty, 248, 309; and the Philadelphia Athletics, 1, 2, 138, 151; salary of, 72, 106
Cochrane, Mickey, 139, 309; and the Detroit Tigers, 127, 140, 142, 264; and the Philadelphia Athletics, 1, 2, 138
Coffman, George "Slick," 297
college football, 31–32, 174, 202–3, 221–22
Collins, Eddie, 1, 2, 138, 262, 310
Combs, Earle, 1, 2, 135
Comiskey, Charles, 82, 140, 261, 310
Comiskey, Lou, 361n9
Comiskey Park, 241, 261. *See also* stadiums
competitive balance: in the American League, xvii, 113, 115–17, 118–19, 120–21, 123–26, 128, 129, 138, 139, 140, 192, 338; and churning, 116–17, 129; and city populations, 118; and the "Golden Era," 113; and loans to franchises, 122, 161, 287, 288, 290, 297;

competitive balance (cont.)
  measuring, 114–15, 338; in the National League, 113, 115, 116, 119, 128–29, 338; and pennant races, 114, 116–17, 118–20, 121, 122–23, 125; and player movement, 120, 121–22, 132; and profitability, 129; and the reserve clause, xvii; and revenue sharing, 160–61, 168; and scheduling, 180, 184–85, 188, 192; and trade restrictions, 122, 124–25, 126–27; and trades, 138
concessions, 46–48, 266, 271, 320, 324, 378n40, 392n82; and night baseball, 47, 229; at Yankee Stadium, 45, 50. *See also* revenue
Congressional hearings, xxi, xxiii, 12–13, 61, 160
Conigliaro, Tony, 253
consumer expenditures, xiv, 9–11, 315, 316
Cooke, Dusty, 142
Courtney, Ernie, 120
Coveleski, Stan, 2
Cox, William, 288–89
Cramer, Doc, 139, 140, 142, 143
Cronin, Joe, 67, 137, 141, 143, 155
Crosetti, Frankie, 125
Crosley, Powel, Jr., 17, 24, 226, 310, 382n78
Crosley Field, 264. *See also* stadiums
Cullenbine, Roy, 104, 127, 152

Dahlgren, Babe, 125
Daniel, Dan, 46, 125, 126, 128, 192, 357n26, 360n73; and the Yankees' financial records, 13, 44–45, 70, 75
Davis, Curt, 145, 147
Dean, Dizzy, 32, 154, 229, 310; and the Chicago Cubs, 16–17, 20, 149; salary of, 80–81
Dean, Paul, 80–81
designated hitter proposal, 249–50
Detroit Tigers, 24, 94, 264; and attendance, 32, 207–8, 358n33; and competitive balance, 121, 127; and farm system, 105; and home game revenue, 164; and night baseball, 241, 243; pennant wins, 32, 33, 84, 142, 358n33; and player movement, 138, 142, 374n49; and profitability, 20, 21; and radio broadcasts, 206, 207–8, 393n2; and revenue sharing, 164; and salaries, 81, 84; and scheduling, 181–82
DeWitt, William, 167, 295, 299
Dickey, Bill, 2, 119, 136
DiMaggio, Joe, 19, 122, 136, 301, 303, 310; salary of, 73–74, 365n79
Dressen, Charley, 84
Dreyfuss, Barney, 193, 224, 250, 275, 310
Dugan, Joe, 120, 152–53, 374n52
Dunn, Jack, 103
Durocher, Leo, 2, 85
Durst, Cedric, 135
Dykes, Jimmy, 138, 192

Earnshaw, George, 136, 190
Ebbets, Charles H., 175–76
Ebbets Field, 40, 45, 46, 210; capacity of, 42–43, 263–64, 360n73; and night baseball, 234, 243. *See also* stadiums
Eckert, Al, 268
economic indicators, 7–11, 315–16
Elberfield, Kid, 120
electric lights. *See* night baseball
Evans, Billy, 68, 273
exhibition games, 45–46, 175, 290, 320, 324, 328
expenses (gross operating), 91–92, 93, 94, 320, 335, 367n131. *See also* revenue

fans, xvii–xviii, 32–33; children, 270–72; and "colorful" teams, 32, 80–81, 272; and holiday doubleheaders, 184–85; polling of, 273; and rowdiness, 265–68; and scoring, 247, 249, 252; women, 37, 53, 56–57, 201, 203, 223, 230, 268–70, 271–72, 277. *See also* ballpark experience
Farley, James, 25
farm system, 134–35, 152; cost of the, 105–7, 320, 337; development of the, 16, 17, 95–101; and free agency, 152;

New York Yankees, 98–100, 102–3, 105, 107, 124, 134–35; opposition to, 101–5, 124; and trading ban, 125–27. *See also* Minor Leagues; player movement

Farrington, Dick, 85

Federal League, xiii, xvii

Feller, Bob, 19, 100, 103, 151–52, 238, 301

female fans. *See* women fans

Fenway Park, 21, 24, 144; capacity of, 182–83, 262; and concessions, 46, 47; and Sunday games, 191–92. *See also* stadiums

Ferrell, Rick, 152

Fette, Lou, 146

Fetter, Henry, xxiii–xxiv

Finley, Charlie, xix, 133, 139, 311

Fletcher, Art, 88

Ford, Whitey, 100

Fort, Rodney, xviii, 115

Foxx, Jimmie, 1, 2, 79–80, 138, 247, 310; and the Boston Red Sox, 137, 140, 143, 155; salary of, 79–80

Frain, Andy, 267

franchise relocation, 353n1; and the Boston Braves, 289–92; and city populations, 285; and loans, 287, 288, 290, 297, 299; and the Philadelphia Phillies, 287–89; rules governing, 285–86; and the St. Louis Browns, 292–300, 302

franchise values, 23–25. *See also* profitability

Frazee, Harry, 13

free agency, 132, 150–53, 155, 374n49. *See also* player movement

Freedman, Andrew, xvi

free passes, 30, 37–38, 39. *See also* ticket prices

Frey, Lon, 146

Frick, Ford, 266, 287, 288, 290, 291, 310; and night baseball, 230, 232; and Sunday games, 174

Frisch, Frankie, 104, 148–49, 150

Fuchs, Emil "Judge," 175, 281, 289–91, 310; and purchase of Babe Ruth, 33, 78, 290; and Sunday games, 190–91, 280

Gallagher, Joe, 296

Garrett, Thomas, 9

gate-sharing rules. *See* revenue sharing

Gehrig, Lou, 1–2, 80, 123, 136, 311; salary of, 72–73, 81, 334

Gehringer, Charlie, 81

Gibson, Josh, 154

Giles, Warren, 18, 71, 129, 146

Glick, Jeffrey, 286

"Golden Era," 113, 353n1

Gomez, Vernon "Lefty," 75–76, 87, 100, 136

Goslin, Goose, 82–83, 141, 142

Graham, Frank, 99, 239, 267

Grant, Charley, 153

Greenberg, Hank, 121, 127, 142, 247, 301; salary of, 81

Gregory, Paul, 67

Gregory, Robert, 80

Griffith, Clark, 118, 138, 143, 252, 272, 276, 297, 304, 311; and farm system, 101, 124–25, 126; and night baseball, 224, 231, 233, 235, 237–38, 241–42, 243, 244, 245, 283–84; and profitability, 18, 109, 140–41; and radio broadcasts, 205; and salaries, 67, 69, 82–83, 84–85; and scheduling, 174, 183

Grimes, Burleigh, 122

Grimm, Charlie, 84

Grissom, Lee, 127

gross domestic product (GDP), 7–8, 315, 316

gross national product (GNP), 8, 10, 11, 315, 316

gross operating income, 43–44, 322. *See also* revenue

Grove, Robert "Lefty," 103, 140, 143, 155, 311; and the Philadelphia Athletics, 1, 2, 63, 136–37, 138, 139, 190; salary of, 63, 69, 365n87

Haas, George "Mule," 138, 192

Hadley, Bump, 137

Hagan, James, 93

Haines, Jesse, 148

Hallahan, Bill, 149

Hanes, Christopher, 90
Harridge, William, 32, 148, 251, 286, 311; and franchise relocation, 293, 294–95, 297, 298; and night baseball, 235, 236; and player salaries, 69, 84–85
Harris, Bucky, 249
Hart, James, xvi, 170
Hartman, Harry, 197
Hartnett, Gabby, 260
Hassett, Buddy, 128
Haupert, Michael, xxi, xxii, xxiii, 82
Haupert Hall of Fame Salary Database (Haupert Database), xxii, 60, 63–64, 69, 71, 79
Heidenry, John, 80
Helyar, John, 60–61
Henrich, Tommy, 74, 104, 152, 296
Herman, Babe, 84
Herman, Billy, 70, 147
Herrmann, Garry, 275
Heydler, John A., 68, 91, 251, 272, 311; and designated hitter proposal, 249, 250; and ticket prices, 35–36, 39, 52–53
Hickey, Thomas J., 274
Higbe, Kirby, 145, 147
Higgins, Pinky, 139, 140
Hoag, Myril, 74, 99, 148, 297
Hogan, Shanty, 150
Honig, Donald, 131
Hornsby, Rogers, 72, 74, 106, 147, 149–50
Howard, Elston, 102, 103
Hoyt, Waite, 1, 2, 87, 88, 374n52
Hubbell, Carl, 75, 154, 239
Huggins, Miller, 1, 87, 248
Hughes, Tommy, 288
Hulbert, William, xiv, 311
Hunter, Jim "Catfish," xix, 150
Huston, T. L., 260

income. *See* revenue
innovations. *See* ballpark experience
integration, 153–55, 231, 272, 288, 302
interleague games, 274–76
International League, 105
Irving, Ira, 153
Irwin, Robert, 93
Isaminger, James, 79

Johnson, Ban, 120
Johnson, Bob, 71, 139, 142
Johnson, Hank, 142
Johnson, Walter, 154
Jolley, Smead, 120
Jorgens, Arndt, 135
Judnich, Walt, 125, 148, 297

Kauff, Benny, xvii
Keller, Charlie, 124
Kelly, John B., 287
Keyser, Lee, 103, 220–21, 311
Klein, Chuck, 79, 144–45, 251, 311, 389n15
Koenig, Mark, 87, 372n6
Konstanty, Jim, 125
Kurowski, Whitey, 134

Laabs, Chet, 148, 297
"ladies' days," 37, 53, 56–57, 268–70, 277. *See also* ticket prices; women fans
Landis, Kenesaw Mountain, 32, 62, 83, 127, 311; and farm system, 102, 103–5, 152; and free agency, 131, 150, 151, 152, 153; and gambling, 289; and integration, 288; and night baseball, 242, 384n32; and radio broadcasts, 200, 215; salary of, 68, 76
Lane, F. C., 15, 63, 69, 118–19, 275
Lannin, Joe, 151
Lary, Lyn, 87, 96, 135–36, 137, 141, 142
Lazzeri, Tony, 1, 2, 135, 372n6
Levitt, Daniel, xxiv, 96, 99
Lieb, Fred, 275
lights. *See* night baseball
Litwhiler, Danny, 288
loans, franchise, 122, 161, 287, 288, 290, 297, 299. *See also* franchise relocation
Lollar, Sherm, 102–3
Lombardi, Ernie, 146
Long, Herman, 120

Mack, Connie, xx, 1, 109, 118, 134, 142, 151, 152, 248, 261, 284, 304, 311; and night baseball, 225, 231, 235, 236, 237, 238, 241, 242, 245; and player salaries, 63–64, 71, 79–80; and radio broad-

casts, 205, 282; and selling of players, 133, 136–37, 138–40, 143; and Sunday baseball, 177, 190, 192–94, 280, 281, 308; and ticket prices, 36, 39
MacPhail, Larry, 17, 25, 33, 40, 126, 267, 291, 304, 311, 353n1, 385n64; and air travel, 274; and interleague games, 275; and night baseball, 226–27, 228, 230, 233–35, 239, 244, 282, 308, 384n32; and player pension plan, 63; and player salaries, 83–84, 152; players purchased by, 146–47; and radio broadcasts, 207, 210; and scheduling, 187; and ticket prices, 36–37, 42–43, 270, 271
MacPhail, Leland Stanford. *See* MacPhail, Larry
Mahaffey, Roy, 140
Malone, Pat, 137
Marcantonio, Vito, 90–91
Marcum, Johnny, 139, 140
Maris, Roger, 143, 250, 310
Martin, Pepper, 32
McCarthy, Joe, 78, 126, 248, 290, 311; and night baseball, 225; salary of, 87–88
McCoy, Benny, 104, 127, 152
McDonald, John, 40
McGraw, John, 120, 150, 153, 248, 250, 311; and air travel, 273–74; and night baseball, 225
McKechnie, William, 78, 231
McKeever, Steve, 231, 312
McManus, Charles, 264
McNair, Eric, 139, 142, 143
McNally, Dave, 150
McQuillan, Hugh, 150
McQuinn, George, 125, 147–48, 299
media. *See* radio broadcasts
Medwick, Joe, 146, 147, 149, 252, 264
Melton, Rube, 288
Messersmith, Andy, 150
Meusel, Bob, 62
Minor Leagues, 3, 31, 124, 251, 274, 276; attendance, 199–200, 221, 222, 225; as farm system, 95, 96–98, 99, 100–107, 148; and franchise relocations, 285–86, 298; and free agency, 151–52; and night baseball, 220–24, 225, 244; and the player draft, 103–4; purchase of players from the, xv–xvi, 96, 98, 99, 103–5, 132, 134–36, 137, 372n6; and radio broadcasts, 199; and revenue sharing, 161; and salaries, 131; and scheduling, 179; and ticket prices, 39. *See also* farm system
Mize, Johnny, 71, 125, 149
monopsony (single-employer bargaining power), xx, 59, 60, 86. *See also* salaries, player
Moore, Wilcy, 1
Morris, Peter, 256, 258, 376n11
motion pictures, 10–11, 354n4
Municipal Stadium, 33, 237, 238, 263. *See also* stadiums
Musial, Stan, 134

National Association of Base Ball Players, 170, 171, 179
National Football League, 131–32, 212; and revenue sharing, 160–61, 167; and scheduling, 170, 186
National League, 144, 273, 376n11; and antitrust laws, xiii–xiv, xvi, xix; and attendance, 11, 29, 31, 32, 33, 34, 253–54, 317, 340; competitive balance in the, 113, 115, 116, 119, 128–29, 338; and farm system, 106, 107, 337; and franchise relocation, 287–88; and gross operating expenses, 92, 335; and interleague games, 274–76; and interlocking team ownership, xvi; and night baseball, 231–32, 236, 240, 243; and profitability, 11, 21, 66, 119, 121, 123, 127–28, 129, 340; and radio broadcasts, 198
National League revenue: from concessions, 46, 325; from home games, 44, 321, 323; from away games, 323, 345, 376n13; from radio, 326; and real gross operating income, 43–44, 322; and real net income, 318, 319; and revenue sharing, 160, 162–64, 344;

National League revenue (cont.)
and the sacrifice fly rule, 250–51; and salaries, 66, 74–75, 91–92, 109, 331; and scheduling, xviii, 172–73, 174, 177–78, 185–86, 187; and scoring, 247–48, 249, 250–52, 253–54, 357n11; and ticket prices, 37, 56; and win-loss percentages, 339, 340. See also American League; American League revenue
Navin, Frank, 264, 292, 312
Navin Field, 264. See also stadiums
Negro Leagues, 153–54, 224
Nehf, Art, 150
net income, 21–22, 318, 319. See also revenue
Newark Bears, 124
Newsome, Bobo, 127
newspapers, 197, 201, 213. See also radio broadcasts
New York Giants, 2–3, 37, 134, 265; and attendance, 29, 33; and competitive balance, 120; and farm system, 100, 107; and games at home revenue, 45; and night baseball, 233, 236, 238–39, 283; pennant wins, 145; and player movement, 96, 145, 150; and public address system, 257, 258; and radio broadcasts, 48, 206, 209–11, 212, 213; and road attendance, 31; and salaries, 69–70, 74–75; and ticket prices, 42, 52; and win-loss percentage, 117
New York Yankees, 1–2, 3, 24–25, 37, 49, 133, 134, 265, 329; and attendance, 2, 29, 50, 123, 212–13, 303, 327, 330, 357n26, 378n42; and competitive balance, 113, 118–19, 122–28, 129; and concessions, 48, 50; and exhibition games, 45; and expenses (gross operating), 92, 93, 94, 335, 336; and farm system, 98–100, 102–3, 105, 107, 124, 134–35; financial records of the, xxi, xxii, xxiv, 49; and ladies' days, 270; and loudspeakers, 257; and night baseball, 57, 233, 236, 238, 239, 241; pennant wins, 49, 113, 116, 122–23, 127, 129, 304; and player movement, 134–38, 372n6; and profitability, 12, 19–20, 21, 22, 50, 302–3; and radio broadcasts, 48, 50, 206, 209–11, 212–13, 326
New York Yankees' revenue, 332; from away games, 49, 328; from concessions, 50, 328; from home games, 44–45, 49, 50, 53–54, 55, 328; from radio, 48, 50, 212, 326; and revenue sharing, 164, 165–67, 346; and road attendance, 31, 164, 165, 166–67, 378n41, 378n42; and salaries, 13–14, 65–66, 67, 70–71, 72–74, 75–78, 81–82, 86–89, 135–36, 332, 333, 334; and scheduling, 178–79, 182–83, 186–87; and ticket prices, 41, 42, 51–57; and uniform numbers, 256; and win-loss percentage, 115–16, 117, 326
night baseball, 57, 267, 308, 387n91, 387n94; and attendance, 226, 229, 234, 237, 238–39, 240–41, 282–84, 298–300, 351; banning of, 233, 236; and concessions, 47; and cost of lights, 219, 223, 225, 227–28, 229, 232, 233–34, 237, 238, 239, 241–42, 283; introduction of, 220–25, 226–28, 230–33, 237; in the Minor Leagues, 220–24, 225, 244; popularity of, 244–45; and profitability, 146, 219, 229, 282–84, 308; and scheduling, 173–74; and women, 223, 230. See also Sunday baseball
Nugent, Gerald, 14, 39, 79, 145, 261, 287–88; salary of, 93
Nugent, Mary, 14, 93

O'Connor, Leslie, 98
O'Doul, Lefty, 145
Ogden, Johnny, 93
O'Malley, Walter, 46, 98
O'Rourke, J. J. "Patsy," 93
Ott, Mel, 248, 251
Owen, Mickey, 147

Pacific Coast League, 78, 99, 104, 174, 273; and radio broadcasts, 200; and revenue sharing, 161; and ticket

prices, 39, 269. *See also* Minor Leagues
Padden, Tom, 136
Paige, Satchel, 154
Passeau, Claude, 145
payroll. *See* salaries, player
Pearson, Monte, 137
Peckinpaugh, Roger, 249
Pennock, Herb, 1, 75, 88, 289
Perini, Lou, 98, 292
Perry, Charles D., 154
personal consumption expenditures (PCE). *See* consumer expenditures
Philadelphia Athletics, 1–2, 3, 300; and attendance, 138–39, 237; and competitive balance, 118–19, 121; and exhibition games, 45; and night baseball, 237, 282; and pennant wins, 136; and player movement, 133, 134, 136–37, 138–40, 143, 192–93; and profitability, 22; and radio broadcasts, 206, 207, 212, 282; and salaries, 63–64, 69, 71, 79–80; and Sunday baseball, 190, 192–93, 280–81, 308; and ticket prices, 36, 39; and win-loss percentage, 117
Philadelphia Phillies, 14, 24, 79, 128, 261; financial records of, xxi–xxii; and gross operating expenses, 92–93; and night baseball, 236, 238, 282–83, 308; and pennant wins, 289; and player movement, 144–46; in the postwar era, 353n1; and profitability, 12, 18; and radio broadcasts, 206, 207, 212; and relocation, 287–89; and revenue sharing, 163, 164; and Sunday baseball, 190, 193, 280–81; and win-loss percentage, 116, 117
Pietrusza, David, 220
Pipgras, George, 137, 142
Pittsburgh Pirates: and concessions, 48; and night baseball, 240, 283; in the postwar era, 353n1; and profitability, 19; and radio broadcasts, 207, 208–9, 214; and revenue sharing, 163, 164; and salaries, 67; and Sunday baseball, 190, 193

player movement, 133, 342; and the Boston Red Sox, 137, 138, 140, 141, 142–44; and the Brooklyn Dodgers, 145, 146, 147; and the Cincinnati Reds, 145, 146; and competitive balance, 120, 121–22, 132; and the Detroit Tigers, 138, 142, 374n49; and the draft, 103–4, 132; and free agency, 132, 150–53, 155; frequency of, 133–34, 149–50; and integration, 153–55; and the Minor Leagues, xv–xvi, 96, 103–5, 132; and the New York Giants, 96, 145, 150; and the New York Yankees, 134–38, 372n6; and the Philadelphia Athletics, 133, 134, 136–37, 138–40, 143, 192–93; and the Philadelphia Phillies, 144–46; and the reserve clause, xv; and the St. Louis Browns, 122, 140, 147–48, 296, 297; and the St. Louis Cardinals, 134, 147, 148–49; and taxes, 132; and the Washington Senators, 138, 140–42. *See also* farm system
player salaries. *See* salaries, player
player tryout system, 97–98. *See also* farm system
Polo Grounds, 45, 46, 50, 238–39, 243; and public address system, 257, 258; and ticket prices, 36, 40, 42, 52. *See also* stadiums
populations, city, 118, 341
Powell, Albert, 291
Powell, Jake, 137, 154
Power, Albert, xxiv
pricing. *See* ticket prices
Priddy, Gerald, 125
profitability, 11–12, 16–23, 59, 109; and accounting principles, 13–15, 21; in the American League, 11, 21–22, 66, 119, 121, 123, 127–28, 129, 340; and attendance, 16, 17, 22, 27, 35, 50, 57; determining, 279–80; and expenses (gross operating), 92, 109; and franchise values, 23–25; and loans, 122, 161, 287, 288, 290, 297; in the National League, 11, 21, 66, 119, 121, 123, 127–28,

profitability (cont.)
129, 340; and night baseball, 146, 219, 229, 282–84, 308; and pennant races, 18–19, 32; reporting of, xviii–xix, xxi–xxii, 12–13, 14–15, 21–22, 32; and salaries, 22–23, 59–60, 66–67, 90–91; and Sunday baseball, 307–8. See also revenue
promotion and relegation, 276–77
promotions, ticket. See ticket prices

Quinn, Bob, 24, 135, 224, 292
Quirk, James, 115

radio broadcasts, 197–99, 393n2, 393n4, 397n2; and attendance, 199–201, 202–3, 204, 206–8, 211, 212–13, 217, 350; banning, 205–6; and censorship, 201–2; and college football, 202; and ownership rights, 213–14; and revenue, 48, 50, 198–99, 281–82, 320, 326; and sponsorships, 203–4, 207, 208, 209, 211, 212, 213, 214–15; and the World Series, 215–16
recreational expenditures. See consumer expenditures
Redland Field. See Crosley Field
Reese, Jimmy, 96, 135–36
Reese, Pee Wee, 147
Reiser, Harold "Pete," 104, 147, 152, 252
reserve clause, xv, xix, xx, 60–61, 91, 131, 155; and competitive balance, xvii. See also salaries, player
revenue, 318, 319, 322, 376n13; and broadcasting rights, 48, 50, 198–99, 208, 210, 211–12, 217, 320, 326; from concessions, 45, 46–48, 50, 229, 320, 324, 325, 328, 378n40; from doubleheaders, 175–76; from exhibition games, 45–46, 320, 324, 328; and expenses (gross operating), 91–93, 94, 109, 320; and gross operating income, 43–44, 322; and net income, 21–22, 318, 319; and the New York Yankees, 44–45, 49–57, 321, 323, 328; and night baseball, 229; and population bases, 44,

45, 117–18; postwar, 301; and scheduling, 169–71, 177, 179–84, 187, 194; and ticket prices, 43–45, 50–56; and win-loss records, 165. See also profitability; revenue sharing
revenue sharing, xxiv–xxv, 51, 159, 160–64, 167, 181–82, 344; and attendance, 164–65, 166–67, 378n41; and competitive balance, 160–61, 168; efficacy of, 164–66, 167–68; National Football League, 160–61, 167; and the New York Yankees, 346; purpose of, 159, 167–68. See also revenue
Reynolds, Carl, 143
Rhodes, Gordon, 142
Rickey, Branch, 17, 149–50, 193, 287, 288–89, 312; and competitive balance, 126, 128–29; and farm systems, 96–98, 100, 102, 104, 147; and integration, 231; and player salaries, 80–81; and the St. Louis Browns, 295; and uniform numbers, 256
Ring, Jimmy, 150
Risberg, Swede, 151
Rizzuto, Phil, 125
Robinson, Jackie, 100, 155
Rommel, Eddie, 134
Roosevelt, Franklin, 9, 228, 242–43, 300, 301
Rottenberg, Simon, 60, 102
Rowe, Schoolboy, 121, 127, 142
Royal, John, 215
Ruffing, Charles "Red," 126, 128, 135, 136, 137
Ruppert, Jacob, xxi, xxiv, 120, 128, 136–37, 251, 290, 312; and competitive balance, 123–25; death of, 25, 125; and farm systems, 99–100; and night baseball, 221, 227; and player salaries, 13, 65, 70–71, 73, 74, 76–77, 87; and profitability, 19–20, 44–45, 49; and radio broadcasts, 205, 206, 211; salary of, 92; and ticket prices, 52, 53, 54–56; and Yankee Stadium, 14, 19, 260, 302–3
Ruth, Babe, xxiii, 1, 2, 50, 68, 73, 80, 90,

Index 415

136, 149, 247, 250, 310, 312; and barnstorming, 62; and the Boston Braves, 33, 290; and exhibition game revenues, 45; salary of, 13–14, 65–66, 72, 74, 76–78, 81, 87, 89, 333, 334, 365n79
Ryan, Rosey, 135

salaries, management, 68, 87–88, 93
salaries, player, xv, 63–65, 93–94, 98; and bonuses, 82–86, 88–89, 151, 361n9; decreases in, 65–66, 67, 68–69, 78–80, 86–87, 90, 301, 303; determining, 89; increases in, 66–67, 69, 70–72, 91–92; limits on, 65, 67; in the Minor Leagues, 131; New York Yankees, 13–14, 65–66, 67, 70–71, 72–74, 75–78, 81–82, 86–89, 333, 334; perceptions of, 61–64; and profitability, 22–23, 59–60, 66–67, 90–91; reporting of, xix, 13–14, 15; and the reserve clause, 60–61, 91; and revenue sharing, 161; and scoring, 253–54; and star players, 72–82, 87, 89, 90; and unionization, 90–91; and World War II, 72
Salsinger, H. G., 207–8
Sanborn, Irving, 28, 193
San Francisco Seals, 78, 223, 271. *See also* Minor Leagues
scheduling, 170–72, 177–78; and the cartel, xviii; challenges in, 172–75; college football, 174; exhibition games, 175; holiday doubleheaders, 169–70, 178–86, 188, 194, 378n33, 378n37; make-up games, 175, 186–87; National Football League, 170, 186; night baseball, 173–74, 242, 243; and number of games, 172, 175, 377n16; pennant races, 173; road trips, 173, 174; and special requests, 173, 174–75, 187; Sundays, 173–74, 177, 179, 188–94, 280–81, 397n2; synthetic doubleheaders, 175–76; and transportation costs, 184, 194
scoreboards, 255, 257, 258. *See also* ballpark experience

scorecards, xxii, 46, 47, 255. *See also* concessions
scoring, 247–50, 388n7; and attendance, 253–54; and batting helmets, 252–53; and the "dead ball," 250–52, 253–54, 357n11; and home runs, 247; and the sacrifice fly rule, 250–51; and salaries, 253–54
Selkirk, George, 136
Seymour, Harold, xxiii, 160
Shawkey, Robert, 87, 225
Sherman Antitrust Act (1890), xiii–xiv
Shibe, John, 192
Shibe Park, 47, 236, 261, 287. *See also* stadiums
Shocker, Urban, 1
Simmons, Al, 1, 2, 64, 138, 140, 192, 373n30; salary of, 64, 362n18
Simons, Herbert, 85
Slaughter, Enos, 125
Sloan, J. W., 276
Smith, Lowell D., 208
Southern Association Minor League, 179
Spalding, Albert, 160
Speaker, Tris, 1, 2, 72, 138, 151, 312
Spink, C. C., 66
Sportsman's Park, 261–62, 294. *See also* stadiums
stadiums, 44, 118, 187, 266; building, xviii, xxiii, 259–61, 262–63; capacity, 182–83, 259–62, 263–64, 357n8, 378n41. *See also* ballpark experience; night baseball; *individual stadium names*
Stengel, Casey, 88, 292
Stevens, Harry, 46–47, 50
St. Louis Browns, 24, 147–48, 227–28, 261–62; and attendance, 33, 166–67, 188, 240, 272, 283, 294, 296, 298–99, 378n42; and competitive balance, 121, 123; and concessions, 48; and exhibition games, 45, 48–49; and farm system, 295; and night baseball, 232–33, 240–41, 242, 243, 244–45, 283, 297, 298–300; and player movement, 122, 140, 147–48, 296, 297; and profitabil-

St. Louis Browns (cont.)
  ity, 16, 295–96; and radio broadcasts, 206–7, 282; and relocation, 292–300, 301, 302; and revenue sharing, 164, 166–67; and salaries, 71–72, 83, 85; and scheduling, 174, 180–82, 188; and ticket selling, 265; and win-loss percentage, 117
St. Louis Cardinals, 2–3, 24, 121, 149, 174; and attendance, 16, 17, 31, 32, 34, 271–72; and children's promotions, 270–72; and concessions, 48; and farm system, 16, 17, 96–98, 107, 148–49, 152; and night baseball, 240; pennant wins, 16, 17, 31, 32, 97, 98, 148, 343; and player movement, 134, 147, 148–49; and profitability, 16–17; and radio broadcasts, 206–7, 282; and relocation, 292–93; and revenue sharing, 163, 164; and salaries, 68, 71, 79, 80–81, 98; and ticket prices, 42; and tryout system, 97–98; and uniform numbers, 256
Stone, John, 141
Stoneham, Charles, 74, 100, 150, 238, 275, 312; and night baseball, 226, 227
Stoneham, Horace, 100, 210, 238–39, 245, 283
Sunday baseball, 179, 188–92, 280–81, 307–8, 349, 397n2; and doubleheaders, 173–74, 177, 194; and the Philadelphia Athletics, 192–94, 280. *See also* night baseball

taxes, xviii; and ticket prices, 38–39, 42, 51, 52–53, 55, 359n50
television, 198, 215–16, 217, 301–2. *See also* radio broadcasts
Terry, Bill, 74–75, 152, 227, 291
Texas League, 200, 222, 223, 274. *See also* Minor Leagues
Thomas, Fay, 99, 135
ticket prices, xiv, 39, 43–45, 191, 259, 265; and arbitraging, 40–41, 42; for children, 270–71; decreases in, 35–37, 53; determining, xx, 35, 37, 40, 43, 359n43; and free passes, 30, 37–38, 39; increases in, 43, 50, 55; Minor League, 39; and revenue sharing, 162, 163; and seat classifications, 36, 37, 40, 43, 45, 51–52, 53, 54, 55–56, 191, 304, 353n8, 357n8; and taxes, 38–39, 42, 51, 52–53, 55, 359n50; for women ("ladies' days"), 37, 53, 56–57, 268–70, 277; and the World Series, 41–43. *See also* attendance
transportation, 184, 194, 286; air travel, 273–74, 286
Trautman, George, 224, 312
Triandos, Gus, 102, 103
Trout, Paul "Dizzy," 105
Turner, Jim, 146
Tygiel, Jules, 155

uniform numbers, 254, 255–57. *See also* ballpark experience

Vance, Dazzy, 75, 81
Vander Meer, Johnny, 234
Vaughan, Irving, 84
Veeck, William "Bill," Jr., 47, 255, 257, 288, 303, 312, 353n11; and women fans, 268
Veeck, William, Sr., 275, 276, 304, 312; and night baseball, 224–25; and women fans, 268
Vidmer, Richard, 141
Vila, Joe, 76, 77
Voigt, David, xxiii
Von der Ahe, Chris, 258–59

Walberg, Rube, 137, 143
Walker, Dixie, 147
Walters, Bucky, 145, 230
war tax. *See* taxes
Washington Senators, 183; and attendance, 31, 141; and night baseball, 241–42, 283–84; pennant wins, 18, 31, 121, 140–41; and player movement, 138, 140–42; and profitability, 18, 140, 304; and radio broadcasts, 48, 207,

Index 417

208–9; and revenue sharing, 164; and salaries, 65, 69, 82–83
Webb, Del, 98
Weil, Sidney, 24
Weiss, George, 92, 99, 107, 304, 312, 372n14
Welch, Jimmy, 150
Wells, Ed, 135
Werber, Billy, 137, 142, 146
Wheelock, David, 9
Williams, Joe, 56
Williams, Ken, 76
Wilson, Hack, 78–79, 247, 313
Winter, Kenneth, xxi, xxiii
Witt, Whitey, 293
women fans, 223, 230, 271–72; and "ladies' days" promotions, 37, 53, 56–57, 268–70, 277; and motion pictures, 354n4; and radio broadcasts, 201, 203. *See also* fans
World Series, 16, 69, 116–17, 125, 370n3; and attendance, 28–29, 30, 33, 358n36; and radio broadcasts, 215–16, 382n78; and scheduling, 377n16; and ticket prices, 41–43, 357n8
World War II, 301–2; and attendance, 34–35; and night baseball, 242–43; and player rosters, 65; and player salaries, 72; and television, 216

Wright, Harry, 171, 189
Wrigley, Philip "P. K.," 61, 84, 175, 270, 273, 304; and night baseball, 241; and profitability, 20; and radio broadcasts, 209
Wrigley, William, Jr., 20, 84, 261, 268–69, 304, 313; and radio broadcasts, 198, 204
Wrigley Field, 47, 241, 245, 260–61, 273, 357n8
Wyatt, Whit, 147

Yankee Network, 204
Yankee Stadium, 45, 46, 50, 182–83, 302–3; building of, xxiii, 14, 19; capacity of, 260, 357n8; and night baseball, 239; and special events, 187; and ticket prices, 40, 53; valuation of, 25. *See also* stadiums
Yawkey, Thomas "Tom," 24, 121, 262, 289, 313; and farm system, 100; players purchased by, 137, 141, 142–44, 155, 295; and profitability, xx, 21, 22, 109; and salaries, 70, 83
Yorke, Frank, 263

Zachary, Tom, 135
Zimbalist, Andrew, xxii

CPSIA information can be obtained at www.ICGtesting.com
Printed in the USA
BVOW07s1158070813

327901BV00001B/1/P